Advanced C++

Advanced C++

Namir Clement Shammas

SAMS PUBLISHING
A Division of Prentice Hall Computer Publishing
11711 North College, Carmel, Indiana 46032 USA

To my dear and special friends George and Rocio Salinas.

FIRST EDITION
FIRST PRINTING—1992

International Standard Book Number: 0-672-30158-X

Library of Congress Catalog Card Number: 92-62270

95 94 93 92 4 3 2 1

Interpretation of the printing code: the rightmost double-digit number is the year of the book's printing; the rightmost single-digit, the number of the book's printing. For example, a printing code of 92-1 shows that the first printing of the book occurred in 1992.

Trademarks

Screen reproductions in this book were created by means of the program Collage Plus, from Inner Media, Inc., Hollis, NH.

Composed in AGaramond and MCPdigital by Prentice Hall Computer Publishing

Printed in the United States of America

Publisher
Richard K. Swadley

Acquisitions Manager
Jordan Gold

Acquisitions Editor
Gregory S. Croy

Development Editor
Stacy Hiquet

Production Editor
Erik Dafforn

Editors
Anne Clarke, Mary Corder, Sandy Doell, Grant Fairchild, Fran Hatton, Dean Miller, Hugh Vandivier

Editorial Coordinators
Rebecca S. Freeman
Bill Whitmer

Editorial Assistants
Rosemarie Graham
Lori Kelley

Technical Editor
Bruce Graves

Cover Designer
Tim Amrhein

Director of Production and Manufacturing
Jeff Valler

Production Manager
Corinne Walls

Imprint Manager
Matthew Morrill

Book Designer
Michele Laseau

Production Analyst
Mary Beth Wakefield

Proofreading/Indexing Coordinator
Joelynn Gifford

Graphics Image Specialists
Jerry Ellis
Dennis Sheehan
Sue VandeWalle

Production
Debra Adams, Julie Brown, Christine Cook, Lisa Daugherty, Mark Enochs, Dennis Clay Hager, Carla Hall-Batton, John Kane, Sean Medlock, Juli A. Pavey, Linda Quigley, Caroline Roop, Michelle Self, Susan Shepard, Greg Simsic, Marcella Thompson, Suzanne Tully, Alyssa Yesh

Indexer
Loren Malloy

About the Author

Namir Clement Shammas is a software engineer and an expert in object-oriented programming. He has written many articles for leading computer magazines and is responsible for many books on object-oriented and Windows programming, including *Turbo Pascal 6 Object-Oriented Programming* and *Windows Programmer's Guide to ObjectWindows Library.*

Overview

Contents

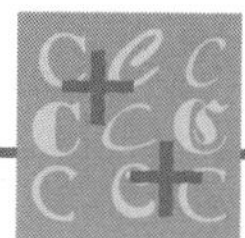

Acknowledgments

I would like to acknowledge the participation of the many people who made this book possible. I wish to thank Stacy Hiquet for putting her knowledge and vision into the development of this book. Many thanks also to Production Editor Erik Dafforn and all the Editors, especially Anne Clarke, Dean Miller, Hugh Vandivier, Mary Corder, Grant Fairchild, Sandy Doell, and Fran Hatton, for their patience and skill. In addition, I would like to thank Bruce Graves for his valuable technical review and recommendations. Finally, I would like to thank all those who were involved in producing the book at Sams Publishing.

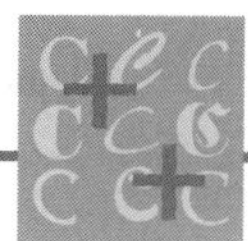

Introduction

C++ is a relatively new language. The practicing C++ programmer undergoes a learning curve to master it. However, C++ continues to evolve. New features, such as templates and exceptions, were recently approved but are not fully defined. In writing this book, I've included material that challenges the limits of C++ and the intended uses of some of its language features. This challenge might not sit well with the so-called C++ gurus. I feel that some of the advice given by these people is more subjective and comes from a desire to set themselves in positions of authority. Often, we are limited by our imagination and by the belief that it can't be done simply because someone else says so. In this book, I try to stretch your imagination while using C++ and modeling real-world objects.

Advanced C++ contains 21 chapters grouped into three parts:

Part I, "Language Components of C++," comprises the first ten chapters and discusses various issues related to the different language components of C++.

Part II, "C++ Object-Oriented Programming," comprises Chapters 11 through 13 and discusses object-oriented programming issues using C++.

Part III, "C++ Template Classes," comprises Chapters 14 through 21 and presents template classes that implement various data structures.

Here are the contents of Part I:

- Chapter 1, "C++ Functions," examines the C++ function and discusses parameter passing, default arguments, overloading functions, and template functions. This chapter gives an overview of the C++ function in general, not just as a class member.
- Chapter 2, "Constructors and Destructors," covers various topics related to class constructors and destructors. Among the topics discussed are the advantages of using pointers to classes, arrays of objects, data conversion using constructors, and inheritance schemes.
- Chapter 3, "Public, Protected, and Private Declarations," investigates the strategies for declaring members as public, protected, or private. I also present valuable tables that illustrate access of the class instance, the subclasses, and the instances of the subclasses to the various members of a class.

- Chapter 4, "Member Functions," focuses on the member functions of a class. The chapter discusses the various roles of member functions, examines virtual functions, and looks at special techniques to pacify member functions.
- Chapter 5, "Static Members," covers the role of static data members and static member functions. The text shows that these member functions conceptually belong to the class rather than the class instances. The chapter includes examples of using static members.
- Chapters 6 and 7 look at overloading the various C++ operators. Chapter 6, "C++ Operators," presents a more general discussion on how the operators may be overloaded in the case of popular structures. Chapter 7, "C++ Dynamic Allocation," focuses on the `new`, `delete`, and `->` operators and offers more specific discussions and examples.
- Chapter 8, "Nested Declarations," discusses local declarations and offers examples. Such declarations include enumerated types, structures, and classes.
- Chapter 9, "Template Classes," examines templates, a new feature in the C++ language. The text discusses how to declare, define, and instantiate a template class. In addition, the chapter looks at inheritance and template classes.
- Chapter 10, "Exception Handling," introduces you to the other new feature in C++, *exceptions.* The text discusses the new mechanism that empowers your code to raise and handle error conditions.

Part II contains the following chapters:

- Chapter 11, "Inheritance," discusses single inheritance, containment, and multiple inheritance. This chapter pays special attention to comparing the use of containment versus multiple inheritance.
- Chapter 12, "Object Behavior," delves into the behavior of special objects. Such objects require special coding or a special sequence for calling their member functions. The text offers examples of state-engine, disabled, transformed, and modular objects.
- Chapter 13, "Objects and Event Handling," discusses the suitability of using objects to handle events. The chapter presents two versions of a simple Microsoft Windows program and illustrates how language extensions and macros support a sophisticated system of sending, intercepting, and handling messages. This chapter also discusses implementing your own simple event handling scheme.

Finally, Part III contains the following chapters:

- Chapter 14, "The String Class," presents an extensive and practical class for strings. The operations of this class include many functions found in the string.h header file, as well as new functions.
- Chapter 15, "Words, Items, and Tokens," looks at a class hierarchy that handles special strings. These strings support space-delimited words, comma-delimited items, and user-defined delimited tokens.
- Chapter 16, "Sorting and Searching Arrays," discusses the searching and sorting methods for arrays. The class presents a template array class that contains a rich set of searching and sorting member functions. Such functions include ones that implement a new sort method and a heuristic linear search algorithm.
- Chapter 17, "Lists," contains template classes that implement unsorted and sorted double-linked list structures.
- Chapter 18, "Basic and Advanced Binary Trees," presents template classes that model various kinds of binary trees. These trees include the simple binary, the AVL tree, and the red-black tree. The chapter presents a new node structure used to simplify the code for the binary tree. In addition, the chapter presents an array-based binary tree.
- Chapter 19, "The Character Set Class," contains a class that models sets of characters. The operations of the class use overloaded functions to offer alternate ways to manipulate the character sets.
- Chapter 20, "Internal and External Search Tables," presents template classes that implement internal and external hash tables. The internal hash tables can handle dynamic data. By contrast, the external hash tables deal with fixed-size data structures and classes with no pointer members.
- Chapter 21, "The M-Way Tree and the B-Tree," discusses the multiway tree and the B-tree. These trees share many structures and algorithms. The multiway trees handle data in memory, whereas the B-tree uses mass storage to save its data.

While the book uses the standard input and output streams in the example programs, some of these programs need additional screen and cursor control. To support such features, you need to create the video.h header file. If you are using the Borland C++ compiler on an MS-DOS machine, you can simply place the following directive in the video.h header file:

```
#include <conio.h>
```

For all other compilers, you need to declare the following prototypes:

```
void gotoxy(int x, int y)  // move cursor to screen position (x, y)
void clrscr() // clear the screen
void clreol() // clear to the end of the line
int getch() // read a character from the keyboard
```

Because Part III deals with numerous data strutures, I am including the following list of textbooks you may want to consult on the topic of data structures:

Aho, A.V., J.E. Hopcroft, and J.D. Ullman. *Data Structures and Algorithms.* Addison-Wesley Publishing Company, 1983.

Baase, S. *Computer Algorithms Introduction to Design and Analysis, 2nd Ed.* Addison-Wesley Publishing Company, 1988.

Brassard, G. and P. Bratley. *Algorithmics Theory and Practice.* Prentice Hall, 1988.

Cormen, T.H., C.E. Leiserson, and R.L. Rivest. *Introduction to Algorithms.* McGraw-Hill, 1990.

Kruse, R. *Data Structures and Program Design, 2nd Ed.* Prentice Hall, 1984.

Sedgewick, R. *Algorithms, 2nd Ed.* Addison-Wesley Publishing Company, 1988.

———. *Algorithms in C++.* Addison-Wesley Publishing Company, 1992.

Tenenbaum, A.M., Y. Langsam, and M.J. Augenstein. *Data Structures Using C.* Prentice Hall, 1990.

Van Wyk, C.J. *Data Structures and C Programs.* Addison-Welsey Publishing Company, 1988.

Weiskamp, K., N. Shammas, and R. Pronk. *Turbo Algorithms: A Programmer's Reference.* John-Wiley, 1989.

Weiss, M.A. *Data Structures and Algorithm Analysis.* Benjamin/Cummings, 1992.

Wirth, N. *Algorithms + Data Structures = Programs.* Prentice Hall, 1976.

Part I

Language Components of C++

C++ Functions

Functions and procedures are tools that extend a programming language, injecting user-defined routines needed by an application. This chapter gives a general overview of the special features of C++ functions and discusses the following topics:

- Reference parameters
- Default arguments
- Overloading functions
- Template functions

Reference Parameters

Functions in C pass everything by value, including addresses. So, if a C function needs to alter the address of a pointer beyond its scope, it must return the new address of that pointer. This scheme commonly occurs in functions that handle dynamic structures, such as linked lists and binary trees where the head or root of the structure is likely to change. The following function prototypes illustrate this point:

```
enum Boolean { false, true };
/* insert in a binary tree */
struct TreeNode* insertInTree(const char* data,
                              struct TreeNode* root,
                              enum Boolean* insertedOK);
/* insert in a list */
struct ListNode* insertInList(const char* data,
                              struct ListNode* head,
                              enum Boolean* insertedOK);
```

The `insertInTree` function returns the current pointer to the root to ensure that the client program maintains an updated root pointer. In the same manner, the `insertInList` function returns the current list-head pointer. The `insertedOK` parameter is a pointer to an enumerated Boolean type acting as a flag that reports the success of the insertion functions.

By introducing the reference type, C++ creates a new and valuable parameter type. In general, a reference variable is an alias of the variable to which it refers. Similarly, a reference parameter is an alias of its argument within the scope of the host function. It's as if the reference parameter has a temporary power of attorney for its argument.

Using reference parameters, you can rewrite the previous data insertion functions as

```
enum Boolean { false, true };
// insert in a binary tree
Boolean insertInTree(const char* data, TreeNode* &root);
// insert in a list
Boolean insertInList(const char* data, ListNode* &head);
```

The `root` and `head` parameters are now reference parameters and can automatically update the root and head pointers. Notice that the `insertedOK` parameter is removed. Instead, the functions return a `Boolean` value that indicates whether the data insertion occurred. Using reference parameters proves beneficial in several ways. The preceding example demonstrates how it helps you write more intuitive functions that you can use in test conditions. For example:

```
if (!insertInTree(aData, root))
    cout << "Cannot insert duplicate data";
```

The preceding examples show how a pointer reference parameter absolves a function from returning that pointer. If a function needs to return multiple pointers,

reference parameters prove even more versatile. As an example, consider a double-linked list structure that maintains pointers to the head and tail. The prototype of a C++ function that inserts new data in a double-linked list might look like this:

```
enum Boolean { false, true };
Boolean insertInDoubleList(const char* data, ListNode* &head,
                           ListNode* &tail);
```

Compare the preceding C++ function with the equivalent C function:

```
struct headAndTail {
     ListNode* theHead;
     ListNode* theTail;
};
enum Boolean { false, true };
struct headAndTail insertInDoubleList(
              const char* data,
              struct ListNode* head,
              struct ListNode* tail,
              enum Boolean* insertedOK);
```

The code for the C++ function is definitely cleaner.

Another benefit of the reference parameter is that it saves code space and processing time. This increase in efficiency occurs in the following areas:

- The parameter passes an array or structure that is not altered by the host function. Passing such data types by value means placing duplicated information in the stack. The runtime system must use time and memory to accomplish this task. By contrast, when you pass such data types by reference, you create a small, pointer-sized alias that accomplishes the same purpose.
- The parameter passes a class that is not altered by the host function. In this case, the runtime system needs to call the class constructor to make a copy. If the class is a descendant of other classes or contains data members that are instances of other supporting classes, the runtime system must make a battery of constructor calls. You can avoid all this effort if you pass the class argument by reference.

Passing parameters by value is justified when the host function must alter the value of the argument in the function's scope alone. An alternate and more efficient scheme for member functions uses the following approach: First, use a reference parameter to pass the argument. Then copy the argument to a data member belonging to the host class. This data member acts as a scratch pad, is created once, and remains during the lifetime of the host object.

Here is an example of the preceding scheme:

```
class MathEval
{
     private:
          StringClass tempString;

     protected:
          // other data members

     public:
          MathEval();
          ~MathEval();
          // other member functions
          double evaluateExpression(StringClass &s,
                                    double *varVector);

};

double MathEval::evaluateExpression(StringClass &s, double *varVector)
{
  double result;

  // copy reference parameter s to private data member
  tempString = s;

  // function alters tempString

  return result;
}
```

The MathEval class evaluates mathematical expressions. The tempString private data member is an instance of the StringClass class. When a program creates an instance of the MathEval class, the tempString member is also instantiated. The evaluateExpression member function passes the StringClass-typed s parameter by reference. Because the function must alter the s parameter, it assigns s to the tempString member. Altering that scratch-pad member does not affect the argument of the s parameter. This approach minimizes the use of stack space and increases the execution speed by reducing the number of calls to the constructor of StringClass.

Default Arguments

C++ allows functions to have default arguments. When you use this feature in a C++ function, the parameters are divided into two separate groups. Parameters lacking default arguments are placed first, and those with default arguments are placed next. What follows is an example of a C++ function with default parameters:

```
enum Boolean { false, true };
void replaceText(const char* filename,
                 const char* findStr,
                 const char* replaceStr = "",
                 Boolean caseSense = true,
                 Boolean forward = true);
```

The first two parameters, filename and findStr, have no default arguments. The other parameters—replaceStr, caseSense, and forward—have default arguments. The following are legitimate function calls:

```
// no argument for the forward parameter
replaceText("text.doc", "1991", "1992", false);

// no argument for the caseSense and forward parameters
replaceText("text.doc", "THe", "The");

// no argument for the replaceStr, caseSense, and forward
// parameters
replaceText("text.doc", "IIII");
```

The first function call performs a backward case-insensitive replacement of the 1991 string with 1992 in the TEXT.DOC file. The function call has no argument for the forward parameter. The second function call carries out a forward case-sensitive replacement of THe with The in the TEXT.DOC file. The function uses the default arguments for the caseSense and forward parameters. The last function call deletes occurrences of the IIII string in the TEXT.DOC file. The search is case-sensitive and proceeds in the forward direction. The function uses all of its default arguments.

The preceding example shows the typical form for assigning default arguments. Such default arguments are fixed values that are assigned using either literal or symbolic constants. In some applications, the default arguments vary depending on certain conditions. If so, the default argument value is provided by a separate variable. In the case of simple C++ functions, global variables store and provide the default arguments. In the case of functions that are class members, private or protected data members maintain the default arguments.

Shortly, I will present an example for the preceding scheme applied to a nonmember function. This function performs a binary search on ordered arrays of integers. The parameters of the binarySearch function are

- The pointer to the array, intArray.
- The array size, arraySize.
- The search data, searchData.
- The index of lower search limit; firstSearchIndex.
- The Boolean flag, updateDefArg, which indicates whether the value of the default argument should be updated using the function's result.

The global variable, lastMatch, stores the current default argument for the firstSearchIndex parameter. The lastMatch variable is initialized as 0, the index of the first array. The binarySearch function is coded to work more efficiently under these conditions:

- The function receives the same arguments of the intArray and arraySize parameters.
- The function receives, in ascending order, the arguments for the searchData parameters.

These conditions mean that the function returns nondecreasing indices for the matching elements of intArray. The following example of the binarySearch function shows that, by updating the default lower search index, the function becomes more efficient:

```
// initialize the global constant
unsigned lastMatch = 0;

enum Boolean (false, true);

unsigned binarySearch(int* intArray, // pointer to an array of int
                      unsigned arraySize,  // array size
                      int searchData, // search data
                      unsigned firstSearchIndex = lastMatch,
                      Boolean updateDefArg = true)
{
  int median;
  unsigned m;
  unsigned first = firstSearchIndex;
  unsigned last = arraySize - 1;

  do {
    // calculate the index of the median element
    m = (first + last) / 2;
    if (searchData < *(intArray + m))
      last = m - 1;
    else
      first = m + 1;
  } while (!(searchData == *(intArray + m) || first > last));

  // return the index of the matching element or 0xffff if no
  // match was found
  if (searchData == *(intArray + m)) {
    if (updateDefArg)
       lastMatch = m; // update the default argument
    return m;
  }
  else
    return 0xffff;
}
```

The preceding scheme is more suitable for classes because the default argument can be stored in a nonpublic data member. Hiding this data prevents client programs from tampering with the global variables that store the various default arguments. What follows is a class of integers that implements the special default argument scheme:

```
class IntArray
{
     protected:
          unsigned lastMatch;
          int* intArray;
          unsigned arraySize;

     public:
          IntArray(unsigned size);
          ~IntArray();

          // other member functions
          unsigned binarySearch(int searchData,
                                unsigned firstSearchIndex = 0xffff,
                                Boolean updateDefArg = true);
};

IntArray::IntArray(unsigned size)
{
  intArray = new int[arraysize = size];
  lastMatch = 0; // initialize the default argument
}

unsigned IntArray::binarySearch(int searchData,
                               unsigned firstSearchIndex,
                               Boolean updateDefArg)
{
  int median;
  unsigned m;
  unsigned first = (firstSearchIndex != 0xffff) ?
                   firstSearchIndex : lastMatch;
  unsigned last = arraySize - 1;

  do {
    // calculate the index of the median element
    m = (first + last) / 2;
    if (searchData < *(intArray + m))
      last = m - 1;
    else
      first = m + 1;
  } while (!(searchData == *(intArray + m) ¦¦ first > last));
```

```
   // return the index of the matching element or 0xffff if no
   // match was found
   if (searchData == *(intArray + m)) {
     if (updateDefArg)
        lastMatch = m; // update the default argument
     return m;
   }
   else
     return 0xffff;
}
```

The `lastMatch` identifier is now a protected data member. The class constructor initializes the `lastMatch` identifier with 0. Notice also the declaration of the `binarySearch` member function and the default argument for the `firstSearchIndex`. The default value is the `0xffff` constant and not the `lastMatch` data member. The default argument cannot be a protected data member—the C++ compiler complains that the `lastMatch` member has no object associated with it. A solution to this problem is to use a special value that acts as a dummy argument. The code of the `binarySearch` function determines whether the argument for the `firstSearchIndex` parameter is `0xffff`. If it is, the function first assigns the `lastMatch` member to the local variable.

Overloading Functions

C++ enables you to overload functions by declaring versions with parameters that differ in sequence and type. The purpose of overloading a function is to provide different data types with similar operations. Here is a simple example of overloaded `sqr` functions:

```
double sqr(int n);
double sqr(unsigned n);
double sqr(double n);
double sqr(float x);
```

The preceding versions differ in parameter types. These versions of the `sqr` function return the double type. The compiler does not consider the function's return type as a component used to distinguish between overloaded functions. The reason is simple: C++ enables you to discard the returned type. Therefore, the following overloaded versions of `sqr` generate a compile-time error:

```
double sqr(int n);
long sqr(int n);
```

Because the parameter list of both versions has the same number and type of parameters, the compiler cannot distinguish between the two versions.

Another example of overloading functions is the following function that replaces text in a file:

```
enum Boolean { false, true };
void replaceText(const char* filename,
                 const char* findStr,
                 const char* replaceStr,
                 Boolean caseSense,
                 Boolean forward);

void replaceText(const char* filename,
                 const char* findStr,
                 const char* replaceStr,
                 Boolean caseSense);

void replaceText(const char* filename,
                 const char* findStr,
                 const char* replaceStr);
```

This example was deliberately chosen (you may recall that the `replaceText` function was presented earlier in this chapter) to show that this kind of function overloading can be eliminated or reduced by using the default arguments. The preceding declarations of the overloaded function can be replaced with the following single declaration that uses default arguments:

```
enum Boolean { false, true };
void replaceText(const char* filename,
                 const char* findStr,
                 const char* replaceStr,
                 Boolean caseSense = true,
                 Boolean forward = true);
```

In some cases, calls to an overloaded function do not result in the invocation of the function's intended version. This situation arises when the arguments supplied are constants with values that lead to a different interpretation by the runtime system. For instance, overloaded functions might have parallel parameters, one a pointer and the other an integer type:

```
void loadWindow(Window* parent, int resourceID);
void loadWindow(Window* parent, char* resourceFile);
```

The `resourceID` and `resourceFile` parameters contain two distinct data types. Accordingly, the compiler accepts that the two functions are overloaded versions of each other. The problem arises when you make the following type of function call:

```
loadWindow(mainWindow, NULL);
```

Is the `NULL` argument interpreted as an `int` or a pointer? The answer is: `NULL` is interpreted as an `int`. Consequently, the runtime system calls the first version of the overloaded function. To call the second version of the function with a `NULL` argument, you must write the statement

```
loadWindow(mainWindow, (char*) NULL);
```

The typecasting of the `NULL` argument invokes the current version.

Overloading functions with default arguments can lead to ambiguity that is flagged by the C++ compiler. Consider the following example:

```
// general logarithm to any base
double log(double x, int base = 10);
// natural log
double log(double x);
```

The first overloaded `log` function returns the logarithm to any base (common bases are 2, 10, and *e*—which is approximately 2.718282). The second overloaded function systematically returns the natural logarithm (of base *e*). The ambiguity arises when you invoke the first overloaded function and don't include an argument for the base parameter. The compiler cannot tell whether you intend to invoke the first or second overloaded function. Three possible solutions to this problem follow:

- Remove the default argument from the first overloaded function. This solution enables you to always supply the first overloaded function with two arguments.
- Simply eliminate the second overloaded function.
- Eliminate the second overloaded function and change the default argument from 10 to *e*.

Template Functions

Object-oriented programming appeals to many programmers because they can reduce the size of code by using classes and inheritance. The new C++ templates provide another means of reducing code. With templates, you can develop generic functions and classes that support the same operations but for different data types. You can write template functions that sort, search, and swap various data types. You can create template classes that model generic data structures, such as arrays, matrices, hash tables, lists, trees, and graphs. This book contains template classes that model most of these data structures.

The most common types of functions used by programmers are those that swap, search, and sort data. What follows are three versions of the swap function, which swaps data for various typical data types:

```
void swap(int &i, int &j)
{
  int temp = i;
  i = j;
  j = temp;
}

void swap(char &i, char &j)
{
  char temp = i;
  i = j;
  j = temp;
}
```

```
void swap(double &i, double &j)
{
  double temp = i;
  i = j;
  j = temp;
}
```

The preceding functions can coexist in a C++ program because the compiler regards them as overloaded functions. You can add more overloaded versions of swap functions to cover the other predefined data types as well as the ones you create. The result is a long list of similar code. The C++ template feature enables you to substitute the code for all these hundreds of overloaded functions with the single following template function:

```
template<class T>
void swap(T& i, T& j)
{
  T temp = i;

  i = j;
  j = temp;
}
```

Notice that the declaration of a template function begins with the `template` keyword, followed by a list of template class names. In this case, the list includes the `T` class (which I call the template class). `T` is a dummy class that is not yet defined but can still be used by the template function. The swapped data type of the previous versions of the function is replaced with the `T` template class. When the compiler sees a template function and a template class, it stores the template code for future reference. The template code itself is not compiled because the template classes are not yet defined. To employ the template function, you need to associate it with a data type or class. The compiler then instantiates a copy of the template function for the data type you specify. This process can bring out any compile-time error for the instantiated template function when the compiler detects incompatible or missing code.

The C libraries include generic (C-style) functions for searching and sorting. The ANSI C standard specifies the following functions to support generic sorting of arrays and to perform binary searches of arrays:

```
/* the generic QuickSort function */
void qsort(void *base, // the pointer to the array
           size_t nelem, // number of array items
```

```
         size_t width, // size of each element
         // the element-comparison function
         int (*fcmp)(const void *, const void *));

/* the binary search function */
void *bsearch(const void *key, // search key
              const void *base, // pointer to the array
              size_t nelem, // number of elements
              size_t width, // size of each element
              // the element-comparison function
              int (*fcmp)(const void*, const void*));
```

What follows is a template function that sorts a generic array using the new Combsort method (the `Combsort` method is discussed further in Chapter 16, "Sorting and Searching Arrays"):

```
template<class T>
void combSort(T array[], unsigned num)
{
  unsigned i, j, n, offset;
  long k;
  Boolean isSorted;

  offset = num; // get the initial offset
  // start loop to sort the array elements in the
  // range [first..last]
  do {
    // update the offset, making sure that it
    // does not become less than 1
    k = (offset * 8L) / 11;
    offset = (k == 0) ? 1 : (unsigned)k;
    isSorted = true;
    // start comparing array elements that are
    // offset members apart
    for (i = 0; i < (num - offset); i++) {
      j = i + offset;
      // need to swap elements i and j?
      if (array[i] > array[j]) {
        // swap the elements i and j
        isSorted = false;
        swap(array[i], array[j]);
      }
```

```
    }
  } while (!(isSorted && offset == 1));
}
```

Here is a template function that supports generic search in arrays:

```
template<class T>
unsigned binarySearch(T& searchData, T array[], unsigned num)
{
  T median;
  unsigned m = (num - 1) / 2;

  do {
    m = (first + last) / 2;
    if (searchData < array[m])
      last = m - 1;
    else
      first = m + 1;
  } while (!(searchData == array[m] || first > last));

  // found a match
  return (searchData == array[m]) ? m : 0xffff;
}
```

Compare the parameter lists of the `qsort` and `combSort` functions and of the `bsearch` and `binarySearch` functions. Notice that the C++ template functions require fewer parameters. The size of each element and the comparison functions are not necessary. The template class provides these items. You can readily instantiate a template function with a predefined data type. A user-defined class must already be defined before you can use it to instantiate a template function or a template class. This means defining a class containing the relational operators <, <=, >, >=, ==, and `!=` so that all possible ways of comparing elements in the template class are covered.

Summary

This chapter presented topics that focus mainly on the nonmember function in C++. You learned the following:

- Reference parameters (a new type of parameter introduced by C++) can effectively reduce stack usage and effort in parameter passing.

- Default arguments enable you to shorten the argument list in a function call by eliminating redundant values.
- Overloading functions enables you to create a family of functions that performs similar tasks on different data types. This chapter also showed some of the pitfalls that result from ambiguous calls to overloaded functions.
- With template functions, you can develop generic routines to handle a wide variety of data types. They also enable you to consolidate your code and to maintain it easier.

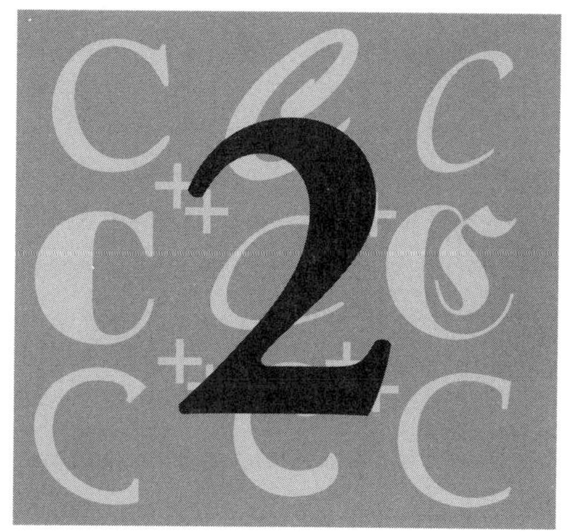

Constructors and Destructors

The sophistication of C++ classes dictates mechanisms for nontrivial object initialization and removal. C++ offers the constructor and destructor as special class members involved in these mechanisms. This chapter examines the various aspects of C++ constructors and destructors and covers the following topics:

- Using multiple constructors
- Using default parameters
- Using an alternate mechanism for passing arguments
- Creating objects
- Initializing static members
- Using C++ destructors

- Using pointers to classes
- Creating arrays of objects
- Using constructors for type conversion
- Using constructors and single inheritance
- Using constructors and multiple inheritance

Using Multiple Constructors

Constructors can be conceptually (using SmallTalk OOP terminology) viewed as messages that are sent to the class itself and ask it to create a new instance. C++ constructors are typeless functions with the same name as the classes with which they are associated. A class cannot have a declared constructor, nor can it have multiple constructors. Each constructor enables the instance of a class to be initialized in a specific way in order to attain a particular state. The following example illustrates the use of multiple constructors to initialize the components of a complex-number class:

```
class complex {
     private:
          double real;
          double imag;
     public:
          complex()
               { real = 0; imag = 0; }                    // #1A
          complex(double x)
               { real = x; imag = 0; }                    // #1B
          complex(double x, double y)                     // #1C
               { real = x; imag = y; }
          complex(complex& c)                             // #1D
               { real = c.real; imag = c.imag; }
     // other members
};
```

The first constructor for the complex class is the default constructor with a void parameter list. It is used to initialize an instance of class complex with the default `0` values assigned to both the real and imaginary components. The second constructor initializes the real part of a complex number with the value of the `x` parameter while

systematically assigning `0` to the imaginary part. The third constructor provides parameters for both components of the complex number. The fourth constructor initializes an instance of class `complex` by copying the contents of an existing one.

Using Default Parameters

Like other C++ functions, constructors admit the use of default parameters. For example, consider the following `XX` class and its constructor:

```
class XX {
     public:
          XX(char* message, int p1 = 1, int p2 = 2, int p3 = 3);
};
```

The `p1`, `p2`, and `p3` parameters have the default values of `1`, `2`, and `3`. Default parameters are listed from left to right in order of their increasing likelihood of using the default values. In the preceding example, the `p3` parameter is most likely to use its default value. The `p2` parameter is less likely to use its default value than `p3`, but more likely than `p1`. Using default parameters enables you to reduce the number of constructors. Without the default parameters used in the preceding `XX` class, the constructors for `XX` would be as follows:

```
class XX {
     public:
          XX(char* message);
          XX(char* message, int p1);
          XX(char* message, int p1, int p2);
          XX(char* message, int p1, int p2, int p3);
};
```

Default parameters, applied to the previous `complex` class, reduce the number of constructors from four to two:

```
class complex {
     private:
          double real;
          double imag;
     public:
          complex(double x = 0, double y = 0)     // #2A
               { real = x; imag = y; }
```

```
        complex(complex& c)                    // #2B
            { real = c.real; imag = c.imag; }
    // other members
};
```

The original two constructors, labeled #1A and #1B, are eliminated because the compiler flags an ambiguity error. Such a condition arises when a constructor's default parameters make it indistinguishable from other constructors when instances are being created. Consider the following declaration:

```
complex c1, c2(10), c3(1,8);
```

The #2A constructor declares instances c1 and c2 as do the #1A and #1B constructors. The removal of these two constructors resolves the ambiguity.

Has the removal of the explicit default constructor, #1A, stripped the complex class of a default constructor? The answer is no. The #2A constructor has default values for all its parameters. This parameter setup permits it to become the default constructor when it is invoked without specifying any arguments.

Using an Alternate Mechanism for Passing Arguments

C++ offers another mechanism for passing parameter values to data members. The preceding examples employ assignment operators. The alternate technique is to initialize data members with parameters. The general form follows:

```
class CLASS {
        type1 d1;
        type2 d2;
        type3 d3;
    public:
        CLASS(type1 p1, type2 p2, type3 p2)
        : d1(p1), d2(p2), d3(p3)
        { /* zero or more statements */ }
        // other members
};
```

The constructor parameter list is followed by a list of data member initialization. A colon separates the parameter list from the initialization list, which is followed by braces containing any statement required to complete the constructor's action. Using this approach for passing values to data members, the complex constructors are rewritten:

```
complex(double x = 0, double y = 0) : real(x), imag(y) { }
complex(complex& c) : real(c.real), imag(c.imag) { }
```

The C++ compiler creates a default constructor if a class declares no constructors.

Creating Objects

The two forms for using constructors to create instances of a class are abbreviated and explicit. Examples of using the abbreviated form to declare instances of the `complex` class follow:

```
complex c1, c2(10), c3(3,4);
```

In the abbreviated form, arguments for constructors accompany the name of the instance they create. The explicit form uses the general syntax

```
className instance = className(<list of constructor arguments>);
```

Examples of using the explicit form to declare the same instances of the complex class follow:

```
complex c1 = complex();
complex c2 = complex(10);
complex c3 = complex(3,4);
```

The explicit form uses the constructor and its argument list to create a temporary object assigned to the declared instance. The explicit form can omit the name of the constructor when one argument is used to create the class instance. The `c2` instance can be declared as

```
complex c2 = 10;
```

The compiler can deduce which constructor to use and which parameters use the default values.

Initializing Static Members

In the course of creating class instances, constructors perform a variety of jobs, among which is assigning values to nonstatic data members. By contrast, static data members must not be initialized by constructors. Static members should be initialized outside the class declaration, even if they are not public. This departure from regular initialization is justified because a static data member occurs only once regardless of the number of existing class instances.

The next version of the `complex` class contains the `count` private static data member, which counts the number of times the class constructors are called. Notice that the static data member is initialized to `0` outside the class declaration. Like nonstatic data members, the `count` data member is accessed by class member functions. By contrast, its initialization requires that it be qualified by a class name (not a class instance). The value of the `count` data member is reported by the `getCount` static member function. The class name is used to qualify the call to `getCount`.

```
#include <iostream.h>
#include <stdio.h>

class complex {
        double real, imag;
        static unsigned count;
     public:
        complex(double x = 0, double y = 0)
          : real(x), imag(y) { count++;}
        complex(complex& c) : real(c.real), imag(c.imag)
          { count++; }
        static unsigned getCount()
          { return count; };
        friend complex operator +(complex& c1, complex c2);
        friend ostream& operator <<(ostream& o, complex& c);
};

unsigned complex::count = 0;

main()
{
   complex c1, c2(10), c3(3,4);
   c1 = c2 + c3;
   cout << c1 << '\n';
```

```
   cout << "The constructors were called "
        << complex::getCount() << " times\n";
   return 0;
}
```

Using C++ Destructors

C++ destructors reverse the action of constructors. This is especially true when the class instances involve dynamic heap data or file I/O. The destructors enable the runtime system to terminate file I/O that is associated with the removed class instance, to recover the heap space, or to perform both operations. C++ allows only one destructor per class. The name of the destructor begins with the tilde character (~) followed by the class name. Destructors have no parameters and are called automatically at the end of the scope of the corresponding class instances. What follows is the `String` class with two constructors and a single destructor:

```
class String {
   private:
     unsigned len;
     char* sstr;
   public:
     String(const char* s);     // constructor
     String(String& s);         // constructor
     ~String() { delete [] sstr; } // destructor
     // other members
};

// definitions of member functions

main()
{
   String Greetings("Hello World!");
   // process string
}
```

The `Greetings` instance invokes the first constructor to allocate the heap space for storing the `"Hello World!"` string. When the main function terminates, the destructor is automatically called to regain the heap space created for the `Greetings` instance. Destructors can be explicitly called with pointers to classes. The next section discusses this further.

Using Pointers to Classes

What about using pointers to classes? Previous examples use variables to create class instances. C++ enables you to create dynamic instances using pointers to classes. The new operator is used with a class constructor to create the dynamic instances. Consider the following pointer to the String class:

```
main()
{
  String *p = new String("C++ is the best language");
  p->upper();
  cout << *p << '\n';
  delete p;
}
```

The p pointer is declared to handle the String class. The new operator allocates heap space for the String data members, whereas the String constructor initializes the dynamic instance and allocates additional heap space to store the string characters. The resulting instance of the String class is accessed by the p pointer. The delete statement reverses the steps of the new operator. The ~String destructor is invoked to deinitialize the instance accessed by p and to regain the heap space for storing the string characters. The delete operator then removes the heap space occupied by the class data members.

Using pointers to classes has an additional advantage that is not otherwise available. You can explicitly invoke the class destructor to remove a dynamic instance. You then create another instance. This aspect is shown in the following code:

```
main()
{
  String *p = new String("C++ is the best language");
  p->upper();
  cout << *p << '\n';
  p->String::~String(); // removes dynamic instance
  p = new String("The New C++");
  p->lower();
```

```
    cout << *p << '\n';
    delete p;
}
```

> The p pointer is first used to create the dynamic instance that stores the "C++ is the best language" text. The fourth statement destroys the instance accessed by the p pointer (notice the syntax for explicitly calling the class destructor) but leaves the dynamic space for class data members intact. This sanctions the fifth statement to create a new instance that stores the "The New C++" string. This new instance is removed when the program reaches the statement with the delete operator.

Creating Arrays of Objects

The preceding examples deal with single instances accessed by either variables or pointers. What about declaring arrays of objects? The rules for declaring both arrays and objects apply to arrays of objects. Suppose you want to declare an array of three complex numbers. The declaration is written

```
complex c[3] = { complex(), complex(10), complex(1,1) };
```

The elements `c[0]`, `c[1]`, and `c[2]` are initialized with `complex()`, `complex(10)`, and `complex(1,1)`. You can substitute `10` for `complex(10)`. If you omit the explicit array size as shown in the following example, the compiler uses the size of the initialization list as the size of the array:

```
complex c[] = { complex(1,2), complex(), complex(8) };
```

If the initialization list contains fewer constructor calls than the specified array size, the compiler uses the default constructor to initialize the remaining elements. The following example demonstrates that the first two elements are explicitly initialized. The compiler applies `complex()` to the rest of the array elements:

```
complex c[10] = { complex(10), complex(1,1) };
```

If class `complex` lacks a default constructor, the initialization list must be complete.

What about a dynamic array of objects? Using a pointer to create and access such an array complicates things a bit. Such an array cannot be initialized explicitly, and its class must define a default constructor.

What is the sequence of initializing an array of objects? The class constructors are applied to the array elements from the lowest to highest index.

The removal of an array of objects is similar to the removal of individual class instances. If the array is not dynamic, you need not perform any special task—just let the destructor handle it. If the array of objects is dynamic, you need to use the `delete` operator. The following example shows the deletion of a dynamic array:

```
complex *p = new complex[10];
// process the dynamic array
delete [] p; // remove the dynamic array
```

Using Constructors for Type Conversion

Examine the following instantiations of objects:

```
String s("Hello There");
String m = String("Hi There");
complex c(10);
complex d = complex(10);
```

Notice that class instances are created using constructors with single arguments. Each single argument represents information of a certain data type (character or double) that is converted into data used by created objects. This reveals the role of constructors as agents for type conversion with the target being an object. To be a conversion agent, a constructor must have only one argument. Constructors can convert data from subclass instances to ancestor class instances. For example, if you create the `complex3` class as a subclass of `complex`, and if `complex3` adds the `z` data member, you can do the following:

```
complex c(1,1);          // c.real = 1, c.imag = 1
complex3 d(9,9,9);       // d.real = 9, d.imag = 9, d.z = 9
c = complex(d);          // c.real is now 9, c.imag is also 9
```

The last statement applies the `complex` constructor to the instance of the `complex3` class. This assigns `9` to both the `real` and `imag` data members of the `c` instance. This is allowed because a subclass has at least the same number of data fields as its parent class (usually a subclass has more data members than its ancestors). Therefore, the information in the subclass data members is mapped onto existing superclass data members.

Using Constructors and Single Inheritance

Single inheritance creates a linear class hierarchy. Each class has one parent class and one child class. This makes tracing the sequence of constructor calls rather easy. The following hierarchy consists of three classes:

```
class A {
     protected:
          int fa;
     public:
          A(int va) : fa(va) {}
          // other members
};

class B : public A {
     protected:
          int fb;
     public:
          B(int va, int vb) : fb(vb), A(va) { }
          // other members
};
class C : public B {
     protected:
          int fc;
     public:
          C(int va, int vb, int vc) : fc(vc), B(va,vb) { }
          // other members
};
```

Constructor A initializes the instances of class A by initializing the fa data member with the va parameter. Constructor B initializes the fb data member with the value of parameter vb then invokes the A constructor with the va argument. Constructor C initializes the fc data member with the value of parameter vc, then invokes the B constructor with the argument list (va, vb).

What is the sequence of invoking the constructors when an instance of class C is created? Constructors C, B, and A are invoked in the following sequence. Constructor C is called first. It passes the value of vc to data member fc and then invokes the B constructor with the argument list (va, vb). Next, constructor B is called to action while constructor C waits for it to finish. The B constructor performs data member initialization and invokes constructor A. When constructor A finishes, execution returns first to B and then to C.

This depicts a smooth sequence of initializing an instance of class C using the constructor of that class as well as that of its ancestor classes. This makes sense because each ancestor class should contribute something to the instance of C. In the preceding hierarchy example, the entire chain of constructors is explicitly invoked. This is not always the case. Consider the following modified version of the three-class hierarchy:

```
class A {
     protected:
          int fa;
     public:
          A(int va = 1) : fa(va) {}
          // other members
};

class B : public A {
     protected:
          int fb;
     public:
          B() { fv = 2; }
          B(int va, int vb = 2) : fb(vb), A(va) { }
          // other members
};

class C : public B {
     protected:
          int fc;
     public:
```

```
        C(int vc) : fc(vc) { }
        // other members
};
```

Here C constructor simply initializes the fc data member with the value of the vc parameter. Constructors for classes A or B are not mentioned. In this case, the compiler invokes the default constructor of the parent class. Coincidentally, the new version of B has an explicit default constructor. This constructor is invoked to initialize the data members of B. Before the assignment in the B constructor begins, the constructor of A must be called. Because the B constructor makes no explicit call to the constructor of A, the default A constructor is called. This call invokes the A constructor with its single default value parameter. If the parameter of the A constructor is stripped of its default value, a compiler error occurs.

> The initialization of a class instance involves the constructors of the target class and its ancestors. The constructor of a class can specify which parent class constructor to call. If the constructor doesn't specify, the default constructor of the parent class is invoked. This rule applies to every member of the hierarchy that is an ancestor of the target class.

The removal of a subclass instance employs a sequence of destructors that starts with the target subclass and proceeds up the class hierarchy. The last constructor invoked is that of the base class.

Using Constructors and Multiple Inheritance

C++ supports multiple inheritance, allowing two or more classes to be parents of a subclass. The sequence of invoking the constructors for the target class and ancestor classes dictates that, as with single inheritance, all constructors of the contributing class hierarchy are called to initialize the subclass instances. How are the constructors invoked in the case of multiple inheritance? The following simple case of multiple inheritance outlines the sequence of constructor invocations. Classes A, B, C, and D are independent from one other. Class A is declared as follows:

```
class A {
    protected:
        int fa;
    public:
        A(int va = 1) : fa(va) { }
        ~A() { fa = 0; }
        // other members
};
```

The other classes are declared in a similar fashion. Now consider the X class, which is a subclass of B, A, D and C (in that sequence):

```
class X : public B, public A, public D, public C {
    protected:
        int fx;
    public:
        X(int vx = 100) : fx(vx), D(-4), A(-1) {}
        ~X() { fx = 0; }
        // other members
};
```

The X constructor explicitly invokes the D and A constructors. The default constructors for B and C are implicitly invoked. Given the preceding information, what is the sequence of constructors when an instance of X is initialized? Because the explicitly invoked constructor takes precedence, logic seems to indicate that the sequence starts with X constructor (of course) and resumes with the D, A, B and C constructors. The actual sequence depends only on the sequence of the inheritance list, which is B, A, D, and C.

The first superclass constructor to be invoked is that of B. Because the X constructor does not explicitly invoke a constructor of B, the default constructor is called. The second superclass constructor called is that of A. Because the X constructor calls A with a -1 argument, that call is used. Similarly, the constructor for D is called with a -4 argument, and the default constructor for class C is invoked. If classes A, B, C, and D are subclasses, the same rule applies to them. Table 2.1 summarizes the sequence of constructor calls.

Table 2.1. The sequence of constructor calls.

Parent Classes	Does constructor X explicitly invoke the class constructor?	Call Form
`B`	No	default
`A`	Yes	`A(-1)`
`D`	Yes	`D(-4)`
C	No	default

The sequence of destructors is called, starting with that of `X` followed by those of `C`, `A`, `D`, and `B`. This is the reverse order of calling the class constructors.

Summary

This chapter discussed various aspects of using C++ constructors and destructors and covered the following topics:

- Using multiple constructors offers diverse ways of building a class instance.
- Using default parameters reduces the number of constructors. The default parameters are listed from left to right in the order of their increasing likelihood of using the default values. If you first assign default arguments to all parameters of a constructor, don't supply it with arguments when creating a class instance; it automatically becomes the default constructor.
- You can use an alternate mechanism for passing arguments. Constructors enable you to pass the values of their arguments by initialization in addition to the more traditional assignment. The initialization mechanism uses a special syntax.
- With C++, you can create class instances in either of the following forms:

  ```
  aClass instance1(parameter);
  aClass instance = aClass(parameter);
  ```

  The first form combines the declaration of a class instance with the invocation of the appropriate constructor. The second form creates a class instance by explicit initialization using the constructor as a typecast agent.

- Static members, including nonpublic members, cannot be initialized by a class constructor. They must be initialized outside the class declaration.
- C++ destructors enable you to remove the dynamic space allocation of a class instance. This action prevents bleeding of the free store, or heap.
- Using pointers to classes enables you to create dynamic instances of a class. In addition, you can explicitly invoke the class destructor to remove these dynamic instances. With pointers to classes, you can create an instance, delete it, and then re-create it using a different constructor.
- You can create an array and specify constructor calls in a list of constructors. If the list contains fewer items than the size of an array, the remaining objects are created using the default constructor. If no list is used, the default constructor initializes every member of the object array.
- You can use constructors as explicit typecasting agents. Typecasting constructors are typically constructors with a single parameter. The parameter represents the data type to typecast into the target class.
- The initialization of a class instance involves the constructors of the target class and its ancestors. The constructor of a class can specify which parent class constructor to call. If it doesn't, the default constructor of the parent class is invoked. This rule applies to every hierarchy member that is an ancestor of the target class.
- The sequence of calling the constructor of the parent classes depends on the sequence of these classes in the inheritance list.

Public, Protected, and Private Declarations

C++ permits classes to control the level of access to their members. Classes have three levels of access: public, protected, and private. In this chapter, I discuss the following topics related to the public, protected, and private declarations:

- Design considerations
- Accessing inherited member functions
- Using `friend` functions
- Using `friend` classes

Design Considerations

The three levels of class member declarations empower the class to determine which instances and subclasses can access the class members. The following sections investigate each access level and discuss the category of data members and member functions that you can place in that level.

Public Members

Declaring a member as public gives open access to all instances of the class, all subclasses, and all instances of the subclasses. Most C++ programmers avoid placing data members in the public section. This rule is basically sound, although I've seen a few cases in which a declared public data member makes the coding of a class hierarchy much easier. This is generally true when you are extending classes in a hierarchy developed by another programmer or a team of programmers.

The member functions that should be declared public are the ones that enable the class instances and subclasses to manipulate the various data members and perform diverse tasks.

Protected Members

Declaring a member as protected prevents the instances of the class and its subclasses from accessing that member. Typically, classes declare most data members as protected. To allow client instances access to these data members, the classes provide public member functions for this purpose. Typically, more functions query data members than the ones that assign values to them. Frequent cases arise where you provide public member functions for reading and writing data to a protected data member. To justify such functions, the function that assigns a value to the data member performs data validation, manipulates other data members, or does both. Otherwise, using such functions merely adds overhead to the class.

The member functions that should be declared protected are the auxiliary functions, which should also be accessed by the subclasses.

Private Members

Private members read like top secret members. Only the member functions of the host class can directly access these members. Place the data members and member functions in the private section in the following cases:

- Only when you are absolutely sure they serve the host class and only the host class.
- Only when you are certain that no subclass should access these functions.

Accessing Members

In this section, I present three tables that classify the access of public, protected, and private members by the host classes and their instances and of the subclasses and their instances.

Table 3.1 shows the access rules for the various levels of members of a class. The table indicates what the class can access (which is everything) and what its instances can access.

Table 3.1. The access rules for a class and its instances.

	Class	Class	Instance
Declaration	***declares***	***accesses***	***accesses***
public	`pubData`	Yes	Yes
	`pubFunc`	Yes	Yes
protected	`pubData`	Yes	No
	`pubFunc`	Yes	No
private	`pubData`	Yes	No
	`pubFunc`	Yes	No

Table 3.2 shows the access rules for a class, its `public` subclass, and the instances of the subclass. The subclass accesses the public and protected members of the parent class. The instances of the subclass access the public members of its class and of the parent class.

Table 3.2. The access rules for a `public` subclass and its instances.

	Parent Class	Public SubClass	SubClass	Instance
Declaration	*declares*	*declares*	*accesses*	*accesses*
public	`pubData1`		Yes	Yes
	`pubFunc1`		Yes	Yes
		`pubData2`	Yes	Yes
		`pubFunc2`	Yes	Yes
protected	`proData1`		Yes	No
	`proFunc1`		Yes	No
		`proData2`	Yes	No
		`proFunc2`	Yes	No
private	`priData1`		No	No
	`priFunc1`		No	No
		`priData2`	Yes	No
		`priFunc2`	Yes	No

Table 3.3 shows the access rules for a class, its nonpublic class, and the instances of the subclass. The rules in this table are similar to that of Table 3.2, except the instances of the subclass do not access the public members of the parent class.

Table 3.3. The access rules for a nonpublic subclass and its instances.

	Parent Class	SubClass	SubClass	Instance
Declaration	*declares*	*declares*	*accesses*	*accesses*
public	`pubData1`		Yes	No
	`pubFunc1`		Yes	No
		`pubData2`	Yes	Yes
		`pubFunc2`	Yes	Yes
protected	`proData1`		Yes	No
	`proFunc1`		Yes	No
		`proData2`	Yes	No
		`proFunc2`	Yes	No

	Parent Class	SubClass	SubClass	Instance
Declaration	*declares*	*declares*	*accesses*	*accesses*
private	`priData1`		No	No
	`priFunc1`		No	No
		`priData2`	Yes	No
		`priFunc2`	Yes	No

Making a subclass a nonpublic child works in cases where the parent class gives an auxiliary type of support. Here is an example. Listing 3.1 contains the source code for the FIXSTAK2.CPP program. The listing declares two template classes—an `Array` class that models generic arrays and `fixedStack`, `Array`'s child class that models fixed-size stacks. The listing declares `Stack` as a nonpublic subclass. This kind of declaration prevents the instances of `Stack` from calling the public member functions of `Array` and possibly circumventing the functions of `Stack`.

Listing 3.1 shows that a change of context in a class hierarchy justifies the declaration of nonpublic subclasses.

Listing 3.1. The source code for the FIXSTAK2.CPP program.

```
#include <iostream.h>

enum boolean { false, true };

template<class T>
class Array
{
  protected:
    unsigned workSize;
    unsigned arrSize;
    T* arrPtr;

  public:
```

continues

Listing 3.1. continued

```
        Array()
          { arrSize = 0;
            workSize = 0;
            arrPtr = NULL;
          }
        ~Array()
          { if (arrPtr) delete [] arrPtr; }
        void create(unsigned ArrSize)
          { arrPtr = new T[arrSize = ArrSize];
            workSize = 0;
          }
         boolean insert(T x)
           {
             if (arrPtr && workSize < arrSize) {
               arrPtr[workSize++] = x;
               return true;
             }
             else
               return false;
           }
         boolean remove(T& x)
           {
             if (arrPtr && workSize > 0) {
               x = arrPtr[--workSize];
               return true;
             }
             else
               return false;
           }
         void erase()
           {  workSize = 0; }
    };

    template<class T>
    class fixedStack : Array<T>
    {

      protected:

        Array<T>* p;
        unsigned height;   // height of stack
```

```
  public:
    fixedStack(unsigned MaxSize = 10)
      { p = new Array<T>;
        p->create(MaxSize);
      }
    ~fixedStack()
      { delete p; }
    /* ****************** state query methods ***************** */
    boolean isempty() {
        return (height == 0) ? true : false;
    }

    /* ************** object manipulation methods ************* */
    void push(T x)
      { if (p->insert(x))
          height++;
      }
    boolean pop(T& x)
      { boolean ok = p->remove(x);
        if (ok) height--;
        return ok;
      }
    void clear()
      { p->erase(); }
};


main()
{
  fixedStack<int> stk(10);
  int i;

  stk.push(1);
  stk.push(10);
  stk.push(100);
  stk.push(1000);
  stk.push(10000);

  while (stk.pop(i))
    cout << i << "\n";

  return 0;
}
```

Friend Functions

Friend functions (and operators) are nonmember functions that have the privilege of accessing the members of a class. C++ requires that you avoid using the `this` pointer in a `friend` function. The return type of the `friend` function need not be the host class. Here is an example of the `friend` function. The `String` class has three overloaded + operators to concatenate `String` class instances, a `String` instance with a `char`, and a `char` type with a `String` instance. The + operators return a `String` result:

```
#include <string.h>

class String
{

 protected:
   char *str;          // pointer to characters
   unsigned maxSize;       // total number of bytes allocated
   unsigned len;           // current String size

 public:
   String(const char* s);
   String(const String&);
   ~String();

   // other member functions

   friend String operator +(String&, String&);
   friend String operator +(String&, char);
   friend String operator +(char, String&);
};

String operator +(cString& s1, cString& s2)
{
   String result(s1.len + s2.len + 1);

   strcpy(result.str,s1.str);
   strcat(result.str,s2.str);
   result.len = s1.len + s2.len;

   return result;
}
```

```
String operator +(cString& s, char c)
{
   String result(s.len + 2);

   strcpy(result.str,s.str);
   result.len = s.len;
   *(result.str+result.len+1) = '\0';
   *(result.str+result.len) = c;
   result.len++;
   return result;
}

String operator +(char c, cString& s)
{
   String result(2 + s.len) ;

   *(result.str+1) = '\0';
   *(result.str) = c;
   strcat(result.str,s.str);
   result.len = s.len + 1;
   return result;
}
```

Notice that each overloaded + operator accesses the `str` and `len` data members of the `String` class. Using friend functions and operators enables you to write routines that cannot be implemented by member functions.

Friend Classes

Using `friend` functions and operators raises little controversy regarding programming techniques. Moreover, utilizing `friend` functions adds practically no complexity to the design of classes. By contrast, using `friend` classes raises all kinds of caution flags. The basic assumption is that a good class interface should, in most cases, help you avoid using `friend` classes. These classes tend to lure you into lowering the class design standards because they provide an easy way to access data members. Object-oriented purists (who, of course, program in languages other than C++) may criticize the idea of `friend` classes as nonhierarchical links between classes that violate pure OOP inheritance rules. Critical application speed may provide the reason to use `friend` classes to bypass the overhead of member functions that access or assign value in the befriended class.

Table 3.4 shows the access rules for a `friend` class and its instances. Notice that the `friend` class gains access to all members of the befriended class. The instances of the `friend` class have access to only the `public` members of the befriended class. Concerning the `public` subclasses of the `friend` class, what can they access? They can access the `public` members of the befriended class. The instances of these subclasses access the same members. You can draw the conclusion that subclasses of `friend` classes only retain the privilege of accessing the `public` members of the befriended class.

Table 3.4. The access rules for a `friend` class and its instances.

	Class	Friend Class	Friend Class	Instance
Declaration	*declares*	*declares*	*accesses*	*accesses*
public	`pubData1`		Yes	Yes
	`pubFunc1`		Yes	Yes
		`pubData2`	Yes	Yes
		`pubFunc2`	Yes	Yes
protected	`proData1`		Yes	No
	`proFunc1`		Yes	No
		`proData2`	Yes	No
		`proFunc2`	Yes	No
private	`priData1`		Yes	No
	`priFunc1`		Yes	No
		`priData2`	Yes	No
		`priFunc2`	Yes	No

Now look at an example that uses a `friend` class. Listing 3.1, which I presented earlier, shows you a `Stack` class template that is a subclass of the `Array` template class. The next example shows the two classes as separate, with `Stack` class as a friend of `Array` class. Listing 3.2 shows the source code for the FIXSTAK3.CPP program.

Listing 3.2. The source code for the FIXSTAK3.CPP program.

```
#include <iostream.h>

enum boolean { false, true };
```

```
template<class T>
class Array
{
  friend class fixedStack<T>;

  protected:
    unsigned workSize;
    unsigned arrSize;
    T* arrPtr;

  public:
    Array()
      { arrSize = 0;
        workSize = 0;
        arrPtr = NULL;
      }
    ~Array()
      { if (arrPtr) delete [] arrPtr; }
    void create(unsigned ArrSize)
      { arrPtr = new T[arrSize = ArrSize];
        workSize = 0;
      }
     boolean insert(T x)
       {
         if (arrPtr && workSize < arrSize) {
           arrPtr[workSize++] = x;
           return true;
         }
         else
           return false;
       }
     boolean remove(T& x)
       {
         if (arrPtr && workSize > 0) {
           x = arrPtr[--workSize];
           return true;
         }
         else
           return false;
       }
    void erase()
```

continues

Listing 3.2. continued

```
        {  workSize = 0; }
};

template<class T>
class fixedStack
{

  protected:

    Array<T>* p;

  public:
    fixedStack(unsigned MaxSize = 10)
      { p = new Array<T>;
        p->create(MaxSize);
      }
    ~fixedStack()
      { delete p; }
    /* ****************** state query methods ***************** */
    boolean isempty() {
        return (p->workSize == 0) ? true : false;
    }

    /* ************** object manipulation methods ************* */
    void push(T x)
      { p->insert(x); }
    boolean pop(T& x)
      { return p->remove(x); }
    void clear()
      { p->workSize = 0; }
};


main()
{
  fixedStack<int> stk(10);
  int i;

  stk.push(1);
```

```
  stk.push(10);
  stk.push(100);
  stk.push(1000);
  stk.push(10000);

  while (stk.pop(i))
    cout << i << "\n";

  return 0;
}
```

Examine the code in Listing 3.2 and notice the following changes that I made because of the friendship between the `Array` and `Stack` classes :

1. The `Stack` class has no `height` data member. I removed this member because it's redundant with the `workSize` member of `Array` class.
2. The `push` and `pop` member functions are simpler than in the previous version, because the data member `height` is not used.
3. The new version of the `isempty` member function compares the `p->workSize` expression to zero.
4. The new version of the `clear` member function assigns zero to the `workSize` data member, accessed using the `p` pointer.

Summary

This chapter discussed topics related to the `public`, `protected`, and `private` members of a class. The text presented the following points:

- Design considerations are popularly used to place the various kinds of data members and member functions in the public, protected, and private sections of a class.
- This chapter presented tables that make it easy to understand the access rules of various members by their own classes, the class instance, the subclasses, and the instances of these subclasses.

- Using `friend` functions provides functions that support operations and calls that are not possible with member functions. C++ requires that at least one parameter in the `friend` function have the host class type. The return type of the `friend` function need not be the host class.
- Using `friend` classes enables classes to establish access outside the OOP inheritance scheme. `friend` classes enable you to speed up applications, but they can complicate the design of your classes. The text also presents a table that explains the access rules of class members by their `friend` classes and their instances.

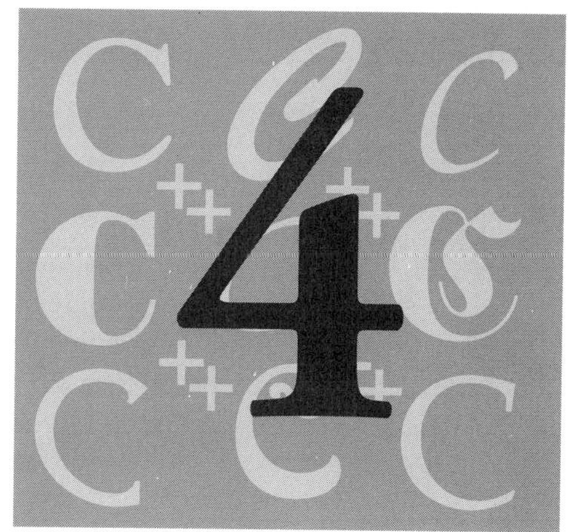

Member Functions

The member functions of a class manipulate the instances of that class. Without member functions, classes become C-style structures. This chapter looks at the following topics that are related to member functions:

- The various roles of member functions
- The virtual member functions
- The dormant member functions

Roles of Member Functions

Member functions support the operations of a class by providing various services. The need of a class for the various kinds of member functions depends, of course, on the features and functionality of that class. The next subsections present the various kinds of member functions.

Instantiation Functions

This category of functions contains the class constructor at the top of its list. Constructors are the most prominent instantiation functions. Typically, constructors serve to initialize important data members, allocate dynamic memory, open streams, and perform other tasks that create a class instance. Here is a simple example of a `String` string class:

```
#include <string.h>
const unsigned DEFAULT_STRING_SIZE = 20;

class String
{
     protected:
          char* str;
          unsigned size;
          unsigned len;

          String& copy(String& s);

     public:
          String();
          String(const char* s);
          String(String& s)
               { copy(s); }
          // other constructors
          ~String();

          // other member functions
          String& operator =(String&)
          {
               copy(s);
               return *this;
          }
          String& operator =(const char);
};

String::String()
{
  len = 0;
  str = new char[size = DEFAULT_STRING_SIZE];
```

```
  str[0] = '\0';
}

String::String(const char* s)
{
  unsigned n = strlen(s);

  if (n == 0) {
     len = 0;
     str = new char[size = DEFAULT_STRING_SIZE];
     str[0] = '\0';
  }
  else {
     len = n;
     str = new char[size = n + 1];
     strcpy(str, s);
  }
}
```

The preceding example shows a typical usage of a constructor to initialize data members and to allocate dynamic memory.

Another type of instantiation function involves a multistage initialization of an object. In this case, the constructor merely performs the first stage and creates a class instance that needs additional initialization steps. Let me explain this type of function with the following example.

Consider a class that models a statistical linear regression object. Linear regression correlates two observed variables, the independent variable X and the dependent variable Y, using the following simple model:

```
Y = A + B X
```

Linear regression attempts to estimate the values of the slope (coefficient B) and the intercept (coefficient A) of the straight line that relates the Y observations with the X observations. The following equation calculates the regression intercept, A:

```
A = (_Y _X2 - _X _XY) / (N _X2 - (_X)2)
```

The following equation calculates the regression slope, `B`:

```
B = (N _XY - _X _Y) / (N _X2 - (_X)2)
```

The previous two equations contain five summations (`N` is the sum of observation pairs `(X, Y)`). This means that to obtain the regression coefficients you need to perform the following tasks:

- Initialize the summations.
- Update the summations with observations.
- Optionally remove bad observations.
- Calculate the regression slope and intercept.

The preceding outline indicates that at least three stages (or states, if you prefer) exist: initialization, summation, and calculation. The regression model and its multistage initialization translate into the following class:

```
class linearRegression
{
     enum Boolean { false, true };
     enum LRstate { initState, sumState, readyState };

     protected:
          double N;
          double sumX;
          double sumX2;
          double sumY;
double sumXY;
          double slope;
          double intercept;
          LRState state;

     public:
          linearRegression() { clearSums() }
          void clearSums();
          void addData(double x, double y);
          void removeData(double x, double y);
          Boolean calcRegressionCoeff(double &Slope,
                                      double &Intercept);
          double projectX(double x);
};
```

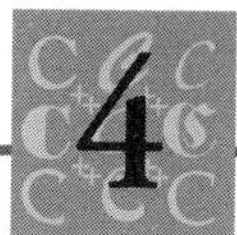

```
void linearRegression::clearSums()
{
  N = 0;
  sumX = 0;
  sumX2 = 0;
  sumY = 0;
  sumXY = 0;
  state = initState;
}

void linearRegression::addData(double x, double y)
{
  N++;
  sumX += x;
  sumX2 += x * x;
  sumY += y;
  sumXY += x * y;
  // shift state to sumState if at least 3
  // observations are summed
  if (N > 2)
    state = sumState;
}

void linearRegression::removeData(double x, double y)
{
  if (N == 0) return;
  N--;
  sumX -= x;
  sumX2 -= x * x;
  sumY -= y;
  sumXY -= x * y;
  // shift the state back to the initialization state if
  // fewer than 3 observations are summed
  if (N < 3)
    state = initState;
}

Boolean linearRegression::calcRegressionCoeff(double &Slope,
                                              double &Intercept);
{
  double d;
```

```
    // exit if the state of the class instance is not ready
    // for calculation
    if (state == initState) {
       Slope = 0;
       Intercept = 0;
       return false;
    }

    // shift state to ready state
    state = readyState;
    // calculate coefficients
    d = (N * sumX2 - sumX * sumX);
    slope = (n * sumXY - sumX * sumY) / d;
    intercept = (sumY * sumX2 - sumX * sumXY) / d;
    Slope = slope;
    Intercept = intercept;
}

double linearRegression::projectX(double x)
{
    return (state == readyState) ? intercept + slope * x : -1.0E+30;
}
```

The class constructor performs the first step in initializing the statistical summations by calling the `clearSums` member function. The member functions `addData`, `calcRegression`, and, to a lesser degree, `removeData`, contribute to completing the instantiation of the instances of the `linearRegression` class. You can invoke the `projectX` member function only when the class instance is completely instantiated. The `projectX` function calculates the estimated Y value for an X value. This operation is not possible unless the regression coefficients are available. In turn, the availability of these coefficients is possible only if enough observations exist in the summations data members. This multistage initialization requires that the `linearRegression` class use the data member state to track the progress in instantiating a class instance. A more complete implementation class might include additional member functions that depend on the results of `calcRegression`.

Data Broker Functions

This type of member function performs assignment, memory management, and type conversion (recall from Chapter 2, "Constructors and Destructors," that constructors can also perform type conversion). Recall the `copy` member function in the `String` class that I presented earlier in this chapter. This member function performs the actual assignment of one `String` instance to another. This process involves allocation and deallocation of dynamic data, as shown:

```
String& String::copy(String& s)
{
  delete [] str;
  size = s.size;
  len = s.len;
  str = new char[size];

  strcpy(str, s.str);
}
```

The `String` class also provides the = operator as a public member function that enables you to assign String instances. This member function and the `String(String&)` constructor call the protected copy member function to perform the actual copying.

Implementation Functions

With implementation functions, you can manipulate the instances of a class. This category of member functions appears in the public section of class and makes the functions accessible to the client applications. Here is another version of the string class `String` that shows a few implementation functions. These functions convert the characters of an instance into uppercase or lowercase, reverse the order of characters, and search for a substring:

```
#include <string.h>

class String
{
     protected:
          char* str;
          unsigned size;
          unsigned len;

          String& copy(
```

```
    public:
        String();
        String(const char* s);
        String(String& s)
            { copy(s); }
        // other constructors
        ~String();

        // implementation member functions
        void stringUpper()
            { strupr(str); }
        void stringLower();
            { strlwr(str); }
        void stringReverse();
            { strrev(str); }
        unsigned pos(String& s, unsigned offset);
        // other member functions
};
```

Access Functions

One of the first rules you learn about declaring data members in a class is to make them nonpublic. This data hiding approach is essential for protecting important data members against unwarranted access by client applications. The client applications need to set and possibly query certain data members. To support a limited access, you need to use access functions.

Because classes can model a large number of real objects, the only general rules on limiting access to data members deal with protecting them. A good, typical example is the following version of the `String` class. (Think of each version of a `String` class that I present in this chapter as part of the same class with specific member functions focused.)

```
class String
{
    protected:
        char* str;
```

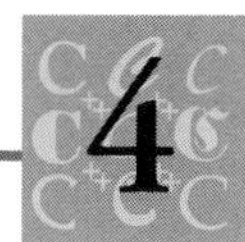

```
        unsigned size;
        unsigned len;

        String& copy(String &s);

    public:
        String();
        String(const char* s);
        String(String& s)

            { copy(s); }
        // other constructors
        ~String();

        // other member functions
        String& operator =(String&)
        {
            copy(s);
            return *this;
        }
        char* getString()
            { return str; }
        unsigned getSize()
            { return size; }
        unsigned stringLen()
            { return len; }
        char& operator [](unsigned index)
            { return *(str + index); }
};
```

The class enables you to query the values of the `size`, `len`, and `str` data members using the `getSize`, `stringLen`, and `getString` member functions. Because you don't need to assign values to the `size` and `len` data members, no counterpart functions that assign values to these two members exist. On the other hand, the class enables you to assign a new string of characters to the class instance. At first, this two-way access seems to defeat the purpose of making the `str` data member protected. Nevertheless, such two-way access functions perform controlled access and enable themselves to update other data members, particularly `len`, when you write a new `string` to a `String` object.

The `[]` operator provides a two-way access to the individual characters of the string. The previous implementation does not perform error-checking on the argument of the parameter index in order to keep the code short. The `[]` access operator works well with classes containing members that are either static arrays or pointers to dynamic arrays.

Auxiliary Functions

Auxiliary functions assist the implementation functions in performing their tasks. Therefore, auxiliary functions should be declared nonpublic because they are never intended to be invoked by the class instance.

Here is an example of auxiliary functions that play a significant role in implementing the operations of an integer class array, `IntArray`. The class models a dynamic array and includes public member functions that store, recall, sort, and search the data in the array. Typically, an instance of the `IntArray` class is not sorted (the class stores the status of the array order in the `isSorted` member). The `QuickSort` member function sorts the array by using the recursive Quicksort method. The `QuickSort` function is a public function that invokes the protected and recursive `Qsort` member function. The latter is an auxiliary member function that actually orders the array. Calling the `QuickSort` function is safer than calling the `Qsort` method because:

- The `QuickSort` function needs no arguments.
- The `QuickSort` function calls the `Qsort` function with the valid arguments.

The `IntArray` class provides the `Search` public member function to search for a value in the dynamic array. This member function is an abstract one. It invokes the protected member function `binSearch` if the array is sorted. Otherwise, the `Search` function calls the protected `linSearch` member function. The `binSearch` and `linSearch` member functions are auxiliary functions that actually perform the binary and linear search, respectively. Making these functions inaccessible to instances of `IntArray` ensures that these instances prevent the following calls:

- Calling the `binSearch` function when the array is unordered; such an invocation leads to false results.
- Calling the `linSearch` function when the array is sorted; this call uses the less efficient linear search method.

Here is the code fragment for the `IntArray` class:

```
class IntArray
{

    enum boolean ( false, true };
```

```
    protected:
        int* dataPtr;
        unsigned size;
        unsigned maxSize;
        boolean isSorted;

        // performs recursive QuickSort
        void Qsort(unsigned left, unsigned right);
        // performs binary search on sorted array
        unsigned binSearch(unsigned searchData);
        // performs linear search on unsorted array
        unsigned linSearch(unsigned searchData);

    public:
        IntArray(unsigned theMaxSize);
        ~IntArray();

        unsigned expand(unsigned newSize);
        void store(int n, unsigned index);
        int recall(unsigned index);
        void QuickSort()
            { Qsort(0, size - 1); }
        unsigned Search(unsigned searchData)
        { return (isSorted) ? binSearch(searchData)
                            : linSearch(serachData);
        }
}
```

const Functions

With C++, you can declare class instances that are constant. Naturally, this means that the data members of these classes cannot be altered. Consequently, you must provide the targeted class with a group of functions that pledge, so to speak, not to change data members. To support this read-only pledge scheme, C++ enables you to append the `const` keyword after the parameter list of a member function in the class declaration. Such a declaration tells the compiler that the targeted function cannot and does not alter a data member. This impacts the compilation process, during which the compiler ensures that the statements in the `const` member function live up to the read-only pledge. If the compiler detects a pledge violation, it generates a compile-time error. In addition, when the compiler handles a constant object, it ensures that the object only calls constant functions. Otherwise, the compiler flags an error.

Look at a code fragment that implements a class with constant member functions. Here is a version of the `String` class, which uses constant functions to provide formal read-only access member functions:

```
class String
{
     protected:
          char* str;
          unsigned size;
          unsigned len;

          String& copy(String &s);

     public:
          String();
          String(const char* s);
          String(String& s)

               { copy(s); }
          // other constructors
          ~String();

          // other member functions
          String& operator =(String&)
          {
               copy(s);
               return *this;
          }
          char* getString() const
               { return str; }
          unsigned getSize() const
               { return size; }
          unsigned stringLen() const
               { return len; }
          char& operator [](unsigned index) const
               { return *(str + index); }
};
```

The class declares the `getString`, `getSize`, `stringLen`, and the `[]` operator as constant functions. These constant functions do not alter any data member. The first three member functions are easy to grasp. What about the `[]` operator? Making the `[]` operator constant means that you can only use it to obtain a character from a class instance. You cannot place the `[]` operator to the left of an assignment operator.

Virtual Functions

With C++, you can override an inherited nonvirtual member function by declaring a new version of this function that has the same name but possesses a different parameter list. In other words, you can override a nonvirtual member function by one that changes its signature. This scheme of overriding nonvirtual member functions throws abstract class behavior out the window. Virtual functions provide a hierarchy of classes with an abstract response. This advantage requires that the parameter list of a virtual function remains the same across a class hierarchy. Each class can define its own virtual function to provide a custom response to that function's call. A good example for using virtual functions is a graphics drawing routine (call it `Draw`) for a geometric shape. Consider a class hierarchy that contains geometric shapes. In this hierarchy, each shape-modeling class defines its own `Draw` virtual function to ensure that it correctly responds to the calls for the `Draw` function. These calls are issued by higher level member functions.

The rule for declaring a virtual function is "once virtual always virtual." In other words, once you declare a function to be virtual in a class, any subclass that declares the same function with the same signature (that is, the number, types, and sequence of arguments) must also be virtual. The virtual declaration is mandatory for the descendant classes. At first this rule seems to lock you in. This limitation is certainly true for object-oriented programming languages that support virtual functions but not overloaded functions. In the case of C++, the work-around is interesting. You can declare nonvirtual and overloaded functions that have the same name as the virtual function but bear a different signature. Moreover, you cannot inherit nonvirtual member functions that share the same name with a virtual function. Here is a simple example that illustrates the point:

```
#include <iostream.h>

class A
{
  public:
    A() {}

    virtual void foo(char c)
      { cout << "virtual A::foo() returns " << c << '\n'; }
};

class B : public A
{
  public:
    B() {}

    void foo(const char* s)
      { cout << "B::foo() returns " << s << '\n'; }
    void foo(int i)
      { cout << "B::foo() returns " << i << '\n'; }
    virtual void foo(char c)
      { cout << "virtual B::foo() returns " << c << '\n'; }

};

class C : public B
{
  public:
    C() {}


    void foo(const char* s)
```

```
      { cout << "C::foo() returns " << s << '\n'; }
    void foo(double x)
      { cout << "C::foo() returns " << x << '\n'; }
    virtual void foo(char c)
      { cout << "virtual C::foo() returns " << c << '\n'; }

};

main()
{
  int n = 100;
  A Aobj;
  B Bobj;
  C Cobj;

  Aobj.foo('A');
  Bobj.foo('B');
  Bobj.foo(10);
  Bobj.foo("Bobj");
  Cobj.foo('C');
  // if you uncomment the next statement
  // the program does not compile
  // Cobj.foo(n);
  Cobj.foo(144.123);
  Cobj.foo("Cobj");

  return 0;
}
```

The previous code declares three classes—`A`, `B`, and `C`—to form a linear hierarchy of classes. Class `A` declares function `foo(char)` as virtual. Class `B` also declares its own version of the virtual `foo(char)` function. In addition, the `B` class declares the nonvirtual overloaded functions `foo(const char* s)` and `foo(int)`. Class `C`, the descendant of `B`, declares the virtual `foo(char)` function and the nonvirtual and overloaded `foo(const char*)` and `foo(double)` functions. Notice that `C` must declare the `foo(const char*)` function if it needs it because it cannot inherit the `B::foo(const char*)` member function. C++ supports a different function inheritance scheme when an overloaded and virtual function is involved. The `main` function creates an instance for each of the three classes and involves the various versions of the `foo` member function.

Dormant Member Functions

The private and protected declarations empower classes to determine the level of member hiding for subclasses and for class instances. The C++ compiler ensures that your code complies with the member hiding scheme. Beyond the compilation and linking steps, no formal mechanism exists to implement a scheme for hiding a member function at runtime. In other words, you cannot conditionally toggle the access of one or more member functions for a specific class instance. To implement a simple yet effective scheme that pseudo-hides a member function (a situation in which the function can be called, but it does not perform its normal task), you need the following components:

- A private data member that acts as a flag or as an access level for the various class instances.
- The constructors for the client class must assign an access level or flag to each instance.
- The pseudo-hidden member functions first examine the access flag or level to determine whether to proceed with their normal tasks. If the access flag or level is in a prohibitive mode, the member function exits.

The previous scheme essentially deactivates the pseudo-hidden member function. Although any instance from the same class (or a subclass) can invoke that member function, it cannot necessarily make that function perform its tasks.

Using an access flag implements a simple access scheme—an instance either can make the pseudo-hidden member function perform its tasks or it cannot. Employing an access level enables you to classify the member functions (and the tasks they perform) as different privileges that are available for different instances.

Now, look at a simple example that implements the previous scheme for deactivating pseudo-hidden member functions.

```
#include <iostream.h>

enum boolean { false, true };

class X
{
  protected:
    unsigned accessLevel;
```

```
    boolean accessErr;

  public:
    X(unsigned AccessLevel)
      : accessLevel(AccessLevel)
    {
      accessErr = false;
    }
    boolean getAccessErr()
      { return accessErr; }

    unsigned demote(unsigned newAccessLevel);
    void anyInstance();
    void privilege();
    void wizard();

};

unsigned X::demote(unsigned newAccessLevel)
{
  if (accessLevel > newAccessLevel)
    accessLevel = newAccessLevel;
  return accessLevel;
}


void X::anyInstance()
{
  cout << "Any instance can call this function\n";
  accessErr = false;
}

void X::privilege()
{
   if (accessLevel >= 1) {
     cout << "This is for the privileged\n";
     accessErr = false;
   }
   else
     accessErr = true;
}
```

```
void X::wizard()
{
   if (accessLevel >= 2) {
     cout << "This is for the wizards\n";
     accessErr = false;
   }
   else
     accessErr = true;
}

main()
{
  X x(0), y(1), z(2);


  x.anyInstance();
  x.privilege();
  if (x.getAccessErr())
    cout << "Object x cannot invoke function privilege()\n";
  x.wizard();
  if (x.getAccessErr())
    cout << "Object x cannot invoke function wizard()\n";

  y.anyInstance();
  y.privilege();
  if (y.getAccessErr())
    cout << "Object y cannot invoke function privilege()\n";
  y.wizard();
  if (y.getAccessErr())
    cout << "Object y cannot invoke function wizard()\n";

  z.anyInstance();
  z.privilege();
  if (z.getAccessErr())
    cout << "Object z cannot invoke function privilege()\n";
  z.wizard();
  if (z.getAccessErr())
    cout << "Object z cannot invoke function wizard()\n";

  return 0;
}
```

The X class declares two data members, accessLevel and accessErr. The accessLevel member stores the access level that determines whether an instance can invoke a member function and successfully use that function. The accessErr member is a Boolean flag that stores the state of the access error. The X class contains a constructor that assigns the various class instances with a class level.

The getAccessErr member function returns the access error status for the last invocation of a member function in an instance.

The demote member function illustrates how you can explicitly demote the access of an instance. Implicit promotion and demotion of class instances should take place in special member functions that perform critical tasks and may result in altering the access privilege of an instance.

The anyInstance member function is an ordinary member function that has no access restrictions.

The privilege member function performs its task only if the accessLevel member for an instance is 1 or greater. Similarly, the wizard member function performs its task only if the accessLevel member for an instance is 2 or greater. Invoking the last two member functions with the wrong access level assigns a true Boolean value to the accessErr member and then exits.

The main function declares three instances of the X class: x, y, and z. These instances have the access levels of 0, 1, and 2 respectively. The main function invokes the anyInstance, privilege, and wizard member functions with each instance of X. In the case of the last two member functions, the main function uses an if statement to determine whether the access is successful. Here is the output of the previous program:

```
Any instance can call this function
Object x cannot invoke function privilege()
Object x cannot invoke function wizard()
Any instance can call this function
This is for the privileged
Object y cannot invoke function wizard()
Any instance can call this function
This is for the privileged
This is for the wizards
```

Summary

This chapter presented selected discussions on member functions and covered the following topics:

- The various roles of member functions. These roles include instantiation functions, data broker functions, implementation functions, access functions, and auxiliary functions.
- The virtual member functions. This chapter discussed how C++ enables you to declare functions that overload virtual member functions. Such nonvirtual functions cannot be inherited because of the enforcement of the virtual function scheme.
- Dormant member functions. This topic discusses how you can use simple techniques to implement pseudo-hidden member function for specific class instances. This scheme enables you to determine the operations that are allowed for the various instances of class. This plan resembles the access levels in electronic bulletin boards.

Static Members

With C++, you can declare class data members and member functions that are static. The data members represent common data for all the instances of the host class. The compiler creates a single storage space for the static members of a class. C++ also enables you to declare static member functions so you can set and query the static members. In this chapter, I discuss static members and their applications. I cover the following topics in this chapter:

- Declaring static data members
- Initializing static data members
- Declaring static member functions
- Use of static members
- Examples of using the static members

Declaring Static Data Members

Declaring static data members involves placing the `static` keyword before the member's data type. This declaration tells the compiler to reserve a special memory location for each static data member. All instances of that class share the same static data members. Static data members can be single variables, arrays, or structures.

Initializing Static Data Members

C++ requires that you initialize the static data members—regardless of their access level—outside the declaration of their class. Usually, you should initialize static members in the implementation file. In addition, C++ requires that you qualify the static data member by stating its data type and class in the initialization statement.

Declaring Static Member Functions

You can manipulate static data members using ordinary member functions. If a member function operates mainly on a static data member, it makes sense to declare that function as static. To declare a member function as static, place the `static` keyword before its return type. Using the static member function in the definition of other member functions and client functions requires that you qualify the function's name with the name of the host class.

Why Use Static Members?

The notion of static variables has its roots in C. Incorporating static data members in C++ classes opens new doors. At the heart of static data members is the concept of commonality between the various instances of a class. Static members provide a kind of link between the class instances. In purist object-oriented thinking, static data members are owned by the class itself and accessible to the various class instances. By viewing static members this way, you can better explore their roles and applications. The kinds of applications for the static members vary and are limited only by the programmer's imagination. Here is a small list of how static data members can be applied:

- Counting the number of class instances. This application allows a static member to keep track of the number of instances. The instance counting member is incremented in the class constructors and decremented in the class destructor.
- Shared error status or error message. Some classes can consolidate the error status flags and error messages using static members. The instances of such classes need not identify the offending instance. Rather, these instances are more concerned with whether an error has occurred. I will clarify this application with an example in the next section.
- Instance communications. In case the various instances of a class interact with each other, you can use static data members to flag requests between the various instances. The static data member stores an index or a pointer to the consumer instance, which requires a service from a supplier instance.
- Shared information. This kind of application deals with a class having instances that share fixed and/or basic data. Think of this data as a miniature database. Rather than using ordinary data members that contain duplicated data, static members offer a better support for such common data.
- Iterators. You can store the pointers to the various instances of a class in a linked list accessed by a static member. You can then implement an iterator function to process all or some of the instances.

Examples

In this section I present various examples that help you to further clarify the rules and concepts related to static members.

Instance Counter

The first example shows you how a static member is used to track the number of class instances. Listing 5.1 shows the source code for the STATIC1.CPP program. The simple `IntArray` class models a dynamic array of integers. The class declares the `numInstances` static data member to track the number of instances. Because this data member is protected, the class offers the `getNumInstances` static member function to return the value stored in the `numInstances` member.

Listing 5.1. The source code for the STATIC1.CPP program.

```
#include <iostream.h>

class IntArray
{
   protected:
     static unsigned numInstances;
     unsigned size;
     int* dataPtr;

   public:
     IntArray(unsigned Size);
     ~IntArray();

     unsigned getSize() const
       { return size; }
     int& operator [](unsigned index)
       { return dataPtr[index]; }

     static unsigned getNumInstances() const
       { return numInstances; }
};

IntArray::IntArray(unsigned Size)
{
  size = (Size > 0) ? Size : 1;
  dataPtr = new int[size];
  numInstances++;
}

IntArray::~IntArray()
{
  delete [] dataPtr;
  numInstances--;
}

unsigned IntArray::numInstances = 0;

const unsigned size1 = 10;
const unsigned size2 = 20;
```

```
const unsigned size3 = 30;

main()
{
  IntArray ar1(size1);
  unsigned i;
  int n;

  n = 1;
  for (i = 0; i < size1; i++)
    ar1[i] = (int) i + n;

  cout << "There are currently " << IntArray::getNumInstances()
       << " instances of the IntArray class\n";

  IntArray ar2(size2);
  {
    n = 1;
    for (i = 0; i < size2; i++)
      ar2[i] = (int) i + n;

    cout << "There are currently " << IntArray::getNumInstances()
         << " instances of the IntArray class\n";

    IntArray ar3(size3);

    n = 1;
    for (i = 0; i < size3; i++)
      ar3[i] = (int) i + n;

    cout << "There are currently " << IntArray::getNumInstances()
         << " instances of the IntArray class\n";

  }

  cout << "There are currently " << IntArray::getNumInstances()
       << " instances of the IntArray class\n";

  return 0;
}
```

The class constructor and destructor increment and decrement the value in numInstances.

The listing initializes the static member using the following statement, which is placed outside the class declaration:

```
unsigned IntArray::numInstances = 0;
```

Notice that this statement includes the data type of the member and fully qualifies the member by stating its host class.

The main function declares various instances of the IntArray class. The ar2 instance is declared in a nested block. When the program execution reaches the end of that block, it removes the ar2 instance. Here is the output of the program, which indicates the number of instances of the IntArray class at various locations in the main function:

```
There are currently 1 instances of the IntArray class
There are currently 2 instances of the IntArray class
There are currently 3 instances of the IntArray class
There are currently 2 instances of the IntArray class
```

To obtain the sought number of instances, the code uses the fully-qualified IntArray::getNumInstances() function call.

Common Error Status

In the last example, I wrote the code for the [] operator without checking for out-of-range indices. In the next example, I present a new version of the intArray class that verifies the argument for the parameter index. If the argument is not valid, the operator returns the reference to the special dummy data member (that stores the integer 32767) and sets an error flag. The error flag is the static member accessError. This Boolean member is shared by the various instances of the IntArray class. This approach is justified by the desire to determine whether an expression that involves multiple instances of IntArray was evaluated without error. In other words, the IntArray class is not concerned about finger-pointing at the guilty instance.

IntArray declares two static Boolean member functions, getAccessError and clearAccessError. The first function returns the value stored in the accessError

protected static member. The second function assigns `false` to the `accessError` member, thus clearing any previous error.

The listing initializes the `accessError` static member using the following statement located outside the class declaration:

```
boolean IntArray::accessError = false;
```

The `main` function in Listing 5.1 creates three instances of the `IntArray` class. Each instance stores a different number of integers. The program uses three `for` loops to assign values to each instance of the `IntArray` class. Then, the program uses the following `for` loop to add the elements of the `ar1` array to `ar2` and store them in `ar3`:

```
for (i = 0; i < size3; i++)
  ar3[i] = ar1[i] + ar2[i];
```

The loop iterates beyond the size of `ar1` and `ar2`. When the value of the `i` loop control variable reaches the `size1` constant (the size of `ar1`), the class sets the `accessError` static member to `true`. Further iterations also assign `true` to the same static member. After the loop, the `main` function invokes the `getAccessError` static function to determine whether the previous `for` loop generated any error. The `getAccessError` function returns `true`. Consequently, the program displays an error message. Following the output, the `main` function calls the `clearAccessError` static member function to reset the error flag of `IntArray`.

Next, the program uses a `for` loop similar to the previous one except that it iterates until the loop control variable reaches the value in `size1`. This limit ensures that the `[]` operator returns value references for all the instances involved in the loop statement. This time, all invocations of the `[]` operator proceed without an error, and the `accessError static` member retains the `false` value assigned to it by the `clearAccessError` function. The `main` function then calls the `getAccessError static` function to inquire once more about the `static` error of the last loop. This time, the `static` function returns `false`, and the program displays an affirmative message. Here is the program output:

```
There are currently 3 instances of the IntArray class
The first loop to add ar1 and ar2 generated an error
The second loop to add ar1 and ar2 generated no error
```

Listing 5.2. The source code for the STATIC2.CPP program.

```
#include <iostream.h>

enum boolean { false, true };

class IntArray
{
   protected:
     static boolean accessError;
     static unsigned numInstances;
     unsigned size;
     int* dataPtr;
     int dummy;

   public:
     IntArray(unsigned Size);
     ~IntArray();

     unsigned getSize() const
       { return size; }
     int& operator [](unsigned index);

     static unsigned getNumInstances() const
       { return numInstances; }
     static boolean getAccessError() const
       { return accessError; }
     static void clearAccessError()
       { accessError = false; }
};

IntArray::IntArray(unsigned Size)
{
  size = (Size > 0) ? Size : 1;
  dataPtr = new int[size];
  dummy = 32767;
  numInstances++;
}

IntArray::~IntArray()
{
```

```
  delete [] dataPtr;
  numInstances--;
}

int& IntArray::operator [](unsigned index)
{
   if (index < size)
     return dataPtr[index];
   else {
     accessError = true;
     return dummy;
   }
}

unsigned IntArray::numInstances = 0;
boolean IntArray::accessError = false;

const unsigned size1 = 10;
const unsigned size2 = 20;
const unsigned size3 = 30;

main()
{
  IntArray ar1(size1);
  IntArray ar2(size2);
  IntArray ar3(size3);
  unsigned i;
  int n;

  n = 1;
  for (i = 0; i < size1; i++)
    ar1[i] = (int) i + n;

  n = 1;
  for (i = 0; i < size2; i++)
    ar2[i] = (int) i + n;

  n = 1;
  for (i = 0; i < size3; i++)
    ar3[i] = (int) i + n;
```

continues

Listing 5.2. continued

```
    cout << "There are currently " << IntArray::getNumInstances()
         << " instances of the IntArray class\n";

    for (i = 0; i < size3; i++)
      ar3[i] = ar1[i] + ar2[i];

    if (IntArray::getAccessError())
      cout << "The first loop to add ar1 and ar2 generated an error\n";
    else
      cout << "The first loop to add ar1 and ar2 generated no error\n";

    IntArray::clearAccessError();

    for (i = 0; i < size1; i++)
      ar3[i] = ar1[i] + ar2[i];

    if (IntArray::getAccessError())
      cout << "The second loop to add ar1 and ar2 generated an error\n";
    else
      cout << "The second loop to add ar1 and ar2 generated no error\n";

    return 0;
}
```

Instance Communications

The next example shows how static members enable the various instances of a class to communicate and interact. The class models a power station that is normally a producer of electrical power. However, power stations frequently experience an inability to satisfy the demands of the consumer—which really rubs folks like you and me the wrong way. Power stations are often connected by a network of power cables so they can supplement each other's needs. The class in the next example models this type of power station. Listing 5.3 contains the source code for the STATIC3.CPP program.

Listing 5.3. The source code for the STATIC3.CPP program.

```
#include <iostream.h>
#include <stdlib.h>

const long MAX_CAPACITY = 1000;
const unsigned MAX_STATIONS = 10;
const long MIN_LOCAL_POWER_DEMAND = 200;

enum boolean { false, true };

long random(long n)
{
  return rand() % n;
}

class powerStation
{
  protected:
    static long neededCapacity;
    static unsigned stationID;

    long capacity;

  public:
    powerStation() {}

    void generatePower()
      { capacity = random(MAX_CAPACITY + 1); }
    long getCapacity()
      { return capacity - MIN_LOCAL_POWER_DEMAND; }

    static void setNeededCapacity(long cap)
      { neededCapacity = cap; }
    static void setStationID(unsigned ID)
      { stationID = ID; }
    static long getNeededCapacity()
      { return neededCapacity; }
    static unsigned getStationID()
      { return stationID; }
```

continues

Listing 5.3.continued

```
};

long powerStation::neededCapacity = 0xffffffff;
unsigned powerStation::stationID = 0xffff;

main()
{
  powerStation pwr[MAX_STATIONS];
  const unsigned maxIters = 4;
  unsigned i, j, k;
  boolean found;

  for (k = 0; k < maxIters; k++) {
    for (i = 0; i < MAX_STATIONS; i++)
      pwr[i].generatePower();
    // get the index for the station that needs power
    srand(k);
    powerStation::setStationID(unsigned(rand() % MAX_STATIONS));
    // assign the needed capacity
    powerStation::setNeededCapacity(long(rand() % 501));
    found = false;
    j = 0;
    while (j < MAX_STATIONS &&
           j != powerStation::getStationID()
           && !found) {
      if (pwr[j].getCapacity() >
          labs(powerStation::getNeededCapacity()))
        found = true;
      else
        j++;
    }

    if (found)
      cout << "Station " << j
           << " can supply station "
           << powerStation::getStationID()
           << " with "
           << powerStation::getNeededCapacity()
           << " Gega units of power\n";
    else
```

```
        cout << "No station could help station "
             << powerStation::getStationID()
             << " obtain "
             << powerStation::getNeededCapacity()
             << " Gega units of power\n";

    }

    return 0;
}
```

The powerStation class declares the following data members:

- The capacity member stores the current capacity of a power-produced power station.
- The neededCapacity static member contains the power required by an instance of powerStation that is falling behind in its production.
- The stationID static member stores the index number of the station that requires supplemental power.

The powerStation class declares the following member functions:

- The generatePower function assigns a random number to the member capacity to simulate the power generated by a class instance.
- The getCapacity function returns the free capacity of a power station. This value is the difference between the power generated (stored in member capacity) and the MIN_LOCAL_POWER_DEMAND constant.
- The setNeededCapacity static function assigns a value to the neededCapacity static member.
- The setStationID static function assigns an integer to the stationID static member.
- The getNeededCapacity static function returns the value stored in the neededCapacity static member.
- The getStationID static function returns the value stored in the stationID static member.

To simulate the supply and demand scenario, the `main` function performs the following tasks:

1. Declares the `MAX_STATIONS (10)` instance of the `powerStation` class.
2. Performs the following steps four times.
3. Invokes the `generatePower` member function for all instances of `powerStation`.
4. Selects, using a random number, the index of the power consumer station. This task calls the `setStationID` static function for this purpose.
5. Assigns the needed capacity for the consumer station, using a random number. This task calls the `setNeededCapacity` static function.
6. Initializes the `found` and `j` search variables.
7. Uses a `while` loop statement to search for the first power producing station that can meet the need for the power consumer station.
8. If the search in the previous step is successful, the program displays the index of the matching power station, the index of the consumer station, and the required power. By contrast, if the previous search fails, the program displays the index of the consumer station and the required power.

Shared Information

The next example presents a class that models the character set. This set includes the first 128 standard ASCII characters as well as the next 128 characters. The class stores the members of the character set as bits. Consequently, bit manipulation is required to set, clear, and test certain bits. These operations can be performed using a static array of bit values. Such a member enables all class instances to share the same basic data. Listing 5.4 shows the abbreviated source code for the STATIC4.CPP program (the companion disk has the complete listing).

Listing 5.4. The abbreviated source code for the STATIC4.CPP program.

```
#include <iostream.h>

enum boolean { false, true };
```

```
const unsigned CHAR_SIZE = 8;
const unsigned CHAR_ARRAY_SIZE = 256 / CHAR_SIZE;

class CharSet
{
   private:
     static unsigned char bitVal[CHAR_ARRAY_SIZE];

     void setbit(unsigned char bitnum);
     void clearbit(unsigned char bitnum);
     boolean testbit(unsigned char bitnum);

   protected:
     unsigned char cset[CHAR_ARRAY_SIZE];
     unsigned char setSize;

   public:
     CharSet()
       { clear(); }
     CharSet(unsigned char first, unsigned char last);
     unsigned char getSetSize()
       { return setSize; }
     CharSet& clear();
     boolean ismember(CharSet& cs);
     CharSet& add(CharSet& cs);
     CharSet& remove(CharSet& cs);
};

unsigned char CharSet::bitVal[CHAR_ARRAY_SIZE] =
                   { 1, 2, 4, 8, 16, 32, 64, 128 };

CharSet& CharSet::clear()
{
  // clear the bits
}

void CharSet::setbit(unsigned char bitnum)
{
    cset[bitnum / CHAR_SIZE] |= bitVal[bitnum % CHAR_SIZE];
}
```

continues

Listing 5.4. continued

```
void CharSet::clearbit(unsigned char bitnum)
{
    cset[bitnum / CHAR_SIZE] ^= bitVal[bitnum % CHAR_SIZE];
}

boolean CharSet::testbit(unsigned char bitnum)
{
    return ((cset[bitnum / CHAR_SIZE] &
             bitVal[bitnum % CHAR_SIZE]) > 0) ? true : false;
}

CharSet::CharSet(unsigned char first, unsigned char last)
{
  // create an instance of CharSet that contains
  // characters first to last.
}

boolean CharSet::ismember(CharSet& cs)
{
  // returns true if the members of
  // instance cs are in this instance
}

CharSet& CharSet::add(CharSet& cs)
{
  // add the members of instance cs to this instance
}

CharSet& CharSet::remove(CharSet& cs)
{
  // remove members of instance cs from this instance
}

main()
{
  CharSet cs1('A', 'H');
  CharSet cs2('I', 'Z');
  CharSet cs3('B', 'X');
```

```
  CharSet cs4('M', 'P');
  CharSet cs5('A', 'G');

  cs1.add(cs2);
  if (cs1.ismember(cs3))
    cout << "Characters B to X are in set 1\n";
  else
    cout << "Characters B to X are NOT in set 1\n";

  cs1.remove(cs4);
  cout << "After removing characters M to P\n";
  if (cs1.ismember(cs3))
    cout << "Characters B to X are in set 1\n";
  else
    cout << "Characters B to X are NOT in set 1\n";

  if (cs1.ismember(cs5))
    cout << "Characters A to G are in set 1\n";
  else
    cout << "Characters A to G are NOT in set 1\n";

  return 0;

}
```

The `CharSet` class declares the `bitVal`, `cset`, and `setSize` data members. The `bitVal` member is a static array that stores the values for bits 0 to 7 in a byte. The listing initializes the elements of this static member using the following statement:

```
unsigned char CharSet::bitVal[CHAR_ARRAY_SIZE] =
                   { 1, 2, 4, 8, 16, 32, 64, 128 };
```

The `cset` member is a 32-element array that stores the bits for the 256 characters. The `setSize` member stores the actual number of members (I am referring to set membership here) of a character set.

The `setbit`, `clearbit`, and `testbit` member functions illustrate how the `bitVal` static array is used to set, clear, and test specific bits in a byte.

Summary

This chapter discussed the declaration, initialization, and use of static data members in C++ classes. The chapter also discussed the declaration and use of static member functions. Static members may be regarded as items owned by the class itself and shared by all class instances. The text also examined the various kinds of applications that use static members:

- Counting the number of class instances
- Common error status or error messages
- Instance communications
- Shared information
- Iterators

C++ Operators

Many years ago the U.S. Department of Defense (DOD) launched the Ada language for all its contractors to use. One of Ada's interesting features was the implementation of operators that made the language itself "programmable." User-defined operators enable you to create expressions involving user-defined data types in a manner similar to the predefined ones. Although languages such as C, Pascal, and Modula-2 were popular when Ada appeared, they lacked Ada's operators. I was very glad to see that the creators of C++ included operators in the language. This chapter discusses the following topics:

- Surveying the C++ operators
- Exploring traditional and nontraditional use of the operators
- Discussing error-handling as related to operators

A Survey of C++ Operators

Implementing operators in a language goes hand-in-hand with function overloading. After all, an operator is a special type of function. In fact, the compiler translates the operator symbols into predefined function names. For example, the + operator might be an alias for the `_plus` function. Because you can define multiple versions of the same operator for the same class, function overloading must be implemented. The C++ operators that you can define as member functions and friend functions of a class are the following:

```
+      -      /      %      !      ^      &       |
~      *      ,      =      <      >      <=      >=
++     --     <<     >>     ==     !=     &&      ||
+=     -=     /=     %=     ^=     &=     |=      <<=
>>=    []     ()     ->     ->*    new    delete  *=
```

C++ requires you to observe the following rules when defining new operators:

1. You cannot override the operators for the predefined types in C++. Although this might seem obvious at first, think of those programmers who would like to implement better or different versions of these operators.

2. The operators you define work only with classes, either as member functions or as friend functions; therefore, you cannot add new operators for the predefined data types.

3. At least one of the arguments of an operator must be a class argument. This further clarifies the previous point—you cannot create operators that take predefined data types and yield a class.

4. The result of an operator need not be a class. This complements the previous step.

5. The class operators observe the same standard operator precedence. C++ provides no special mechanism to alter the precedence of an operator as it is being defined. For example, consider the following instances of a complex class:

   ```
   #include <iostream.h>
   #include <complex.h>
   ```

```
main()
{
   complex c1(1,1), c2(2,2), c3(3,3), c4(0,0);
   c4 = c1 + c2 * c3;
   cout << c4 << '\n'; // displays (1,13)
   return 0;
}
```

The * operator is performed first, yielding an intermediate result of (0,12). The + operator is performed next to produce the complex number (1,13). Using parentheses, you can alter the effective operator precedence, as shown here:

```
#include <iostream.h>
#include <complex.h>

main()
{
   complex c1(1,1), c2(2,2), c3(3,3), c4(0,0);
   c4 = (c1 + c2) * c3;
   cout << c4 << '\n'; // displays (0, 18)
   return 0;
}
```

The `c1` and `c2` objects are added first to obtain the complex number (3,3), which is then multiplied by `c3` to yield (0,18).

6. You cannot alter the *arity* (in other words, the number of arguments) of the C++ operators. Some operators, such as `+`, `-`, `*`, and `&`, can be either unary or binary operators. Others, like the `!` operator, are strictly unary. Most C++ operators are binary.

Rather than abstractly surveying the C++ operators that you can overload, I will view them in light of the hypothetical `Complex`, `Array`, `Matrix`, `String`, linked `List`, and `BitSet` classes. These classes are representative of the popular data structure classes. For now, view these classes in general terms. I will introduce class declarations as needed.

The Binary + Operator

The binary + operator is probably the most frequently used with classes. The scalar numerical classes, such as `Complex`, use the + operator to mathematically add two complex numbers. Such classes frequently define the + operator as a friend function instead of a member function, allowing the class instances to appear on either side of the operator. This is done using the following versions of the + operators:

```
class Complex
{
     private:
          double real, imag;
          int mathError;

     public:
          // constructors and other methods
          friend Complex operator +(Complex& c1, Complex& c2);
          friend Complex operator +(Complex& c, double realX);
          friend Complex operator +(double realX, Complex& c);
};
```

The classes of numerical arrays and matrices use the + operator to perform a more elaborate version of the mathematical addition. I say elaborate because it is an operation that requires the arrays (or matrices) to have the same sizes. Otherwise, a mathematical error will occur. How do you handle adding arrays (or matrices) of different sizes? There are a few approaches:

1. Display an error message and halt the program. Take this step if the error occurs in a critical stage and you cannot reiterate the process with healthy data.
2. Relax the mathematical rules of adding arrays or matrices and use the following pragmatic approach—the smaller array is first expanded to match the size of the bigger array by adding zero elements. Then, vector addition proceeds normally. A similar approach is used with matrices. This method assumes that such expansions do not introduce errors elsewhere in the application.
3. Return a single-element array or matrix. You can use this unusual size to flag the attempt at adding incompatible arrays or matrices. Moreover, you can assign a specific value (say, a very large negative number like -1e+30) to the single-element array or matrix to stress the error condition. This approach permits execution of the addition without halting the application before the expression is fully evaluated. The application program examines the size and content of the result to decide whether to stop or to try and obtain better data. The following code illustrates how this method works:

```
class Array
{
     private:
          unsigned size;
          // other data members
     public:
          // constructors, destructor, and other methods
          double& operator [](unsigned);
          friend Array& operator +(Array&, Array&);
};

Array& operator +(Array& ar1, Array& ar2)
{
     Array result((ar1.size == ar2.size) ? ar1.size : 1);

     if (ar1.size != ar2.size)
          result[0] = -1.0e+30;
     else
          for (unsigned i = 0; i < ar1.size; i++)
               result[i] = ar1[i] + ar2[i];

     return result;
}
```

You can use this method with other math operators, allowing an expression to return a temporary result without halting the program.

You can also use the + operator to concatenate items, such as character strings. Indeed, language implementations such as QuickBASIC and Turbo Pascal use the + operator to concatenate strings and characters. You need five versions of the + operator for the `String` class to add string objects, character strings, and characters:

```
class String
{
     private:
          unsigned maxLen;
          unsigned len;
          char* str;

     public:
          // constructors, destructors, and other methods
          friend String operator +(String& s1, String& s2);
```

```
        friend String operator +(String& s1, const char* s2);
        friend String operator +(const char* s1, String& s2);
        friend String operator +(String& s, const char c);
        friend String operator +(const char c, String& s1);
};
```

This enables you to write expressions such as:

```
String s1("Hello"), s2("World"), s3(80);
s3 = s1 + ' ' + s2 + ".  I love you!";
cout << s3 // displays "Hello World.  I love you!"
```

The previous string expression observes the rule requiring the operator to have at least one class argument. You can still concatenate two characters, two C strings, or a character and a C string by typecasting one of them into a `String` object. In this case, the `String` class must define a constructor that uses a character or C string as a parameter. An example of this type of concatenation appears as follows:

```
String s1, s2("Hello");
char s = "World";
char c1 = ' ', c2 = '!';
s1 = s2 + c1 + String(s) + c2; // C-string "s" is type casted
cout << s1; // displays "Hello World!"
```

Some implementations of BASIC use the `&` operator to concatenate strings. You can define an additional set of `&` operators for that purpose to accommodate new C++ programmers who are more comfortable with the `&` operator.

You can use the `+` operator with the `BitSet` class (and with any other class that models a set of items) to add new set members. If a member exists in both added sets, it is simply carried over to the resulting set without any type of "carry." This differentiates set addition in general from mathematical addition. The `+` and `¦` operators produce the same effect with `BitSet` and other set classes.

The `+=` operator provides a shortcut for adding two numbers, appending two strings, or adding new set members. Cases exist where using the `+=` operator makes more sense than the `+` and `=` operators. Adding data to dynamically linked lists is an example:

```
List orderedList;
orderedList += "Turbo"; // list has "Turbo"
orderedList += "Ada";   // list has "Ada"->"Turbo"
orderedList += "C++";   // list has "Ada"->"C++"->"Turbo"
```

You can use the += operator with such list classes to append or insert new data. If the list is unordered, the += operator simply appends the new data. By contrast, if the list is ordered, the += operator inserts the new data in such a way that preserves the list order. Using operators with dynamic data structures deprives you of promptly knowing if the data insertion is successful (especially in the case of an ordered linked list that does not accept data with duplicate key fields). That information must be stored in a Boolean data member that you can query later with a function call. Adding new data using a member function enables you to promptly deduce the success of the operation by examining the function's returned value. The two approaches are compared in the following code:

```
class List
{
     private:
          int insertedOk; // insertion flag
          // other data members

     public:
          // constructors, destructor, and various methods
          int getInsertedOk() const { return insertedOK; }
          int insert(void* data);
          List& operator +=(void* data);
};

List orderedList;
orderedList += "Turbo";

if (orderedList.getInsertedOK)
     cout << "'Turbo' was not inserted\n";

if (orderedList.insert("Turbo"))
     cout << "'Turbo' was not inserted\n";
```

There are applications that will tolerate duplicate key data. In such cases, using the += operator is smoother.

The - Operator

The - operator basically reverses the effect of the + operator. The - operator's communicative capability can impose some restrictions on using it in a way that parallels the + operator. This is true when handling arrays or matrices of incompatible sizes. Remember that I presented three methods for dealing with the problem when I discussed the + operator. The first and third methods work fine with the - operator, but the second method will likely raise some disagreement, especially when you attempt to subtract a bigger array or matrix from a smaller one.

In the case of strings I suggest that you implement the - operator to delete the first occurrence of a substring in a string. The following code shows this:

```
String aString(80), subStr(" Clement");
aString = "Namir Clement Shammas" - subStr;
cout << aString; // displays "Namir Shammas"
aString = aString - "Loren";
cout << aString; // again displays "Namir Shammas"
```

If the substring is not found, the main string is unchanged.

In the case of the `BitSet` class, the - operator removes existing members from the bit set. Attempting to remove a nonexistent member has no effect on the left operand.

In the case of the dynamic `List` class, the -= operator, rather than the - operator, is more suitable for deleting members. The same comments for the += operators and list classes can be made regarding the need to flag the success or failure of the -= operator.

The Binary * Operator

The binary * operator is highly dedicated to multiplying mathematical types. This includes the `Complex`, `Array`, and `Matrix` classes in our selected set of classes. You can use the * operator to work between arrays, between matrices, between arrays and matrices, between scalars and arrays, and between scalars and matrices. You must strictly obey size compatibility when both operands are not scalar—you cannot apply the previously suggested method that relaxes such rules here. Therefore, the method that returns a single-element array or matrix is probably the best one.

Regarding the `String` class, you can use the * operator for creating big strings from smaller string patterns or from characters, as shown:

```
bigString = smallString * numberOfTimes;
bigString = aSingleChar * numberOfTimes;
```

Because the * operator has higher precedence than the + or - operators, mixing String operators is no problem:

```
String bigString, aString("Hello");
char padChar = '+';
unsigned paddingCount = 10;
bigString = aString + padChar * paddingCount;
```

The string of padded characters is created first. Then, it is concatenated to the aString object.

The / Operator

The / operator works with numerical classes in a manner similar to the * operator. However, you should watch out for the famous division-by-zero errors. In the case of the scalar numeric class Complex, the best approach is one that returns a small complex number and raises a divide-by-zero flag. This is better than returning a large complex number. Why? Consider the following expression:

```
Complex c1(1,1), c2(0,0), c3(3,3), c4(0,0), c5(0,0);
c5 = c1 / c2 * c3 / c4;
if (c5.haveMathError())
     cerr << "Divide by zero!";
```

Both divisions involve zero complex numbers. If you return a large temporary result, you risk an overflow due to the multiplication. Therefore, it is better to return a reasonable value to permit the uninterrupted evaluation of the expression. This allows the program to reach the if statement where the truth of the matter is uncovered.

Concerning arrays and matrices, the / operator is used for division by a scalar. You also can define the / operator to solve a system of linear equations. Division-by-zero errors should be dealt with in a manner similar to the Complex class.

The String class can use the / operator in a rather untraditional way—truncating a string at the first occurrence of a substring. Here's an example:

```
String Astring("The quick brown fox"), subStr(" brown"), newString;
newString = Astring / subStr;
cout << newString; // displays "The quick"
```

You might choose to implement the / operator for including the matching substring if it makes more sense for your applications. If the substring finds no match, the operator returns the left operand.

The % Operator

The % operator is frequently used to return the modulus of two integers. Some applications involve floating-point versions of the % operator. Because division is involved in evaluating the result of a % operator, you need to handle division-by-zero errors.

The String class can use the % operator in a way that complements the / operator—the result includes the remaining characters from the first string. The following example shows the suggested use of the % operator:

```
String Astring("The quick brown fox"), subStr("brown"), newString;
newString = Astring % subStr;
cout << newString; // displays "The quick  fox"
```

Again, you might choose to implement a version of the % operator that excludes the matching substring from the result.

The Relational Operators

With C++, you can declare the ==, !=, <, >, <=, and >= operators to compare instances of classes. You can apply the first two operators (== and !=) to just about every class—the concept of equality for the state of two objects is universal. You can apply the other relational operators (<, >, <=, and >=) to the classes where the concept of "magnitude" comparison holds. I will focus on the latter relational operators because their use varies widely between classes.

The Complex, Array, and Matrix classes are examples of numeric classes for which the comparative relational operators make no sense. Classes that implement OOP versions of the predefined numerical data types can certainly benefit from the comparative relational operators to make the class instances more abstract.

The String class definitely benefits from all relational operators. The implementation of these operators is almost effortless—just make a simple call to the appropriate

C comparison function. An example follows:

```
int string::operator <(const String& s)
{
     return strcmp(str, s.str) < 0;
}
```

Comparative relational operators don't make sense with lists or even other dynamic data structures like trees, graphs, and hash tables. By contrast, set classes can use <= and >= to test if a set is a subset or superset of another one.

The ++ and -- Operators

The C and C++ languages use these operators to increment and decrement by one value of the predefined numeric types as well as pointer addresses. The use of the ++ and -- operators with classes will in most cases require that you specify the "value change" before using these operators. Consider the case of the `Complex` type. You can have the constructors set the change in the `real` and `imag` field to default values, say 1. The `Complex` class can use a member function to alter the changes made to the `real` and `imag` fields when the ++ or -- operators are applied. You can use a similar approach with arrays and matrices—the ++ and -- operators alter the value of every element by a specified magnitude.

Concerning the `String` class, you can use the ++ operator to append a specific character to the string:

```
// create string s with default padding character (say, ' ')
String s("Hello");
s++; // s is now "Hello "
s.setPadChar('+');
s++; // s is now "Hello +"
```

Using a member function (`setPadChar` in the previous example) you can alter the appending character.

The role of the -- operator with the `String` class might be to delete the last character. You can make the action of the ++ and -- operators more elaborate by using a special data member that indicates whether the operators should act on the first or the last character. This enables you to either prepend or append characters and to delete leading or trailing characters.

The Index [] Operator

Classes that store collections of similar items, such as strings, arrays, and bit sets, can greatly benefit from the `[]` operator. The power of this operator comes from the fact that by returning a reference type, the operator can appear on either side of the = operator. For example, you can write the following statement:

```
String s1("Hello"), s2("Tomorrow");
s1[1] = s2[4]; // s1 is now "Hollo"
```

The `[]` operator offers a good level of abstraction. You can index elements in a class without being concerned about the actual implementations.

Please observe these rules when using the `[]` operator:

- The `[]` operator takes a single integer-type argument. This limits the `[]` operator to indexing one-dimensional arrays, making it unsuitable for matrix classes.
- You must provide your own mechanism for detecting out-of-range indices. I'll talk about this next.

The `[]` operator works very well with string classes. With it, you can access the individual characters as though you were dealing with C strings. This also raises the concern for out-of-range indices. A very simplistic approach merely terminates the program. I compare this to being sentenced to death just for running a stop sign. I suggest the following approach, which can easily be applied to other classes. Because the `[]` operator returns a reference to a `char`-type element, you need to fulfill this requirement for all index values. The trick is to return the reference of a special element for all out-of-range indices. This special element can be an extra array element that you allocate to deal with this problem. I prefer the declaration of a separate dummy data member to handle out-of-range indices. This approach is a bit clearer because it does not upset the count for the actual size of the dynamic character array—something that might make you frown when looking at the code six months later. Here is an "updated" skeleton declaration for the `String` class:

```
class String
{
     private:
        char badindex;
```

```
protected:
     enum stringErrors { NO_ERR, NULL_STRING, BAD_INDEX };
     char *str;         // pointer to characters
     unsigned maxLen;   // total number of bytes allocated
     unsigned len;      // current string size
     stringErrors strErr;

public:
     // constructors here
     // class destructor here
     int checkBounds(unsigned i) { return ((i < len) ? 1 : 0); }
     stringErrors getError()
     char& operator [](const unsigned);
     // other methods
};

stringErrors String::getError()
{
     stringErrors temp = strErr;
     strErr = NO_ERR; // reset error flag
     return temp;
}
```

The private `badindex` data member is the name for the dummy member I just mentioned. A descriptive name helps in self-documenting the class declaration. The local enumerated `stringErrors` type gives a sample list of the error types. The query method `getError` returns the state of the last error and also resets the error state stored in the `strErr` data member. The `checkBounds` member function examines the validity of a given index with respect to the current length of the `String` object. It returns 1 if the index is within ranges; otherwise, it emits 0. The `checkBounds` member function is used by the `[]` operator, shown as follows:

```
char& String::operator [](const unsigned i)
{
     if (checkBounds(i))
          return *(str + i);
     else {
          strErr = BAD_INDEX;
          return badindex;
     }
}
```

The badindex data member should be initialized by the class constructors, just in case the first out-of-range index occurs when the [] operator is used on the left-hand side of an assignment operator.

The question that may be raised is this: Given an expression with multiple occurrences of the [] operator, how do you spot the offending call? An example of such an expression is

```
String s1(10), s2("AAAAAAA");, s2("BBBBBBB");
unsigned i, j, k;
// statements that assign values to i, j, and k
s1[k] = (s2[i] > s3[j]) ? s1[i] : s2[j];
```

You can use the checkBounds function member to trap an out-of-range index before it appears in a [] operator. The following is an example of an early detection of bad indices for the s2 instance:

```
if (s2.checkBounds(i))
     // statements to obtain a better value for i
s1[k] = (s2[i] > s3[j]) ? s1[i] : s2[j];
```

The [] operator works with numeric arrays (as well as other kinds of arrays) in a manner very similar to the String class. You can apply the string class mechanism for handling out-of-range indices to the array classes.

List classes and other linear dynamic data structures can also benefit from the [] operator. You can access a list member by its positional index. This enhances dynamic list classes by giving them an array-like access feature. The result is a hybrid structure that can occupy memory space as needed.

My first inclination was to dismiss applying the [] operator to the Complex class. However, a closer look at the class reveals an interesting case. The Complex class has two similar data members to store the real and imaginary components of a complex number. You can implement a complex number class using a two-member array, as shown:

```
class MyComplex
{
     protected:
          double[2] X;

     public;
```

```
        MyComplex(double x, double y)
        { X[0] = x; X[1] - y; }
        // other methods
    };
```

This leads me to think that `Complex` belongs to a category of classes that are characterized by a small and fixed number of similar data fields. These individual data fields can be treated as a pseudo-array using the `[]` operator. To illustrate this aspect consider the `spaceCoord` class that models spacial coordinates:

```
#include <iostream.h>

class spaceCoord
{
    protected:
        double x, y, z;

    public:
        spaceCoord(double xx, double yy, double zz) :
                 x(xx), y(yy), z(zz) {}
        double& operator[](unsigned);
};

double& spaceCoord::operator[](unsigned i)
{
    i = (i+1) % 3;
    switch (i) {
    case 0 :
        return z;
    case 1 :
        return x;
    case 2 :
        return y;
    }
}

main()
{
    spaceCoord c(1, 2, 3);
```

```
    cout << c[0] << ' ' << '+' << ' ' << 'i'
         << c[1] << ' ' << '+' << ' ' << 'j'
         << c[2] << '\n';

    return 0;
}
```

The [] operator returns a reference to the x, y, and z data members when supplied the respective 0, 1, and 2 indices. To solve the out-of-range index problem in this case, I used the % operator to guarantee that i contains the range of 0 to 2 in the switch structure. The main function shows how the indices can access their individual coordinates.

The () Iterator Operator

The () iterator operator is extremely versatile. In the beginning of this chapter, I mentioned that C++ imposes rules on using operators to prevent unusual uses. The () operator is the exception (might there be other ones?). I feel that the name *iterator* really comes across as part of an official name. The real name of the operator should be the *anything-goes* or the *Baghdad-Genie* operator, and I mean it. You can declare the () operator with any number and any type of parameter. In addition, the return type can be either a reference, a pointer, or a normal type. In fact, the () operator can outmatch the [] operator. If you have any complaints about using the [] operator, just switch to the () operator. This operator aims to please.

As the () operator's official role, it sequentially accesses the members of a collection in an object. A class that makes such a use of the () operator needs an additional data member to act as a sequential-access index. The class constructors should initialize this index (usually to 0).

The () operator works with the String class to access the next character. Assuming that the class declaration contains an iterIndex data member for the () operator, the following is an implementation of the () operator:

```
char String::operator()()
{
     if (iterIndex < len)
          return *(str + iterIndex++);
     else
          return (iterIndex = 0);
}
```

Notice that the operator has no arguments. It relies on the `iterIndex` data member to cycle through the stored characters. In addition, notice that the returned result is a `char` type. At the end of an iteration cycle, the value of `iterIndex` equals that of the `len` data member, the string length. This makes the `else` clause reset the value of `iterIndex` to 0 and return that value as the function result. The iterator operator is usually placed in a `while` loop. Consequently, a returned zero value is a convenient way to terminate the loop iteration. An example follows:

```
String s("Hello World!");
char c;
while (c=s()) // loop displays "Hello World!"
     cout << c;
cout << '\n';
```

Another use of the `()` operator with the `String` class is to access a substring. The following implementation shows the `()` operator with two arguments, the starting index and the size of the substring. The reference type of result enables you to use the operator on either side of an assignment:

```
String& String::operator ()(const unsigned start, unsigned count)
{
     if (start < len) {
          count = ((start+count) <= len) ? count : len - start;
          count = (count != 0) ? count : 1;
          strncpy(str, (str + start), count); // from "string.h"
          str[count] = '\0';
          // calculate len based on the actual length of str
          len = strlen(str);
     }
     return *this;
}
```

The previous declaration of the () operator enables you to write the following statements:

```
String s1("Hello World!"), s2("011111222");
s1(0, 4) = s2(1, 5); // s1 is now "11111 World!"
```

The second through the sixth characters of s2 object overwrite the first five characters of s1 object.

Iterating with numeric (noninteger) arrays requires a slightly different approach. To use the () operator in a while loop, you need the () operator to return an integer-compatible result (int, char, or unsigned char). In addition, the accessed element must be returned by a reference parameter:

```
unsigned char spaceArray::operator()(double& x)
{
     if (iterIndex < 3) {
          x = *(dataptr + iterIndex++);
          return 1;
     }
     else {
          iterIndex = 0;
          return 0;
     }
}
```

With this approach, you can write the following while loop, which processes the various members of the A array object:

```
Array A(10);
double x;
// statements to assign values to the object A
while (A(x))
     cout << x << ' ';
cout << '\n';
```

Arrays can use the () operator to implement *associative arrays* or *tables*—arrays indexed by strings. This involves hashing techniques that convert the string argument for the () operator to a storage address. The () operator implementation, using an ideal hashing function, appears as follows:

```
double& Array::operator()(const char* name)
{
```

```
     unsigned i = idealHashingFunction(name);
     rcturn *(dataptr + i);
}
```

Using the previous version of the `()` operator, you can write statements such as

```
Array A(100);
A("C") = 23;
A("Pascal") = 200;
A("C++") = A("C") + A("Pascal");
```

The `Complex` class and similar classes can benefit from the `()` operator in ways similar to arrays, once you regard that some of their data members can be indexed.

Matrices benefit from the `()` operator in various ways. First, the `()` operator can do for matrices what the `[]` operator has failed to do. The following code shows how the `()` operator is used to access individual matrix elements by specifying the matrix row and column. You can use the `()` operator this way with all classes of matrices. The following code creates a matrix object, assigns data to its members, and displays the matrix elements:

```
#include <iostream.h>

class Matrix
{
     protected:
          double* dataPtr;
          unsigned maxrows;
          unsigned maxcols;
     public:
          matrix(unsigned rows, unsigned cols) :
          maxrows(rows), maxcols(cols)
               { dataPtr = new double[rows * cols]; }
          double& operator()(unsigned row, unsigned col)
               { return *(dataPtr + row + col * maxrows); }
};

main()
{
     matrix m(10, 5);
     unsigned row, col;
```

```
    // assign values to the various matrix elements
    for (row = 0; row < 10; row++)
         for (col = 0; col < 5; col++)
              m(row, col) = row * 10.0 + col + 100.0;

    // display the matrix
    for (row = 0; row < 10; row++) {
         for (col = 0; col < 5; col++)
              cout << m(row, col);
         cout << '\n';
    }

    return 0;
}
```

You can also use the `()` operator to iterate through the various matrix elements. You need data members to keep track of the current row and column traversal indices. Here, you have a few options depending on what you want the iteration cycle to do:

- Visit all the matrix elements. The traversal can be row-wise or column-wise. The traversal direction can be fixed, or it can be influenced by other special data members. These members influence the direction of traversal.
- Visit the elements of a specific row or column.

List classes as well as other linear and even nonlinear dynamic structure classes can really put the `()` operator to work. The parameter for the `()` operator represents the key data to select the sought element of a list, graph, binary tree, and so on. If these dynamic structures are implemented to tolerate duplicate keys, you need to add a counter parameter to access the various occurrences.

There are other operators, such as `new`, `delete`, and `->`. I will discuss these operators in the next chapter, using more specific examples.

Summary

This chapter discussed various aspects of the user-defined C++ operators and covered the following topics:

- Surveying the C++ operators. This chapter presented the operators that you can define in your classes either as member functions or as friend functions. The discussion also stated the general rules for using these operators.
- Exploring traditional and nontraditional uses of the operators. By using hypothetical classes, the chapter explored how a selection of the operators can be used. The hypothetical classes represent complex numbers, numerical arrays, numerical matrices, strings, linked lists, and bitsets. The discussion showed how you can push some of the operators, particularly the `()` operator, to the limit. In addition, the chapter proposes nontraditional uses of the `-`, `*`, `/`, and `%` operators with string classes.
- Discussing error-handling related to operators. The discussion presented methods to handle errors while using a variety of operators with different classes. The chapter made some suggestions that enable your programs to resume execution and decide what to do with the error.

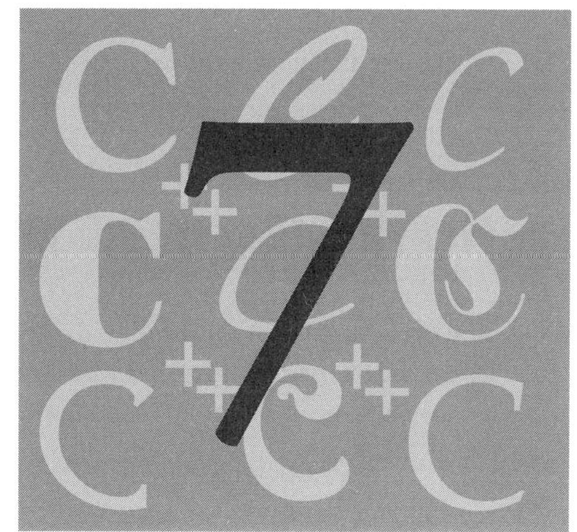

C++ Dynamic Allocation

In Chapter 6, "C++ Operators," I discussed overloading many of the operators in C++. In this chapter, I focus on overloading the `new`, `delete`, and `->` operators. The early versions of C++ (including version 1.2) were unable to overload the `new` and `delete` operators. Subsequent versions, however, can overload these operators and implement custom dynamic allocation schemes. This chapter covers the following topics:

- Overloading the `new` operator
- Overloading the `delete` operator
- Uses for overloaded `new` and `delete` operators
- Overloading the `->` operator

Overloading the new Operator

The predefined (also called global) new operator provides adequate dynamic allocation in the heap (or free store). Occasionally, however, you may need to implement a custom dynamic memory management scheme that suits your application's needs.

The new operator can be overloaded in C++. The C++ compiler automatically regards the new operator as static because the operator is often called to create class instances. The first parameter of the overloaded new operator must be `size_t`, a type declared in the stddef.h header file, and the operator must return a `void*` pointer. The argument for the first parameter is the name of a class or data type. For example, consider the following class declaration that contains

```
class X
{
     public:
          X() {}
          void* operator new(size_t size);
};

main()
{
     X* x = new X;
     // other statements
     delete x;
     return 0;
}
```

The class name X that appears after the new operator is the argument for the parameter size. The compiler translates the class name into its size and passes that information to the parameter size.

C++ enables you to declare additional parameters that may be required by the new operator. Because the new operator is treated as static by the compiler, it cannot access nonstatic data members. (The following example contains two versions of the overloaded new operator.)

```
class Matrix
{
     protected:
          unsigned maxRow;
          unsigned maxCol;
          double* dataPtr;

     public:
          Matrix(unsigned Rows, unsigned Cols)
          {
               maxRows = Rows;
               maxCols = Cols;
               dataPtr = new double[maxRows * maxCols];
          }
          void* operator new(size_t size);
          void* operator new(size_t size, unsigned Rows, Cols);
};

main()
{
     Matrix *mat = new Matrix(10, 20);
     // other statements
     delete mat;
     return 0;
}
```

The first version of the new operator is the same one I showed you in the previous code fragment. The second version of the operator includes parameters for the rows and columns of a matrix. The class constructor invokes the second version of new operator to create the dynamic data for the matrix. The function main declares the pointer mat, which creates a dynamic instance of class Matrix. The call to new in main invokes the first overloaded version of the new operator to create a dynamic instance of Matrix. The creation of the instance involves the constructor, which invokes the second version of the new operator to allocate additional dynamic space, accessed by the pointer dataPtr.

To invoke the global new operator, use the ::new syntax.

Overloading the delete Operator

You can also overload the `delete` operator in C++. In contrast to the `new` operator, you may declare only one overloaded version per class. The general syntax for declaring the delete operator is

```
void delete(void* [, size_t])
```

The first parameter is the pointer to the object being destroyed. The second parameter is optional and is initialized by the compiler as the size of the object addressed by the first argument. You need to include the second parameter in a class hierarchy that inherits the overloaded `delete` operator. The `delete` operator returns the type `void`.

Uses for Overloading new and delete Operators

It is necessary to overload the `new` and `delete` operators to control dynamic allocation and deallocation. A general purpose of overloading the new and delete operators is to implement a special dynamic storage scheme (such a scheme may use special memory or devices—such as hard disks—for storage or allocate heap space in chunks). Another general purpose for overloading the `new` and `delete` operators is to monitor dynamic allocation and deallocation statistics.

As an example of monitoring the statistics of the dynamic allocation and deallocation, Listing 7.1 shows the source code for the NEWDEL1.CPP program. The program declares the class `UINT` (unsigned integer). The class declares the static data members `total` and `current` to store, respectively, the total and current number of dynamic instances of class `UINT`. You can further modify the class by including a static fixed array to store the sequence of calling the `new` and `delete` operators. The static functions `getTotal` and `getCount` return, respectively, the values stored in the static members `total` and `count`.

The class `UINT` declares the overloaded `new` operator with a single parameter. The operator allocates the dynamic space for an instance of `UINT` by calling the global operator `new`. If the allocation is successful, the `new` operator increments the `total` and `count` static members. The operator then returns the local pointer `p` that accesses the newly allocated class instance.

The `delete` operator decrements the value stored in the static member `count`. The operator then invokes the global operator `delete` to remove the object accessed by pointer `ptr`.

The `UINT` class declares the data member value to store the unsigned integer value. The class uses the assign and get member functions to assign and retrieve an integer from the value data member.

The function `main` intermittently creates and removes various dynamic instances of class `UINT`. The function invokes the static functions `getTotal` and `getCount` to obtain the present statistics on the total and current number of dynamic instances of class `UINT`. The function `main` also assigns values to the dynamic instances of class `UINT` and then displays these values.

Listing 7.1. The source code for the NEWDEL1.CPP program.

```
#include <iostream.h>
#include <stddef.h>

enum boolean { false, true };

class UINT
{
   protected:
     unsigned value;

     // total number of instances created
     static unsigned total;
     // the current number of instances
     static unsigned count;

   public:
     UINT() {}

     void assign(unsigned Value)
       { value = Value; }
     unsigned get()
       { return value; }

     static unsigned getTotal()
       { return total; }
```

continues

Listing 7.1. continued

```
    static unsigned getCount()
      { return count; }
    void* operator new(size_t);
    void operator delete(void*, size_t);
};

void* UINT::operator new(size_t)
{
  UINT* p;

  // create an instance using the global new operator
  p = ::new UINT;
  if (p) {
    // update static counters
    total++;
    count++;
  }
  return p;
}

void UINT::operator delete(void* ptr, size_t)
{
   if (ptr) {
     // decrement instance counter
     count--;
     // delete instance using the global delete operator
     ::delete ptr;
   }
}

unsigned UINT::total = 0;
unsigned UINT::count= 0;

main()
{
  UINT *num1, *num2, *num3, *num4;

  num1 = new UINT;
  cout << "Instances: total = " << UINT::getTotal()
       << " current = " << UINT::getCount() << "\n";
  num2 = new UINT;
```

```
    cout << "Instances: total = " << UINT::getTotal()
         << " current = " << UINT::getCount() << "\n";
    num3 = new UINT;
    cout << "Instances: total = " << UINT::getTotal()
         << " current = " << UINT::getCount() << "\n\n";

    num1->assign(10);
    num2->assign(200);
    num3->assign(300);

    cout << "num1 has " << num1->get() << "\n";
    cout << "num2 has " << num2->get() << "\n";
    cout << "num3 has " << num3->get() << "\n\n";

    delete num2;
    num2 = new UINT;
    cout << "Instances: total = " << UINT::getTotal()
         << " current = " << UINT::getCount() << "\n\n";
    num2->assign(200);
    cout << "num1 has " << num1->get() << "\n";
    cout << "num2 has " << num2->get() << "\n";
    cout << "num3 has " << num3->get() << "\n\n";

    delete num1;
    num4 = new UINT;
    cout << "Instances: total = " << UINT::getTotal()
         << " current = " << UINT::getCount() << "\n\n";

    num4->assign(4000);

    cout << "num2 has " << num2->get() << "\n";
    cout << "num3 has " << num3->get() << "\n";
    cout << "num4 has " << num4->get() << "\n\n";

    delete num2;
    delete num3;
    delete num4;
    cout << "Instances: total = " << UINT::getTotal()
         << " current = " << UINT::getCount() << "\n";

    return 0;
}
```

The next example, Listing 7.2, presents a modified version of Listing 7.1. This version uses the overloaded operators `new` and `delete` to manage the allocation and deallocation of dynamic instances from a chunk of heap space that I'll call *microheap*—a chunk of dynamic space that can accommodate up to a certain number of dynamic instances at any given time. Microheap reserves space in the heap. Listing 7.2 shows the source code for the NEWDEL2.CPP program. The program declares a new version of `UINT`. This class contains two static members, `usedFlag` and `microHeap`. `usedFlag` is an array of `MICRO_HEAP_SIZE` Boolean elements that stores in-use flags. The `micro Heap` member is the pointer to the dynamically allocated microheap. These two static members are initialized outside the class declaration. The listing assigns false to the elements of array `usedFlag`. The listing also initializes the pointer `micro Heap` by dynamically allocating `MICRO_HEAP_SIZE` elements.

The class declares an overloaded `new` operator to tap into the microheap. The operator searches for the first element in the microheap that is vacant. The search employs a `while` loop that sequentially examines the elements of `usedFlag` to locate the first empty slot in the microheap. The operator returns the address of the matching microheap location or yields 0 if no match is found. The `new` operator does not perform dynamic allocation.

The class also declares an overloaded `delete` operator. This operator determines the index of the deleted element. This index is the difference between the addresses of the argument of the parameter `ptr` and the static member `microHeap`. The operator then assigns the Boolean value `false` to the element of `usedFlag` that corresponds to the index of the deleted element. The delete operator does not perform dynamic deallocation.

The function `main` intermittently creates and removes various dynamic instances of class `UINT`. To understand how the `new` and `delete` operators work, trace the program execution at these operators. Observe the value of the indices of the elements in the micro heap.

Listing 7.2. The source code for the NEWDEL2.CPP program.

```
#include <iostream.h>
#include <stddef.h>

enum boolean { false, true };

const MICRO_HEAP_SIZE = 10;
```

```
class UINT
{
   protected:
     unsigned value;

     static boolean usedFlag[MICRO_HEAP_SIZE];
     static UINT *microHeap;

   public:
     UINT() {}

     void assign(unsigned Value)
       { value = Value; }
     unsigned get()
       { return value; }

     void* operator new(size_t);
     void operator delete(void*, size_t);
};

void* UINT::operator new(size_t size)
{
   boolean notFound = true;
   unsigned i = 0;

   while (i < MICRO_HEAP_SIZE && notFound)
     if (usedFlag[i])
       i++;
     else {
       notFound = false;
       usedFlag[i] = true;
     }

   return (!notFound) ? &microHeap[i] : 0;
}

void UINT::operator delete(void* ptr, size_t dummy)
{
   unsigned offset = (UINT*) ptr - microHeap;
   usedFlag[offset] = false;
}
```

continues

Listing 7.2. continued

```
boolean UINT::usedFlag[MICRO_HEAP_SIZE] = { false };
UINT* UINT::microHeap = new UINT[MICRO_HEAP_SIZE];

main()
{
  UINT *num1, *num2, *num3, *num4;

  num1 = new UINT;
  num2 = new UINT;
  num3 = new UINT;

  num1->assign(10);
  num2->assign(200);
  num3->assign(300);

  cout << "num1 has " << num1->get() << "\n";
  cout << "num2 has " << num2->get() << "\n";
  cout << "num3 has " << num3->get() << "\n\n";

  delete num2;
  num2 = new UINT;
  num2->assign(200);
  cout << "num1 has " << num1->get() << "\n";
  cout << "num2 has " << num2->get() << "\n";
  cout << "num3 has " << num3->get() << "\n\n";

  delete num1;
  num4 = new UINT;
  num4->assign(4000);

  cout << "num2 has " << num2->get() << "\n";
  cout << "num3 has " << num3->get() << "\n";
  cout << "num4 has " << num4->get() << "\n";

  delete num2;
  delete num3;
  delete num4;

  return 0;
}
```

The next example, Listing 7.3, presents a class that models dynamic numerical matrices. This class uses two versions of the overloaded operator `new`. One version allocates dynamic space for the instance itself, and the second version allocates dynamic space for the matrix data. For the sake of making the program shorter and clearer, the overloaded new and `delete` operators invoke the global operators `new` and `delete`. You can modify the program so that the overloaded operators `new` and `delete` use random-access streams for storing dynamic data.

The program declares the class `Matrix` that contains the data members `maxRows`, `maxCols`, and `dataPtr`. The first two members, `maxRows` and `maxCols`, store, respectively, the maximum number of rows and columns of the dynamic matrix. The `dataPtr` member is the pointer to the dynamic data of the matrix.

The class `Matrix` declares a constructor, a destructor, two access member functions, and the overloaded operators `new` and `delete`. The class constructor has parameters that specify the maximum number of rows and columns and the fill value used to initialize a class instance. The constructor creates the dynamic space for the matrix data by invoking the operator `new(size_t,unsigned,unsigned)`. The constructor also assigns the matrix dimensions to their respective data members and uses nested `for` loops to initialize the matrix instance.

The class destructor calls the global operator `delete` to deallocate the matrix data space. The member functions `store` and `recall` enable you to access the matrix elements by specifying the row and column indices. The member functions return a Boolean value to indicate the validity of your arguments for the row and column indices.

The first version of the overloaded operator `new` allocates a number of bytes that is equal to the object type. The second version of the operator allocates a number of bytes that accommodates a matrix of any given type. The overloaded operator `delete` simply invokes the global operator `delete`. If you modify the program to use disk storage, you need to replace the calls to the global operators `new` and `delete` with calls to your own functions that manage space on disk.

The function `main` creates a dynamic instance of `Matrix` with 10 rows and 20 columns and initializes the elements of the dynamic matrix with 1. The function then assigns arbitrary values to arbitrary matrix elements and uses nested loops to calculate and display the sum of each column.

Listing 7.3. The source code for the NEWDEL3.CPP program.

```
#include <iostream.h>
#include <stddef.h>

enum boolean { false, true };

class Matrix
{
   protected:
     unsigned maxRows;
     unsigned maxCols;
     double *dataPtr;

   public:
     Matrix(unsigned Rows, unsigned Cols, double fillValue = 0);
     ~Matrix()
       { ::delete [] dataPtr; }

     boolean store(unsigned row, unsigned col, double x);
     boolean recall(unsigned row, unsigned col, double& x);

     void* operator new(size_t size)
       { return ::new unsigned char[size]; }
     void* operator new(size_t size, unsigned Rows, unsigned Cols)
       { return ::new unsigned char[size * Rows * Cols]; }
     void operator delete(void* ptr, size_t dummy)
       { ::delete ptr; }

};

Matrix::Matrix(unsigned Rows, unsigned Cols, double fillValue)
{
  maxRows = Rows;
  maxCols = Cols;
  // invoke the Matrix::operator new(size_t, unsigned, unsigned)
  dataPtr = new double[maxRows * maxCols];
  // fill the matrix
  for (unsigned row = 0; row < maxRows; row++)
    for (unsigned col = 0; col < maxCols; col++)
      *(dataPtr + row * maxCols + col) = fillValue;
}
```

```
boolean Matrix::store(unsigned row, unsigned col, double x)
{
  if (row < maxRows && col < maxCols) {
    *(dataPtr + row * maxCols + col) = x;
    return true;
  }
  else
    return false;
}

boolean Matrix::recall(unsigned row, unsigned col, double& x)
{
  if (row < maxRows && col < maxCols) {
    x = *(dataPtr + row * maxCols + col);
    return true;
  }
  else
    return false;
}

const unsigned numRows = 10;
const unsigned numCols = 20;

main()
{
  Matrix *mat = new Matrix(numRows, numCols, 1.0);
  double sumX, x;

  // assign arbitrary values to arbitrary matrix elements
  mat->store(3, 4, 2.0);
  mat->store(5, 2, 3.0);
  mat->store(9, 4, 4.0);
  mat->store(1, 0, 9.0);
  mat->store(6, 9, 2.0);
  mat->store(2, 6, 3.0);
  mat->store(0, 1, 4.0);
  mat->store(7, 2, 9.0);

  // loop to obtain the sum of each row
```

continues

Listing 7.3. continued

```
for (unsigned row = 0; row < numRows; row++) {
  sumX = 0;
  for (unsigned col = 0; col < numCols; col++) {
    mat->recall(row, col, x);
    sumX += x;
  }
  cout << "Sum of row " << row << " = " << sumX << "\n";
}

delete mat;

return 0;
}
```

Overloading the -> Operator

C++ enables you to overload the `->` operator to access the public members of a non-publicly contained instance of another class. Consider the classes `X` and `Y` in the next example (Listing 7.4). Class `X` has two protected data members, `data1` and `data2`, as well as the public data member (for the sake of demonstration) `data3`. The class declares four member functions to access the two protected data members. The class also declares the function `whoAreYou` to identify the class name of an instance.

The program also declares class `Y`, which includes the protected data member `x`. This member is a pointer to class `X`. Class `Y` declares the `->` operator as:

```
X* operator->()
  { return x; }
```

The previous operator allows the instances of class `Y` to access the public data members and the member function of class `X`. Class `Y` also declares a member function, `whoAreYou`, to identify the instances of class `Y`.

The function `main` declares `y` as the instance of class `Y`. The instance `y` manipulates the protected data members of class `X` using the `->` operator and the functions `setData1`, `setData2`, `getData1`, and `getData2`. The instance `y` also manipulates the public data member `data3` of class `X` using `->data3`.

The last statements of function `main` invoke the `whoAreYou` functions of classes `X` and `Y` using the following statements:

```
cout << "Who are you instance y? ";
y.whoAreYou();
cout << "Who are you instance y->? ";
y->whoAreYou();
```

The program generates the following output:

```
called constructor X()
called constructor Y()
123
321
1000
Who are you instance y? I am an instance of class Y
Who are you instance y->? I am an instance of class X
```

Listing 7.4. The source code for the DEREF1.CPP program.

```
#include <iostream.h>

class X
{
  protected:
    unsigned data1;
    unsigned data2;

  public:
    unsigned data3;

    X()
      { cout << "called constructor X()\n"; }

    void setData1(unsigned newData1)
      { data1 = newData1; }
    unsigned getData1()
      { return data1; }
    void setData2(unsigned newData2)
      { data2 = newData2; }
    unsigned getData2()
      { return data2; }
```

continues

Listing 7.4. continued

```
     void whoAreYou()
       { cout << "I am an instance of class X\n"; }
};

class Y
{
  protected:
    X* x;

  public:
    Y()
       { x = new X;
         cout << "called constructor Y()\n";
       }
    ~Y()
      { delete x; }
    X* operator->()
      { return x; }
     void whoAreYou()
       { cout << "I am an instance of class Y\n"; }
};

main()
{
  Y y;

  y->setData1(123);
  y->setData2(321);
  y->data3 = 1000;

  cout << y->getData1() << "\n";
  cout << y->getData2() << "\n";
  cout << y->data3 << "\n";
  cout << "Who are you instance y? ";
  y.whoAreYou();
  cout << "Who are you instance y->? ";
  y->whoAreYou();


  return 0;
}
```

Summary

This chapter discusses the special operators `new`, `delete`, and `->` and addresses the following topics:

- Overloading the `new` operator—you can create multiple versions of the overloaded `new` operator in C++. The general syntax for the overloaded operator is

  ```
  void* operator new(size_t [,other parameters])
  ```

  The operator must declare the first parameter as `size_t`, a data type declared in the stddef.h header file that allows the compiler to substitute the class name with its size. You can include additional parameters to provide the `new` operator with needed information. C++ treats the `new` operator as static and denies it access to non-static data members of the host class.

- Overloading the `delete` operator—C++ also enables you to overload the `delete` operator. You can only declare one overloaded version per class. The general syntax for declaring the `delete` operator is

  ```
  void delete(void* [, size_t])
  ```

  The first parameter is the pointer to the object being destroyed. The second parameter is optional and is initialized by the compiler as the size of the object addressed by the first argument. The `delete` operator returns the type `void`.

- Using the overloaded operators `new` and `delete`—these operators can be used to control memory management, support alternate storage, and obtain statistics for allocating and deallocating dynamic data.

- Overloading the `->` operator—you can overload the `->` operator in C++ to access the public members of a nonpublicly contained instance of another class.

Nested Declarations

C++ permits classes to declare nested enumerated types, structures, and even classes. These nested declarations enable the class to create data types for its own consumption. The scope of these nested data types is limited to the class and does not add more global data types to modules and the application. Consequently, using nested declarations minimizes the probability of conflicting global data types. This chapter looks at the following local declarations:

- Nested types
- Nested enumerated data types
- Nested structures
- Nested classes

Declaration of Nested Types

Nested data types may be declared as public, protected, or private in the host class. Consequently, access by member functions, class instances, member functions of subclasses, and instances of subclasses follows the access rules of ordinary class members. You may declare a data type in the public section to make it accessible to the various instances, member functions of subclasses, and subclass instances. The reference of the nested data types must be qualified using the host class name. These kinds of nested types are very similar to global data types.

You can also declare a nested type as protected or private. A nested type is considered more hidden if it is declared as protected or private rather than public. The private nested types are strictly for internal use by the host class. The protected nested types allow the member functions of the subclasses to access these types.

If a nested data type appears in the declaration of a public member function, that data type must be declared public. A protected nested type can be accessed by the protected member functions of the host class and its subclasses. A private nested type can be accessed by the private and protected member functions of the host class.

Nested Enumerated Types

Nested enumerated data types provide a class with local enumerated types. The following example, Listing 8.1, which contains the source code for the NESTENUM.CPP program, shows nested enumerated types that are declared public and protected. The class `Days` manipulates the weekdays. The class communicates with its clients using strings that represent the names of the weekdays. However, the class uses the protected nested enumerated type `weekDays` to store and manipulate the weekdays. For the purpose of demonstrating a public nested enumerated type, the class `Days` declares the Boolean type.

The class Days has two data members, dayEnum and dayStr. The dayEnum member stores enumerated weekday values. The dayStr member helps the member function getDay to return a string that represents the name of a weekday.

The class declares a constructor that assigns the default argument Sunday to the class instances. The constructor calls the assignDay member function to perform the actual assignment. The assignDay function uses a series of if statements to translate the name of the weekday into its corresponding enumerated value. The function stores the translated value in the dayEnum member. When the function is successful, it returns the Boolean value true. Otherwise, the function returns false and assigns the enumerated value Sunday to the dayEnum member. I chose to handle erroneous weekdays this way because it simplifies the code.

The member functions nextDay, prevDay, and addDays manipulate the enumerated value stored in the member dayEnum. These functions increment, decrement, and advance the weekday. The function getDay returns the string that contains the name of the weekday.

The function main in the program declares today as an instance of class Days. The program initializes this instance with the string Monday. The function main also declares the Boolean variable ok. Notice that the reference to Boolean is qualified by the Days class name.

The function main tests the various member functions of class Days and uses the variable ok to test whether or not the string Tusday (which I deliberately misspelled) is a valid weekday name. Notice that the if statement, which compares the variable ok with the enumerated value true, actually uses Days::true. This qualification is needed for both the enumerated data type and its enumerated values.

Listing 8.1. The source code for the NESTENUM.CPP program.

```
#include <iostream.h>
#include <string.h>

class Days
```

continues

Listing 8.1. continued

```
{
   public:
     enum boolean { false, true };

   protected:
     enum weekDays { Sunday = 1, Monday, Tuesday, Wednesday,
                     Thursday, Friday, Saturday };

     weekDays dayEnum;
     char dayStr[10];

   public:
     Days(const char* d = "Sunday")
       { assignDay(d); }

     boolean assignDay(const char* d = "Sunday");
     char* getDay();
     void nextDay();
     void prevDay();
     void addDays(unsigned moreDays);

};

Days::boolean Days::assignDay(const char* d)
{
  boolean ok = true;

  if (strcmpi(d, "Sunday") == 0)
    dayEnum = Sunday;
  else if (strcmpi(d, "Monday") == 0)
    dayEnum = Monday;
  else if (strcmpi(d, "Tuesday") == 0)
    dayEnum = Tuesday;
  else if (strcmpi(d, "Wednesday") == 0)
    dayEnum = Wednesday;
  else if (strcmpi(d, "Thursday") == 0)
    dayEnum = Thursday;
  else if (strcmpi(d, "Friday") == 0)
    dayEnum = Friday;
```

```
  else if (strcmpi(d, "Saturday") == 0)
    dayEnum = Saturday;
  else {
    dayEnum = Sunday;
    ok = false;
  }

  return ok;
}

char* Days::getDay()
{
  switch (dayEnum) {
    case Sunday:
      strcpy(dayStr, "Sunday");
      break;
    case Monday:
      strcpy(dayStr, "Monday");
      break;
    case Tuesday:
      strcpy(dayStr, "Tuesday");
      break;
    case Wednesday:
      strcpy(dayStr, "Wednesday");
      break;
    case Thursday:
      strcpy(dayStr, "Thursday");
      break;
    case Friday:
      strcpy(dayStr, "Friday");
      break;
    case Saturday:
      strcpy(dayStr, "Saturday");
      break;
  }
  return dayStr;
}

void Days::nextDay()
{
  if (dayEnum == Saturday)
```

continues

Listing 8.1. continued

```
    dayEnum = Sunday;
  else
    dayEnum = weekDays(dayEnum + 1);
}

void Days::prevDay()
{
  if (dayEnum == Sunday)
    dayEnum = Saturday;
  else
    dayEnum = weekDays(dayEnum - 1);
}

void Days::addDays(unsigned moreDays)
{
  moreDays = moreDays % 7;
  while (moreDays > 0) {
    nextDay();
    moreDays--;
  }
}

main()
{
  Days today("Monday");
  Days::boolean ok;
  char s[10] = "Tusday"; // Tuesday deliberately misspelled

  cout << "Today is " << today.getDay() << "\n";
  today.nextDay();
  cout << "Tomorrow is " << today.getDay() << "\n";
  today.prevDay(); today.prevDay();
  cout << "Yesterday was " << today.getDay() << "\n";
  today.addDays(4);
  cout << "Three Days from today is " << today.getDay() << "\n";

  ok = today.assignDay(s);
  if (ok == Days::true)
    cout << s << " is a valid day\n";
```

```
  else
    cout << s << " is NOT a valid day\n";

  return 0;
}
```

Nested Structures

Classes use nested structures to implicitly implement supportive data structures such as lists and trees. Listing 8.2 shows the declaration of the template class `Stack` in the stack.hpp header file. Notice that the class `Stack` declares the nested structure `StackNode`. This structure models the nodes of a linked list that stores and manages the stack elements. The `StackNode` structure consists of two members: `nodeData` and `nextPtr`. The `nodeData` member stores data in a stack element. The member `nextPtr` is the pointer to the next list node that represents the next stack element.

Declaring the `StackNode` member as protected hides it from the instances of `Stack` and its subclasses. To support this kind of declaration, the `StackNode` structure does not appear in the declaration of any public member function in `Stack`. However, as Listing 8.3 shows, most of the member functions of `Stack` use local pointers to the `StackNode` structure. This structure is vital to maintaining the dynamic linked list that stores and manages the generic stack elements.

Listing 8.2. The source code for the stack.hpp header file.

```
#ifndef _STACK_HPP
#define _STACK_HPP

#ifndef BOOLEAN
#define BOOLEAN
enum boolean { false, true };
#endif

template<class T>
class Stack
{
```

continues

Listing 8.2. continued

```
protected:
  // nested structure
  struct StackNode {
      T nodeData;
      StackNode *nextPtr;
  };

  unsigned height;    // height of stack
  boolean allocateError; // dynamic allocation error
  StackNode *top; // pointer to the top of the stack
  Stack<T>& copy(Stack<T>&);

public:
  Stack();
  ~Stack()
    { clear(); }
  /* ****************** state query methods ***************** */
  boolean isempty() const {
      return (height == 0) ? true : false;
  }
  boolean getAllocateError() const
    { return allocateError; }

  /* ************** object manipulation methods ************* */
  void push(T);
  boolean pop(T&);
  void clear();
  Stack<T>& operator =(Stack<T>& g)
    { copy(g); return *this; }
};

#endif
```

Listing 8.3. The source code for the STACK.CPP library file.

```
#include <string.h>
#include "stack.hpp"
```

```
template<class T>
Stack<T>::Stack()
{
    height = 0;
    allocateError = false;
    top = NULL;
}

template<class T>
Stack<T>& Stack<T>::copy(Stack<T>& g)
{
    StackNode *p, *q, *r;

    // clear the stack if not already empty
    if (top)
        clear();
    // copy the stack heights
    height = g.height;
    allocateError = false;
    // assign NULL to top of the target stack
    top = NULL;
    // exit if the source stack is empty
    if (!g.top)
        return *this;
    // allocate a new stack element
    top = new StackNode;
    // exit if error in allocation
    if (!top) {
        allocateError = true;
        return *this;
    }
    // initialize pointers for deep copy
    top->nextPtr = NULL;
    top->nodeData = g.top->nodeData;
    q = g.top->nextPtr;
    p = top;
    // loop to duplicate the source stack elements
    while (q) {
        // create new stack element
        r = new StackNode;
        if (!r) {
```

continues

Listing 8.3. continued

```
                allocateError = true;
                return *this;
            }
            r->nodeData = q->nodeData; // copy data
            r->nextPtr = NULL;
            p->nextPtr = r;
            p = p->nextPtr;
            q = q->nextPtr;
        }
        return *this;
}


template<class T>
void Stack<T>::clear()
{
    T x;

    while (pop(x))
     /* do nothing */;
}

template<class T>
void Stack<T>::push(T x)
{
    StackNode *p;

    allocateError = false;
    if (top) {
        p = new StackNode; // allocate new stack element
        if (!p) {
         allocateError = true;
         return;
     }
        p->nodeData = x;
     p->nextPtr = top;
     top = p;
    }
    else {
```

```
        top = new StackNode;
        if (top == NULL) {
         allocateError = true;
         return;
     }
     top->nodeData = x;
     top->nextPtr = NULL;
    }
    height++;
}

template<class T>
boolean Stack<T>::pop(T& x)
{
    StackNode *p;

    if (height) {
        x = top->nodeData;
     p = top;
     top = top->nextPtr;
     delete p; // deallocate stack node
     height--;
     return true;
    }
    else
     return false;
}
```

Nested Classes

You can declare a class within a class in C++. The nested classes are defined within the scope of their host class. You might expect that nesting classes fosters a special access privilege for members between the host and nested classes. This expectation, however, is unfounded. Host and nested classes follow the access rules for members that exist between nonnested classes. You should use nested classes to hide specialized classes and their instances within a host class. C++ enables you to obtain similar operations by using friend classes (except the friend classes that are not hidden).

Listing 8.4 contains the source code for the FIXSTACK.CPP program. This program declares the template class `fixedStack` that models fixed-size generic stacks. This implementation uses an underlying dynamic array to store the various stack elements. The `fixedStack` class declares the nested class `Array`. This class has both protected and public members and comes complete with a constructor, destructor, and various implementation member functions.

The class `Array` has three members: `workSize`, `arrSize`, and `arrPtr`. The member `workSize` is similar to the stack height member. The member `arrSize` stores the size of the fixed size (this size is fixed at runtime). The `arrPtr` member is the pointer to the dynamic array that stores the stack elements.

The constructor for the nested class allocates the dynamic space for the supporting array, sets `arrSize` to the array size, and sets the `workSize` member to 0. The constructor for the nested class deallocates the dynamic space accessed using the pointer `arrPtr`.

The nested class `Array` offers the member functions `insert`, `remove`, and `erase`. These functions support the member functions `push`, `pop`, and `clear` that are declared for the host class `fixedStack`.

The host class `fixedStack` declares two members, `height` and `p` (`height` stores the current stack height; `p` is a pointer to an instance of the nested class `Array`). The constructor of the host class creates a dynamic instance of the nested class. The member functions `push`, `pop`, and `clear` invoke the member functions of the nested class using the pointer `p`. In fact, this pointer provides the link between the host class and its nested class. The functions of `fixedStack` manipulate the dynamic instance of `Array` by invoking its member functions—the functions of `fixedStack` have no direct access to the data members of `Array`.

The function `main` creates an instance of `fixedStack` that is instantiated using the `int` type. The function `main` then invokes the `push` and `pop` member functions of the `fixedStack`. The nested `Array` remains invisible to the function `main`.

Listing 8.4. The source code for the FIXSTACK.CPP program.

```
#include <iostream.h>

enum boolean { false, true };
```

```
template<class T>
class fixedStack
{

  protected:
    // declare nested class Array
    class Array
    {
      protected:
        unsigned workSize;
        unsigned arrSize;
        T* arrPtr;

      public:
        Array(unsigned ArrSize)
          { arrPtr = new T[arrSize = ArrSize];
            workSize = 0;
          }
        ~Array()
          { delete [] arrPtr; }
         boolean insert(T x)
           {
             if (workSize < arrSize) {
               arrPtr[workSize++] = x;
               return true;
             }
             else
               return false;
           }
         boolean remove(T& x)
           {
             if (workSize > 0) {
               x = arrPtr[--workSize];
               return true;
             }
             else
               return false;
           }
        void erase()
           {  workSize = 0; }
    };
```

continues

Listing 8.4. continued

```
    Array* p;
    unsigned height;   // height of stack

  public:
    fixedStack(unsigned MaxSize = 10)
      { p = new Array(MaxSize); }
    ~fixedStack()
      { delete p; }
    /* ****************** state query methods ***************** */
    boolean isempty() {
        return (height == 0) ? true : false;
    }

    /* ************** object manipulation methods ************* */
    void push(T x)
      { if (p->insert(x))
          height++;
      }
    boolean pop(T& x)
      { boolean ok = p->remove(x);
        if (ok) height--;
        return ok;
      }
    void clear()
      { p->erase(); }
};


main()
{
  fixedStack<int> stk(10);
  int i;

  stk.push(1);
  stk.push(10);
  stk.push(100);
  stk.push(1000);
  stk.push(10000);
```

```
  while (stk.pop(i))
    cout << i << "\n";

  return 0;
}
```

Summary

This chapter discusses declaring enumerated types, structures, and classes within classes and addresses the following points:

- Declarations of nested types can be declared public, protected, or private. Nested types that are declared public can be accessed by various kinds of class instances and even normal functions. Nested types that are declared protected or private impose more control on their access. Nested data types enable you to minimize the conflict in auxiliary data types that serve classes.
- Nested enumerated data types provide classes with nonglobal enumerated values. Protected and private nested enumerated types become invisible to class instances and client functions.
- Nested structures provide classes with nonglobal structures. Protected and private nested structure types become invisible to class instances and client functions.
- Nested classes offer the convenience of hiding a class. There are no special access privileges, however, between the host and nested classes for each other's members.

Template Classes

Object-oriented programming eliminates redundant coding through inheritance. Subclasses inherit functions from their parent and ancestor classes. In Chapter 4, "Member Functions," I discussed template functions and showed you how these functions can replace numerous nontemplate functions that perform similar tasks on different data types.

C++ also supports template classes. These classes model generic objects that provide similar operations for different data types. The best example of using template classes is data structures. By using a template class you can create a generic stack, for example, that can be instantiated for various predefined and user-defined data types. You can also have template classes for queues, arrays, matrices, lists, trees, hash tables, graphs, and any other general-purpose data structure. The chapters in Part III of this book present a whole series of template classes. This chapter also presents template classes and discusses the following topics:

- Template class declarations
- Template class instances

- Template parameters
- Class derivation and templates

Template Class Declarations

Declaring template classes is similar to, but more complex than, declaring a template function. An example of a simple template class, Listing 9.1, shows the source code for the stack.hpp header file.

Listing 9.1. The source code for the stack.hpp header file.

```
#ifndef _STACK_HPP
#define _STACK_HPP

#ifndef BOOLEAN
#define BOOLEAN
enum boolean { false, true };
#endif

template<class T>
class Stack
{

  protected:
    // nested structure
    struct StackNode {
        T nodeData;
        StackNode *nextPtr;
    };

    unsigned height;       // height of stack
    boolean allocateError; // dynamic allocation error
    StackNode *top;        // pointer to the top of the stack
    Stack<T>& copy(Stack<T>&);

  public:
    Stack();
    ~Stack()
```

```
        { clear(); }
    /* ****************** state query methods ***************** */
    boolean isempty() const {
        return (height == 0) ? true : false;
    }
    boolean getAllocateError() const
      { return allocateError; }

    /* ************** object manipulation methods ************* */
    void push(T);
    boolean pop(T&);
    void clear();
    Stack<T>& operator =(Stack<T>& g)
      { copy(g); return *this; }
};

#endif
```

The keyword `template` informs the compiler that you are about to declare a template class or function. The `template` keyword is followed by a template parameter list that is enclosed in angle brackets. Typically, the list contains a single class item. The type `T` is the popular choice for the template class. The template parameter list may include additional template classes and other data types (predefined or user-defined structures). The template class `Stack` declares a nested structure `StackNode`. This structure contains two members, `dataNode` and `nextPtr`. The `dataNode` member has the template type, and the `nextPtr` member is the pointer to a stack node. This structure also tells you that the generic stack is implemented using an unordered, single-linked list.

The template class `Stack` implements a simple, generic stack that pushes and pops data and clears the stack. Secondary operations enable you to copy stack objects and access the dynamic allocation error state.

Notice that the reference to the class itself inside its declaration requires the use of `Stack<T>` (not `Stack`, the name of the template class). The member functions `copy` and `operator =` use this type of class reference. You should also notice the use of the template class `T` with member functions that manipulate the basic, undefined data type.

What about the definition of member functions? Does this require any special syntax? The answer is yes. Examine the source code for the STACK.CPP library file shown in Listing 9.2 and notice that the definition of every member function begins with `template<class T>`. The class name qualifier is `Stack<T>`, not `Stack`. A good example is the member function `copy`:

```
template<class T>
Stack<T>& Stack<T>::copy(Stack<T>& g)
```

The template class declaration and the definition of its member functions require the use of the class name and parameter identifiers when making a reference to the template class.

You will notice in Listing 9.2 that the statements involving the `nodeData` member of the `StackNode` structure use the assignment operator. This means that if you apply the template class `Stack` to a user-defined class, that class must define an = operator that contains the following general declaration:

```
T& operator =(T&)
```

The stack operations do not involve relational operators. Most other data structures do employ various relational operators. Therefore, it is a good practice to declare your class with the = operator and various relational operators.

Listing 9.2. The source code for the STACK.CPP library file.

```
#include <string.h>
#include "stack.hpp"

template<class T>
Stack<T>::Stack()
{
    height = 0;
    allocateError = false;
    top = NULL;
}
```

```
template<class T>
Stack<T>& Stack<T>::copy(Stack<T>& g)
{
    StackNode *p, *q, *r;

    // clear the stack if not already empty
    if (top)
        clear();
    // copy the stack heights
    height = g.height;
    allocateError = false;
    // assign NULL to top of the target stack
    top = NULL;
    // exit if the source stack is empty
    if (!g.top)
        return *this;
    // allocate a new stack element
    top = new StackNode;
    // exit if error in allocation
    if (!top) {
        allocateError = true;
        return *this;
    }
    // initialize pointers for deep copy
    top->nextPtr = NULL;
    top->nodeData = g.top->nodeData;
    q = g.top->nextPtr;
    p = top;
    // loop to duplicate the source stack elements
    while (q) {
        // create new stack element
        r = new StackNode;
        if (!r) {
            allocateError = true;
            return *this;
        }
        r->nodeData = q->nodeData; // copy data
        r->nextPtr = NULL;
        p->nextPtr = r;
```

continues

Listing 9.2. continued

```
        p = p->nextPtr;
        q = q->nextPtr;
    }
    return *this;
}


template<class T>
void Stack<T>::clear()
{
    T x;

    while (pop(x))
     /* do nothing */;
}

template<class T>
void Stack<T>::push(T x)
{
    StackNode *p;

    allocateError = false;
    if (top) {
        p = new StackNode; // allocate new stack element
        if (!p) {
         allocateError = true;
         return;
     }
        p->nodeData = x;
     p->nextPtr = top;
     top = p;
    }
    else {
        top = new StackNode;
     if (top == NULL) {
         allocateError = true;
         return;·
     }
     top->nodeData = x;
```

```
      top->nextPtr = NULL;
      }
     height++;
}

template<class T>
boolean Stack<T>::pop(T& x)
{
    StackNode *p;

    if (height) {
        x = top->nodeData;
     p = top;
     top = top->nextPtr;
     delete p; // deallocate stack node
     height--;
     return true;
    }
    else
     return false;
}
```

Template Class Instances

To instantiate template classes, you must follow a few rules:

1. The C++ compiler does not compile template classes. Instead, the compiler reads and stores them until they appear in the code. Therefore, you need to include the code to declare the template class and to define its member functions. You can put these two code segments in one file or you can use a header file and a .CPP file. I choose to apply the latter approach, simply to be more consistent with nontemplate classes. Using this approach, you need to include the .CPP in your client programs. Of course, the .CPP file needs to include the related header file.

2. The template class is instantiated by specifying predefined data types or user-defined classes. The general syntax for instantiating a simple template class is:

   ```
   templateClass<type> instance(constructorArguments);
   ```

Listing 9.3, containing the source code for the TSSTACK.CPP test program, illustrates the instantiation of the class `Stack`. The program creates three instances of the template class `Stack`, and these instances are instantiated using the `int`, `double`, and class `String10`. The `String10` class is also declared in the test program to model a simple 10-character string. Notice that the class declares the `=` operators. The template class uses the first overloaded version, and the statements in function `main` use the second version. Attempting to use the template class `Stack` with a simple array of characters does not work. The program illustrates the use of the member functions `push` and `pop` with the various instances of class `Stack`. The program pushes data in each instance and then pops them off. The program uses a `while` loop to pop off and display the stack elements for each stack.

Listing 9.3. The source code for the TSSTACK.CPP test program.

```
#include <iostream.h>
#include <string.h>
#include "stack.cpp"

class String10
{
  protected:
    char str[11];

  public:
    String10()
      { str[0] = '\0'; }
    String10(const char* s)
      { strcpy(str, s); }

    char* getString() const
      { return str; }
    unsigned getLen() const
      { return strlen(str); }
    String10& operator =(String10& s)
    {
      strcpy(str, s.str);
      return *this;
    }
    String10& operator =(const char* s)
    {
```

```
        strcpy(str, s);
        return *this;
      }
};

main()
{
  int i;
  double x;
  String10 s;
  Stack<int> intStk;
  Stack<double> dblStk;
  Stack<String10> strStk;

  intStk.push(1);
  intStk.push(10);
  intStk.push(100);
  intStk.push(1000);
  intStk.push(10000);

  cout << "Popping off data from integer stack\n";
  while (intStk.pop(i)) {
    cout << i << "\n";
  }
  cout << "\n";

  dblStk.push(2.2);
  dblStk.push(4.4);
  dblStk.push(8.8);
  dblStk.push(16.16);
  dblStk.push(32.32);

  cout << "Popping off data from floating-point numbers stack\n";
  while (dblStk.pop(x)) {
    cout << x << "\n";
  }
  cout << "\n";
  s = "Windows";
  strStk.push(s);
  s = "MS-DOS";
  strStk.push(s);
```

continues

Listing 9.3. continued

```
    s = "UNIX";
    strStk.push(s);
    s = "X-Windows";
    strStk.push(s);
    s = "CP/M";
    strStk.push(s);

    cout << "Popping off data from strings stack\n";
    while (strStk.pop(s)) {
      cout << s.getString() << "\n";
    }
    cout << "\n";


    return 0;
}
```

If you compile and run the test program, it produces the following output:

```
Popping off data from integer stack
10000
1000
100
10
1

Popping off data from floating-point numbers stack
32.32
16.16
8.8
4.4
2.2

Popping off data from strings stack
CP/M
X-Windows
UNIX
MS-DOS
Windows
```

Template Parameters

The template parameter list enables you to specify multiple classes and/or additional data types. Most template classes that model generic data structures have only one template class. A few employ more than one template class. The following code fragment contains the declaration of a template class that models the directed graph data structure. The code also includes the declarations of two template structures.

```
template<class T>
struct graphRec {
    unsigned gindex;
    T edgeValue;
    graphRec<T>* nextPtr;
};

template<class T, class L>
struct vertexRec {
   L graphLabel;
   graphRec<T>* head;
};

template<class T, class L>
class Graph
{

  protected:
    unsigned        maxSize,          // maximum number of vertices
                    workSize;         // the working size
    graphRec<T>*    currentVertex;    // traversal pointer
    vertexRec<T,L>* graphData;        // pointer to list heads
    string80        errorMessage;     // error message string

  public:
    // ************** state manipulation methods **************
    Graph() {}
    Graph(unsigned maxVertices);
    ~Graph();

    // ***************** state query methods ****************
    char* getErrorMessage() const;
```

```
    unsigned getWorkSize() const { return workSize; }

    // ************** object manipulation methods *************
    boolean expand(unsigned newMaxSize);
    boolean linkVertex(unsigned source,
                       unsigned target,
                       T& linkValue);
    boolean getLinkValue(unsigned source,
                         unsigned target,
                         T& linkValue);
    boolean unlinkVertex(unsigned source,
                         unsigned target);
    boolean store(L& x, unsigned index);
    boolean recall(L& x, unsigned index);
    unsigned search(L& key);
    unsigned visitFirst(unsigned startingVertex);
    unsigned visitNext();
};
```

The class `Graph` models graphs that are made up of connected nodes. Each node (also called a *vertex*) has a value called the *label value*. In addition, each connection between any two vertices (called a *link*) has a value. The best example of a graph is a vendor's geographical map. The map contains cities (the vertices) that are connected by highways (the links). The cities have values that represent potential dollar sales, and the highways have values that represent miles. To implement a template graph, you need to use two template classes, one to represent the vertex values and one to represent the link values.

The template parameter list may contain nonclass data types. The next example illustrates a template class with multiple template parameter lists. Listing 9.4 shows the source code for the pstack.hpp header file. This file declares the template class `priorStack` with the template parameter list `<class T, unsigned L>`. The parameter `L` represents a priority access for the various class instances. If the argument for `L` is 0, the class instances can only push and pop data and clear the stack. If the argument for `L` is 1, the class instances can also invoke the `rollDown` and `rollUp` member functions to rotate the stack. If the argument for `L` is 2 or more, the class instances can also invoke the `deque` member function to turn the stack into a queue. This example shows how a template parameter like `L` is used to specify critical information that greatly influences the template class instances. To shorten the implementation, I chose

to make the template class priorStack a descendant of the template class Stack. The class priorStack stores the access level passed by template parameter L in the data member level. I coded the class so that you can alter the access level of an instance when you clear it by invoking the member function clear. The new version has the parameter newLevel. Thus, you can clear a stack and assign a new access level.

Listing 9.4. The source code for the pstack.hpp header file.

```
#include "stack.cpp"

#ifndef _PSTACK_HPP
#define _PSTACK_HPP
template<class T, unsigned L>
class priorStack : public Stack<T>
{
   protected:
     unsigned level;
     priorStack<T,L>& copy(priorStack<T,L>& g);

   public:
     priorStack();
     ~priorStack()
       { clear(0); }

    void clear(unsigned newLevel);
    void rollUp();
    void rollDown();
    boolean deque(T& x);
    priorStack<T,L>& operator =(priorStack<T,L>& g);

};

#endif
```

Listing 9.5 shows the source code for the PSTACK.CPP library file. The defined member functions either set or test the value of the level data member. The member functions push and pop are inherited from the parent template class.

Listing 9.5. The source code for the PSTACK.CPP library file.

```
#include <string.h>
#include "pstack.hpp"

template<class T, unsigned L>
priorStack<T,L>::priorStack()
{
    level = L;
    Stack<T>::Stack();
}

template<class T, unsigned L>
priorStack<T,L>& priorStack<T,L>::copy(priorStack<T,L>& g)
{
  level = g.level;
  Stack<T>::copy(g);
  return *this;
}


template<class T, unsigned L>
void priorStack<T,L>::clear(unsigned newLevel)
{
    T x;

    while (pop(x))
     /* do nothing */;
    level = newLevel;
}

template<class T, unsigned L>
void priorStack<T,L>::rollUp()
{
    StackNode *old_top, *next_one;

    if (level < 1 || !top || height < 2)
     return;
    old_top = top;
    top = top->nextPtr;
    old_top->nextPtr = NULL; // new bottom NULL pointer
```

```
    next_one = top->nextPtr;
    while (next_one->nextPtr != NULL)
     next_one = next_one->nextPtr;
    next_one->nextPtr = old_top;
}

template<class T, unsigned L>
void priorStack<T,L>::rollDown()
{
    StackNode *last_one, *next_one;

    if (level < 1 || !top || height < 2)
     return;
    last_one = NULL;
    next_one = top;
    while (next_one->nextPtr != NULL) {
        last_one = next_one;
     next_one = next_one->nextPtr;
    }
    next_one->nextPtr = top;
    top = next_one;
    last_one->nextPtr = NULL;
}

template<class T, unsigned L>
boolean priorStack<T,L>::deque(T& x)
{
    if (level >= 2) {
      rollDown();
      return pop(x);
    }
    else
      return false;
}
```

Listing 9.6 contains the source code for the TSPSTACK.CPP test program. This program creates an instance of the template class `priorStack` to store integers. The program assigns the initial stack instance an access level of 0, and it makes this assignment as it creates the stack instance. The program uses a `for` loop to push data in the stack and test the accessing member functions `rollDown` and `deque` for the levels 0, 1, and 2. The second and third loop iteration begin by clearing the stack and assigning a new access level. The following program output illustrates the different access privileges of the stack as the program alters its access level.

```
**************** level 0 ***************
The current top of the stack is: 10000
After rolling down the stack, top element is:
Error! Cannot use rollDown function
After dequeueing the stack, top element is:
Error! Cannot use deque function
**************** level 1 ***************
The current top of the stack is: 10000
After rolling down the stack, top element is: 1
After dequeueing the stack, top element is:
Error! Cannot use deque function
**************** level 2 ***************
The current top of the stack is: 10000
After rolling down the stack, top element is: 1
After dequeueing the stack, top element is: 1
```

Listing 9.6. The source code for the TSPSTACK.CPP test program.

```
#include <iostream.h>
#include "pstack.cpp"

main()
{
  int i, j;
  boolean ok;
  priorStack<int, 0> intStk;

  for (unsigned k = 0; k < 3; k++) {
    // clear stack and assign a new level if k is not 0
    if (k != 0)
       intStk.clear(k);
    // push data in the stack
    intStk.push(1);
    intStk.push(10);
    intStk.push(100);
    intStk.push(1000);
    intStk.push(10000);
```

```
    cout << "**************** level " << k << " ***************\n";
    cout << "The current top of the stack is: ";
    if (intStk.pop(i)) {
      cout << i << "\n";
      intStk.push(i);
      j = i;
    }
    cout << "After rolling down the stack, top element is: ";
    intStk.rollDown();
    intStk.pop(i);
    if (i != j) {
      cout << i << "\n";
      intStk.push(i);
      j = i;
    }
    else
      cout << "\nError! Cannot use rollDown function\n";

    // test the deque function
    cout << "After dequeueing the stack, top element is: ";
    if (intStk.deque(i)) {
      intStk.pop(i);
      cout << i << "\n";
      intStk.push(i);
    }
    else
      cout << "\nError! Cannot use deque function\n";
  }
  return 0;
}
```

Class Derivation and Templates

Listing 9.5 shows the declaration of the template class `priorStack` as the descendant of template class `Stack`. The following declaration shows that the reference to the parent class is `Stack<T>`, not `Stack`.

```
template<class T, unsigned L>
class priorStack : public Stack<T>
```

The general rule for declaring descendant template classes, therefore, is to use the fully qualified reference to the parent class. C++ enables you to develop hierarchies of template classes that are similar to those of nontemplate classes. The base template class is often an abstract class that simply lays the specification for the main member functions. The descendant template classes offer the implementations of the member functions.

The hierarchy of template classes need not exclude nontemplate classes. You can declare the first nontemplate in the hierarchy. All the descendants of that class are also nontemplate classes. The transition between template and nontemplate classes is very easy.

```
template<class T>
class unorderedList
{
     struct listNode {
          T data;
          listNode* next;
     };

     protected:
          unsigned listSize;
          listNode* head;

     public:
          unorderedList();
          ~unorderedList();

          boolean addData(T& x);
          boolean deleteAdata(T& x);
          boolean searchData(T& x);
          boolean visitFirst(T& x);
          boolean visitNext(T& x);
};

template<class T>
class orderedList : public unorderedList<T>
{
     public:
          orderedList();
          ~orderedList();
```

```
        boolean addData(T& x);
        boolean searchData(T& x);
};

class DOSfileList : public orderedList<DOSfile>
{
    public:
        DOSfileList();
        ~DOSfileList();

        void addFiles(const char* wildcards);
        void deleteFiles(const char* wildcards);
};
```

The preceding code fragment contains a three-class hierarchy. The base class is the template class `unorderedList`. This class models generic unordered lists. The first descendant class is `orderedList`. This template class models generic ordered lists. The descendant of `orderedList` is class `DOSfileList`, a nontemplate class that models sorted lists of MS-DOS files. Notice that the declaration of class `DOSfileList` is

```
class DOSfileList : public orderedList<DOSfile>
```

The parent template class, `orderedList`, appears not as `orderedList<T>` but as the instantiated class `orderedList<DOSfile>`. It is this instantiation that provides the critical transition between template classes and nontemplate classes in the hierarchy.

Summary

Templates are a relatively new language feature in C++. This chapter discussed template class use and covered the following topics:

- Template class declarations—this step states that a class is generic using the general syntax:

  ```
  template<parameterList>
  class className
  {
     // declarations of members
  };
  ```

- `parameterList` is a list of one or more template classes. The list may also include predefined data types and user-defined structures. The class declaration requires the use of a fully qualified class name.
- The definition of the various member functions must employ a special syntax. The general form is

```
template<parameterList>
type className<paramNamesList>::memberFunction(
                                          functionParameterList)
```

- `paramNamesList` is the list of parameter names and does not include the associated classes and data types.
- Template class instances—this is a process that creates an instance from the template class by specifying the instantiating data type. The general syntax for the instantiation of a template class is

```
className<instantiatingType>
classInstance(constructurArguments);
```

- Template parameters—these include one or more classes as well as any other valid data type. This chapter illustrates how generic directed graphs are modeled using a C++ class with two template classes. The text also presents an implementation of a generic stack that supports various access levels for different instances.
- Class derivation and templates—C++ supports the normal rules of deriving classes and inheritance for template classes. C++ enables you to create template class hierarchies that are solely made up of template classes or both template and nontemplate classes. The chapter offers an example of how a hierarchy of linked lists can switch from template to nontemplate classes.

Exception Handling

This chapter serves as a quick introduction to the new error handling mechanism in C++. As the language evolves, C++ designers are providing it with a better error handling mechanism—namely, exceptions. This chapter addresses the following topics:

- Introduction to exceptions
- Discrimination of exceptions
- Naming of exceptions
- Exceptions and non-error code jumps
- Unhandled exceptions
- Alternatives for exception handling

Introduction to Exceptions

C and Pascal are examples of languages that lack any formal mechanism to deal with errors. Programmers using these languages must rely on defensive programming techniques. Such programming methods require that the library developer warn its client functions of any errors. At the same time, the client functions are expected to test every likely error occurrence. This approach has frustrated many programmers.

Among the early language implementations that provided PC error handling was Microsoft Basic. This implementation enabled you to declare a general error trap and specify how to handle the error. Although this approach freed the source code from the overhead of defensive programming, the compiler code was full of low-level instructions for error detection. Another version of Basic, called True Basic, provided special structures that resemble the new C++ exception constructs to handle errors. Ada is one of the prominent languages that uses exceptions (in name and concept). Because the new C++ exceptions look very similar, it seems likely that C++ designers have been influenced by Ada's exceptions.

The new exceptions mechanism uses new reserved words and the new `try-catch` construct. These new language aspects can be illustrated using the following example. Consider the class of dynamic arrays of floating-point numbers declared below:

```
class DblArray
{
     protected:
          unsigned size;
          double* dataPtr;

     public:
          class OutOfRange {}; // exception class

          DblArray(unsigned Size);
          // other member functions
          double& operator [](unsigned index)
          {
               if (index < size)
                    return dataPtr[index];
               throw OutOfRange();
          }
};
```

The operator `[]` returns the reference to the element number index when the specified index is within the valid range. What happens when the index is out of range? In Chapter 6, "C++ Operators," I suggested using a dummy data member and returning the reference to that member if the index is out of range. The new C++ exception offers a different solution. Notice that the second statement in the operator `[]` is thrown `OutOfRange()`. The `throw` identifier is a reserved word that tells the compiler to raise (or throw) an array using the object `OutOfRange()`. The class `DblArray` also declares the exception class `OutOfRange` as a public nested class. Throwing an exception is like launching a cruise missile in hopes that it finds the target. The `throw` statement in the `[]` operator raises an error condition that must be handled by the client functions.

How do client functions handle raised exceptions? C++ uses the new `try-catch` construct to monitor one or more function calls and deals with exceptions that might be raised by these functions. The general syntax for the `try-catch` construct is

```
try {
     // statements with functions that may raise errors
}
catch (exception) {
     // statements that attempt to deal with the error
}
```

The following function, for example, adds two numerical arrays assumed to be of equal size. The `for` loop statement, which adds the elements of the second array, `ar2`, to the elements of the first array, `ar1`, might raise an error if `ar2` is smaller than `ar1`:

```
void addDblArrays(DblArray& ar1, DblArray& ar2)
{
  unsigned sz = ar1.getSize();
  try {
     for (unsigned i = 0; i < sz; i++)
          ar1[i] += ar2[i];
  }
  catch (DblArray::OutOfRange()) {
    // ar2 is smaller than ar1
    cerr << "Array ar2 is smaller than ar1\n";
  }
}
```

Discrimination of Exceptions

In order to deal with errors properly, you first need to identify them. Simply raising an exception only addresses part of the problem. You can determine the error by declaring various exception classes. For example, the `DblArray` class can declare exception classes to handle out-of-range indices, overflow errors, and array size errors, as shown here:

```
class DblArray
{
     protected:
          unsigned size;
          double* dataPtr;

     public:
          // exception classes
          class OutOfRange {};
          class OverflowError {};
          class ArraySizeError {};

          DblArray(unsigned Size);
          // other member functions
};
```

A client function can then detect the error and determine its type:

```
void solve(DblArray& array)
{
     try {
     }
     catch (DblArray::OutOfRange) {
          // deal with out-of-range error
     }
     catch (DblArray::OverflowError) {
          // deal with overflow error
     }
     catch (DblArray::ArraySizeError) {
          // deal with an error in the array size
     }
}
```

The preceding code also demonstrates that C++ enables you to include multiple catch clauses. C++ also allows you to select the errors to handle. In other words, you don't have to catch every exception.

Naming of Exceptions

In many cases, thrown exceptions do not result in fatal errors that make it necessary to halt a program. Instead, the exception handler is able to resolve the problem. In order for the handler to do so, however, it needs information to classify the offending condition. To pass information with the exception class, C++ enables you to declare public data members in the exception class. The following example is a modified version of the `DblArray` class that includes such a data member:

```
class DblArray
{
     protected:
          unsigned size;
          double* dataPtr;

     public:
          // exception class
          class OutOfRange
          {
               public:
                    unsigned badIndex;
                    OutOfRange(unsigned index)
                         : badIndex(index) { }
          };

          DblArray(unsigned Size);
          // other member functions
          double& operator [](unsigned index)
          {
               if (index < size)
                    return dataPtr[index];
               throw OutOfRange(index);
          }
};
```

The exception class `OutOfRange` declares the public data member index. The new version of class `DblArray` passes the parameter index in operator `[]` with the thrown exception. As shown in the following example, the client function can then use the information on the bad index to handle the out-of-range exception:

```
void addDblArrays(DblArray& ar1, DblArray& ar2)
{
  unsigned sz = ar1.getSize();
  try {
     for (unsigned i = 0; i < sz; i++)
          ar1[i] += ar2[i];
  }
  catch (DblArray::OutOfRange(i)) {
    // ar2 is smaller than ar1
    cerr << "Array ar2 has " << i-1 << " elements\n";
  }
}
```

Exceptions and Non-Error Code Jumps

The `throw` statement may be regarded as a sophisticated form of a *jump in* statement. The `try-catch` construct specifies the jump destination. Therefore, you can use the `try-catch` construct to monitor the state of data members in class instances. For example, the following code fragment monitors the sizes of three matrices and ensures that their sizes remain above a minimum number of rows and columns. The code fragment assigns the function `processMatrices` to call functions in class `Matrix` that are able to shrink the matrix size:

```
void processMatrices(Matrix& mat1, Matrix& mat2, Matrix& mat3)
{
     try {
          // manipulate the matrices mat1, mat2, and mat3
     }
     catch(Matrix::SmallSize(matPtr, currentSize) {
          // statements to resize the matrix accessed
          // by pointer matPtr to a minimum size
          return;
     }
}
```

Unhandled Exceptions

What happens to an unhandled exception? The answer is that the compiler C++ code calls the `terminate()` function. In turn, this function executes the last-resort, error handling function that you specify using the `set_terminate` function. The argument for `set_terminate` is a void function with no parameters. The `set_terminate` function returns the previous last-resort, error handling function. Using such a function enables you to save critical data or perform a smart shutdown of your system. By default, the `terminate()` function calls the `abort()` function.

Alternatives for Exception Handling

The catch clauses contain statements that handle certain exceptions. These statements enable you to apply various solutions:

1. Abort the program after displaying the proper diagnosis messages and saving any critical data.
2. Pass the exception by using the `throw;` statement. Subsequent catch clauses will attempt to handle the exceptions. This alternative enables various exception handlers to make an attempt to solve the problem.
3. Throw another exception after transforming the problem (if possible) from one form to a simpler one that can be resolved by another exception handler.
4. Resolve the problem and reexecute the original statements. In this case, the error-generating statements should be placed in a separate function.
5. If the host function requires a result, return a value.

Summary

This chapter introduced you to the new C++ error handling features and discussed the following topics:

- Introduction to exceptions—C++ now supports the `throw` statement and the `try-catch` construct. The `throw` statement raises an exception. The try clause in the `try-catch` construct executes one or more statements that might raise an exception. If this happens, the subsequent catch clause (or clauses) attempts to resolve the exception.

- Discrimination of exceptions—C++ enables you to declare several public nested classes to model different exception categories.
- Naming of exceptions—C++ enables you to declare public data members in the exception classes. These members assist in passing information to the catch clause in an exception handler.
- Using exceptions to handle non-error code jumps—the `try-catch` construct can be used to monitor and handle non-error conditions.
- Unhandled exceptions—C++ invokes the `terminate()` function, which by default calls the `abort()` function to deal with unhandled exceptions. You can use the `set_terminate` function to specify the non-default function which is called by the `terminate()` function.
- Alternatives for exception handling—the catch clauses in the `try-catch` constructs enable you to perform various error handling tasks such as aborting the program, passing the error, and retrying the offending statements after fixing the problem.

Part II

C++ Object-Oriented Programming

Inheritance

C++ supports single and multiple inheritance schemes. There are many programmers and developers who argue strongly against multiple inheritance. They regard multiple inheritance as a language feature inviting abuse and misuse. In addition, they feel that good class design can use single inheritance and containment to model any object. In this chapter, I discuss the following topics:

- Single inheritance
- Containment
- Multiple inheritance

Single Inheritance

Single inheritance is the simplest and most widely used inheritance scheme. Each subclass has one—and only one—parent class. The single inheritance scheme uses the *isA* model. This means that conceptually each subclass is an enhanced version of its parent class. Listing 11.1 shows the source code for the SINHERIT.CPP program and demonstrates and clarifies the isA concept. The listing contains the following hierarchy of classes: `Circle`, `Cylinder`, `HollowCylinder`. You can say that a cylinder object *is a* circle with a height. This conceptual relationship translates into making the `Cylinder` class a child of the `Circle` class. Similarly, you can say that a hollow cylinder *is a* cylinder with a hollow space inside it. This conceptual relationship translates into making the `HollowCylinder` class a child of `Cylinder`.

The conceptual relationship between a subclass and its ancestor classes may not be as obvious as the one with the parent class. Nevertheless, it is sufficient to clearly define the conceptual relationship between parent and child classes.

The single inheritance scheme used to define the class hierarchy in Listing 11.1 is straightforward. Each subclass has access to the protected and public members of its ancestor classes. This access feature succeeds in reducing the number of member functions in a subclass.

Compile and run the program. Here is the program output.

```
Circle data
Radius: 1 ft
Area: 3.141593 sqft
Circumference: 6.283185 ft

Cylinder data
Radius: 1 ft
Height: 2 ft
Area: 18.849556 sqft
Volume: 6.283185 cuft

Hollow cylinder data
Outer radius: 1 ft
Inner radius: 0.5 ft
Height: 2 ft
Area: 23.561945 sqft
Volume: 4.712389 cuft
```

Listing 11.1. The source code for SINHERIT.CPP.

```
#include <iostream.h>
#include <math.h>

const double pi = 4 * atan(1);
```

```
inline double sqr(double x)
{
  return x * x;
}

class Circle
{
   protected:
     double radius;

   public:
     Circle(double aRadius) : radius(aRadius) {}

     void setRadius(double aRadius)
       { radius = aRadius; }
     double getRadius() const
       { return radius; }
     double getArea() const
       { return pi * sqr(radius); }
     double getCircumf() const
       { return 2 * pi *radius; }

};

class Cylinder : public Circle
{
  protected:
    double height;

  public:
    Cylinder(double aRadius, double aHeight) :
      Circle(aRadius), height(aHeight) {}

   void setHeight(double aHeight)
     { height = aHeight; }
   double getHeight() const
     { return height; }
   double getVolume() const
     { return height * getArea(); }
   double getSurfaceArea() const
     { return 2 * getArea() + height * getCircumf(); }
```

continues

Listing 11.1. continued

```
};

class HollowCylinder : public Cylinder
{
  protected:
    double innerRadius;

  public:
    HollowCylinder(double InnerRadius,
                   double OuterRadius,
                   double aHeight) :
    Cylinder(OuterRadius, aHeight), innerRadius(InnerRadius) {}

     void setInnerRadius(double InnerRadius)
       { innerRadius = InnerRadius; }
     double getInnerRadius() const
       { return innerRadius; }

    double getVolume() const
      { return pi * (sqr(radius) - sqr(innerRadius)) * height; }
    double getSurfaceArea() const
      { return 2 * pi * (sqr(radius) - sqr(innerRadius)) +
              height * getCircumf() +
              height * 2 * pi * innerRadius;
      }

};

main()
{
   Circle circle(1.0);
   Cylinder cylinder(1.0, 2.0);
   HollowCylinder hollow(0.5, 1.0, 2.0);

   cout << "Circle data\n";
   cout << "Radius: " << circle.getRadius() << " ft\n";
   cout << "Area: " << circle.getArea() << " sqft\n";
   cout << "Circumference: " << circle.getCircumf() << " ft\n\n";

   cout << "Cylinder data\n";
   cout << "Radius: " << cylinder.getRadius() << " ft\n";
```

```
    cout << "Height: " << cylinder.getHeight() << " ft\n";
    cout << "Area: " << cylinder.getSurfaceArea() << " sqft\n";
    cout << "Volume: " << cylinder.getVolume() << " cuft\n\n";

    cout << "Hollow cylinder data\n";
    cout << "Outer radius: " << hollow.getRadius() << " ft\n";
    cout << "Inner radius: " << hollow.getInnerRadius() << " ft\n";
    cout << "Height: " << hollow.getHeight() << " ft\n";
    cout << "Area: " << hollow.getSurfaceArea() << " sqft\n";
    cout << "Volume: " << hollow.getVolume() << " cuft\n\n";

    return 0;
}
```

Containment

Containment is the inclusion of instances or pointers to instances of a class as data members of another class. Behind containment is the *HasA* model or concept. The host class includes components that are themselves instances of other classes. For example, the windows of a graphical user interface show text or graphics, scroll bars, and other windows components. You can model the main window with a class as follows:

```
class Window
{
    protected:
        ScrollBarClass *scrollBar;
        EditorClass *Edit;
        MenuClass *menu;
        // other protected members

    public:
        Window();
        ~Window();
        // other constructors and public members
};
```

Containment relates various classes by a connection that crosses the boundaries of class hierarchies. The common factor is that the contained classes are components of the host class.

Containment is regarded by some programmers as a good substitute for multiple inheritance. These programmers argue that containing class instances offers good control for the contribution of each contained class.

Containment, like multiple inheritance, can be a double-edged sword. One of the problems with containment is that it can impose additional overhead. Listing 11.2, which shows the source code for the program CINHERIT.CPP, is an example. This program is a version of the previous one, but it uses containment rather than single inheritance. The `Cylinder` class contains the data member circle, an instance of `Circle` class. The justification for this relationship is merely that the cylinder contains a circular base. Likewise, the `HollowCylinder` class contains two members that are instances of `Cylinder`. The argument behind this containment is that the hollow cylinder contains two cylinders.

To offer an equivalent set of operations of the classes in Listing 11.2 requires overhead. Because the contained instances are protected, the host classes need to declare additional member functions that invoke the functions of the contained class. Under single inheritance, instances of `Cylinder` invoke the inherited function `Circle::getArea()`. Using containment requires the `Cylinder` class to declare its own `getArea()` function as

```
double getArea() const
  { return circle.getArea(); }
```

The same requirement is true for all other member functions of class `Circle`. This duplication becomes complicated in the case of class `HollowCylinder`. This class must declare member functions that parallel member functions of both the `Circle` and `Cylinder` classes!

Listing 11.2. The source code for CINHERIT.CPP.

```
#include <iostream.h>
#include <math.h>

const double pi = 4 * atan(1);

inline double sqr(double x)
{
```

```
  return x * x;
}

class Circle
{
   protected:
     double radius;

   public:
     Circle()
       { radius = 0.0; }
     Circle(double aRadius) : radius(aRadius) {}

     void setRadius(double aRadius)
       { radius = aRadius; }
     double getRadius() const
       { return radius; }
     double getArea() const
       { return pi * sqr(radius); }
     double getCircumf() const
       { return 2 * pi *radius; }

};

class Cylinder
{
  protected:
    Circle circle;
    double height;

  public:
    Cylinder()
      { circle.setRadius(0.0);
        height = 0.0;
      }
    Cylinder(double aRadius, double aHeight) :
      height(aHeight) { circle.setRadius(aRadius); }

   void setRadius(double aRadius)
     { circle.setRadius(aRadius); }
   double getRadius() const
```

continues

Listing 11.2. continued

```
      { return circle.getRadius(); }
    void setHeight(double aHeight)
      { height = aHeight; }
    double getHeight() const
      { return height; }
    double getArea() const
      { return circle.getArea(); }
    double getCircumf() const
      { return circle.getCircumf(); }
    double getVolume() const
      { return height * circle.getArea(); }
    double getSurfaceArea() const
      { return 2 * circle.getArea() +
               height * circle.getCircumf();
      }

};

class HollowCylinder
{
  protected:
    Cylinder innerCyl;
    Cylinder outerCyl;
    double innerRadius;

  public:
    HollowCylinder(double InnerRadius,
                   double OuterRadius,
                   double aHeight) :
      innerRadius(InnerRadius)
      {
        innerCyl.setRadius(InnerRadius);
        innerCyl.setHeight(aHeight);
        outerCyl.setRadius(OuterRadius);
        outerCyl.setHeight(aHeight);
      }

     void setRadius(double aRadius)
       { outerCyl.setRadius(aRadius); }
     double getRadius() const
       { return outerCyl.getRadius(); }
```

```
      void setHeight(double aHeight)
        { outerCyl.setHeight(aHeight); }
      double getHeight() const
        { return outerCyl.getHeight(); }
      void setInnerRadius(double InnerRadius)
        { innerRadius = InnerRadius; }
      double getInnerRadius() const
        { return innerRadius; }

     double getVolume() const
       { return outerCyl.getVolume() - innerCyl.getVolume(); }
     double getSurfaceArea()
       { return 2 * (outerCyl.getArea() - innerCyl.getArea()) +
                outerCyl.getHeight() * outerCyl.getCircumf() +
                innerCyl.getHeight() * innerCyl.getCircumf(); }

};

main()
{
   Circle circle(1.0);
   Cylinder cylinder(1.0, 2.0);
   HollowCylinder hollow(0.5, 1.0, 2.0);

   cout << "Circle data\n";
   cout << "Radius: " << circle.getRadius() << " ft\n";
   cout << "Area: " << circle.getArea() << " sqft\n";
   cout << "Circumference: " << circle.getCircumf() << " ft\n\n";
   cout << "Cylinder data\n";
   cout << "Radius: " << cylinder.getRadius() << " ft\n";
   cout << "Height: " << cylinder.getHeight() << " ft\n";
   cout << "Area: " << cylinder.getSurfaceArea() << " sqft\n";
   cout << "Volume: " << cylinder.getVolume() << " cuft\n\n";

   cout << "Hollow cylinder data\n";
   cout << "Outer radius: " << hollow.getRadius() << " ft\n";
   cout << "Inner radius: " << hollow.getInnerRadius() << " ft\n";
   cout << "Height: " << hollow.getHeight() << " ft\n";
   cout << "Area: " << hollow.getSurfaceArea() << " sqft\n";
   cout << "Volume: " << hollow.getVolume() << " cuft\n\n";

   return 0;
}
```

The problem of declaring member functions that invoke the functions of contained instances can be significantly reduced by using pointers to contained classes. Listing 11.3 shows the source code for the program CINHERI2.CPP. This listing uses a pointer to class `Circle` in class `Cylinder`, and pointers to `Cylinder` in class `HollowCylinder`. `Cylinder` and `HollowCylinder` contain new functions that set and assign the pointers of the contained classes. Consequently, you can access the pointer to the contained classes and invoke the member functions of the contained classes. The listing shows the unnecessary member functions that I commented out.

The member functions of classes `Cylinder` and `HollowCylinder` use the pointers of the contained classes. The function `main` also uses pointers to `Circle` and `Cylinder` to create, set, and query the instances of classes `Cylinder` and `HollowCylinder`.

Using pointers to contained classes is a scheme that assumes you want to reveal the contained class to the client classes and functions. If you wish to hide the contained classes, you must be willing to use the additional overhead or a class hierarchy. The conclusion is that containment is generally not a good substitute for single inheritance.

Listing 11.3. The source code for CINHERI2.CPP.

```
#include <iostream.h>
#include <math.h>

const double pi = 4 * atan(1);

inline double sqr(double x)
{
  return x * x;
}

class Circle
{
   protected:
     double radius;

   public:
```

```
      Circle()
        { radius = 0.0; }
      Circle(double aRadius) : radius(aRadius) {}

      void setRadius(double aRadius)
        { radius = aRadius; }
      double getRadius() const
        { return radius; }
      double getArea() const
        { return pi * sqr(radius); }
      double getCircumf() const
        { return 2 * pi *radius; }

};

class Cylinder
{
  protected:
    Circle *circle;
    double height;

  public:
    Cylinder()
      { height = 0.0; }
    Cylinder(Circle *c, double aHeight) :
      height(aHeight) { circle = c; }

   void setCircle(Circle *c)
     { circle = c; }
   Circle* getCircle() const
     { return circle; }

// The following commented member functions are optional
// to the setCircle and getCircle functions
/*
   void setRadius(double aRadius)
     { circle->setRadius(aRadius); }
   double getRadius() const
     { return circle->getRadius(); }
*/
   void setHeight(double aHeight)
```

continues

Listing 11.3. continued

```
      { height = aHeight; }
    double getHeight() const
      { return height; }

// The following commented member functions are optional
// to the setCircle and getCircle functions
/*
    double getArea() const
      { return circle->getArea(); }
    double getCircumf() const
      { return circle->getCircumf(); }
*/
    double getVolume() const
      { return height * circle->getArea(); }
    double getSurfaceArea() const
      { return 2 * circle->getArea() +
               height * circle->getCircumf();
      }

};

class HollowCylinder
{
  protected:
    Cylinder *innerCyl;
    Cylinder *outerCyl;

  public:
    HollowCylinder(Cylinder *inCyl,
                   Cylinder *outCyl) :
      innerCyl(inCyl), outerCyl(outCyl) {}

     void setOuterCyl(Cylinder *c)
       { outerCyl = c; }
     Cylinder* getOuterCyl() const
       { return outerCyl; }
     void setInnerCyl(Cylinder *c)
       { innerCyl = c; }
     Cylinder* getInnerCyl() const
       { return innerCyl; }
```

```
// The following commented member functions are optional
// to the setInnerCyl, getInnerCyl, setOuterCyl, and getOuterCyl
// functions
/*
     void setRadius(double aRadius)
       { outerCyl->setRadius(aRadius); }
     double getRadius() const
       { return outerCyl->getRadius(); }
     void setHeight(double aHeight)
       { outerCyl->setHeight(aHeight); }
     double getHeight() const
       { return innerCyl->getHeight(); }
     void setInnerRadius(double InnerRadius)
       { innerCyl->setRadius(InnerRadius); }
     double getInnerRadius() const
       { return innerCyl->getRadius(); }
*/
    double getVolume() const
      { return outerCyl->getVolume() - innerCyl->getVolume(); }
    double getSurfaceArea() const
      { Circle *pInCirc, *pOutCirc;
        pInCirc = innerCyl->getCircle();
        pOutCirc = outerCyl->getCircle();

        return 2 * (pOutCirc->getArea() - pInCirc->getArea()) +
               outerCyl->getHeight() * pOutCirc->getCircumf() +
               innerCyl->getHeight() * pInCirc->getCircumf(); }

};

main()
{
   Circle circle(1.0);
   Circle innerCircle(0.5);
   Cylinder cylinder(&circle, 2.0);
   Cylinder innerCyl(&innerCircle, 2.0);
   HollowCylinder hollow(&innerCyl, &cylinder);


   cout << "Circle data\n";
   cout << "Radius: " << circle.getRadius() << " ft\n";
```

continues

Listing 11.3. continued

```
    cout << "Area: " << circle.getArea() << " sqft\n";
    cout << "Circumference: " << circle.getCircumf() << " ft\n\n";

    // declare access pointers
    Circle *pCirc = cylinder.getCircle();
    cout << "Cylinder data\n";
    cout << "Radius: " << pCirc->getRadius() << " ft\n";
    cout << "Height: " << cylinder.getHeight() << " ft\n";
    cout << "Area: " << cylinder.getSurfaceArea() << " sqft\n";
    cout << "Volume: " << cylinder.getVolume() << " cuft\n\n";

    // declare access pointers
    Cylinder *pInCyl, *pOutCyl;
    Circle *pInCirc, *pOutCirc;
    pOutCyl = hollow.getOuterCyl();
    pInCyl = hollow.getInnerCyl();
    pInCirc = pInCyl->getCircle();
    pOutCirc = pOutCyl->getCircle();

    cout << "Hollow cylinder data\n";
    cout << "Outer radius: " << pOutCirc->getRadius() << " ft\n";
    cout << "Inner radius: " << pInCirc->getRadius() << " ft\n";
    cout << "Height: " << pOutCyl->getHeight() << " ft\n";
    cout << "Area: " << hollow.getSurfaceArea() << " sqft\n";
    cout << "Volume: " << hollow.getVolume() << " cuft\n\n";

    return 0;
}
```

Multiple Inheritance

Multiple inheritance enables a class to have multiple parent classes. The relationship in this kind of class hierarchy is modeled by the *HasA* model or concept (as is containment). That is why some programmers prefer using containment rather than multiple inheritance. Unlike containment, multiple inheritance does not require additional overhead to access the members of the contained classes.

The parent classes may be part of completely separate or intertwined hierarchies. In the latter case, the parent class shares a common ancestor class. Consider the following simple case. Class `A` is the parent of Classes `B` and `C`. Class `X` is the subclass of both Classes `B` and `C`. This means that Class `X` has the same ancestor (Class `A`), because it is the parent class of `B` and `C`. In this case, the C++ compiler requires you to use the keyword `virtual` in declaring Classes `B` and `C` (see the following code). The `virtual` keyword warns the compiler of the connected class hierarchies.

```
class A
{
  protected:
  // protected member declarations
  public:
  // constructor and other public members
  virtual void foo();
};

class B : virtual public A
{
  protected:
  // protected member declarations
  public:
  // constructor and other public members
  virtual void foo();
};

class C : virtual public A
{
  protected:
  // protected member declarations
  public:
  // constructor and other public members
  virtual void foo();
};

class X : public B, public C
{
  // member declarations
};
```

To add more complexity to the picture, consider the `virtual` functions that are declared in class `A`, `B`, and `C`. The previous code fragment specifies the `virtual` function `foo` as an example. The member functions of class `X` can specify the exact `virtual` function by qualifying it with the class name. Thus, `A::foo()`, `B::foo()`, and `C::foo()` specify the versions of functions `foo()` in classes `A`, `B`, and `C`, respectively.

Let's look at an example of using multiple inheritance. Listing 11.4 shows the source code for MINHERIT.CPP. This program emulates a class that solves simultaneous equations (I say emulates because I actually use less code to perform a simple matrix-array manipulation). The solution of simultaneous equations involves the following equation:

```
A X = B
```

where `A` is the matrix of coefficients, `B` is the righthand-side vector (array), and `X` is the solution vector (array).

The listing declares the following classes:

Class `Array`—models a dynamic numerical array.
Class `Matrix`—models a dynamic numerical matrix.
Class `SimultEqn`—a child of classes `Array` and `Matrix`, that models a simultaneous-equations solver.

The `SimultEqn` class inherits the data members to support array `B` and matrix `A` from the classes `Array` and `Matrix`, respectively. To manage the dynamic array of solutions `X`, the class declares the protected pointer `solnPtr`. This pointer is similar to the `arrPtr` in class `Array`. The class `SimultEqn` declares a constructor, a destructor, and a few functions.

The constructor for class `SimultEqn` invokes the constructors of classes `Array` and `Matrix`. In addition, the constructor allocates the dynamic space for the array `X` using the `solnPtr` member. The class destructor deletes the dynamic space accessed by member `solnPtr`. The dynamic space for matrix `A` and array `B` is deallocated by the destructors of classes `Matrix` and `Array`, respectively.

The member function `SimultEqn::solnRecall` enables you to recall dynamic data for the solution array `X`. The function solve simulates solving the simultaneous equations. This function uses the array and matrix access functions inherited from classes `Array` and `Matrix`.

The function `main` creates `se`, an instance of class `SimultEqn`, with 2 rows and 2 columns. `main` uses `for` loop statements to assign values to array `B` and matrix `A`. Then `main` calls the function `SimultEqn::solve` to manipulate the arrays and matrix. Finally, `main` uses another set of `for` loops to display array `B`, matrix `A`, and array `X`.

Listing 11.4. The source code for MINHERIT.CPP.

```
#include <iostream.h>

class Array
{
  protected:
    unsigned arrSize;
    double *arrPtr;

  public:
    Array(unsigned ArraySize)
      { arrPtr = new double[arrSize = ArraySize]; }
    ~Array()
      { delete [] arrPtr; }

    void arrStore(double x, unsigned index)
      { arrPtr[index] = x; }
    void arrRecall(double& x, unsigned index)
      { x = arrPtr[index]; }
};

class Matrix
{
  protected:
    unsigned maxRows;
    unsigned maxCols;
    double *matPtr;

  public:
    Matrix(unsigned Rows, unsigned Cols)
      { maxRows = Rows;
        maxCols = Cols;
        matPtr = new double[Rows * Cols];
      }
    ~Matrix()
      { delete [] matPtr; }

    void matStore(double x, unsigned row, unsigned col)
      { matPtr[row + maxRows * col] = x; }
    void matRecall(double& x, unsigned row, unsigned col)
      { x = matPtr[row + maxRows * col]; }
};
```

continues

Listing 11.4. continued

```
class SimultEqn : public Array, public Matrix
{
   protected:
     double *solnPtr;

   public:
     SimultEqn(unsigned Rows, unsigned Cols) :
       Array(Cols), Matrix(Rows, Cols)
     { solnPtr = new double[Rows]; }

     ~SimultEqn()
      { delete [] solnPtr; }
    void solve();
    void solnRecall(double& x, unsigned index)
      { x = solnPtr[index]; }

};

void SimultEqn::solve()
{
  double x, y;

  for (unsigned row = 0; row < maxRows; row++) {
    solnPtr[row] = 0;
    for (unsigned col = 0; col < maxCols; col++) {
      matRecall(x, row, col);
      arrRecall(y, col);
      solnPtr[row] += x * y;
    }
  }
}

main()
{
   SimultEqn se(2,2);
   double z;
   for (unsigned i = 0; i < 2; i++)
     se.arrStore(1.0 + i, i);
```

```
    for (i = 0; i < 2; i++)
      for (unsigned j = 0; j < 2; j++)
        se.matStore(2.5 + i + j, i, j);

    se.solve();

    cout << "Array A:\n";
    for (i = 0; i < 2; i++) {
      se.arrRecall(z, i);
      cout << z << "\n";
    }

    cout << "\nMatrix A:\n";
    for (i = 0; i < 2; i++) {
      for (unsigned j = 0; j < 2; j++) {
        se.matRecall(z, i, j);
        cout << z << "  ";
      }
      cout << "\n";
    }

    cout << "\nArray X:\n";
    for (i = 0; i < 2; i++) {
      se.solnRecall(z, i);
      cout << z << "\n";
    }

    return 0;
}
```

Let's compare the `SimultEqn` class in the previous program with a version that uses containment. The justification behind using containment is that a simultaneous-equations solver has a matrix and two arrays. Listing 11.5 shows the source code for the program MINHERI2.CPP. The listing shows that class `Array` is not affected by using containment. By contrast, I added the member functions `getRows` and `getCols` in class `Matrix`.

The class `SimultEqn` looks quite different using containment. There are three data members: two of these are pointers to class `Array` and the other one is a pointer to class `Matrix`. The class constructor passes instance-pointers to the data members. The new version of the class declares functions that access the data members. The class still has the member function solve. I adjusted the code of this function to use the data members in order to access various functions in classes Array and Matrix.

The function main has different statements than Listing 11.4. First, the function declares two dynamic instances of class Array and one dynamic instance of class Matrix. MINHERIT.CPP creates the instance of class SimultEqn using the pointers for the previous dynamic instances.

The function main uses the same loops to assign values to array B and matrix A. The code employs pointer-dereferencing to invoke the access functions of classes Array and Matrix. After main calls the function SimultEqn::solve, it calls the function SimultEqn::getX to obtain the updated pointer to the solution array X. After main displays the arrays and matrix, it removes the dynamic instances by using three delete statements.

Listing 11.5. The source code for MINHERI2.CPP.

```
#include <iostream.h>

class Array
{
  protected:
    unsigned arrSize;
    double *arrPtr;

  public:
    Array(unsigned ArraySize)
      { arrPtr = new double[arrSize = ArraySize]; }
    ~Array()
      { delete [] arrPtr; }

    void arrStore(double x, unsigned index)
      { arrPtr[index] = x; }
    void arrRecall(double& x, unsigned index)
      { x = arrPtr[index]; }
};

class Matrix
{
  protected:
    unsigned maxRows;
    unsigned maxCols;
    double *matPtr;
```

```
  public:
    Matrix(unsigned Rows, unsigned Cols)
      { maxRows = Rows;
        maxCols = Cols;
        matPtr = new double[Rows * Cols];
      }
    ~Matrix()
      { delete [] matPtr; }

    unsigned getRows()
      { return maxRows; }
    unsigned getCols()
      { return maxCols; }
    void matStore(double x, unsigned row, unsigned col)
      { matPtr[row + maxRows * col] = x; }
    void matRecall(double& x, unsigned row, unsigned col)
      { x = matPtr[row + maxRows * col]; }
};

class SimultEqn
{
   protected:
     Array *X;
     Array *B;
     Matrix *A;

   public:
     SimultEqn(Array *x, Array *b, Matrix *a)
     {
       X = x;
       B = b;
       A = a;
     }

    Array* getX()
      { return X; }
    Array* getB()
      { return B; }
    Matrix* getA()
      { return A; }
    void solve();
};
```

continues

Listing 11.5. continued

```
void SimultEqn::solve()
{
  double x, y, z;

  for (unsigned row = 0; row < A->getRows(); row++) {
    X->arrStore(0, row);;
    for (unsigned col = 0; col < A->getCols(); col++) {
      A->matRecall(x, row, col);
      B->arrRecall(y, col);
      X->arrRecall(z, row);
      X->arrStore(z + x * y, row);
    }
  }
}

main()
{
   Array *x = new Array(2);
   Array *b = new Array(2);
   Matrix *a = new Matrix(2,2);
   SimultEqn se(x, b, a);
   double z;

   for (unsigned i = 0; i < 2; i++)
     b->arrStore(1.0 + i, i);

   for (i = 0; i < 2; i++)
     for (unsigned j = 0; j < 2; j++)
       a->matStore(2.5 + i + j, i, j);

   se.solve();
   x = se.getX();

   cout << "Array B:\n";
   for (i = 0; i < 2; i++) {
     b->arrRecall(z, i);
     cout << z << "\n";
   }

   cout << "\nMatrix A:\n";
```

```
    for (i = 0; i < 2; i++) {
      for (unsigned j = 0; j < 2; j++) {
        a->matRecall(z, i, j);
        cout << z << " ";
      }
      cout << "\n";
    }

    cout << "\nArray X:\n";
    for (i = 0; i < 2; i++) {
      x->arrRecall(z, i);
      cout << z << "\n";
    }

    delete a;
    delete b;
    delete x;

    return 0;
}
```

The `SimultEqn` class shows that containment is more intuitive because the class contains the required two arrays and matrix. The multiple inheritance version inherits the data members to support a single array. To make up the difference, the first `SimultEqn` class has to declare an additional pointer to a double-typed dynamic array. Moreover, the same class has to implement an access function for the second dynamic array.

Summary

This chapter discussed the following schemes of linking classes:

- Single inheritance—This is the most common scheme for creating a hierarchy of classes in which each subclass has only one parent class.
- Containment—This scheme models real-world objects where a big object contains one or more components that are well-defined objects. Using pointers to contained classes works more efficiently than using contained instances of the same classes.

- Multiple inheritance—This scheme enables you to create a subclass from multiple subclasses. Most programmers warn against using multiple inheritance because it invites careless class hierarchy design. Such a design is complicated and difficult to maintain.

Whatever class linkage scheme you employ, remember what Albert Einstein said: "Keep it simple, but no simpler."

Object Behavior

Object-oriented programming's claim to fame is that it models real-world objects much better than structured programming does. This chapter examines cases of objects that possess special behavior—a specific way or sequence for invoking member functions. The chapter looks at the following cases of object behavior:

- State-engine objects
- Disabled objects
- Transformed objects
- Modular objects

State-Engine Objects

This type of object requires a specific sequence of operations. The classes that model state-engine objects need special member functions that bring the state of the class instance to a fully operative level. Chapter 4, "Member Functions," offered an example of a linear regression class that models a state-engine object. This section presents a similar example, a class that models basic statistics and simple statistical testing. This example typifies state-engine objects where user interaction (usually data input) supplies information in batches. This gradual build-up of data enables the state-engine object to reach a mature state, so to speak, where it is able to be fully operational. State-engine objects usually enable you to shift or reset the state to a lower level.

Listing 12.1 shows the source code for the STATENG.CPP program. The class `basicStat`, declared in the listing, offers basic statistics (the mean and standard deviation) and tests the mean value of a sample set of observations (also known as sample population).

Listing 12.1. The source code for STATENG.CPP.

```
#include <iostream.h>
#include <math.h>

const double BAD_RESULT = -1.0E+30;

enum stateEnum { reset, summing, hasBasicStat };
enum statTest { testError, cannotReject, cannotAccept };

class basicStat
{
  protected:
    unsigned count;
    double sumX;
    double sumX2;
    double mean;
    double sdev;
    stateEnum state;

  public:
    basicStat()
      { clear(); }

    void clear();
    void addData(double X);
    void delData(double X);
    void calcStat();
```

```
    double getMean()
      { return (state > hasBasicStat) ? mean : BAD_RESULT; }
    double getSdev()
      { return (state > hasBasicStat) ? sdev : BAD_RESULT; }
    unsigned getCount()
      { return count; }
    statTest testMean(double testedMean, double studentT);
};

void basicStat::clear()
{
  count = 0;
  sumX = 0;
  sumX2 = 0;
  state = reset;
}

void basicStat::addData(double X)
{
  count++;
  sumX += X;
  sumX2 += X * X;
  if (count > 2)
    state = summing;
}

void basicStat::delData(double X)
{
  if (count > 0) {
    count--;
    sumX -= X;
    sumX2 -= X * X;
    if (count <= 2)
      state = reset;
    else
      state = summing;
   }
}

void basicStat::calcStat()
{
```

continues

Listing 12.1. continued

```
    if (state >= summing) {
      mean = sumX / count;
      sdev = sqrt((sumX2 - sumX * sumX / count) / (count - 1));
      state = hasBasicStat;
    }
  }

  statTest basicStat::testMean(double testedMean, double studentT)
  {
    if (state == hasBasicStat) {
      return (fabs(mean - testedMean) * sqrt((double(count)) / sdev)
            > studentT) ? cannotAccept : cannotReject;
    }
    else
      return testError;
  }

  void showData(basicStat& s, double testedMean)
  {
    statTest r;

    cout << "\n"
         << "Mean = " << s.getMean() << "\n"
         << "Sdev = " << s.getSdev() << "\n"
         << "N    = " << s.getCount() << "\n\n"
         << "Testing the following hypothesis\n"
         << "H0: " << s.getMean() << " == " << testedMean << "\n"
         << "H1: " << s.getMean() << " != " << testedMean << "\n"
         << "Conclusion: ";
    r = s.testMean(testedMean, 3.182);
    switch (r) {
      case testError:
        cout << "Insufficient data!\n";
        break;
      case cannotAccept:
        cout << "Cannot accept null hypothesis H0\n";
        break;
      case cannotReject:
        cout << "Cannot reject null hypothesis H0\n";
        break;
```

```
    }
}

main()
{
  basicStat s;
  double testedMean = 8.32;

  cout << "Adding 8.1 to data\n";  s.addData(8.1);
  cout << "Adding 8.5 to data\n";  s.addData(8.5);
  cout << "Adding 7.9 to data\n";  s.addData(7.9);
  cout << "Adding 8.3 to data\n";  s.addData(8.3);

  showData(s, testedMean);
  cout << "\n\n";
  s.calcStat();
  showData(s, testedMean);


  return 0;
}
```

The `basicStat` class declares the following members:

- The `count`, `sumX`, and `sumX2` members store the number of observations accumulated and the statistical summations.
- The `mean` and `sdev` members store the mean and standard deviation statistics.
- The `state` member stores the state of the class instance. This member has the enumerated type `stateEnum` which represents the three object states:

  The `reset` enumerated value indicates that the object is either newly created or has been reset. At this state, the class instance needs to accumulate data.

  The `summing` enumerated value signals that the class instance has accumulated enough data to proceed to the next state and calculate the basic statistics.

  The `hasBasicState` enumerated value indicates that the class instance has obtained the basic statistics and is ready to test the mean value of the accumulated data.

The `basicStat` class declares the following member functions that both affect and are affected by the state of the class instances:

- The `clear` member function initializes and resets the state of the class instances. The function assigns zeros to the summation members and assigns the enumerated value `reset` to the data member `state`.
- The `addData` function accumulates data in the summation data members, `count`, `sumX`, and `sumX2`. If the value in member `count` is greater than 2, the function assigns the enumerated value `summing` to the member `state`. This assignment plays two roles:

  After the initialization or resetting of a class instance, the `addData` function promotes the state from `reset` to `summing`.

  After obtaining the basic statistics, the `addData` function demotes the state from `hasBasicStat` to `summing`. This demotion flags the update in the summation of observations, which also requires updating the mean and standard deviation statistics.
- The `delData` function enables you to remove erroneous or biased data from the accumulated observations. The function sets the state member to `reset` if the member `count` is less than or equal to 2. Otherwise, the function assigns the enumerated value `summing` to the member `state`. The latter assignment plays the same role as the assignment in the function `addData`.
- The `calcStat` member function calculates the mean and standard deviation statistics and stores the values in the members `mean` and `sdev`, respectively. This calculation takes place if the enumerated value in the member `state` is greater than `summing`.
- The `testMean` member function performs a two-sided statistical test for the mean if the member `state` has the enumerated value `hasBasicStat`. The function returns the test state which can be `testError` (wrong class instance state), `cannotAccept`, and `cannotReject`. The function tests the following null hypothesis:

  ```
  H0:  mean = tested_mean
  ```

  versus

  ```
  H1:  mean ≠ tested_mean
  ```

The null hypothesis is tested at a certain level of probability. Because statistics deals with uncertainty, the outcome of the test is either not rejecting the null hypothesis or not accepting it. The `statTest` enumerated values `cannotReject` and `cannotAccept` reflect the two terms used to describe the test outcome. The first parameter of the function `testMean` is the tested mean. The second parameter is the inverse student-t probability distribution function taken for the tested confidence level.

Listing 12.1 also contains the ordinary function `showData`, which displays the basic statistics, tests the mean value, and displays the outcome. `main` declares `s` as an instance of the class `basicStat` and performs the following tasks:

- Adds four observations to the instance `s` by calling the `addData` member function.
- Invokes the function `showData` to prematurely test the mean statistic (which is not yet calculated) against the value 8.32. The output of `showData` indicates that the state of instance `s` is not ready for the statistical test.
- Calculates the basic statistics by calling the member function `calcStat`.
- Calls function `showData` to test the mean statistic against the value 8.32. This call produces meaningful results. The second argument of 3.182 in the `testMean` function call is the value of the inverse student-t probability distribution for a 95 percent confidence level.

Here is the output of Listing 12.1:

```
Adding 8.1 to data
Adding 8.5 to data
Adding 7.9 to data
Adding 8.3 to data

Mean = -1e+30
Sdev = -1e+30
N    = 4

Testing the following hypothesis
H0: -1e+30 == 8.32
H1: -1e+30 != 8.32
Conclusion: Insufficient data!
```

```
Mean = 8.2
Sdev = 0.258199
N    = 4

Testing the following hypothesis
H0: 8.2 == 8.32
H1: 8.2 != 8.32
Conclusion: Cannot reject null hypothesis H0
```

Disabled Objects

Classes model real-world objects. The data members keep track of the state of an object, and the member functions implement the associated functionality. What about modelling a malfunction (which occurs when the state of an object exceeds a critical level) which might occur during the operation of an object? There are two general scenarios. In the first scenario the object malfunction is fatal, causing the application to halt. The second scenario deals with contained classes malfunctioning. In this case, all might not be lost. It is possible to shut down the offending contained class and still maintain a level of functionality. One example is an airplane with four engines. Should one engine malfunction, the pilot shuts it down and keeps flying with the other three engines. It does not make sense to crash the airplane just because one engine fails! To implement shutting down a contained class, a special `shutdown` data member monitors the status of the contained class. As long as the `shutdown` field is `false`, the contained class responds normally to the messages it receives. The `shutdown` member is set to `true` when the state of the contained class indicates damage. Beyond this point, the members of the malfunctioning class give minimal or no response.

Listing 12.2 shows the source code for the program FLY.CPP, which simulates the airplane example just mentioned. The `TEngine` class models an airplane engine. The `Fuel` data member keeps track of the remaining fuel used by the engine. `FuelRate` is the current rate of burning fuel. The `ShutDown` data member keeps track of engine malfunction. The `Start` member function supplies the initial values for the `Fuel` and `FuelRate` data members, and sets the `shutDown` data member to `false`. The member function `GetFuel` returns the amount of remaining fuel. The functions `SetFuelRate` and `GetFuelRate` set and return the rate of burning fuel, respectively. The member function `UpdateFuel` updates the value of the `Fuel` data member based on the given `BurnTime`. This member function is used to decrement the amount of remaining fuel.

Finally, the `ShutDown` member function irreversibly shuts down the engine. When `ShutDown` is set to `true`, the member functions `SetFuelrate`, `GetFuelRate`, and `UpdateFuel` cease to respond in the normal fashion. Consequently, the instance of `TEngine` stops functioning.

Listing 12.2. The source code for the FLY.CPP program.

```
#include <iostream.h>
#include <stdlib.h>
#include "video.h"

const double CRITICAL_FUEL_RATE = 10; // lb/hr
const double DeltaTime = 1; // hour

enum boolean { false, true };

class TEngine
{
  protected:
    double Fuel;
    double FuelRate;
    boolean ShutDown;

  public:
    boolean GetShutDown()
      { return ShutDown; }
    void Start(double FuelAdded, double TheFuelRate);
    double GetFuel()
      { return Fuel; }
    void SetFuelRate(double TheFuelRate);
    double GetFuelRate()
      { return (ShutDown) ? 0 : FuelRate; }
    void UpdateFuel(double BurnTime);
    void ShutEngine();
};
class TFly
{
  public:
    TEngine Engine[4];
    boolean WillCrash();
```

continues

Listing 12.2. continued

```
};

void TEngine::Start(double FuelAdded, double TheFuelRate)
{
    Fuel = FuelAdded;
    FuelRate = TheFuelRate;
    ShutDown = false;
}

void TEngine::SetFuelRate(double TheFuelRate)
{
    if (!GetShutDown())
      FuelRate = TheFuelRate;
}

void TEngine::UpdateFuel(double BurnTime)
{
    if (GetShutDown()) return;
    Fuel -= BurnTime * FuelRate;
    if (FuelRate < CRITICAL_FUEL_RATE ¦¦ Fuel <= 0)
         ShutEngine();
}

void TEngine::ShutEngine()
{
    ShutDown = true;
}

boolean TFly::WillCrash()
{
    return (Engine[0].GetShutDown() &&
            Engine[1].GetShutDown() &&
            Engine[2].GetShutDown() &&
            Engine[3].GetShutDown()) ? true : false;
}

void ShowData(TFly& Airplane, double& X, double& FlightTime)
{
    clrscr();
```

```
    cout << "Time : " << FlightTime << " hours\n";
    for (unsigned i = 0; i < 4; i++) {
        X = double(rand() % 10000) / 10000;
        if (X > 0.95) // trouble
            Airplane.Engine[i].ShutEngine();
        cout << "Engine " << i
             << " Fuel = " << Airplane.Engine[i].GetFuel()
             << " lbs "
             << " Burn Rate = " << Airplane.Engine[i].GetFuelRate()
             << " lb/hr\n";
        Airplane.Engine[i].UpdateFuel(DeltaTime);
    }
}

main()
{
    TFly Airplane;
    double FlightTime, X;
    char aKey;

    for (unsigned i = 0; i < 4; i++)
        Airplane.Engine[i].Start(1000, 100);
    FlightTime = 0;
    do {
        FlightTime += DeltaTime;
        ShowData(Airplane, X, FlightTime);
        cout << "\n"
             << "Your choices are: Land now, Set fuel rate\n";
        cout << "\n> ";
        aKey = getche();
        aKey = (aKey <= 'a' && aKey <= 'z') ?
                    aKey + 'A' - 'a' : aKey;
        if (aKey == 'S') {
            cout << "\n";
            cout << "Enter engine and new fuel rate : ";
            cin >> i >> X;
            Airplane.Engine[i].SetFuelRate(X);
        }
    } while  (!Airplane.WillCrash() && aKey != 'L');
    ShowData(Airplane, X, FlightTime);
    if (Airplane.WillCrash())
```

continues

Listing 12.2. continued

```
        cout << "\nYou crashed!";
    else {
        cout << "\nYou landed after flying "
             << FlightTime << " hours";
    }

    getch();
    return 0;
}
```

The class `TFly` contains a four-member array of type `TEngine`. The `WillCrash` member function checks whether all four engines have stopped, leading to an imminent crash.

The program uses a `do-while` loop to simulate the increment of time. Each engine is initially supplied with 1000 pounds of fuel and set to burn at 100 lb/hr. The updated amount of fuel and fuel burn rate are displayed for all four engines. A small menu below the engine data reminds you that you can type L to land the airplane or S to reset the fuel burn rate of a functioning engine.

To add some excitement to the simulation, the program provides two sources of trouble that lead to an engine shutdown. The first results from setting the fuel burn rate below a critical value (assigned to the constant `CRITICAL_FUEL_RATE`). The second source of malfunction simulates random troubles. A random number between 0 and 1 is generated. If the number exceeds 0.95 (less than a five percent chance), the engine is shut down.

You are welcome to expand on the simulation to make it more interesting. The main point made by the program is to show how to deal with malfunctioning object variables.

Transformed Objects

Typical classes model objects that are themselves persistent. The operations involving these objects simply alter their states. This section looks at applying classes to reacting chemicals. This kind of application represents objects that are partially or completely diminished in a chemical reaction. This variation cannot be simply modeled by using null pointers. To keep the discussion simple, I focus on the following popular reaction that synthesizes water from oxygen and hydrogen:

$$2H_2 + O_2 = 2H_2O$$

Now consider a mixture of hydrogen (an object) and oxygen (another object). When these chemical elements combine to form a quantity of water (yet another object), the instances of hydrogen and of oxygen diminish, or even disappear. The chemical reaction also creates an equivalent amount of water.

The object-oriented analysis of the above reaction yields some interesting notes. The first step in the analysis creates the classes that model the various objects. Hydrogen and oxygen are basic elements that can be modeled by a common class. This class defines the properties that are used in modeling the reaction. Similarly, water is a simple compound that can be modeled by a separate class. Since elements and compounds possess a large number of properties and characteristics, the analysis must select those attributes needed to model the reaction. These attributes include the following:

1. The atomic or molecular weight.
2. The mass of the chemical.
3. The valence of an element. This attribute tells how many electrons are given or taken by an atom to establish a chemical bond.

Other optional attributes include the name and chemical symbol for the elements and compounds. The classes that model an element and a compound contain data members to represent some of the above attributes. The member functions of these classes enable you to access these attributes.

The interesting part of modeling chemical reactions using classes is the function that calculates the amounts of chemical reactants consumed and chemical products generated. The task involves comparing the number of moles for the reactants to determine which one is in excess. One mole contains an Avagadro number (6.02E+23) of atoms or molecules. This step then determines which reactant is completely consumed by the reaction and the amount of product generated. Which class declares the reaction-calculating function? Is it the class that models the reactants or the product? The answer depends on how biased you want to be toward any one of the above classes. An objective solution chooses either a separate class or a simple function. I prefer the latter solution because a simple function treats the various classes equally.

Look at the code that implements the water synthesis reaction. Listing 12.3 shows the source code for the WATER.CPP program. The listing declares classes `Element` and `Compound` to model the chemical elements and compounds, respectively.

Listing 12.3. The source code for the WATER.CPP program.

```
#include <iostream.h>
#include <math.h>
#include <string.h>

class Element
{
  protected:
    double atomicWeight;
    double mass;
    char name[21];
    char symbol[3];

  public:
    Element(const char* Name,
            const char* Symbol,
            double AtomicWeight,
            double Mass) :
       atomicWeight(AtomicWeight),
       mass(Mass)
       {
         strcpy(name, Name);
         strcpy(symbol, Symbol);
       }

    double getAtomicWeight()
      { return atomicWeight; }
```

```
    double getMass()
      { return mass; }

    char* getName()
      { return name; }
    char* getSymbol()
      { return symbol; }
    void setMass(double Mass)
      { mass = Mass; }
};

class Compound
{
  protected:
    double molecularWeight;
    double mass;
    char name[21];
    char symbol[11];

  public:
    Compound(const char* Name,
             const char* Symbol,
             double MolecularWeight,
             double Mass) :
       molecularWeight(MolecularWeight),
       mass(Mass)
       {
         strcpy(name, Name);
         strcpy(symbol, Symbol);
       }

    double getMolecularWeight()
      { return molecularWeight; }
    double getMass()
      { return mass; }

    char* getName()
      { return name; }
    char* getSymbol()
      { return symbol; }
    void setMass(double Mass)
```

continues

Listing 12.3. continued

```
        { mass = Mass; }
};

void makeCompound(Element *elem1,
                  int valence1,
                  Element *elem2,
                  int valence2,
                  Compound *compound)
{
  double molesElem1, molesElem2;
  double molesReacted;

  valence1 = abs(valence1);
  valence2 = abs(valence2);

  // exit if both elements are not present
  if (fabs(elem1->getMass() * elem2->getMass()) <= 1.0e-7)
    return;

  // get the number of moles
  molesElem1 = elem1->getMass() / elem1->getAtomicWeight();
  molesElem2 = elem2->getMass() / elem2->getAtomicWeight();

  if (molesElem1 / valence2 > molesElem2 / valence2) {
    // there is more of elem1 than elem2.  Calculate the
    // excess of elem1
    molesReacted = molesElem2 / valence1;
    molesElem1 -= molesReacted * valence2;
    elem2->setMass(0);
    elem1->setMass(molesElem1 * elem1->getAtomicWeight());
  }
  else {
    // there is more of elem2 than elem1.  Calculate the
    // excess of elem2
    molesReacted = molesElem1 / valence2;
    molesElem2 -= molesReacted * valence1;
    elem1->setMass(0);
    elem2->setMass(molesElem1 * elem2->getAtomicWeight());
  }
```

```
    // update the compound
    compound->setMass(compound->getMass() +
                     molesReacted * compound->getMolecularWeight());
}

main()
{
  Element hydrogen("Hydrogen", "H", 1, 3);
  Element oxygen("Oxygen", "O", 16, 17);
  Compound water("Water", "H2O", 18, 0.5);

  cout << "Initial amounts of reactants and products are:\n";
  cout << hydrogen.getName() << " : "
       << hydrogen.getMass() << " grams\n"
       << oxygen.getName() << " : "
       << oxygen.getMass() << " grams\n"
       << water.getName() << " : "
       << water.getMass() << " grams\n\n";

  makeCompound(&hydrogen, -1, &oxygen, 2, &water);
  cout << "Final amounts of reactants and products are:\n";
  cout << hydrogen.getName() << " : "
       << hydrogen.getMass() << " grams\n"
       << oxygen.getName() << " : "
       << oxygen.getMass() << " grams\n"
       << water.getName() << " : "
       << water.getMass() << " grams\n";

  return 0;
}
```

The class `Element` declares data members to represent the atomic weight, mass, element name, and chemical symbol. The class constructor creates an instance by assigning values to the various data members. Most of the member functions of class `Element` return the values of the data members. Only the `setMass` function enables you to set the value in the member `mass`.

The class `Compound` contains data members and member functions that are similar to those in the class `Element`. Instead of using references to atomic weight, the class employs molecular weight.

The listing also declares the function makeCompound as the reaction-calculating function. This function has the following parameters:

- elem1 is the pointer to the first reacting element.
- valence1 is the valence of the first reacting element.
- elem2 is the pointer to the second reacting element.
- valence2 is the valence of the second reacting element.
- compound is the pointer to the compound generated by the reaction.

The makeCompound function determines which reactant has the excess amount. This information tells the function that the mass of the other reactant determines how much product is generated. The function calculates the depletion of the reactants and the amount of product generated. The function assumes that the product might be present initially and therefore adds the amount generated by the reaction.

The main() creates the following instances:

- The instance hydrogen, representing 3 grams of hydrogen.
- The instance oxygen, representing 17 grams of oxygen.
- The instance water, with an initial amount of 0.5 grams.

main() displays the initial amounts of reactants and product, calls the function makeCompound, and then displays the post-reaction amounts of reactants and product. The call to makeCompound passes the pointers to the above instances and supplies the valences of +1 and –2 for hydrogen and oxygen, respectively.

Here is the output of Listing 12.3:

```
Initial amounts of reactants and products are:
Hydrogen : 3 grams
Oxygen : 17 grams
Water : 0.5 grams

Final amounts of reactants and products are:
Hydrogen : 0.875 grams
Oxygen : 0 grams
Water : 19.625 grams
```

Modular Objects

This section examines modular objects that are made up of smaller objects. These latter objects are plug-in modules that you can replace. Your computer system is an example of a modular object with its motherboard, CPU, keyboard, memory, video monitor, disk drives, hard disk, and other pieces of hardware. Each of these components in your PC is a well-defined object with a well-developed set of attributes and operations. In addition, these components are replaceable. For example, upgrading the memory, motherboard, and hard drive is somewhat common in the face of technological advances.

Classes can use containment to model such modular objects. Each module is represented by a separate class. The host class (the one that contains all of the modular objects) declares pointers to the contained classes. Such pointers indicate whether a certain module exists (for example, an optional CD-ROM drive). Also, the pointers access the instances that represent the modular objects.

Look at an example that further clarifies the above discussion. Listing 12.4 shows the source code for the PC.CPP program. The listing declares the classes `Memory`, `HardDisk`, and `CPU` to model the memory, hard disk, and CPU. These classes are simple—they enable you to store and recall the data members (that represent the specifications) of their respective instances. Moreover, each class declares a friend operator << to write a data member to an output stream. The listing also declares an enumerated type to represent a family of Intel 80x86 processors.

Listing 12.4. The source code for the PC.CPP program.

```
#include <iostream.h>

enum processor { Intel8088, Intel80286,
                 Intel80386SX, Intel80386DX,
                 Intel80486SX, Intel80486DX,
                 Intel80586SX, Intel80586DX };

class Memory
{
  protected:
    unsigned kRam;
```

continues

Listing 12.4. continued

```
  public:
    Memory() {}

    void setRam(unsigned newRam)
      { kRam = newRam; }
    unsigned getRam()
      { return kRam; }
    friend ostream& operator <<(ostream& os, Memory& m)
    {
       os << m.kRam;
       return os;
    }
};

class HardDisk
{
  protected:
    unsigned megStorage;

  public:
    HardDisk() {}

    void setStorage(unsigned newStorage)
      { megStorage = newStorage; }
    unsigned getStorage()
      { return megStorage; }
    friend ostream& operator <<(ostream& os, HardDisk& h)
    {
       os << h.megStorage;
       return os;
    }
};

class CPU
{
  protected:
    processor CPUtype;

  public:
    CPU() {}
```

```
    void setProcessor(processor newCPUtype)
      { CPUtype = newCPUtype; }
    processor getProcessor()
      { return CPUtype; }
    friend ostream& operator <<(ostream& os, CPU& c);

};

ostream& operator <<(ostream& os, CPU& c)
{
  switch (c.CPUtype) {
    case Intel8088:
      os << "8088";
      break;
    case Intel80286:
      os << "80286";
      break;
    case Intel80386SX:
      os << "80386SX";
      break;
    case Intel80386DX:
      os << "80386DX";
      break;
    case Intel80486SX:
      os << "80486SX";
      break;
    case Intel80486DX:
      os << "80486DX";
      break;
    case Intel80586SX:
      os << "80586SX";
      break;
    case Intel80586DX:
      os << "80586DX";
      break;
    default:
      os << "unknown";
  }
  return os;
}
```

continues

Listing 12.4. continued

```
class PC
{
  protected:
    Memory *memory;
    HardDisk *hardDisk;
    CPU *cpu;

  public:
    PC()
    { memory = 0;
      hardDisk = 0;
      cpu = 0;
    }

    void setMemory(Memory *pMemory)
      { memory = pMemory; }
    Memory* getMemory()
      { return memory; }
    void setHardDisk(HardDisk *pHardDisk)
      { hardDisk = pHardDisk; }
    HardDisk* getHardDisk()
      { return hardDisk; }
    void setCPU(CPU *pCPU)
      { cpu = pCPU; }
    CPU* getCPU()
      { return cpu; }

    friend ostream& operator <<(ostream& os, PC& pc);
};

ostream& operator <<(ostream& os, PC& pc)
{
  os << "Memory: ";
  if (pc.memory)
    os << *pc.memory << " kRam\n";
  else
    os << "0 kRam\n";

  os << "HardDisk: ";
  if (pc.hardDisk)
```

```
    os << *pc.hardDisk << " MBytes\n";
  else
    os << "none installed\n";

  os << "CPU: ";
  if (pc.cpu)
    os << *pc.cpu << "\n";
  else
    os << "No CPU!\n";

  return os;
}
main()
{
  Memory memory;
  HardDisk hardDisk;
  CPU cpu;
  PC pc;

  memory.setRam(16000); // 16 meg
  hardDisk.setStorage(320); // 320 megabytes
  cpu.setProcessor(Intel80486DX);

  pc.setMemory(&memory);
  pc.setHardDisk(&hardDisk);
  pc.setCPU(&cpu);

  cout << pc << "\n";

  pc.setHardDisk(0);
  cout << pc << "\n";

  memory.setRam(32000); // 32 meg
  hardDisk.setStorage(1000); // 1 gigabyte
  cpu.setProcessor(Intel80586DX);
  // reassigns the address of instance hardDisk
  pc.setHardDisk(&hardDisk);
  cout << pc << "\n";

  return 0;
}
```

The listing also declares the class `PC` to represent the host class. The class declaration includes data members that are pointers to the other classes. The constructor of class `PC` initializes these pointers to 0 to indicate the absence of these modular objects. `PC` declares a number of member functions that set and retrieve the data members. In addition, `PC` declares a friend operator << to send the PC configuration (represented by the various modular objects) to an output stream. This version of the operator << indicates whether a module exists in an instance of class `PC`. In addition, it invokes the << operators for the other classes using the data members (pointers to these classes).

`main()` declares instances of the various classes and performs the following tasks:

- Assigns values to the modular objects by calling their respective `setXXXX` member functions.
- Assigns the addresses of the various modular objects to the variable `pc`, an instance of class `PC`. The assignments use the various `setXXXX` member functions of class `PC`.
- Displays the current system configuration by using the operator << with the standard output stream.
- Assigns a null pointer to the `hardDisk` member of class PC. This task uses the `setHardDisk` member function and supplies it an argument of 0.
- Displays the current system configuration by using the operator << with the standard output stream.
- Assigns new values to the modular objects by calling their respective `setXXXX` member functions.
- Assigns the address of the `hardDisk` instance to the `hardDisk` member of `pc`. The assignment uses the member function `PC::setHardDisk`.
- Displays the current system configuration by using the operator << with the standard output stream.

Here is the output of Listing 12.4:

```
Memory: 16000 kRam
HardDisk: 320 MBytes
CPU: 80486DX
```

```
Memory: 16000 kRam
HardDisk: none installed
CPU: 80486DX

Memory: 32000 kRam
HardDisk: 1000 MBytes
CPU: 80586DX
```

Summary

This chapter discussed special object behaviors and how they are modeled using C++ classes. Topics included the following:

- State-engine objects. These objects are modeled by classes that control normal operations with various member functions. You must invoke the member functions in a special order to attain the full capability of the class. State-engine objects are able to reset their state.
- Disabled objects. These objects are modeled by classes that use special Boolean data members. Such members determine whether the member functions can respond in a normal way.
- Transformed objects. These objects have the unique characteristic of being altered as part of their normal operations. Chemical elements and compounds that react with each other represent the most prominent examples of transformed objects.
- Modular objects. These objects model well-developed components (or modules) in a larger object. C++ classes use containment to model these objects. The host class that models the large object declares pointers to the various modular components.

Objects and Event-Handling

Object-oriented programming languages like C++ model real-world objects using classes. In the real world, objects often interact with each other. These interactions are called events and are often triggered by messages. This chapter discusses event-handling using classes and covers the following topics:

- An introduction to event-handling
- Event-handling in Microsoft Windows
- Writing your own simple event-handlers

Introduction

Many programmers regard modeling real-world objects using classes as part of the overall effort to create an application. The other part comes from animating these objects and making them interact with each other. A popular metaphor is that of the working office. The employees (regarded as objects) interact with each other by sending messages to other employees or departments. The recipient of the message then responds by either performing the required task or sending a message to another employee.

Like the employees in a working office, the various objects in an application communicate by sending messages that trigger an event. The original message can be passed from one object to another until it finds an appropriate responsive object. Also, it is possible and acceptable that the message goes unhandled.

Using C++ classes to handle events and respond to messages has proven successful. C++ enables you to write code that is shorter, easier to maintain, and more readable than C. Consequently, the advent of graphical user interfaces, such as Microsoft Windows and X-Windows, makes programming in C++ even more attractive.

Event-Handling in Microsoft Windows

Microsoft developed Windows using C and assembly language and implemented an operating system that relies heavily on event-handling. Windows constantly monitors the user's input and sends a stream of messages to the various visible and invisible objects. For example, when you move the mouse across several opened windows, Windows sends a flurry of messages telling these visible windows that the mouse is entering, moving across, and leaving their area. The window may respond, for example, by altering its color or changing the mouse cursor shape. If the user clicks the mouse button, Windows generates a mouse click message and sends it to the window that contains the mouse. That window responds to the mouse click if it is programmed to do so. Otherwise, the mouse click event is handled by some default action.

Microsoft Windows uses a central message loop to collect and dispatch messages to the various windows and other invisible objects. A system this sophisticated requires special extensions and syntax for C++. In this section, I present two versions of the same simple Windows program. The first version is written for the Microsoft C/C++ 7.0

compiler, whereas the second version is coded for the Borland C++ 3.1 compiler. Both versions represent a trivial, yet typical, Windows application that responds to clicking the left and right mouse buttons. When you click the left mouse button, the application responds by displaying a message dialog box that states you clicked the left mouse button. When you click the right mouse button, the application displays a query dialog box asking you whether you want to exit the application. The dialog box has a Yes button and a No button. Click the Yes button to exit.

Listing 13.1 shows the source code for the SECWINAP.CPP program coded for the Microsoft C/C++ 7.0 compiler. The listing declares the window class `CAppWindow`. Notice that the class declares two special member functions, `OnLButtonDown` and `OnRButtonDown`, and places the identifier `afx_msg` before the return type of these functions. The `afx_msg` identifier tells the C++ compiler to mark these member functions as message handlers. At this point, the compiler does not know which messages are handled by these functions. The program needs additional declarations to map the message-handling functions to their associated messages. The additional information comes in two steps. First, the class `CAppWindow` declares the message-mapping macro `DECLARE_MESSAGE_MAP()`. Second, the program includes the following macro:

```
BEGIN_MESSAGE_MAP(CAppWindow, CFrameWnd)
    ON_WM_LBUTTONDOWN()
    ON_WM_RBUTTONDOWN()
END_MESSAGE_MAP()
```

This second macro tells the compiler that the enclosed message maps belong to the class `CAppWindow`. The message macros `ON_WM_LBUTTONDOWN()` and `ON_WM_RBUTTONDOWN()` tell the compiler that these messages are handled by their default functions, `OnLButtonDown` and `OnRButtonDown`. The Microsoft C/C++ 7.0 compiler declares a rich set of message macros, each with a default response member function. When you create a custom message and declare its own handler, you need to use special message macros that map the message ID with the responding member function. The following is an example.

```
BEGIN_MESSAGE_MAP(CAppWindow, CFrameWnd)
  ON_BN_CLICKED(ID_MEMBER1_BTN, HandleMember1Btn)
  ON_BN_CLICKED(ID_MEMBER2_BTN, HandleMember2Btn)
  ON_BN_CLICKED(ID_MEMBER3_BTN, HandleMember3Btn)
  ON_COMMAND(CM_EXIT, OnExit)
  ON_WM_CREATE()
  ON_WM_CLOSE()
END_MESSAGE_MAP()
```

The `ON_BN_CLICKED` message macro tells the compiler of the various user-defined messages generated by clicking a button and the corresponding functions that respond to these messages. Similarly, the `ON_COMMAND` message macro tells the compiler that the user-defined menu command `CM_EXIT` is handled by the `OnExit` member function.

Listing 13.1. Source code for the Microsoft C/C++ 7.0 version of SECWINAP.CPP.

```
#include <afxwin.h>

// Define a window class derived from CFrameWnd
class CAppWindow : public CFrameWnd
{
public:
    CAppWindow()
    {
      Create(NULL, "A Simple MFC Application",
             WS_OVERLAPPEDWINDOW, rectDefault);
    }

    // handle the left mouse button click
    afx_msg void OnLButtonDown(UINT nFlags, CPoint point);

    // handle the right mouse button click
    afx_msg void OnRButtonDown(UINT nFlags, CPoint point);

    // message map macro
    DECLARE_MESSAGE_MAP()

};

// Define an application class derived from CWinApp
class CWindowApp : public CWinApp
{
public:
        virtual BOOL InitInstance();
};

void CAppWindow::OnLButtonDown(UINT nFlags, CPoint point)
{
```

```
  MessageBox("You clicked the left button!",
             "Mouse Click Event!", MB_OK);
}

void CAppWindow::OnRButtonDown(UINT nFlags, CPoint point)
{
  int result;
  MessageBeep(0); // beep

  // prompt whether user wants to close the application
  result = MessageBox("Want to close this application",
                      "Query", MB_YESNO ¦ MB_ICONQUESTION);

  // if the user clicked the Yes button, send a WM_CLOSE message
  // to the application's window
  if (result == IDYES)
     SendMessage(WM_CLOSE);
}

BEGIN_MESSAGE_MAP(CAppWindow, CFrameWnd)
    ON_WM_LBUTTONDOWN()
    ON_WM_RBUTTONDOWN()
END_MESSAGE_MAP()

// Construct the CWindowApp's m_pMainWnd data member
BOOL CWindowApp::InitInstance()
{
        m_pMainWnd = new CAppWindow();
        m_pMainWnd->ShowWindow(m_nCmdShow);
        m_pMainWnd->UpdateWindow();
        return TRUE;
}

// application's constructor initializes and runs the app
CWindowApp WindowApp;
```

The Borland C++ 3.1 compiler uses a different approach for specifying message-handling member functions. Listing 13.2 shows the source code for the SECWINAP.CPP program coded for the Borland C++ 3.1 compiler. The class `TAppWindow` models the application's window. The member functions `WMLButtonDown` and WMRButtonDown handle the messages generated by clicking the left and right mouse buttons, respectively. Notice that the class declares these functions as virtual and includes a language extension that uses the syntax =[messageID] to indicate the ID of the message handled by a member function. The Borland C++ compiler is less strict than the Microsoft C/C++ 7.0 compiler concerning the names of the message-handling functions.

Listing 13.2. Source code for the Borland C++ 3.1 version of SECWINAP.CPP.

```
#include <owl.h>

// declare the custom application class as
// a subclass of TApplication

class TWinApp : public TApplication
{
public:
  TWinApp(LPSTR  AName,          // application name
       HINSTANCE hInstance,      // instance handle
       HINSTANCE hPrevInstance,  // previous instance handle
       LPSTR  lpCmdLine,      // command-line arguments
       int    nCmdShow) :     // display command
       TApplication(AName, hInstance, hPrevInstance,
                 lpCmdLine, nCmdShow) {};

protected:
  virtual void InitMainWindow();

};

// use the _CLASSDEF macro to declare reference and pointer
// types related to the new TAppWindow class
_CLASSDEF(TAppWindow)

// expand the functionality of TWindow by deriving class TAppWindow
class TAppWindow : public TWindow
{
public:
  TAppWindow(PTWindowsObject AParent, LPSTR ATitle) :
            TWindow(AParent, ATitle) {};
```

```
  // handle the left mouse button click
  virtual void WMLButtonDown(RTMessage Msg)
       = [WM_FIRST + WM_LBUTTONDOWN];

  // handle the right mouse button click
  virtual void WMRButtonDown(RTMessage Msg)
       = [WM_FIRST + WM_RBUTTONDOWN];

};

void TAppWindow::WMLButtonDown(RTMessage Msg)
{
  MessageBox(HWindow, "You clicked the left button!",
             "Mouse Click Event!", MB_OK);
}

void TAppWindow::WMRButtonDown(RTMessage Msg)
{
  int result;
  MessageBeep(0); // beep

  // prompt whether user wants to close the application
  result = MessageBox(HWindow, "Want to close this application",
                      "Query", MB_YESNO | MB_ICONQUESTION);

  // if the user clicked the Yes button, send a WM_CLOSE message
  // to the application's window
  if (result == IDYES)
     SendMessage(HWindow, WM_CLOSE, 0, 0);
}

void TWinApp::InitMainWindow()
{
  MainWindow = new TAppWindow(NULL, Name);
}

int PASCAL WinMain(HINSTANCE hInstance, HINSTANCE hPrevInstance,
             LPSTR lpCmdLine, int nCmdShow)
{
  TWinApp WinApp("A Simple OWL Application", hInstance,
           hPrevInstance, lpCmdLine, nCmdShow);
```

continues

Listing 13.2. continued

```
  WinApp.Run(); // run OWL application
  return WinApp.Status; // return application status
}
```

Custom Event-Handlers

The difficulty of creating custom event-handlers depends on the complexity of the system you want to implement. Simple event-handlers are easy to code using a single-inheritance class hierarchy. First, you need to create a structure that packages the event and includes the ID of the event, a resolved flag, and any other needed data members. Here is a general example of an event-handling structure:

```
struct TEvent {
  unsigned ID;
  int isResolved; // Boolean member
  // other data members
};
```

The scheme for handling events employs a bottom-up design. The bottom subclass receives the message first and attempts to handle it. If the attempt is successful, the message is handled. Otherwise, the scheme invokes the event-handler of the parent class. The same scenario takes place with the parent class, which might end up calling the grandparent class, and so on. Here is a three-class hierarchy that illustrates the bottom-up event-handling scheme:

```
class A
{
  protected:
    // protected members
  public:
    // constructors and destructor
    virtual void handleEvent(TEvent& event)
    {
       switch (eventID) {
         // case labels
         default:
```

```
            // do nothing
         }
      }
}

class B : public A
{
  protected:
    // protected members
  public:
    // constructors and destructor
    virtual void handleEvent(TEvent& event)
    {
       switch (eventID) {
         // case labels
         default:
          A::handleEvent(event);
       }
    }
}

class C : public B
{
  protected:
    // protected members
  public:
    // constructors and destructor
    virtual void handleEvent(TEvent& event)
    {
       switch (eventID) {
         // case labels
         default:
          B::handleEvent(event);
       }
    }
}
```

Each `handleEvent` member function uses a `switch` statement to examine the ID of the message (or event) and determine whether it can respond to the message (or handle the event). The subclasses use the `default` clause in the `switch` statement to invoke the event-handler of the parent class.

To give you a simple example of how the chain of event-handling works, consider the following scenario. Suppose you want to return a stereo system that you had bought from a department store—call it Summer-Mart. You take the merchandise back to the electronics department and request a refund from the salesperson. The salesperson can give you a full refund if you have your sales receipt. If you have lost the sales receipt, the salesperson is able to refund your money as long as it does not exceed $200. In object-oriented terms, this incident creates an "event" which the salesperson successfully handles if you present a sales receipt. Otherwise, the department supervisor must be consulted. The supervisor is authorized to refund your money up to $500. If the amount is larger, you must talk to the store manager. The manager decides whether to refund your money for a sale of less than $10,000. Otherwise, you really need to produce a sales slip!

The salesperson, department supervisor, and store manager form a complete chain of objects that handle the request for a refund. The salesperson is the first store employee presented with the request for the refund. Based on the refund case, the salesperson may be able to take care of the matter or refer you to the department supervisor. In doing so, the event (requesting your refund) is passed to the supervisor. If the latter is able to resolve it, you leave the store with your money. Otherwise, the matter is presented to the store manager. The manager makes the final decision and handles the event, one way or the other.

Listing 13.3 shows the source code for the DEPSTORE.CPP program that models the previous case using C++ classes. The `TEvent` structure contains three members:

- The `salesAmount` member stores the amount of refund due to you.
- The `hasSalesSlip` member stores the Boolean status of the availability of the sales refund.
- The `resolved` member indicates whether the refund request is resolved.

The `TSalesPerson` class models the salesperson. It has two data fields:

- The `dollarLimit` member represents the maximum amount of refund from the salesperson that does not require a sales slip.
- The `needSalesSlip` member indicates whether the sales slip is required to refund an amount greater than `dollarLimit`.

The `HandleEvent` function permits the instances of `TSalesPerson` to deal with the refund request. Noticc that the parameter event is passed by reference. This kind of parameter enables the value of the resolved member to be passed back to the message sender.

The `TSupervisor` is declared as a descendant of `TSalesPerson`. It inherits the data fields of `TSalesPerson` and overrides the inherited `TManager.HandleEvent` function. The `TManager` class is declared as a subclass of `TSupervisor`. The `TManager` class inherits the data members of `TSalesPerson` and overrides the inherited `HandleEvent` function.

To examine how the refund-request model works and how the event-handling chain is implemented, look at the various definitions of the `HandleEvent` procedure. The basic notion used in this model is that the salesperson and the supervisor represent the store manager. If the store was a mom-and-pop operation, the manager, the supervisor, and the salesperson would be one and the same—the store owner. Based on this notion, `TManager::HandleEvent` first sends `TSupervisor.HandleEvent` before presenting the rest of the code for the manager's response. The manager intervenes only if the supervisor is unable to handle the event. Likewise, the first statement in `TSupervisor::HandleEvent` is the `TSalesPerson::HandleEvent` message. This similarly states that the salesperson should first attempt to handle the event before involving the department supervisor.

The `TSalesPerson::HandleEvent` function sets the values for the `dollarLimit` and `needSalesSlip` data fields and executes the `if` statement that decides whether you get your refund or need to see the supervisor. The `TSupervisor::HandleEvent` function employs a similar `if` statement to resolve the matter by either refunding your money or sending you to the store manager. The `TManager::HandleEvent` function implements the manager's response that involves a random number in the range of 0–999. If the generated number is above 499, you get your refund. This random number simulates the personal decision of the manager to refund your money.

The program defines the object manager as an instance of class `TManager`. There is no need for the instances of `TSupervisor` and `TSalesPerson` because the `HandleEvent` functions chain the event-handling. The main program section uses the variable `event` to set up the refund request data. The function `main` sends the message `HandleEvent` to the variable `Manager` to simulate resolving the refund request.

The program starts by prompting you for the value of the returned item and the availability of the sales slip. The program identifies the responses made by the salesperson, the supervisor, and the store manager. A delay of two seconds is used between the responses of the various store employees.

Listing 13.3. The source code for the DEPSTORE.CPP program that demonstrates basic event-handling concepts.

```
#include <iostream.h>
#include "video.h"
#include <dos.h>
#include <stdlib.h>

const unsigned WAIT = 2000;

enum boolean { false, true };

struct TEvent {
   double salesAmount;
   boolean hasSalesSlip;
   boolean resolved;
};

class TSalesPerson
{
   public:
     double dollarLimit;
     boolean needSalesSlip;
     void HandleEvent(TEvent& event);
};

class TSupervisor : public TSalesPerson
{
  public:
    void HandleEvent(TEvent& event);
};

class TManager : public TSupervisor
{
  public:
    void HandleEvent(TEvent& event);
};

void TSalesPerson::HandleEvent(TEvent& event)
{
    dollarLimit = 200;
    needSalesSlip = true;
```

```
    cout << "Salesperson: ";
    event.resolved = false;
    if (needSalesSlip && event.hasSalesSlip ||
       event.salesAmount <= dollarLimit)  {
        cout << "Here is your refund of $"
             << event.salesAmount << "\n";
        event.resolved = true;
    }
    else
        cout << "You need to talk to my supervisor!\n";
    cout << "\n";
    delay(WAIT);
}

void TSupervisor::HandleEvent(TEvent& event)
{
    TSalesPerson::HandleEvent(event);
    dollarLimit = 500;
    needSalesSlip = false;
    if (!event.resolved) {
      cout << "Supervisor: ";
      event.resolved = false;
      if (event.salesAmount <= dollarLimit)  {
          cout << "Here is your refund of $"
               << event.salesAmount << "\n";
          event.resolved = true;
      }
      else
          cout << "You need to talk to the manager!\n";
      cout << "\n";
      delay(WAIT);
    }
}

void TManager::HandleEvent(TEvent& event)
{
    double x;
    TSupervisor::HandleEvent(event);
    dollarLimit = 10000;
    if (!event.resolved) {
        cout << "Store manager: ";
```

continues

Listing 13.3. continued

```
            event.resolved = false;
            if (event.salesAmount <= dollarLimit)  {
                srand(unsigned(event.salesAmount) % 13);
                x = double(rand() % 1000);
                if (x >= 500)
                    cout << "Here is your refund of $"
                         << event.salesAmount << "\n";
                else
                    cout << "Sorry! You need to bring the sales slip!\n";
            }
            else
                cout << "Sorry! You need to bring the sales slip!\n";
            cout << "\n";
            event.resolved = true;
            delay(WAIT);
        }
        cout << "Thank you for shopping at Summer-Mart!\n\n";
    }

    main()
    {
        char Answer;
        TManager manager;
        TEvent event;

        clrscr();
        cout << "Enter the following sales refund information";
        cout << "\n\n";
        cout << "Enter sales amount : ";
        cin >> event.salesAmount;
        cout << "\n";
        cout << "Do you have the sales slip? (Y/N) ";
        cin >> Answer;  cout << "\n";
        event.hasSalesSlip = (Answer == 'Y' || Answer == 'y') ?
                                                    true : false;
        manager.HandleEvent(event);
        delay(WAIT);

        return 0;
    }
```

The following is a sample session with the program:

```
Enter the following sales refund information

Enter sales amount : 600

Do you have the sales slip? n

Salesperson: You need to talk to my supervisor!

Supervisor: You need to talk to the manager!
Store manager: Here is your refund of $600

Thank you for shopping at Summer-Mart!
```

Summary

This chapter discussed how C++ classes offer suitable programming tools to develop applications that employ a sophisticated system of messages and events. The chapter covered the following topics:

- An introduction to event-handling. Object-oriented programming languages are able to handle events or messages in a manner similar to employees of an office. A certain object sends a message to another object. This second object either responds to the message, passes the message to another object, or does nothing. This pattern of response can repeat itself.
- Event-handling in Microsoft Windows. The Microsoft and Borland C++ compilers each use a different approach to extend the C++ syntax and use special message-mapping macros. These macros tell the compiler which member functions handle a specific message or event.
- Writing your own event-handling. This process is simple; it involves cascaded event-handling member functions that either respond to a specific message or invoke the event-handler or the parent classes.

Part III

C++ Template Classes

The String Class

The first chapter in this part of the book addresses the most common need among C++ programmers working with text: a string class. Like C, C++ does not define a formal type or class for strings. Instead, the language leaves that task to the programmer. One of the first C++ projects I completed was creating a somewhat-comprehensive string class. In this chapter I present the `cString` class, an enhanced version of the first string class, and a battery of small test programs. While this chapter is, perhaps, the least advanced in its level, the string class is a cornerstone of later string manipulation.

The cString Class Declaration

Let me introduce the `cString` class by presenting the string.hpp header file, shown in Listing 14.1. The string.hpp header file includes the iostream.h and comndata.h header files. The comndata.h file includes common data declarations I use in this book. In addition, the string.hpp header file declares the following constants and data types:

1. The unsigned constant `NO_SUBSTR_FOUND`, which has the value of `0xffff`. This value hints that the length of the instances of the `cString` class can store up to `0xfffe` characters. The index `0xffff` is reserved to flag a "no matching substring" search outcome.

2. The unsigned constant `DEFAULT_STRING_SIZE`, which specifies the default string size. Feel free to alter this constant to either conserve string space or allocate string space more generously.

3. The unsigned constant `DEFAULT_STRING_SIZE_INCREM`, which determines the increments by which the maximum string size grows. If you don't wish to waste memory space (and aren't concerned about heap-space fragmentation), you can assign a lower value to this constant.

4. The enumerated type `stringErrors`. This data type defines the error state of a string operation.

The `cString` class declares the following data members:

1. The `badindex` member is a special member, retrieved by the operator `[]` when you supply an out-of-range character index. Using the `badindex` member enables the operator `[]` to return a reference to a `char` (see the description of the `[]` operator later in this chapter) for all arguments of parameter `index`. This approach is less disruptive than not returning a value and allows your application to decide whether the error is fatal. To assign a value to the `badindex` member, use the `[]` operator with a high index. The index value of `0xffff` is guaranteed to work. Consider the following example:

   ```
   cString s;
   char badIndexVal = '~';

   s[0xffff] = badIndexVal;
   ```

2. The `str` data member points to the dynamic array of characters.

3. The `maxSize` data member stores the maximum number of characters that can be stored in an instance of `cString` (not counting the `'\0'` character).

4. The `len` data member stores the current number of characters stored.

5. The `sizeIncr` data member stores the increment in string size.

6. The enumerated data member `strErr` stores the error state for the last operation performed on an instance of `cString`.

The `cString` class uses unsigned integers to determine the maximum size, current length, and character indices. The limit offered by the unsigned integer type should be adequate for most cases. If your application needs longer strings (which your system can provide), you may alter the code of `cString` to handle long integers. In that case, you can make the constant `NO_SUBSTR_FOUND` a –1 instead of a large positive integer. You also should check the implementation of the `cString` member functions that use the constant `NO_SUBSTR_FOUND`.

The `cString` class has the following sets of functions:

1. Four constructors and a class destructor.
2. Functions that are wrappers to C-style string functions found in the header file string.h.
3. Functions that implement new and additional string manipulation.
4. Assignment and access operators.
5. Relational operators.
6. Concatenation, deletion, and string-slicing operators. The deletion and string slicing operators use the `-`, `/`, and `%` operators in a nontraditional manner on strings. More about these operators appears later in this chapter.

Listing 14.1. The source code for the string.hpp header file.

```
//////////////////////////////////////////////////////////////////////
//                                                                  //
//                        NCS String Library                        //
//                                                                  //
//              Copyright (c) 1992  Namir Clement Shammas           //
//                                                                  //
// Version 1.1.0                                            3/25/91 //
//                                             Last Update: 6/16/92 //
//                                                                  //
// Comprehensive C++ string library that provides a variety of      //
// member functions to manipulate string classes.                   //
//                                                                  //
//////////////////////////////////////////////////////////////////////
```

continues

Listing 14.1. continued

```
#ifndef _STRING_HPP
#define _STRING_HPP

#include <iostream.h>
#include "comndata.h"

const unsigned NO_SUBSTR_FOUND = 0xffff;
const unsigned DEFAULT_STRING_SIZE = 41;
const unsigned DEFAULT_STRING_SIZE_INCREM = 10;

enum stringErrors { NO_ERR, NULL_STRING, BAD_INDEX };

class cString
{
 private:
   char badindex;

 protected:

   cString& replaceOneChar(char findchar,
                           char replacechar,
                           unsigned first = 0,
                           unsigned last = 0xffff);

   char *str;         // pointer to characters
   unsigned maxSize;      // total number of bytes allocated
   unsigned len;          // current cString size
   unsigned sizeIncr; // increment
   stringErrors strErr;

 public:
   // ******* constructors *******
   cString();
   cString(const unsigned size,
          const unsigned sizeIncrement = DEFAULT_STRING_SIZE_INCREM);
   cString(const char* s,
          const unsigned sizeIncrement = DEFAULT_STRING_SIZE_INCREM);
   cString(const cString&,
          const unsigned sizeIncrement = DEFAULT_STRING_SIZE_INCREM);
   // class destructor
```

```
~cString();

boolean checkBounds(unsigned i) { return (i < len) ? true : false; }
stringErrors getError() {
    stringErrors temp = strErr;
    strErr = NO_ERR; // reset error flag
    return temp;
}
char* getstr() { return str; }
unsigned hash(unsigned modulo);
cString& insert(const cString&, const unsigned);
unsigned lastpos(cString& s,
                 const boolean caseSense = true);
cString& left(unsigned, const char padchar = ' ');
cString& mapChars(const cString& findchar,
                  const cString& replacechar,
                  const unsigned first = 0,
                  const unsigned last = 0xffff);
cString& overwrite(const cString& substr, const unsigned start);
cString& padends(unsigned countAtEachEnd, const char c = ' ');
cString& padleft(unsigned count, const char c = ' ');
cString& padright(unsigned count, const char c = ' ');
unsigned pos(const cString& s,
         const boolean caseSense = true,
         const unsigned start = 0);
void print(const cString& str1,
           const char c,
           const cString& str2);
cString& remove(const unsigned start, unsigned count = 0xffff);
cString& repeatChar(const char, const unsigned);
cString& repeatString(cString&, const unsigned);
cString& replace(const cString& findstr,
                 const cString& replacestr,
                 unsigned& count,
                 const boolean caseSense = true,
                 const unsigned start = 0,
                 unsigned freq = 0xffff);
cString& replaceChars(const cString& findchar,
                      const char replacechar,
                      const unsigned first = 0,
                      const unsigned last = 0xffff);
```

continues

Listing 14.1. continued

```
cString& replaceRangeChars(const char firstChar,
                           const char lastChar,
                           const char replacechar,
                           const unsigned first = 0,
                           const unsigned last = 0xffff);
cString& resize(unsigned new_size);
cString& right(unsigned count, const char padchar = ' ');
cString& stringchr(const char);
unsigned stringcspn(const cString&);
unsigned stringlen() const { return len; }
cString& stringlwr();
cString& stringncat(const cString& , const unsigned);
cString& stringnset(const char, const unsigned);
cString& stringpbrk(const cString&);
cString& stringrchr(const char);
cString& stringrev();
cString& stringset(const char);
unsigned stringspn(const cString&);
cString& stringstr(const cString&);
cString& stringtok(cString&,
                   const char*,
                   const boolean getFirst = true);
cString& stringupr();
friend cString substring(const cString&, unsigned, unsigned);
cString& trimends(const char c = ' ');
cString& trimleft(const char c = ' ');
cString& trimright(const char c = ' ');
cString& trimSequenceChars(const char c = ' ');

// assignment operators
cString& operator =(const cString&);
cString& operator =(const char*);
cString& operator =(const char);
char& operator[](const unsigned);
cString operator ()(const unsigned start,
                    unsigned count);
// comparative operators with other cString classes
int operator >(const cString&);
int operator >=(const cString&);
int operator ==(const cString&);
```

```
    int operator <(const cString&);
    int operator <=(const cString&);
    int operator !=(const cString&);
    // comparative operators with standard cStrings
    int operator >(const char*);
    int operator >=(const char*);
    int operator ==(const char*);
    int operator <(const char*);
    int operator <=(const char*);
    int operator !=(const char*);
    // friend function to add strings and text/chars
    friend cString operator +(cString&, cString&);
    friend cString operator +(cString&, char*);
    friend cString operator +(char*, cString&);
    friend cString operator +(cString&, char);
    friend cString operator +(char, cString&);
    cString& operator +=(const cString&);
    cString& operator +=(const char*);
    cString& operator +=(const char);
    // nontraditional operators
    friend cString operator -(cString&, const char*);
    friend cString operator -(cString&, cString&);
    cString& operator -=(const char*);
    cString& operator -=(cString&);
    friend cString operator /(cString&, const char*);
    friend cString operator /(cString&, cString&);
    cString& operator /=(const char*);
    cString& operator /=(cString&);
    friend cString operator %(cString&, const char*);
    friend cString operator %(cString&, cString&);
    cString& operator %=(const char*);
    cString& operator %=(cString&);
    friend ostream& operator <<(ostream& os, cString& s);
};

#endif
```

In the next sections, I present a piecewise implementation of the `cString` class. The companion disk contains the complete source code in the file STRING.CPP.

The cString Constructors

Let's look at the four `cString` class constructors. They are as follows:

The Default cString Class Constructor

Listing 14.2 contains the source code for the default class constructor. This constructor allocates an empty dynamic string of `DEFAULT_STRING_SIZE` characters. This constructor also assigns the previous constant to the `maxSize` data member and assigns the constant `DEFAULT_STRING_SIZE_INCREM` to the `sizeIncr` data member. The `strErr` and `badindex` members are assigned `NO_ERR` and the space character, respectively.

Listing 14.2. The default `cString` class constructor.

```
//////////////////////////////////////////////////////////////////////
//
cString::cString()
//
// Purpose: the default class constructor. Creates a string with
// the default size and the default size increment
//
{
   maxSize = DEFAULT_STRING_SIZE;
   str = new char[maxSize];
   *str = '\0';
   len = 0;
   sizeIncr = DEFAULT_STRING_SIZE_INCREM;
   strErr = NO_ERR;
   badindex = ' ';
}
```

The Second cString Class Constructor

The second constructor, shown in Listing 14.3, creates an empty string with arguments that specify the maximum size and the size increment. This constructor

verifies that the arguments for the maximum size and the size increment are at least 2 and 1, respectively. The `sizeIncrement` has the default value of `DEFAULT_STRING_SIZE_INCREM`.

Listing 14.3. The second `cString` class constructor.

```
//////////////////////////////////////////////////////////////////////
//
cString::cString(const unsigned size, const unsigned sizeIncrement)
//
// Purpose: customizing constructor. Creates a string object with
// a specific size and size increment. The string has no characters
// assigned to it.
//
// Parameters:
//
//    input: size - the size of the string.
//           sizeIncrement - the increment in the string size
//
{
   // verify the size parameter and assign it to the maxSize member
   maxSize = (size < 2) ? 2 : size;
   str = new char[maxSize];
   str[0] = '\0';
   len = 0;
   // verify and assign the size increment
   sizeIncr = (sizeIncrement == 0) ? 1 : sizeIncrement;
   strErr = NO_ERR;
   badindex = ' ';
}
```

The Third cString Class Constructor

The third class constructor, shown in Listing 14.4, creates an instance of `cString` using a C-style string. This constructor allows you to specify the size increment, which has the default value of `DEFAULT_STRING_SIZE_INCREM`. The `cString` instance is created with a copy of the characters of parameter `s`.

The third constructor also is used by the C++ compiler to convert C-style strings into `cString` instances. Consequently, this constructor is a valuable tool in reducing the number of overloaded member functions by eliminating the versions that use the parameters of the type `const char*`.

Listing 14.4. The third `cString` class constructor.

```
//////////////////////////////////////////////////////////////////////
//
cString::cString(const char* s, const unsigned sizeIncrement)
//
// Purpose: customizing constructor that creates a string using a
// C-style string. The second parameter also sets the size increment
// of the string object.
//
// Parameters:
//
//    input: s - the pointer to the string used to create this object.
//           sizeIncrement - the size increment of the string.
//
// Comments: if the argument for s is an empty string, the constructor
// creates a string object with the default string size.
//
{
  badindex = ' ';
  len = (s) ? strlen(s) : 0;
  // is the string s not empty?
  if (len > 0) {
    maxSize = len+1;
    str = new char[maxSize];
    strcpy(str, s);
  }
  else {
    maxSize = DEFAULT_STRING_SIZE;
    str = new char[maxSize];
    str[0] = '\0';
  }
  sizeIncr = (sizeIncrement == 0) ? 1 : sizeIncrement;
  strErr = NO_ERR;
}
```

The Fourth cString Class Constructor

The last class constructor, shown in Listing 14.5, creates an instance of `cString` using an existing instance of the `cString` class. This constructor also enables you to specify the size increment, which has the default value of `DEFAULT_STRING_SIZE_INCREM`. The `cString` instance is created with a copy of the characters of `s`.

Listing 14.5. The fourth `cString` class constructor.

```
////////////////////////////////////////////////////////////////////
//
cString::cString(const cString& s, const unsigned sizeIncrement)
//
// Purpose: customizing constructor that creates a string using a
// C-style string. The second parameter also sets the size increment
// of the string object.
//
// Parameters:
//
//    input: s - the pointer to the string used to create this object.
//           sizeIncrement - the size increment of the string.
//
{
  badindex = ' ';
  len = s.len;
  maxSize = len+1;
  str = new char[maxSize];
  strcpy(str, s.str);
  sizeIncr = (sizeIncrement == 0) ? 1 : sizeIncrement;
  strErr = NO_ERR;
}
```

The Class Destructor

The class destructor, shown in Listing 14.6, deallocates the dynamic spaces accessed by the member `str`.

Listing 14.6. The class destructor.

```
///////////////////////////////////////////////////////////////////
//
cString::~cString()
//
// Purpose: class destructor.
//
{
   if (str)
      delete [] str;
   maxSize = 0;
   len = 0;
   sizeIncr = 0;
}
```

NonWrapper Member Functions

In this section we discuss member functions that contain multiple statements and that do more than simply call familiar C-string functions.

The hashing Function

Listing 14.7 shows the source code for the `hashing` function. The parameter `modulo` represents the hash table size. The `hashing` function returns a value in the range of 0 to `modulo-1`.

Listing 14.7. The `hashing` function.

```
///////////////////////////////////////////////////////////////////
//
unsigned cString::hash(unsigned modulo)
//
// Purpose: returns the hashing address 0..modulo-1.
//
// Parameters:
```

```
//
//    input: modulo - the size of the hash table.
//
{
   unsigned y = 0;
   char* p = str;

   while (*p)
      y = (y + len + 13 * *p++) % modulo;
   return y;
}
```

The insert Function

The `insert` function, shown in Listing 14.8, inserts the string argument `substr` at the index `start`. If the argument for `start` is 0, the argument `substr` is prepended to the `cString` instance. If the argument for `start` is greater than the current length of the `cString` instance, the argument for `substr` simply is appended to the instance.

Listing 14.8. The `insert` function.

```
////////////////////////////////////////////////////////////////////////
//
cString& cString::insert(const cString& substr, const unsigned start)
//
// Purpose: inserts or appends substr, starting at index start.
//
// Parameters:
//
//    input: substr - the inserted or appended substring.
//           start - the index of the insertion.
//
{
   unsigned m = substr.len;

   // need to resize this string object?
   if ((len+m+1) > maxSize)
       resize(len+m+1);
```

continues

Listing 14.8. continued

```
      if (start < len) {
         // insert substring
         memmove((str+start+m), (str+start), len+1-start);
         memmove((str+start), substr.str, m);
      }
      else
         // append substring
         memmove((str+len), substr.str, m+1);
      // update string length
      len += m;
      return *this;
   }
```

Testing the insert Function

Listing 14.9 shows the source code for the INSERT.CPP program file, which tests the `insert` function. The test program illustrates how the `insert` function prepends, inserts, and appends the string `insStr`—which stores the string `ABCD`—to instances `s1`, `s2`, and `s3`, respectively. The strings `s2` and `s3` are copies of string `s1`, which contains `1234567890`. The output of the test program is as follows:

```
1234567890
ABCD1234567890
123ABCD4567890
1234567890ABCD
```

The first string shows the contents of string `s1`. The other strings illustrate how the string `ABCD` is prepended, inserted, and appended to the string `1234567890`.

Listing 14.9. The source code for the INSERT.CPP program file.

```
// Test the cString::insert member function

#include <iostream.h>
#include "string.hpp"

main()
```

```
{
  cString s1 - "1234567890";
  cString s2 = s1;
  cString s3 = s1;
  cString insStr = "ABCD";

  cout << "\n\n";
  cout << s1 << '\n';

  // prepend insStr
  s1.insert(insStr, 0);
  cout << s1 << '\n';

  // insert insStr
  s2.insert(insStr, 3);
  cout << s2 << '\n';

  // append insStr
  s3.insert(insStr, 1000);
  cout << s3 << '\n';

  return 0;

}
```

The lastpos Function

The `lastpos` function, shown in Listing 14.10, returns the character index of the last occurrence of string `s` in the `cString` instance. The Boolean parameter `caseSense` indicates whether the search is case-sensitive. If the `lastpos` function finds no match for string `s`, it returns the `NO_SUBSTR_FOUND` value.

The `lastpos` function works by reversing the characters of both this string and the string `s`. The function then searches for the first occurrence of the reversed `s` string in the reversed target string (the instance of `cString` in question). If the function finds a match, it obtains the actual index and then adjusts the index's value to account for the string reversals. The function next restores the strings to their original character order and returns the function result.

Listing 14.10. The lastpos function.

```
//////////////////////////////////////////////////////////////////
//
unsigned cString::lastpos(cString& s, const boolean caseSense)
//
// Purpose: returns the index of the last occurrence of string s
// in this string object.
//
// Parameters:
//
//    input: s - the search string.
//           caseSense - the case-sensitivity mode for the search.
//
{
    unsigned offset;

    if (caseSense) {
        // ******* search IS case-sensitive *******
        // reverse string object s
        s.stringrev();
        // reverse this string
        stringrev();
        // search for string s in this string
        char* ptr = strstr(str, s.str);
        // substring found?
        if (ptr) {
            // calculate character offset
            offset = (unsigned)(ptr - str);
            // adjust offset to account for reversed characters
            offset = len - offset - s.len;
        }
        else
            offset = NO_SUBSTR_FOUND;
        // reverse the characters of string s
        s.stringrev();
        // reverse the characters of this string
        stringrev();
        return offset;
    }
    else {
```

```
        // ******* search IS NOT case-sensitive *******
        unsigned offset;
        // make a copy of this string
        char* str2 = new char[len+1];
        strcpy(str2, str);
        // convert to uppercase
        strupr(str2);
        // reverse characters
        strrev(str2);
        // make a copy of string s
        char* s2 = new char[s.len+1];
        strcpy(s2, s.str);
        // convert to uppercase
        strupr(s2);
        // reverse characters
        strrev(s2);
        // search for string s2 in str2
        char* ptr = strstr(str2, s2);
        // get the character offset
        offset = (unsigned)(ptr - str2);
        // delete the string copies
        delete [] s2;
        delete [] str2;
        // was there a matching substring?
        if (ptr) {
            // calculate and return the adjusted offset
            offset = len - offset - s.len;
            return offset;
        }
        else
            return NO_SUBSTR_FOUND;
    }
}
```

Testing the lastpos Function

Listing 14.11 shows the source code for the LASTPOS.CPP test program, which illustrates using the `lastpos` function. The program creates the string object `s1` and assigns it the characters `hellohellohellohello`. The program assigns the search string `LO` to the string object `s2` and performs the following tasks:

- Displays the string object `s1`.
- Obtains and displays the position of the last occurrence of string `s2` in `s1`. The search is case-insensitive.
- Obtains and displays the position of the last occurrence of string `s2` in `s1`. The search is case-sensitive.

The output of the test program is as follows:

```
                   1         2         3
          0123456789012345678901234567890
Main string is hellohellohellohello
Case-insensitive position of LO is 18
Case-sensitive position of LO is 65535
```

The last output displays the decimal equivalent of `0xffff`, the value of the constant `NO_SUBSTR_FOUND`. This value indicates that the case-insensitive search fails.

Listing 14.11. The source code for the LASTPOS.CPP test program.

```
// Test the cString::lastpos member function

#include <iostream.h>
#include "string.hpp"

main()
{
  cString s1 = "hellohellohellohello";
  cString s2 = "LO";
  unsigned charPos;

  cout << "\n\n";
  cout << "                        1         2         3" << '\n';
  cout << "               0123456789012345678901234567890" << '\n';
  cout << "Main string is " << s1 << '\n';

  charPos = s1.lastpos(s2, false);
  cout << "Case-insensitive position of " << s2 <<
          " is " << charPos << '\n';
```

```
    charPos = s1.lastpos(s2, true);
    cout << "Case-sensitive position of " << s2 <<
            " is " << charPos << '\n';

    return 0;

}
```

The left Function

The `left` function, shown in Listing 14.12, extracts the left portion of a `cString` instance. The parameter `count` specifies the leftmost character to extract. If the argument for parameter `count` is greater than the actual length of the string instance, the function first expands the string and then pads it with the `padchar` character. The default argument for `padchar` is the space character, the most common padding character. The resulting string contains `count` characters.

Listing 14.12. The `left` function.

```
//////////////////////////////////////////////////////////////////////
//
cString& cString::left(unsigned count, const char padchar)
//
// Purpose: extracts the count leftmost characters. If the argument
// for count is greater than the current string length, the function
// appends the fillchar.
//
// Parameters:
//
//    input: count - the final string length
//           padchar - the padding character
//
{
    count = (count == 0) ? 1 : count;
    if (count < len) {
        // extract the leftmost characters
        str[count] = '\0'; // truncate String
```

continues

Listing 14.12. continued

```
        len = count;
    }
    else if (count > len) {
        // pad more characters
        resize(count); // resize the string
        // write the padding characters
        for (unsigned i = len; i < count; i++)
          *(str + i) = padchar;
        str[count] = '\0';
        len = count;
    }
    return *this;
}
```

Testing the left Function

Listing 14.13 contains the source code for the LEFT.CPP program, which tests the `left` function. The program tests various cases of the `left` function by applying the following steps:

1. Extracts the five leftmost characters from the string `s1`, which is initialized with the characters `1234567890`.
2. Extracts the six leftmost characters from string `s1`. Because the string was truncated to five characters in the preceding step, this step appends one character. The function `left` uses the default space argument because the function call to `left` does not specify the padding character.
3. Extracts the ten leftmost characters from string `s1`. Because the string now is six characters long, this step appends four more characters. This time, the call to function `left` specifies appending the plus (+) character.

The program output is as follows:

```
Main string is '1234567890'
'12345'
'12345 '
'12345 ++++'
```

The program encloses the strings in single quotes to enable you to detect the spaces that are part of the string.

Listing 14.13. The source code for the LEFT.CPP program.

```
// Test the cString::left member function

#include <iostream.h>
#include "string.hpp"

main()
{
  cString s1 = "1234567890";

  cout << "\n\n";
  cout << "Main string is '" << s1 << "'" << '\n';

  s1.left(5);
  cout << "'" << s1 << "'" << '\n';

  s1.left(6);
  cout << "'" << s1 << "'" << '\n';

  s1.left(10, '+');
  cout << "'" << s1 <<"'" << '\n';

  return 0;

}
```

The mapchars Function

The `mapChars` function, shown in Listing 14.14, performs a one-to-one character translation for a `cString` instance. The `findchar` and `replacechar` parameters specify the string instances that contain the characters to be mapped and their replacements. The parameters `first` and `last` define the first and last characters of the `cString` instance that are affected by the translation. The default arguments for the parameters `first` and `last` are `0` and `0xffff`, respectively. These default values specify an entire string.

The mapChars function exits if any one of the following conditions is true:

- The argument for first is greater than or equal to the current length of the cString instance.
- The argument for first is greater than the argument for last.
- The strings findchar and replacechar have unequal lengths.
- The string findchar is an empty string.

The mapChars function detects the default argument for the last parameter and assigns the expression len-1 to the local variable Last. The mapChars function uses a for loop to examine each character of findchar in the cString instance. When the function finds a matching character, it replaces that character with the character in string replacechar that has the same index as the current character in string findchar.

Listing 14.14. The mapChars function.

```
//////////////////////////////////////////////////////////////////////
//
cString& cString::mapChars(const cString& findchar,
                           const cString& replacechar,
                           const unsigned first,
                           const unsigned last)
//
// Purpose: maps the characters of findchar into the corresponding
// characters of replacechar, beginning at index first and ending
// at index last.
//
// Parameters:
//
//    input: findchar - the string containing the set of sought
//             characters.
//           replacechar - the string containing the set of the
//             replacement characters.
//           first - the index where character mapping begins.
//           last - the index where character translation ends.
//
{
    unsigned j;
    char c;
    boolean found;
```

```
    if (first >= len ||
        first > last ||
        findchar.stringlen() != replacechar.stringlen() ||
        findchar.stringlen() == 0)
        return *this;

    // adjust the last parameter for the default value
    unsigned Last = (last < 0xffff) ? last : len - 1;

    // scan the characters from first to len-1
    for (unsigned i = first; i <= Last; i++) {
        c = *(str + i); // c = the i'th string character
        j = 0;
        found = false;
        // search for character c in string findchar
        while (j < findchar.len && found == false)
            // c matches the findchar[j] character?
            if (c != *(findchar.str + j))
              j++;
            else {

                *(str + i) = *(replacechar.str + j);
                found = true;
            }
    }
    return *this;
}
```

Testing the mapchars Function

Listing 14.15 contains the source code for the MAPCHARS.CPP program, which tests the `mapChars` function. The program assigns the string to the `s1` string object:

```
[A1 + A2] / A3 * [A0 - A2]
```

Next, the program tests calling function `mapChars` to map the characters `0123456789` to `)!@#$%^&*(`. The mapping takes place for the index range of 10 to 15. The program then tests mapping the same characters for the entire string `s1` by using the default arguments for parameters `first` and `last`. The program output is

```
Main string is [A1 + A2] / A3 * [A0 - A2]
Replacing characters 0123456789 with )!@#$%^&*(
Starting at index 10 to index 15 : [A1 + A2] / A# * [A0 - A2]
Starting at index 0 to the end : [A! + A@] / A# * [A) - A@]
```

Notice that the first call to `mapChars` ends up translating the character `3` to `#`. The rest of the string remains intact. In the second call to `mapChars`, the rest of the digits in the main string are affected.

Listing 14.15. The source code for the MAPCHARS.CPP program.

```
// Test the cString::mapChars member function

#include <iostream.h>
#include "string.hpp"

main()
{
  cString s1 = "[A1 + A2] / A3 * [A0 - A2]";

  cout << "\n\n";
  cout << "Main string is " << s1 << '\n';
  cout << "Replacing characters 0123456789 with )!@#$%^&*(" << '\n';

  s1.mapChars("0123456789", ")!@#$%^&*(", 10, 15);
  cout << "Starting at index 10 to index 15 : " << s1 << '\n';

  s1.mapChars("0123456789", ")!@#$%^&*(");
  cout << "Starting at index 0 to the end : " << s1 << '\n';

  return 0;

}
```

The overwrite Function

The `overwrite` function, shown in Listing 14.16, overwrites a `cString` instance with the string `substr`. The parameter `start` indicates the index of the first overwritten character. The function deals with the five cases of overwriting a string:

- Case 1: the overwriting string, `substr`, completely overwrites the `cString` instance. In this case, the argument for start is `0` and the argument for `substr` has at least as many characters as the targeted `cString` instance.
- Case 2: the argument for `substr` overwrites the leading characters of the targeted `cString` instance. In this case, the argument for start also is `0`, but the string `substr` has fewer characters than the targeted string.
- Case 3: the string `substr` overwrites and extends the targeted `cString` instance. In this case, the argument for `start` is greater than `0` but equal to or greater than the length of the targeted string.
- Case 4: the string `substr` overwrites existing characters of the targeted `cString` instance. The length of the targeted string does not increase.
- Case 5: The string `substr` is appended to the targeted `cString` instance. In this case, the argument for `start` is equal to or greater than the `len` member of the targeted string.

The `overwrite` function examines the length of the argument for `substr` and the argument for `start` to determine which case applies.

Listing 14.16. The `overwrite` function.

```
///////////////////////////////////////////////////////////////////
//
cString& cString::overwrite(const cString& substr,
                            const unsigned start)
//
// Purpose: overwrite string object with substr, starting at
// index start.
//
// Parameters:
//
//    input: substr - the overwriting substring.
//           start - the character index of the first
//             overwritten character.
//
{
   unsigned m = substr.len;
```

continues

Listing 14.16. continued

```
    if (start == 0) {
      if (m >= len) {
        // case 1 : substring completely replaces this string
        resize(m);
        strcpy(str, substr.str);
        len = m;
      }
      else {
        // case 2: substring overwrites the leading
        // characters of this string
        memmove(str, substr.str, m);
      }
    }
    else {
       unsigned newSize = start + m;
       if (start < len && newSize >= len) {
         // case 3 : substring overwrites and extends this string
         // need to resize the string?
         if (newSize >= maxSize)
           resize(newSize);
         memmove(str + start, substr.str, m);
         len = newSize;
         str[len] = '\0';
       }
       else if (start < len && newSize < len)
         // case 4 : overwrite characters inside this string
         memmove(str + start, substr.str, m);
       else {
          // case 5: append substring to this string
          strcat(str, substr.str);
          len += m;
       }
    }
    return *this;
}
```

Testing the overwrite Function

Listing 14.17 shows the source code for the OVERWRITE.CPP program, which tests the `overwrite` function. The program illustrates the five cases of overwriting a string discussed earlier. The main string is `0123456789`, and the overwriting strings are `abcd` and `!!!!!!!!!!!!!!`. The latter string is used to demonstrate Case 1; the first string demonstrates the other cases. The various cases also use varying arguments for parameter `start`. These arguments range from `0` to `0xffff`. The program output, by case, is as follows:

```
Main string is '0123456789'
```

Case 1:

```
String is completely overwritten by string '!!!!!!!!!!!!!!'
!!!!!!!!!!!!!!
```

Case 2:

```
Leading characters are overwritten by string 'abcd'
abcd456789
```

Case 3:

```
Trailing characters are overwritten by string 'abcd'
01234567abcd
```

Case 4:

```
Internal characters are overwritten by string 'abcd'
01abcd6789
```

Case 5:

```
Appending substring 'abcd'
0123456789abcd
```

Listing 14.17. The source code for the OVERWRITE.CPP program.

```
// Test the cString::overwrite member function

#include <iostream.h>
#include "string.hpp"

main()
```

continues

Listing 14.17. continued

```
{
  cString s0 = "0123456789";
  cString s1 = s0;
  cString s2 = "!!!!!!!!!!!!!!";
  cString s3 = "abcd";

  cout << "\n\n";
  cout << "Main string is '" << s1 << "'" << '\n';

  s1.overwrite(s2, 0);
  cout << "Case 1:\n"
       << "String is completely overwritten by string '"
       << s2 << "'\n" << s1 << '\n';
  s1 = s0;

  s1.overwrite(s3, 0);
  cout << "Case 2:\n"
       << "Leading characters are overwritten by string '"
       << s3 << "'\n" << s1 << '\n';
  s1 = s0;

  s1.overwrite(s3, s1.stringlen() - 2);
  cout << "Case 3:\n"
       << "Trailing characters are overwritten by string '"
       << s3 << "'\n" << s1 << '\n';
  s1 = s0;

  s1.overwrite(s3, 2);
  cout << "Case 4:\n"
       << "Internal characters are overwritten by string '"
       << s3 << "'\n" << s1 << '\n';
  s1 = s0;

  s1.overwrite(s3, 0xffff);
  cout << "Case 5:\n"
       << "Appending substring '"
       << s3 << "'\n" << s1 << '\n';

  return 0;

}
```

The padends Function

The `padends` function, shown in Listing 14.18, pads the leading and trailing characters of a `cString` instance. The `countAtEachEnd` parameter clearly specifies the number of padded string at each end. The parameter `c` indicates the padding character (by default, a space). The `padends` function expands the size of the string, if required, before calling the `padleft` and `padright` functions.

Listing 14.18. The padends function.

```
//////////////////////////////////////////////////////////////////////
//
cString& cString::padends(unsigned countAtEachEnd, const char c)
//
// Purpose: pad each end of the string object with countAtEachEnd
// c characters.
//
// Parameters:
//
//    input: countAtEachEnd - the number of characters to pad at
//             each end.
//           c - the padding character.
//
{
    countAtEachEnd = (countAtEachEnd == 0) ?
                         1 : countAtEachEnd;
    // does padding result in a bigger string?
    if ((2 * countAtEachEnd + len + 1) > maxSize)
        resize(2 * countAtEachEnd + len + 1);
    // pad to the left
    padleft(countAtEachEnd, c);
    // pad to the right
    padright(countAtEachEnd, c);
    return *this;
}
```

Testing the padends Function

Listing 14.19 offers the source code for the PADENDS.CPP program, which tests the `padends` function. The program creates the instance of `cString`, `s1`, and initializes it with the string `1234567890`. The test program pads two spaces and three plus (+) characters at each end by calling the `padends` function. Because the `padends` function returns a reference to the `cString` class, it is possible to chain the function calls in one statement. The output of the test program is as follows:

```
Main string is '1234567890'
'+++  1234567890  +++'
```

Listing 14.19. The source code for the PADENDS.CPP program.

```
// Test the cString::padends member function

#include <iostream.h>
#include "string.hpp"

main()
{
  cString s1 = "1234567890";

  cout << "\n\n";
  cout << "Main string is '" << s1 << "'" << '\n';

  // pad two spaces and then pad three + characters on each end
  s1.padends(2).padends(3, '+');
  cout << "'" << s1 << "'" << '\n';

  return 0;

}
```

The padleft Function

The `padleft` function, shown in Listing 14.20, pads the leading characters of a `cString` instance. The `count` parameter specifies the number of padded characters. The

parameter c indicates the padding character (by default, a space.) The `padleft` function expands the size of the string if required. The function then moves the original leading characters toward the tail end by calling the `memmove` function. Next, the function calls the `memset` function to set the count leading characters to the character `c`.

Listing 14.20. The `padleft` function.

```
//////////////////////////////////////////////////////////////////////
//
cString& cString::padleft(unsigned count, const char c)
//
// Purpose: pad the left side of the string object with count c
// characters.
//
// Parameters:
//
//    input: count - the number of characters to pad.
//           c - the padding character.
//
{
    count = (count == 0) ? 1 : count;
    // expand the string?
    if ((count + len + 1) > maxSize)
        resize(count + len + 1);
    // move the string character toward the tail end by
    // count characters
    memmove((str + count), str, len+1);
    // set the first count string characters to c
    memset(str, c, count);
    len += count;
    return *this;
}
```

Testing the padleft Function

Listing 14.21 offers the source code for the PADLEFT.CPP program, which tests the `padleft` function. The program creates the instance of `cString`, `s1`, and initializes it with the string `1234567890`. The test program pads two spaces and three plus (+)

characters to the left of the string by calling the `padleft` function. Because the `padleft` function returns a reference to the `cString` class, it is possible to chain the function calls in one statement. The output of the test program is as follows:

```
Main string is '1234567890'
'+++  1234567890'
```

Listing 14.21. The source code for the PADLEFT.CPP program.

```
// Test the cString::padleft member function

#include <iostream.h>
#include "string.hpp"

main()
{
  cString s1 = "1234567890";

  cout << "\n\n";
  cout << "Main string is '" << s1 << "'" << '\n';

  // pad two spaces and then pad three + characters to the left
  s1.padleft(2).padleft(3, '+');
  cout << "'" << s1 << "'" << '\n';

  return 0;

}
```

The padright Function

The `padright` function, shown in Listing 14.22, pads the leading characters of a `cString` instance. The `count` parameter specifies the number of padded characters. The parameter `c` indicates the padding character (by default, a space). The `padright` function expands the size of the string, if required. The function creates a local dynamic string and fills it with the character `c`. The function then appends the local string to the characters of the `cString` instance.

Listing 14.22. The `padright` function.

```
//////////////////////////////////////////////////////////////////
//
cString& cString::padright(unsigned count, const char c)
//
// Purpose: pad the right side of the string object with count c
// characters.
//
// Parameters:
//
//    input: count - the number of characters to pad.
//           c - the padding character.
//
{
    count = (count == 0) ? 1 : count;
    // create a padding string
    char* s = new char[count+1];
    // expand this string?
    if ((count + len + 1) > maxSize)
        resize(count + len + 1);
    // set the characters of local string s to c
    memset(s, c, count);
    s[count] = '\0';
    // concatenate string s to this string
    strcat(str, s);
    len += count;
    // delete local dynamic string
    delete [] s;
    return *this;
}
```

Testing the padright Function

Listing 14.23 offers the source code for the PADRIGHT.CPP program, which tests the `padright` function. The program creates the instance of `cString`, `s1`, and initializes it with the string `1234567890`. The test program pads two spaces and three plus (+) characters to the right of the string by calling the `padright` function. Because the padright function returns a reference to the cString class, it is possible to chain the function calls in one statement. The output of the test program is as follows:

```
Main string is '1234567890'
'1234567890  +++'
```

Listing 14.23. The source code for the PADRIGHT.CPP program.

```
// Test the cString::padright member function

#include <iostream.h>
#include "string.hpp"

main()
{
  cString s1 = "1234567890";

  cout << "\n\n";
  cout << "Main string is '" << s1 << "'" << '\n';

  // pad two spaces and then pad three + characters to the right
  s1.padright(2).padright(3, '+');
  cout << "'" << s1 << "'" << '\n';

  return 0;

}
```

The pos Function

The pos function, shown in Listing 14.24, returns the character index of the first occurrence of s in a cString instance. The Boolean parameter caseSense indicates whether the search is case-sensitive. The parameter start specifies the first character that participates in the search. If the pos function finds no match for the searched string, it returns the NO_SUBSTR_FOUND value.

Your applications can use a while loop statement and the pos function to detect all matching substrings. Here's a short and general example:

```
cString mainS("hellohellohello   hello");
cString subS("lo");
unsigned i;

i = mainS.pos(subS, true);
while (i != NO_SUBSTR_FOUND) {
// process the information at index i

// find the next match
i = mainS.pos(subS, true, i + 1);
}
```

The pos function uses the strstr function (prototyped in string.h) to obtain the pointer to the first matching occurrence of the search string. This function then uses the difference between the address of that pointer and the string's base address to obtain the index of the matching substring. If a case-insensitive search occurs, the function uses uppercase copies of the targeted and search strings.

Listing 14.24. The pos function.

```
/////////////////////////////////////////////////////////////////////
//
unsigned cString::pos(const cString& s,
                      const boolean caseSense,
                      const unsigned start)

//
// Purpose: finds the index of substring s in the string object. The
// search begins at index start. The caseSense parameter determines
// whether the search is case-sensitive. If no match is
// found, the function returns NO_SUBSTR_FOUND
//
// Parameters:
//
//    input: s - the search string.
//           caseSense - case-sensitivity mode.
//           start - the index of the first searched character.
//
{
   if (start >= len)
```

continues

Listing 14.24. continued

```
        return NO_SUBSTR_FOUND;

    if (caseSense) {
        // ****** search IS case-sensitive ******
        // find the pointer to the matching substring
        char* ptr = strstr((str + start), s.str);
        // match found?
        if (ptr)
            return (unsigned)(ptr - str);
        else
            return NO_SUBSTR_FOUND;
    }
    else {
        unsigned offset;

        // create an uppercase copy of string s
        char* s2 = new char[s.len+1];
        strcpy(s2, s.str);
        strupr(s2);
        // create an uppercase copy of this string
        char* str2 = new char[len+1];
        strcpy(str2, str);
        strupr(str2);
        // find the pointer to the matching substring
        char* ptr = strstr((str2 + start), s2);
        // calculate the offset
        offset = (unsigned)(ptr - str2);
        delete [] s2;
        delete [] str2;
        // found any match?
        if (ptr)
            return offset;
        else
            return NO_SUBSTR_FOUND;
    }
}
```

Testing the pos Function

Listing 14.25 shows the source code for the POS.CPP program, which tests the `pos` function. The program creates the string object `s1` and assigns it the characters `hellohellohellohello`. The program assigns the search string `LO` to the string object `s2` and performs the following tasks:

- Displays the string object `s1`.
- Obtains and displays the position of the first occurrence of `s2` in `s1`. The search is case-insensitive.
- Obtains and displays the position of the first occurrence of `s2` in `s1`. The search is case-sensitive.

The output of the test program is as follows:

```
                         1         2         3
               0123456789012345678901234567890
Main string is hellohellohellohello
Case-insensitive position of LO is 3
Case-sensitive position of LO is 65535
```

Listing 14.25. The source code for the POS.CPP program.

```
// Test the cString::pos member function

#include <iostream.h>
#include "string.hpp"

main()
{
  cString s1 = "hellohellohellohello";
  cString s2 = "LO";
  unsigned charPos;

  cout << "\n\n";
  cout << "                         1         2         3" << '\n';
  cout << "               0123456789012345678901234567890" << '\n';
  cout << "Main string is " << s1 << '\n';
```

continues

Listing 14.25. continued

```
    charPos = s1.pos(s2, false);
    cout << "Case-insensitive position of " << s2 <<
            " is " << charPos << '\n';

    charPos = s1.pos(s2, true);
    cout << "Case-sensitive position of " << s2 <<
            " is " << charPos << '\n';

    return 0;

}
```

The print Function

The `print` function, shown in Listing 14.26, allows you to output the characters of a `cString` instance, along with the following items:

- A leading string that can be used to comment the output.
- A trailing character that can be used to insert a new line after the characters of the targeted `cString` instance. If the argument for this character is `\0`, the character is ignored.
- A trailing string that completes the text of the leading string.

Here are two examples of using the `print` function:

```
// example 1
cString s = "1445";
s.print("Size of file = ", '\0', " bytes");

// example 2
cString s = "Namir";
s.print("My name is ", "\n", "")
```

Listing 14.26. The `print` function.

```
////////////////////////////////////////////////////////////////////
//
void cString::print(const cString& str1,
                    const char c,
                    const cString& str2)
//
// Purpose: prints this string with str1 before it and character c
// and string str after it.
//
// Parameters:
//
//     input: str1 - the string leading this string.
//              c - the character following this string
//           str2 - the string following this string
//
{
  cout << str1.str << str;
  if (c != '\0')
     cout << c;
  cout << str2.str;
}
```

The remove Function

The `remove` function, shown in Listing 14.27, deletes some or all of the characters of a `cString` instance. The parameter `start` indicates the index of the first deleted character. The `count` parameter specifies the number of characters to delete. There are two cases for deleting the characters of a `cString` instance:

- The first case deals with truncating these characters. The function simply assigns a null character at the new string tail.
- The second case handles removing characters inside the string. The deleted character may span from the front end of the string.

The `remove` function moves the undeleted trailing characters to the front to overwrite the deleted characters.

Listing 14.27. The remove function.

```
//////////////////////////////////////////////////////////////////////
//
cString& cString::remove(const unsigned start, unsigned count)
//
// Purpose: removes count characters from the string object, beginning
// at index start.
//
// Parameters:
//
//    input: start - the first character to be removed.
//           count - the number of characters to remove.
//
{
   if (start >= len ¦¦ count == 0)
       return *this;

   count = (count == 0xffff) ? (len - start) : count;
   if ((start+count-1) >= len) {
      // truncate string
      *(str+start) = '\0';
      len = start + 1;
   }
   else {
      // move characters to overwrite deleted substring
      memmove((str+start),
              (str+start+count),
              len-start-count+1);
      len -= count;
   }
   return *this;
}
```

Testing the remove Function

Listing 14.28 contains the source code for the REMOVE.CPP program, which tests the `remove` function. The program assigns the string `0123456789` to the `s0` and `s1` instances of the `cString` class. The program tests two cases of deleting characters:

- Deleting characters inside the string `s0`, such that the original leading and trailing characters appear in the resulting string. In this test, the program deletes the characters at indices 4, 5, and 6.
- Deleting the trailing characters of the string `s1`. In this test, the program truncates the trailing characters starting at index 4.

The program output is as follows:

```
Main string is '0123456789'
Deleting characters at index 4, 5, and 6 '0123789'
Deleting characters at index 4 to the end '0123'
```

Listing 14.28. The source code for the REMOVE.CPP program.

```
// Test the cString::remove member function

#include <iostream.h>
#include "string.hpp"

main()
{
  cString s0 = "0123456789";
  cString s1 = s0;

  cout << "\n\n";
  cout << "Main string is '" << s1 << "'" << '\n';

  s1.remove(4, 3);
  cout << "Deleting characters at index 4, 5, and 6 '"
       << s1 << "'\n";

  s0.remove(4);
  cout << "Deleting characters at index 4 to the end '"
       << s0 << "'\n";

  return 0;

}
```

The repeatChar Function

The `repeatChar` function, shown in Listing 14.29, assigns a sequence of the same character to a `cString` instance. The parameter `c` specifies the repeated character. The parameter count indicates the size of the sequence created. If the argument for the `count` parameter is `0`, the function exits leaving the `cString` instance intact. If the argument for `count` is greater than the maximum size of the `cString` instance, the size of the instance is expanded before writing the repeated characters.

Listing 14.29. The `repeatChar` function.

```
//////////////////////////////////////////////////////////////////////
//
cString& cString::repeatChar(const char c, const unsigned count)
//
// Purpose: fills the string object with count c characters. The
// previous string contents are overwritten.
//
// Parameters:
//
//    input: c - the repeated character.
//           count - the number of times to repeat character c.
//
{
  if (count == 0)
    return *this;

  // expand string?
  if (count > maxSize)
    resize(count+1);
  // set string characters to c
  memset(str, c, count);
  str[count] = '\0';
  len = count;
  return *this;
}
```

Testing the repeatChar Function

Listing 14.30 shows the source code for the .CPP program that tests the `repeatChar` function. The test program assigns a string with ten plus (+) characters to the `cString` instance `s1`. The program also assigns a string with five exclamation mark characters (`!`) to the `cString` instance `s2`. The program then concatenates `s1` and `s2` and assigns the result to `s3`. The output is

```
++++++++++!!!!!"
```

Listing 14.30. The source code for the .CPP program.

```
// Test the cString::repeatChar member function

#include <iostream.h>
#include "string.hpp"

main()
{
  cString s1, s2, s3;

  cout << "\n\n";

  s3 = s1.repeatChar('+', 10) + s2.repeatChar('!', 5);
  cout << s3 << '\n';

  return 0;

}
```

The repeatString Function

The `repeatString` function, shown in Listing 14.31, assigns a repeated sequence of a string to the `cString` instance. The parameter `s` specifies the repeated string. The parameter `count` indicates the number of times to concatenate string `s`. The size of the resulting string is equal to `count` times the length of string `s`. If the final size is greater than the initial maximum size of the targeted `cString` instance, the function increases the maximum size to accommodate the repeated strings. The `repeatString` function uses a `for` loop statement and the `memcpy` function to copy the characters of s quickly to the characters of the targeted `cString` instance.

Listing 14.31. The `repeatString` function.

```
////////////////////////////////////////////////////////////////////////////
//
cString& cString::repeatString(cString& s, const unsigned count)
//
// Purpose: fills the string object with count s strings. The
// previous string contents are overwritten.
//
// Parameters:
//
//    input: s - the repeated string.
//           count - the number of times to repeat string s.
//
{
  unsigned newsize = s.len * count;

  if (count==0)
    return *this;

  // expand string?
  if (newsize > maxSize)
    resize(newsize+1);
  // copy the string s into this string
  for (unsigned i = 0; i < count; i++)
     memcpy(str + i * s.len, s.str, s.len);
  str[newsize] = '\0';
  len = newsize;
  return *this;
}
```

Testing the repeatString Function

Listing 14.32 shows the source code for the REPSTRIN.CPP program, which tests the `repeatString` function. The program creates a `cString` instance, `s1`, which is

initialized with the string `0123456789`. The program assigns three concatenated copies of string `s1` to string `s2`. The program output is

```
Repeating string '0123456789' three times gives
012345678901234567890123456789
```

Listing 14.32. The source code for the REPSTRIN.CPP program.

```
// Test the cString::repeatString member function

#include <iostream.h>
#include "string.hpp"

main()
{
  cString s1("0123456789"), s2;

  cout << "\n\n";

  cout << "Repeating string '" << s1
       << "' three times gives" << '\n';
  s2.repeatString(s1, 3);
  cout << s2 << '\n';

  return 0;

}
```

The replace Function

The `replace` function, shown in Listing 14.33, replaces occurrences of parameter `findstr` with parameter `replacestr`. The argument for parameter `replacestr` can be an empty string. The reference parameter `count` returns the actual number of substrings replaced. The Boolean parameter `caseSense` indicates whether the translation is case-sensitive. The default argument for this parameter is `true` to support case-sensitive translation. The parameter `start` specifies the index of a `cString` instance at which the translation begins. The `freq` parameter indicates the maximum number of substring translations. The default arguments for the start and freq parameters are 0 and 0xffff, respectively. These values support translating all of the occurrences of findstr in a cString instance.

The replace function calls the pos function to locate the first position of findstr in the targeted cString instance. The function then uses a while loop to iterate as long as the matching position of findstr is not NO_SUBSTR_FOUND and the current value of freq is positive. Each iteration of the while loop performs the following tasks:

1. Decrements the freq parameter.
2. Increments the count parameter.
3. Removes the findstr string from the targeted cString instance at index match_pos.
4. Updates the new string length (stored in the local variable new_len). This new value accounts for the difference in lengths between the strings findstr and replacestr.
5. Expands the string if the value of new_len exceeds the current maximum string size.
6. Inserts replacestr at index match_pos if replacestr is not an empty string.
7. Adjusts the value for match_pos to prepare for finding the next occurrence of string findstr.
8. Locates the position of the next findstr.

Listing 14.33. The replace function.

```
//////////////////////////////////////////////////////////////////////
//
cString& cString::replace(const cString& findstr,
                          const cString& replacestr,
                          unsigned& count,
                          const boolean caseSense,
                          const unsigned start,
                          unsigned freq)
//
// Purpose: replace freq occurrences of substring findstr in this
// string with replace substring, starting at index start. The
```

```
// caseSense parameter determines whether the translation
// is case-sensitive. The count parameter returns the actual
// number of translations
//
// Parameters:
//
//    input: findstr - the string to replace.
//           replacestr - the replacement string.
//           caseSense - the case-sensitivity flag.
//           start - the first character affected by the
//             string replacement.
//           freq - the requested number of times to replace string
//             findstr.
//
//     output:
//           count - the number of times string findstr is actually
//             replaced.
//
{
    unsigned findlen = findstr.len;
    unsigned repl_strlen = replacestr.len;
    unsigned new_len;
    unsigned match_pos;

    count = 0;
    //-----------------Argument-checking----------------
    if ( ((findlen * len) == 0) || (start >= len) ) {
       strErr = NULL_STRING;
       return *this;
    }
    // find the first position of findstr in this string
    match_pos = pos(findstr, caseSense, start);
    // loop while there is a matching findstr substring
    while (match_pos != NO_SUBSTR_FOUND && freq > 0) {
        // decrement the freq count
        freq--;
        // increment the reference count parameter
        count++;
        // remove string found
        remove((unsigned)match_pos, findlen);
```

continues

Listing 14.33. continued

```
        // check new string length
        new_len = len + repl_strlen - findlen;
        if ((new_len+1) > maxSize)
            resize(new_len+1);
        // replace it with new string
     if (repl_strlen > 0)
         insert(replacestr, (int) match_pos);

        // find next matching strings
        match_pos += 1 + repl_strlen - findlen;
        if (match_pos > 0)
            match_pos = pos(findstr, caseSense, (unsigned)match_pos);
        else
            match_pos = pos(findstr, caseSense);
    }

   return *this;
}
```

Testing the replace Function

Listing 14.34 contains the source code for the REPLACE.CPP program, which tests the `replace` function. The program creates the `cString` instances `s1` and `s2` and assigns the string `The rain in Spain stays mainly in the plain`. The program then tests the use of the replace function in the following ways:

- Performs a case-sensitive translation by replacing the substring `ain` with `ayn`. The translation starts at index `10` and allows for up to two occurrences of `ain` to be replaced.
- Carries out a case-insensitive translation by replacing the substring `AYN` with `AIN`. The translation starts at index `0`. The default argument for `freq` (`0`) is used in this call to function `replace`; the `freq` parameter is included for the sake of demonstration.
- Performs a case-sensitive translation by replacing the substring `AIN` with `ain`. The translation starts at index `0` and specifies up to 100 replacements. This relatively high number ensures the translation of all the specified substrings.

The output of the test program is as follows:

```
Main string is 'The rain in Spain stays mainly in the plain'
2 occurrences of 'ain' were replaced with 'ayn'
'The rain in Spayn stays maynly in the plain'
2 occurrences of 'AYN' were replaced with 'AIN'
'The rain in SpAIN stays mAINly in the plain'
4 occurrences of 'AIN' were replaced with 'ain'
'The rain in Spain stays mainly in the plain'
```

Listing 14.34. The source code for the REPLACE.CPP program.

```
// Test the cString::replace member function

#include <iostream.h>
#include "string.hpp"

main()
{
  cString s1 = "The rain in Spain stays mainly in the plain";
  cString s2 = s1;
  unsigned count;

  cout << "\n\n";
  cout << "Main string is '" << s1 << "'" << '\n';

  s1.replace("ain", "ayn", count, true, 10, 2);
  cout << count << " occurrences of 'ain' were replaced with 'ayn'"
       << '\n' << "'" << s1 << "'" << '\n';

  s1.replace("AYN", "AIN", count, false, 0);
  cout << count << " occurrences of 'AYN' were replaced with 'AIN'"
       << '\n' << "'" << s1 << "'" << '\n';

  s1.replace("AIN", "ain", count, true, 0, 100);
  cout << count << " occurrences of 'AIN' were replaced with 'ain'"
       << '\n' << "'" << s1 << "'" << '\n';
  return 0;

}
```

The replaceChars Function

The replaceChars function, shown in Listing 14.35, replaces the characters specified in the parameter findchar with the character specified by the replacechar parameter. The parameters first and last indicate the range of indices for the replaced characters.

The replaceChars function uses a for loop to process each character in the findchar parameter. The loop statements include a call to the protected function replaceOnChar to replace a character in findchar with the replacechar parameter. Listing 14.36 shows the replaceOneChar function.

Listing 14.35. The replaceChars function.

```
///////////////////////////////////////////////////////////////////////
//
cString& cString::replaceChars(const cString& findchar,
                               const char replacechar,
                               const unsigned first,
                               const unsigned last)
//
// Purpose: replace the characters of this string that are in
// findchar with replacechar, beginning at index first and
// ending at index last.
//
// Parameters:
//
//    input: findchar - the set of replaced characters.
//           replacechar - the set of replacement characters.
//           first - the index of the first replaced character
//           last - the index of the last replaced character.
//
{
    unsigned findlen = findchar.len;
    unsigned Last = (last != 0xffff) ? last : len - 1;
    char c;

    if (first >= len || first > last)
        return *this;

    if (findlen > 0) {
```

```
        for (unsigned i = 0; i < findlen; i++) {
            c = *(findchar.str + i);
            // call member function replaceOnChar
            replaceOneChar(c, replacechar, first, Last);
        }
    }
    return *this;
}
```

Listing 14.36. The `replaceOneChar` function.

```
//////////////////////////////////////////////////////////////////
//
cString& cString::replaceOneChar(char findchar,
                                 char replacechar,
                                 unsigned start,
                                 unsigned last)
//
// Purpose: replaces a single character with another.
//
// Parameters:
//
//    input: findchar - the character to find.
//           replacechar - the replacement character.
//           first - the character index at which the replacement
//             process begins.
//           last - the character index at which the replacement
//             process ends.
//
// Comments: if the argument for first is not less than the length of
// the string, the function returns the string as is.
{
    char s[] = " ";
    unsigned offset;
    char* ptr;

    last = (last != 0xffff) ? last : len - 1;
```

continues

Listing 14.36. continued

```
    if (start < len) {
        // assign findchar to the first character of string s
        s[0] = findchar;
        do {
           // search for string s in the target string object
           ptr = strstr((str + start), s);
           // found a match?
           if (ptr) {
               // get the character offset
               offset = (unsigned)(ptr - str);
               if (offset <= last)
                 // overwrite the target character with replacechar
                 str[offset] = replacechar;
               else
                 // matching character is beyond the specified range
                 ptr = NULL;
           }
        } while (ptr);
    }
    return *this;
}
```

Testing the replaceChars Function

Listing 14.37 shows the source code for the REPLCHAR.CPP program, which tests the `replaceChars` function. The program assigns the following string to the `cString` instance `s1`:

```
(A1 + A2) / A3 * (A0 - A2)
```

The program tests two cases of replacing the digits in the previous strings with the exclamation mark character (`!`):

- Replacing the digits for the index range of 5 to 15. In this case, the program calls the `replaceChars` function and supplies it with the arguments `5` and `15` for the `first` and `last` parameters, respectively.
- Replacing the digits in the entire string. Here, the program calls the function `replaceChars` and uses the default arguments for parameters `first` and `last`.

The output for the test program is as follows:

```
                      1         2         3
            0123456789012345678901234567890
Main string is (A1 + A2) / A3 * (A0 - A2)
Replacing characters 0123456789 with character '!'
for indices 5 to 15 yields:
(A1 + A!) / A! * (A0 - A2)
Replacing characters 0123456789 with character '!'
for the entire string yields:
(A! + A!) / A! * (A! - A!)
```

Listing 14.37. The source code for the REPLCHAR.CPP program.

```
// Test the cString::replaceChars member function

#include <iostream.h>
#include "string.hpp"

main()
{
  cString s1 = "(A1 + A2) / A3 * (A0 - A2)";

  cout << "\n\n";
  cout << "                         1         2         3\n";
  cout << "               0123456789012345678901234567890\n";
  cout << "Main string is " << s1 << '\n';
  cout << "Replacing characters 0123456789 with character '!'\n"
       << "for indices 5 to 15 yields:\n";

  s1.replaceChars("0123456789", '!', 5, 15);
  cout << s1 << '\n';

  cout << "Replacing characters 0123456789 with character '!'\n"
       << "for the entire string yields:\n";

  s1.replaceChars("0123456789", '!');
  cout << s1 << '\n';


  return 0;

}
```

The replaceRangeChars Function

The `replaceRangeChars` function, shown in Listing 14.38, replaces a range of characters in a specified range of character indices. The parameters `firstChar` and `lastChar` define the range of characters to replace. The parameter `replacechar` specifies the replacement character. The parameters `first` and `last` define the range of characters in the targeted `cString` instance that are affected by the character replacement process.

The function uses a `for` loop statement to scan the characters at the indices `first` to `last`. If the current character is in the range of `firstChar` and `lastChar`, the function replaces that character with `replacechar`.

Listing 14.38. The `replaceRangeChars` function.

```
///////////////////////////////////////////////////////////////////
//
cString& cString::replaceRangeChars(const char firstChar,
                                    const char lastChar,
                                    const char replacechar,
                                    const unsigned first,
                                    const unsigned last)
//
// Purpose: replaces all the characters of this string that are in
// the range [firstChar..lastChar] with replacechar. The replacement
// begins at index first and stops after index last.
//
// Parameters:
//
//    input: firstChar, lastChar - the range of replaced characters.
//           replacechar - the replacement character.
//           first - the index of the first replaced character.
//           last - the index of the last replaced character.
//
{
    char c;
    unsigned Last = (last != 0xffff) ? last : len - 1;

    if (first >= len ||
        first > last ||
        len == 0     ||
```

```
        firstChar > lastChar)
        return *this;

    for (unsigned i = first; i <= Last; i++) {
        c = *(str + i);
        if (c >= firstChar && c <= lastChar)
            *(str + i) = replacechar;
    }
    return *this;
}
```

Testing the replaceRangeChars Function

Listing 14.39 shows the source code for the REPLRANG.CPP program, which tests the `replaceRangeChars` function. The program assigns the following string to the `cString` instance `s1`:

```
(A1 + A2) / A3 * (A0 - A2)
```

The program tests two cases of replacing the digits 0 to 9 in the previous strings with the `!` character:

- Replacing the digits for the index range of 5 to 15. In this case, the program calls the `replaceRangeChars` function and supplies it with the arguments `5` and `15` for the first and last parameters, respectively.
- Replacing the digits in the entire string. Here, the program calls the function `replaceRangeChars` and uses the default arguments for parameters `first` and `last`.

The output for the test program is as follows:

```
                          1         2         3
               0123456789012345678901234567890
Main string is (A1 + A2) / A3 * (A0 - A2)
Replacing characters '0' to '9' with character '!'
for indices 5 to 15 yields:
(A1 + A!) / A! * (A0 - A2)
Replacing characters '0' to '9' with character '!'
for the entire string yields:
(A! + A!) / A! * (A! - A!)
```

Listing 14.39. The source code for the REPLRANG.CPP program.

```
// Test the cString::replaceRangeChars member function

#include <iostream.h>
#include "string.hpp"

main()
{
  cString s1 = "(A1 + A2) / A3 * (A0 - A2)";

  cout << "\n\n";
  cout << "                         1         2         3\n";
  cout << "              0123456789012345678901234567890\n";
  cout << "Main string is " << s1 << '\n';
  cout << "Replacing characters '0' to '9' with character '!'\n"
       << "for indices 5 to 15 yields:\n";

  s1.replaceRangeChars('0', '9', '!', 5, 15);
  cout << s1 << '\n';

 cout << "Replacing characters '0' to '9' with character '!'\n"
      << "for the entire string yields:\n";

  s1.replaceRangeChars('0', '9', '!');
  cout << s1 << '\n';

  return 0;

}
```

The resize Function

The `resize` function, shown in Listing 14.40, has the important task of expanding the maximum string size of a `cString` instance. The `resize` function performs the following basic tasks:

1. Creates the new string.
2. Copies the characters from the old string to the new string.

3. Deletes dynamic space occupied by the characters of the old string.
4. Updates the data members.

The `resize` function calculates the adjusted new size using the `sizeIncr` data member. Therefore, the actual new maximum size of a `cString` instance is most likely slightly larger—by no more than `sizeIncr` bytes—than the requested new size.

Listing 14.40. The `resize` function.

```
//////////////////////////////////////////////////////////////////////
//
cString& cString::resize(unsigned new_size)

//
// Purpose: resize the string object to new_size + 1 bytes.
//
// Parameters:
//
//    input: new_size - the new string size.
//
{
   unsigned current_len = len;

   // exit if new_size is actually smaller than the current size
   if (maxSize >= new_size) return *this;

   // if new_size is not a perfect multiple of sizeIncr,
   // increase new_size
   if (((new_size / sizeIncr) * sizeIncr) < new_size)
       new_size = ((new_size / sizeIncr) + 1) * sizeIncr;

   // create new string
   char* strcopy = new char[new_size+1];
   // copy characters from the current string to the new string
   strcpy(strcopy, str);
   // delete this string
   delete [] str;
   maxSize = new_size;
```

continues

Listing 14.40. continued

```
        // copy pointers
        str = strcopy;
        len = current_len;
        return *this;
}
```

The right Function

The `right` function, shown in Listing 14.41, extracts the right portion of a `cString` instance. The parameter `count` specifies the rightmost characters to extract. If the argument for `count` is greater than the actual length of the string instance, the function pads it with the `padchar` character. The default argument for `padchar` is the space character, the most common padding character. The resulting string contains `count` characters.

Listing 14.41. The right function.

```
//////////////////////////////////////////////////////////////////////
//
cString& cString::right(unsigned count, const char padchar)

//
// Purpose: extracts the count rightmost characters.
//
// Parameters:
//
//    input: count - the new string size.
//           padchar - the padding character.
//
{
    count = (count == 0) ? 1 : count;
    if (count < len) {
      strcpy(str, (str + len - count));
      len = count;
    }
    else if (count > len) {
```

```
        unsigned padlen = count - len;
        char* s = new char[padlen+1];
        memset(s, padchar, padlen);
        s[padlen] = '\0';
        strcat(str, s);
        len = count;
        delete [] s;
    }
    return *this;
}
```

Testing the right Function

Listing 14.42 contains the source code for the RIGHT.CPP program, which tests the `right` function. The program tests various cases of using the `right` function by applying the following steps:

1. Extracts the five rightmost characters from `s1`, which is initialized with the characters `1234567890`.
2. Extracts the six rightmost characters from `s1`. Because the string was truncated to five characters in the previous step, this step actually appends one character. The right function uses the default space argument because the function call to `right` does not specify the padding character.
3. Extracts the ten rightmost characters from `s1`. Because the string is six characters long, this step appends four more characters. This time, the call to the `right` function specifies to append the plus (+) character.

The output of the test program is as follows:

```
Main string is '1234567890'
'67890'
'67890 '
'67890 ++++'
```

The program encloses the strings in single quotes so you can detect the spaces that are part of the string.

Listing 14.42. The source code for the RIGHT.CPP program.

```
// Test the cString::right member function

#include <iostream.h>
#include "string.hpp"

main()
{
  cString s1 = "1234567890";

  cout << "\n\n";
  cout << "Main string is '" << s1 << "'" << '\n';

  s1.right(5);
  cout << "'" << s1 << "'" << '\n';

  s1.right(6);
  cout << "'" << s1 << "'" << '\n';

  s1.right(10, '+');
  cout << "'" << s1 <<"'" << '\n';

  return 0;

}
```

The C-String Wrapper Member Functions

Listing 14.43 contains the set of C-string wrapper functions. These functions are shells for some of the string manipulation functions that are prototyped in the string.h header file. The functions in Listing 14.43 include `stringchr`, `stringcspn`, `stringlwr`, `stringncat`, `stringnset`, `stringpbrk`, `stringrchr`, `stringrev`, `stringset`, `stringspn`, `stringstr`, `stringtok`, and `stringupr`. The names of these functions are derived from the names of the functions they wrap. For example, the function `stringstr` is a wrapper for the `strstr` function. I added the letters `ing` to the name of the functions.

The functions in Listing 14.43 return a reference value to the `cString` class. Consequently, these functions act on the `cString` instance that invokes them. Therefore, to maintain the original `cString` instance and obtain another instance modified by one of these functions, you must create a copy of the original instance and then manipulate the copy.

Listing 14.43. The set of C-string wrapper functions.

```
//////////////////////////////////////////////////////////////////////
//
cString& cString::stringchr(const char c)
{
  strcpy(str, strchr(str, c));
  return *this;
}

//////////////////////////////////////////////////////////////////////
//
unsigned cString::stringcspn(const cString& s)
{
    return strcspn(str, s.str);
}

//////////////////////////////////////////////////////////////////////
//
cString& cString::stringlwr()
{
   strlwr(str);
   return *this;
}

//////////////////////////////////////////////////////////////////////
//
cString& cString::stringncat(const cString& s, const unsigned n)
{
    if (s.str && n)
    {
        resize(len + s.len);
        strncat(str, s.str, n);
```

continues

Listing 14.43. continued

```
    }
    return *this;
}

///////////////////////////////////////////////////////////////////////
//
cString& cString::stringnset(const char c, const unsigned n)
{
  strcpy(str, strnset(str, (int)c, n));
  return *this;
}

///////////////////////////////////////////////////////////////////////
//
cString& cString::stringpbrk(const cString& s)
{
    strcpy(str, strpbrk(str, s.str));
    return *this;
}

///////////////////////////////////////////////////////////////////////
//
cString& cString::stringrchr(const char c)
{
  strcpy(str, strrchr(str, c));
  return *this;
}

///////////////////////////////////////////////////////////////////////
//
cString& cString::stringrev()
{
   strcpy(str, strrev(str));
   return *this;
}

///////////////////////////////////////////////////////////////////////
//
cString& cString::stringset(const char c)
{
```

```
  strcpy(str, strset(str, c));
  return *this;
}

//////////////////////////////////////////////////////////////////
//
unsigned cString::stringspn(const cString& s)
{
    return strspn(str, s.str);
}

//////////////////////////////////////////////////////////////////
//
cString& cString::stringstr(const cString& s)
{
   strcpy(str, strstr(str, s.str));
   len = strlen(str);
   return *this;
}

//////////////////////////////////////////////////////////////////
//
cString& cString::stringtok(cString& source,
                           const char* tokenchars,
                           const boolean getFirst)
{
    char* p = strtok((getFirst == true) ? source.str : NULL,
                     tokenchars);

    if (p) {
        len = strlen(p);
        if ((len+1) > maxSize)
            resize(len+1);
        strcpy(str, p);
    }
    else {
        str[0] = '\0';
        len = 0;
    }
    return *this;
}
```

continues

Listing 14.43. continued

```
//////////////////////////////////////////////////////////////////////
//
cString& cString::stringupr()
{
   strupr(str);
   return *this;
}
```

The substring Function

The `substring` function, shown in Listing 14.44, returns a `cString` result that contains all or part of a `cString` instance. The parameter `s` specifies the source string. The parameters `first` and `last` indicate the range of characters to extract. The substring function performs the following tasks:

1. Returns an empty string if the argument for `first` is greater than that of `last`.
2. Adjusts the arguments of `first` and `last` if either or both arguments exceed the actual length of `s`.
3. Makes a second comparison between the possibly adjusted values of `first` and `last`. If `first` is greater than `last`, the function returns an empty string.
4. Assigns the argument of `s` to the local `cString` instance, `result`.
5. If the value of `first` is positive, the function removes the leading characters in string `results`. This task also adjusts the values of `last` and `result.len` to account for the deleted characters.
6. If the value of `last` is less than `result.len`, the function deletes the unneeded trailing characters.
7. Returns the string `result`.

Listing 14.44. The substring function.

```
//////////////////////////////////////////////////////////////////////
//
cString substring(const cString& s,
                  unsigned first,
                  unsigned last)
//
// Purpose: extracts the characters of string s, starting from
// those at index first to index last.
//
// Parameters:
//
//    input: s - the target string.
//           first - the index of the first extracted character.
//           last - the index of the last extracted character.
//
{
    cString result;

    if (last < first) // bad arguments
       return result;

    if (first > s.len) first = s.len;
    if (last > s.len)  last = s.len;
    // second comparison of first and last values
    if (first > last)
      return result;

    result = s;

    if (first > 0) {
        result.remove(0, first);
        last -= first; // adjust value of last
        // update len with new string length
        result.len -= first;
    }

    if (last < result.len)
      result.remove((last+1), (result.len-last));

    return result;
}
```

Testing the substring Function

Listing 14.45 contains the source code for the SUBSTR.CPP program, which tests the `substring` function. The program assigns the string `1234567890` to the `cString` instance `s1`. The program then tests the following cases of extracting parts of `s1`:

1. Extracting characters that exclude leading or trailing parts of `s1`. The arguments for the first and last parameters are `1` and `5`, respectively.
2. Extracting to the end of the string. The arguments for the first and last parameters are `2` and `0fxxxx`, respectively.
3. Extracting characters starting with the first character in `s1`. The arguments for the `first` and `last` parameters are `0` and `5`, respectively.
4. Extracting the entire string `s1`. The arguments for the `first` and `last` parameters are `0` and `0fxxxx`, respectively.

The output of the test program is as follows:

```
Main string is '1234567890'
Substring from index 1 to 5 is '23456'
Substring from index 2 to the end is '34567890'
Substring from index 0 to 5 is '123456'
Substring from index 0 to the end is '1234567890'
```

Listing 14.45. The source code for the SUBSTR.CPP program.

```
// Test the cString::substring member function

#include <iostream.h>
#include "string.hpp"

main()
{
  cString s1 = "1234567890";
  cString s2;

  cout << "\n\n";
  cout << "Main string is '" << s1 << "'" << '\n';

  s2 = substring(s1, 1, 5);
  cout << "Substring from index 1 to 5 is '" << s2 << "'" << '\n';
```

```
    s2 = substring(s1, 2, 0xffff);
    cout << "Substring from index 2 to the end is '" << s2
         << "'" << '\n';

    s2 = substring(s1, 0, 5);
    cout << "Substring from index 0 to 5 is '" << s2
         << "'" << '\n';

    s2 = substring(s1, 0, 0xffff);
    cout << "Substring from index 0 to the end is '" << s2
         << "'" << '\n';

    return 0;

}
```

The trimends Function

The `trimends` function, shown in Listing 14.46, trims the leading and trailing character `c` from a `cString` instance. The default argument for the `c` parameter is the space character; this is the most common character to trim from strings. The `c` parameter enables you to specify a character other than the space if a different character meets your application's needs. The `trimends` function calls the `trimleft` and `trimright` functions to actually perform the character trimming.

Listing 14.46. The `trimends` function.

```
/////////////////////////////////////////////////////////////////////
//
cString& cString::trimends(const char c)

//
// Purpose: removes character c from both ends of this string.
//
// Parameters:
//
```

continues

Listing 14.46. continued

```
//    input: c - the trimmed character.
//
{
   trimleft(c);
   trimright(c);
   return *this;
}
```

Testing the trimends Function

Listing 14.47 shows the source code for the TRIMENDS.CPP program, which tests the `trimends` function. The test program assigns the string `'+++++1234567890+++++'` to the `cString` instance `s1`. The program trims the leading and trailing spaces by calling the `trimends` function without specifying an argument for parameter `c`. This call removes the leading and trailing spaces. The new string has leading and trailing + characters. To remove these characters, the program calls the `trimends` function with the argument +. The output of the test program is as follows:

```
Main string is '    +++++1234567890+++++    '
After trimming the spaces, the string is '+++++1234567890+++++'
After trimming the + characters, the string is '1234567890'
```

Listing 14.47. The source code for the TRIMENDS.CPP program.

```
// Test the cString::trimends member function

#include <iostream.h>
#include "string.hpp"

main()
{
  cString s1 = "    +++++1234567890+++++    ";

  cout << "\n\n";
  cout << "Main string is '" << s1 << "'" << '\n';
```

```
   s1.trimends();
   cout << "After trimming the spaces, the string is '"
        << s1 << "'" << '\n';
   s1.trimends('+');
   cout << "After trimming the + characters, the string is '"
        << s1 << "'" << '\n';
   return 0;

}
```

The trimleft Function

The `trimleft` function, shown in Listing 14.48, trims the leading characters of a `cString` instance that match the argument of parameter `c`. The default argument for `c` is the space character. The `trimleft` function uses a `for` loop to count the number of leading string characters that match the parameter `c`. The function stores that number in the local variable `count` and then calls the `remove` function to delete these leading characters.

You can create an overloaded version of `trimleft` that has a string parameter. This version enables you to trim the leading characters that match any character in the string parameter. The trimming stops when the overloaded function finds a character that is not in the string parameter. Such a function can replace multiple calls to the `trimleft` function, shown in Listing 14.48.

Listing 14.48. The `trimleft` function.

```
//////////////////////////////////////////////////////////////////
//
cString& cString::trimleft(const char c)
//
// Purpose: removes the leading character c from this string object.
//
// Parameters:
//
//    input: c - the trimmed character.
//
```

continues

Listing 14.48. continued

```
{
   unsigned i, count = 0;

   for (i = 0; ( (*(str+i) != '\0') &&
               (*(str+i) == c) ); i++)
      count++;

   remove(0, count);
   return *this;
}
```

Testing the trimleft Function

Listing 14.49 shows the source code for the TRIMLEFT.CPP program, which tests the `trimleft` function. The program assigns the string `'     +++++1234567890+++++     '` to the `cString` instance `s1`. The program trims the leading spaces by calling the `trimleft` function without specifying an argument for `c`. This call removes the leading spaces. The new string has leading + characters. To remove these characters, the program calls the `trimleft` function with the argument +. The output of the test program is as follows:

```
Main string is '     +++++1234567890+++++     '
After trimming the leading spaces, the string is:
'+++++1234567890+++++     '
After trimming the leading + characters, the string is:
'1234567890+++++     '
```

Listing 14.49. The source code for the TRIMLEFT.CPP program.

```
// Test the cString::trimleft member function

#include <iostream.h>
#include "string.hpp"

main()
{
  cString s1 = "     +++++1234567890+++++     ";
```

```
    cout << "\n\n";
    cout << "Main string is '" << s1 << "'" << '\n';

    s1.trimleft();
    cout << "After trimming the leading spaces, the string is:"
         << "\n'" << s1 << "'\n";

    s1.trimleft('+');
    cout << "After trimming the leading + characters, the string is:"
         << "\n'" << s1 << "'\n";

    return 0;

}
```

The trimright Function

The `trimright` function, shown in Listing 14.50, trims the leading characters of a `cString` instance that match the argument of `c`. The default argument for `c` is the space character. The `trimright` function uses a `for` loop to count the number of trailing string characters that match `c`. The function stores that number in the local variable `count` and then assigns the null character to the appropriate index. The function also decreases the member `len` by the number of trimmed characters.

You can create an overloaded version of `trimright` that has a string parameter. This version enables you to trim the trailing characters that match any character in the string parameter. The trimming stops when the overloaded function finds a character that's not in the string parameter. Such a function can replace multiple calls to the `trimright` function, shown in Listing 14.50.

Listing 14.50. The `trimright` function.

```
////////////////////////////////////////////////////////////////////
//
cString& cString::trimright(const char c)
//
```

continues

Listing 14.50. continued

```
// Purpose: removes the trailing character c from this string
// object.
//
// Parameters:
//
//    input: c - the trimmed character.
//
{
   unsigned i, count = 0;
   if (len == 0) {
      strErr = NULL_STRING;
      return *this; // exit if string is empty
   }
   for (i = len-1; *(str+i) == c; i--)
      count++;

   *(str+len-count) = '\0';
   len -= count;
   return *this;
}
```

Testing the trimright Function

Listing 14.51 shows the source code for the TRIMRIGH.CPP program, which tests the `trimright` function. The test program assigns the string `'    +++++1234567890+++++    '` to the `cString` instance `s1`. The program trims the trailing spaces by calling the `trimright` function without specifying an argument for `c`. This call removes the trailing spaces. The new string has trailing + characters. To remove these characters, the program calls the `trimright` function with the argument `+`. The output of the test program is as follows:

```
Main string is '    +++++1234567890+++++    '
After trimming the trailing spaces, the string is:
'    +++++1234567890+++++'
After trimming the trailing + characters, the string is:
'    +++++1234567890'
```

Listing 14.51. The source code for the TRIMRIGH.CPP program.

```
// Test the cString::trimright member function

#include <iostream.h>
#include "string.hpp"

main()
{
  cString s1 = "     +++++1234567890+++++    ";

  cout << "\n\n";
  cout << "Main string is '" << s1 << "'" << '\n';


  s1.trimright();
  cout << "After trimming the trailing spaces, the string is:"
       << "\n'" << s1 << "'\n";
  s1.trimright('+');
  cout << "After trimming the trailing + characters, the string is:"
       << "\n'" << s1 << "'\n";

  return 0;

}
```

The trimSequenceChars Function

The `trimSequenceChars` function, shown in Listing 14.52, replaces sequences of the same character with a single occurrence of that character. The `c` specifies the trimmed character. The default argument for the parameter is the space character. The function uses a `while` loop to test whether the sequence of two characters matches the parameter `c`. If the previous condition is true, the function uses the `memmove` function to overwrite the second character and decrease the value of member `len`. Otherwise, the function increments the character index variable `i`.

Listing 14.52. The `trimSequenceChars` function.

```
//////////////////////////////////////////////////////////////////////
//
cString& cString::trimSequenceChars(const char c)
//
// Purpose: replaces the sequence of character c with a single
// occurrence.
//
// Parameters:
//
//    input: c - the trimmed character.
//
{
    unsigned i = 0;

    if (len > 0) {
        while (i < len)
            if (str[i] == c && str[i+1] == c) {
                memmove((str+i+1), (str+i+2), len - 1 + i);
                len--;
            }
            else
                i++;
    }
    return *this;
}
```

Testing the trimSequenceChars Function

Listing 14.53 contains the source code for the TRIMSEQ.CPP program, which tests `trimSequenceChars`. The program assigns the string `Namir   Clement    Shammas` to the `cString` instance `s1`. The program then removes the extra spaces by calling the function `trimSequenceChars`. The call specifies no argument because the default argument is adequate. The output of the test program is as follows:

```
Main String is 'Namir   Clement    Shammas'
After removing sequence of spaces, the string is
'Namir Clement Shammas'
```

Listing 14.53. The source code for the TRIMSEQ.CPP program.

```
// Test the cString::trimSequenceChars member function

#include <iostream.h>
#include "string.hpp"

main()
{
  cString s1 = "Namir   Clement    Shammas";

  cout << "\n\n";
  cout << "Main string is '" << s1 << "'" << '\n';


  s1.trimSequenceChars();
  cout << "After removing sequence of spaces, the string is:"
       << "\n'" << s1 << "'\n";

  return 0;

}
```

Operators

The Assignment Operators

Listing 14.54 shows the source code of the three assignment operators (=). These operators return the reference to the `cString` class and enable you to assign:

- A `cString` instance
- A C-style string
- A single character to a `cString` instance

Although the first two versions of the assignment operator may seem redundant (because the compiler can use the constructors to convert `const char*` to `cString`), they offer faster operation because no conversion is involved.

Listing 14.54. The assignment (=) operators.

```
//////////////////////////////////////////////////////////////////////
//
cString& cString::operator =(const cString& s)
{
   len = s.len;
   if ((len+1) > maxSize)
       resize(len+1);
   strcpy(str, s.str);
   return *this;
}

//////////////////////////////////////////////////////////////////////
//
cString& cString::operator =(const char* s)
{
    len = strlen(s);
    if ((len+1) > maxSize)
        resize(len+1);
    strcpy(str,s);
    return *this;
}

//////////////////////////////////////////////////////////////////////
//
cString& cString::operator =(const char c)
{
  len = 1;
  *str = c;
  *(str+1) = '\0';
  return *this;
}
```

The Access Operator

The access operator (`[]`), shown in Listing 14.55, allows you to access a character in a `cString` instance by specifying its index. If the index is out-of-range, the function returns the reference to the badindex data member. I demonstrate the use of the [] operator later in this chapter.

Listing 14.55. The access operator ([]).

```
/////////////////////////////////////////////////////////////////////////
//
char& cString::operator [](const unsigned i)
{
   if (checkBounds(i)) {
      return *(str + i);
   }
   else {
      strErr = BAD_INDEX;
      return badindex;
   }
}
```

The Relational Operators

Listing 14.56 offers the relational operators >, >=, <, <=, ==, and !=. Relational operators enable you to write logical expressions that are easier to read. These operators are simple shells that use the strcmp function prototyped in the header file string.h. Relational operators come in two flavors:

- The first uses const cString& arguments
- The second use the const char* types

Listing 14.56. The relational operators >, >=, <, <=, ==, and !=.

```
/////////////////////////////////////////////////////////////////////////
//
int cString::operator >(const cString& s)
{
   return strcmp(str,s.str) > 0;
}
```

continues

Listing 14.56. continued

```
/////////////////////////////////////////////////////////////////////
//
int cString::operator >=(const cString& s)
{
   return strcmp(str,s.str) >= 0;
}

/////////////////////////////////////////////////////////////////////
//
int cString::operator ==(const cString& s)
{
   return strcmp(str,s.str) == 0;
}

/////////////////////////////////////////////////////////////////////
//
int cString::operator <(const cString& s)
{
   return strcmp(str,s.str) < 0;
}

/////////////////////////////////////////////////////////////////////
//
int cString::operator <=(const cString& s)
{
   return strcmp(str,s.str) <= 0;
}

/////////////////////////////////////////////////////////////////////
//
int cString::operator !=(const cString& s)
{
   return strcmp(str,s.str) != 0;
}

/////////////////////////////////////////////////////////////////////
//
```

```
int cString::operator >(const char* s)
{
   return strcmp(str,s) > 0;
}

//////////////////////////////////////////////////////////////////////
//
int cString::operator >=(const char* s)
{
   return strcmp(str,s) >= 0;
}

//////////////////////////////////////////////////////////////////////
//
int cString::operator ==(const char* s)
{
   return strcmp(str,s) == 0;
}

//////////////////////////////////////////////////////////////////////
//
int cString::operator <(const char* s)
{
   return strcmp(str,s) < 0;
}

//////////////////////////////////////////////////////////////////////
//
int cString::operator <=(const char* s)
{
   return strcmp(str,s) <= 0;
}

//////////////////////////////////////////////////////////////////////
//
int cString::operator !=(const char* s)
{
   return strcmp(str,s) != 0;
}
```

The Concatenation Operator

Listing 14.57 shows the source code for the concatenation operator (+), which enables you to concatenate combinations of cString instances with other cString instances, C-style strings, and characters. There are several versions of this operator; all have a cString parameter as either the first or the second operand. The other parameter belongs to the types mentioned previously. The various forms of the + operator enable you to concatenate several characters and strings in a single statement.

Listing 14.57. The concatenation operator (+).

```
//////////////////////////////////////////////////////////////////////
//
cString operator +(cString& s1, cString& s2)
{
   cString result(s1.len + s2.len + 1);

   strcpy(result.str,s1.str);
   strcat(result.str,s2.str);
   result.len = s1.len + s2.len;

   return result;
}

//////////////////////////////////////////////////////////////////////
//
cString operator +(cString& s1, char* s2)
{
   cString result(s1.len + strlen(s2) + 1);
   unsigned length = strlen(s2);
   strcpy(result.str,s1.str);
   strcat(result.str,s2);
   result.len = s1.len + length;
   return result;
}

//////////////////////////////////////////////////////////////////////
//
cString operator +(char* s1, cString& s2)
{
   cString result(strlen(s1) + s2.len + 1);
```

```
   unsigned length = strlen(s1);

   strcpy(result.str, s1);
   strcat(result.str, s2.str);
   result.len = s2.len + length;
   return result;
}

//////////////////////////////////////////////////////////////////////
//
cString operator +(cString& s, char c)
{
   cString result(s.len + 2);

   strcpy(result.str,s.str);
   result.len = s.len;
   *(result.str+result.len+1) = '\0';
   *(result.str+result.len) = c;
   result.len++;
   return result;
}

//////////////////////////////////////////////////////////////////////
//
cString operator +(char c, cString& s)
{
   cString result(2 + s.len) ;

   *(result.str+1) = '\0';
   *(result.str) = c;
   strcat(result.str,s.str);
   result.len = s.len + 1;
   return result;
}
```

The Append Operator (+=)

The append operator (+=), shown in Listing 14.58, complements the + operator's different uses. You can append characters, C-style strings, and `cString` instances to a `cString` instance using the += operator.

Listing 14.58. The append operator (+=).

```
////////////////////////////////////////////////////////////////////
//
cString& cString::operator +=(const cString& s)
{
   unsigned newlen = len + s.len;

   if ((newlen+1) > maxSize)
       resize(newlen+1);
   strcat(str, s.str);
   len += s.len;

   return *this;
}

////////////////////////////////////////////////////////////////////
//
cString& cString::operator +=(const char* s)
{
   unsigned newlen = len + strlen(s);

   if ((newlen+1) > maxSize)
       resize(newlen+1);
   strcat(str, s);
   len += strlen(s);
   return *this;
}

////////////////////////////////////////////////////////////////////
//
cString& cString::operator +=(const char c)
{
   unsigned newlen = len + 1;

   if ((newlen+1) > maxSize)
       resize(newlen+1);
   str[len] = c;
   str[len++ +1] = '\0';

   return *this;
}
```

The Deletion Operator (-)

Listing 14.59 shows the source code for the deletion operator (-). I've implemented the deletion operator to delete the first occurrence of a substring from a `cString` instance. The two versions of the deletion operator enable you to delete a C-style string or a `cString` instance from a `cString` instance (which appears in the first parameter). The operators simply scan for the existence of the second parameter `substr` in the first one, s. If there is a match, the operator calls the `remove` function to delete the matching substring.

Listing 14.59. The deletion operator (-).

```
//////////////////////////////////////////////////////////////////////
//
cString operator -(cString& s, const char* substr)
//
// Purpose: deletes the first occurrence of substring substr in
// string object s.
//
// Parameters:
//
//    input: s - the target string.
//           substr - the deleted substring.
//
{
    cString result = s;

    unsigned i = s.pos(substr);
    if (i != NO_SUBSTR_FOUND)
        result.remove(i, strlen(substr));
    return result;
}

//////////////////////////////////////////////////////////////////////
//
cString operator -(cString& s, cString& substr)
//
// Purpose: deletes the first occurrence of substring substr in
// string object s.
```

continues

Listing 14.59. continued

```
//
// Parameters:
//
//    input: s - the target string.
//           substr - the deleted substring.
//
{
    cString result = s;

    unsigned i = s.pos(substr);
    if (i != NO_SUBSTR_FOUND)
        result.remove(i, substr.len);
    return result;
}
```

The Delete-First Operator (-=)

The delete-first operator (-=), with source code shown in Listing 14.60, complements the delete operator. The delete-first operator enables you to delete the first occurrence of substring `substr` in the targeted `cString` instance.

Listing 14.60. The delete-first operator (-=).

```
//////////////////////////////////////////////////////////////////////
//
cString& cString::operator -=(const char* substr)
//
// Purpose: deletes the first occurrence of substring substr in
// this string object.
//
// Parameters:
//
//    input: substr - the deleted substring.
//
{
    unsigned i = pos(substr);
    if (i != NO_SUBSTR_FOUND)
```

```
        remove(i, strlen(substr));
    return *this;
}

////////////////////////////////////////////////////////////////////
//
cString& cString::operator -=(cString& substr)
//
// Purpose: deletes the first occurrence of substring substr in
// this string object.
//
// Parameters:
//
//    input: substr - the deleted substring.
//
{
    unsigned i = pos(substr);
    if (i != NO_SUBSTR_FOUND)
        remove(i, substr.len);
    return *this;
}
```

Testing the Deletion and Delete-First Operators

Listing 14.61 shows the source code for the OPMINUS.CPP program, which tests the deletion (-) and delete-first (-=) operators. The program assigns the strings `0123456789ABDC` and `ABDC` to the `cString` instances `s1` and `s2`. The program tests the deletion and delete-first operators in the following way:

1. Subtracts `s2` from `s1`, using the deletion operator, and assigns the result to another `cString` instance, `s3`. The program then displays `s3`, which is `0123456789`.
2. Subtracts the literal string `ABDC` from `s1`, using the deletion operator, and assigns the result to `s3`. The string still contains the characters `0123456789`.
3. Subtracts the substring `123` from the `s1` using the delete-first operator. The `s1` string now contains the characters `0456789ABDC`.

The program output is as follows:

```
String s1 = '0123456789ABDC'
String s2 = 'ABDC'
s1 - s2 = '0123456789'
s1 - 'ABDC' = '0123456789'
After removing substring 123, the string s1 is '0456789ABDC'
```

Listing 14.61. The source code for the OPMINUS.CPP program.

```
// Test the cString::operator - and operator -=

#include <iostream.h>
#include "string.hpp"

main()
{
  cString s1 = "0123456789ABDC";
  cString s2 = "ABDC";
  cString s3;

  cout << "\n\n";
  cout << "String s1 = '" << s1 << "'\n"
       << "String s2 = '" << s2 << "'\n";
  s3 = s1 - s2;
  cout << "s1 - s2 = '" << s3 << "'\n";
  s3 = s1 - "ABDC";
  cout << "s1 - 'ABDC' = '" << s3 << "'\n";
  s1 -= "123";
  cout << "After removing substring 123, the string s1 is "
       << "'" << s1 << "'" << '\n';

  return 0;

}
```

The Truncation Operator (/)

Listing 14.62 shows the source code for the two versions of the truncation operator (/). I've chosen to make the truncation operator truncate a `cString` instance where

the substr parameter occurs in string s. The characters that appear before the first occurrence of substr are deleted. The operator returns the part of the string s that begins with the substring substr. If the substring substr does not occur in the string s, the operator returns string s in its entirety.

Listing 14.62. The truncation operators (/).

```
///////////////////////////////////////////////////////////////////
//
cString operator /(cString& s, const char* substr)
//
// Purpose: extracts the trailing characters of string s that
// include the first occurrence of the substring substr.
//
// Parameters:
//
//    input: s - the target string.
//           substr - the substring used to mark the new beginning
//             of this string.
//
{
    cString result = s;

    unsigned i = s.pos(substr);
    if (i != NO_SUBSTR_FOUND)
        result.remove(0, i);
    return result;
}

///////////////////////////////////////////////////////////////////
//
cString operator /(cString& s, cString& substr)
//
// Purpose: extracts the trailing characters of string s that
// include the first occurrence of the substring substr.
//
// Parameters:
//
//    input: s - the target string.
```

continues

Listing 14.62. continued

```
//          substr - the substring used to mark the new beginning
//            of this string.
//
{
    cString result = s;

    unsigned i = s.pos(substr);
    if (i != NO_SUBSTR_FOUND)
        result.remove(0, i);
    return result;
}
```

The Truncate-First Operator (/=)

The different uses of the `/=` operator, shown in Listing 14.63, complement the truncation operator just presented. The truncate-first operator truncates a `cString` instance at the first occurrence of parameter `substr`. If the substring `substr` does not occur in the targeted `cString` instance, that instance remains intact.

Listing 14.63. The truncate-first operator (/=).

```
//////////////////////////////////////////////////////////////////////
//
cString& cString::operator /=(const char* substr)
//
// Purpose: extracts the trailing characters of this string that
// include the first occurrence of the substring substr.
//
// Parameters:
//
//    input: substr - the substring used to mark the new beginning
//            of this string.
//
{
    unsigned i = pos(substr);
    if (i != NO_SUBSTR_FOUND)
```

```
        remove(0, i);
    return *this;
}

////////////////////////////////////////////////////////////////////
//
cString& cString::operator /=(cString& substr)
//
// Purpose: extracts the trailing characters of this string that
// include the first occurrence of the substring substr.
//
// Parameters:
//
//    input: substr - the substring used to mark the new beginning
//             of this string.
//
{
    unsigned i = pos(substr);
    if (i != NO_SUBSTR_FOUND)
        remove(0, i);
    return *this;
}
```

Testing the Truncation and Truncate-First Operators

Listing 14.64 shows the source code for the OPDIVIDE.CPP program, which tests the truncation (`/`) and truncate-first (`/=`) operators. The program assigns the strings `0123456789ABDC` and `567` to the `cString` instances `s1` and `s2`. The program tests the truncation and truncate-first operators in the following ways:

1. Truncating `s1` at the first occurrence of `s2`, using the truncation operator. The program assigns the result to another `cString` instance, `s3`, and then displays `s3`, which is `567890ABDC`.
2. Truncating `s1` using literal string `567` and the truncation operator and assigning the result to string `s3`. The content of `s3` also is the string `56789ABDC`.
3. Truncating `s1` using the substring `123` and the truncate-first operator. The `s1` string now contains the characters `56789ABDC`.

The output of the test program is as follows:

```
String s1 = '0123456789ABDC'
String s2 = '567'
s1 / s2 = '56789ABDC'
s1 / '567' = '56789ABDC'
After truncating at 567, the string s1 is '56789ABDC'
```

Listing 14.64. The source code for the OPDIVIDE.CPP program.

```
// Test the cString::operator / and operator /=

#include <iostream.h>
#include "string.hpp"

main()
{
  cString s1 = "0123456789ABDC";
  cString s2 = "567";
  cString s3;

  cout << "\n\n";
  cout << "String s1 = '" << s1 << "'\n"
       << "String s2 = '" << s2 << "'\n";
  s3 = s1 / s2;
  cout << "s1 / s2 = '" << s3 << "'\n";
  s3 = s1 / "567";
  cout << "s1 / '567' = '" << s3 << "'\n";
  s1 /= "567";
  cout << "After truncating at 567, the string s1 is "
       << "'" << s1 << "'" << '\n';

  return 0;

}
```

The Truncate-At Operator (%)

Listing 14.65 shows the source code for the two versions of the truncate-at operator (`%`). I've chosen to make the truncate-at operator truncate a `cString` instance where

the substr parameter occurs in string s. The characters that appear after the end of the first occurrence of substr are deleted. The operator returns the part of the string s that ends with the substring substr. If substr does not occur in s, the operator returns s in its entirety.

Listing 14.65. The truncate-at operators (%).

```
//////////////////////////////////////////////////////////////////////
//
cString operator %(cString& s, const char* substr)
//
// Purpose: extracts the leading characters of string object s that
// include the first occurrence of the substring substr.
//
// Parameters:
//
//    input: s - the target string.
//           substr - the substring used to mark the new end of
//             this string.
//
{
    cString result = s;

    unsigned i = s.pos(substr);
    if (i != NO_SUBSTR_FOUND)
        result.remove(i + strlen(substr));
    return result;
}
//////////////////////////////////////////////////////////////////////
//
cString operator %(cString& s, cString& substr)
//
// Purpose: extracts the leading characters of string object s that
// include the first occurrence of the substring substr.
//
// Parameters:
//
//    input: s - the target string.
//           substr - the substring used to mark the new end of
//             this string.
```

continues

Listing 14.65. continued

```
//
{
    cString result = s;

    unsigned i = s.pos(substr);
    if (i != NO_SUBSTR_FOUND)
        result.remove(i + substr.len);
    return result;
}
```

The Truncate-At Assignment Operator (%=)

The truncate-first operators (%=), shown in Listing 14.66, complement the truncate and truncate-at operators just presented. The truncate-first operator truncates a cString instance at the first occurrence of parameter substr. If the substring substr does not occur at the targeted cString instance, that instance remains intact.

Listing 14.66. The truncate-at assignment operators (%=).

```
////////////////////////////////////////////////////////////////////////
//
cString& cString::operator %=(const char* substr)
//
// Purpose: extracts the leading characters that include the first
// occurrence of the substring substr.
//
// Parameters:
//
//    input: substr - the substring used to mark the new end of
//              this string.
//
{
    unsigned i = pos(substr);
    if (i != NO_SUBSTR_FOUND)
        remove(i + strlen(substr));
    return *this;
```

```
}
//////////////////////////////////////////////////////////////////////
//
cString& cString::operator %=(cString& substr)
//
// Purpose: extracts the leading characters that include the first
// occurrence of the substring substr.
//
// Parameters:
//
//    input: substr - the substring used to mark the new end of
//             this string.
//
{
    unsigned i = pos(substr);
    if (i != NO_SUBSTR_FOUND)
        remove(i + substr.len);
    return *this;
}
```

Testing the Truncate-At and Truncate-First Assignment Operators

Listing 14.67 shows the source code for the OPMODULO.CPP program, which tests the truncate-at (`%`) and truncate-first (`%=`) operators. The program assigns the strings `0123456789ABDC` and `567` to the `cString` instances `s1` and `s2`. The program tests the `%` and `%=` operators in the following way:

1. Truncating `s1` at the first occurrence of `s2`, using the `%` operator. The program assigns the result to string, another `cString` instance, `s3`, and then displays `s3`, which is `01234567`.
2. Truncating `s1` using literal string `567` and the `%` operator, and assigning the result to `s3`. The string `s3` still contains the characters `01234567`.
3. Truncating `s1` using the substring `567` and the `%=` operator. The `s1` string now contains the characters `01234567`.

The program output is as follows:

```
String s1 = '0123456789ABDC'
String s2 = '567'
s1 % s2 = '01234567'
s1 % '567' = '01234567'
After truncating at 567, the string s1 is '01234567'
```

Listing 14.67. The source code for the OPMODULO.CPP program.

```
// Test the cString::operator % and operator %=

#include <iostream.h>
#include "string.hpp"

main()
{
  cString s1 = "0123456789ABDC";
  cString s2 = "567";
  cString s3;

  cout << "\n\n";
  cout << "String s1 = '" << s1 << "'\n"
       << "String s2 = '" << s2 << "'\n";
  s3 = s1 % s2;
  cout << "s1 % s2 = '" << s3 << "'\n";
  s3 = s1 % "567";
  cout << "s1 % '567' = '" << s3 << "'\n";
  s1 %= "567";
  cout << "After truncating at 567, the string s1 is "
       << "'" << s1 << "'" << '\n';

  return 0;

}
```

The Multi-Character Access Operator (<<)

The multi-character access operator (<<), shown in Listing 14.68, supports string insertion of a `cString` instance. The insertion operator writes the characters of `s` to the output stream `os`.

Listing 14.68. The multi-character access operator (<<).

```
///////////////////////////////////////////////////////////////////
//
ostream& operator <<(ostream& os, cString& s)
{
    os << s.str;
    return os;
}
```

The Extraction Operator (())

The extraction operator (`()`), shown in Listing 14.69, extracts a substring from the targeted `cString` instance. The parameter `start` specifies the first extracted character. The parameter `count` indicates the number of characters to extract. This operator is similar to the `substring` function; the difference is in the second parameter.

Listing 14.69. The extraction operator (()).

```
///////////////////////////////////////////////////////////////////
//
cString cString::operator ()(const unsigned start,
                             unsigned count)
//
// Purpose: extracts the count characters of this string,
// starting at index start.
//
// Parameters:
//
//    input: start - the index of the first extracted character.
//           count - the number of extracted characters.
//
{
    // create a local copy of this string
    cString result(str);

    if (start < len) {
```

continues

Listing 14.69. continued

```
        // adjust the argument of count, if required
        count = ((start+count) <= len) ? count : len - start;
        count = (count != 0) ? count : 1;
        // copy the extracted characters
        strncpy(result.str, (str + start), count);
        result.str[count] = '\0';
        // update the length of string object result
        result.len = count;
    }
    return result;
}
```

Testing the Access and Extraction Operators

Listing 14.70 shows the source code for the MID.CPP program, which tests the access (`[]`) and extraction (`()`) operators. The program assigns the string `1234567890` to the `cString` instance `s1`. The program then uses the access operator to recall the characters at indices 3 through 6. To test the extraction operator, the program displays the substring obtained by extracting the characters at indices 3 to 6 of string `s1`. The output of the test program is as follows:

```
Main string is '1234567890'
Character 3 is 4
Character 4 is 5
Character 5 is 6
Character 6 is 7

Characters at indices 3 to 6 are 4567
```

Listing 14.70. The source code for the MID.CPP program.

```
// Test the cString::operator [] and operator () member functions

#include <iostream.h>
#include "string.hpp"

main()
{
```

```
  cString s1 = "1234567890";

  cout << "\n\n";
  cout << "Main string is '" << s1 << "'" << '\n';

  for (unsigned i = 3; i < s1.stringlen() - 3; i++)
    cout << "Character " << i << " is " << s1[i] << '\n';

  cout << "\nCharacters at indices 3 to 6 are "
       << s1(3, 4) << '\n';

  return 0;

}
```

Summary

This chapter presented the `cString` class, which models strings. The chapter discussed the various members of the class:

- The data members that manage the class instances.
- The various constructors used in creating the class instance and converting C-style strings to `cString` instances.
- The class destructor.
- Wrapper functions, which are simple shells that call string functions prototyped in string.h.
- Nonwrapper functions that contain string-comparison functions prototyped in the string.h header file.
- Relational operators, which make code comparing `cString` instances much easier to read.
- The concatenation (`+`) and deletion (`-`) operators, which add and remove substrings. The `cString` class contains a rich set of overloaded `+` operators to concatenate combinations of `char*`, `char`, and `cString` types.
- The truncation (`/`) and truncate-at (`%`) operators, which truncate strings.

Words, Items, and Tokens

The last chapter presented the cString class, which implements strings. Often, text-management applications manipulate groups of strings. These groups are classified by the delimiting characters that separate each group member. In addition, each group of strings follows certain rules related to the delimiting characters. This chapter presents classes that manipulate strings as words, items, and tokens. The chapter also explores the C++ implementation of such groups by first developing a class of cString lists that is the base class for these groups.

Words

Let me begin by discussing the properties of words, items, and tokens and the rules applied to manage them. The common denominator among these three groups is that they are special strings. Words, for example, are space-delimited substrings that appear in a string. The string `"The early bird gets the worm"` contains six words. You also can say that the string contains a list of six words. (Here, the term *list* is taken in a general sense and does not refer to a formal data structure.)

The space is the only delimiting character that defines words in a string. The following rules apply to the space character:

- A sequence of multiple spaces has the same effect as a single space.
- Leading and trailing spaces in a string are not significant.

Based on the above two rules, the string `" The early bird gets the worm "` (including the leading and trailing spaces) also contains six words: neither the leading space, the trailing space, nor the sequence of space characters alters either the number of words or the individual words.

Items

Items are substrings that are delimited by commas. For example, the string `"one,two,three"` contains a list of three items. The following rules apply to the comma delimiter:

- Each sequence of two commas contains an empty item.
- Leading and trailing commas are significant. A leading comma character causes the first item to be a null item. Similarly, a trailing comma indicates that there is a trailing null item in a string.

Strings that contain comma-delimited lists are sometimes used in text files to store database records. Because the records are stored in text files, you can view and edit them with a text editor.

Tokens

Tokens are substrings that are delimited by a user-specified set of characters. For example, the string `(X + Y) / Z` contains the tokens `X`, `Y`, and `Z`, assuming the delimiting characters are `()`, `/`, and `+`. By varying the set of delimiting characters, you most likely alter the number and content of tokens. The following rules apply to the delimiting characters:

- A sequence of delimiters has the same effect as a single delimiter.
- Leading and trailing delimiters in a string are not significant.

These rules are similar to those for words; the difference is that you're dealing with a set of delimiting characters instead of just the space character.

The String List Class

There are two approaches to maintaining words, items, and tokens:

- The first approach maintains the source string that contains these words, items, and tokens. Searching, extraction, deletion, replacement, and other tasks are performed on the host string.
- The second approach uses a dynamic linked list that stores the individual words, items, or tokens. This approach, although it requires a bit more memory space, offers faster operations because the process of scanning words, items, and tokens is performed once, during the list initialization.

Earlier I said that the common factor among words, items, and tokens is that they appear in strings. Another common factor among these substrings is that they are, conceptually, lists of substrings (or smaller strings, if you prefer). You can transform the conceptual lists into actual linked lists by scanning the string and building lists that store the individual words, items, and tokens. In this section I present the `strList` class, which implements string lists. The `strList` class is the parent of the classes that model words, items, and tokens.

Listing 15.1 contains the source code for the strlist.hpp header file. Listing 15.2 shows the source code for the STRLIST.CPP library file. The class declares the protected, nested structure `strListNode`. This structure maintains the typical nodes of the dynamic, singly linked list. The `strList` class also declares the following data members:

- The `head` member is the pointer to the head of the list.
- The `tail` member is the pointer to the tail of the list.
- The `listSize` member stores the current number of nodes in an instance of `strList`.

The `strList` class also declares the protected function `copyList`. The `copyList` function copies the dynamic nodes of the `sl` parameter to the targeted instance of the `strList` class.

Listing 15.1. The source code for the strlist.hpp header file.

```
////////////////////////////////////////////////////////////////////
//                                                                //
//                       NCS String Library                       //
//                                                                //
//            Copyright (c) 1992  Namir Clement Shammas           //
//                                                                //
// Version 1.1.0                                          3/25/91 //
//                                           Last Update: 6/16/92 //
//                                                                //
// Implements a class for maintaining a list of cString objects.  //
//                                                                //
////////////////////////////////////////////////////////////////////


#ifndef _STRLIST_HPP
#define _STRLIST_HPP

#include "string.hpp"

class strList
{
  protected:
    // internal list node structure
    struct strListNode {
        cString      data;
        strListNode* nextNode;
    };

    strListNode* head; // head of list
    strListNode* tail; // tail of list
    unsigned listSize;

    void copyList(strList& sl);

  public:
```

```
    // ---------------------- Constructors -----------------
    strList();
    strList(const char* str);
    strList(cString&);
    strList(strList&);
    ~strList();

    unsigned getListSize() const
      { return listSize; }
    void clear();
    void insert(const cString& s, unsigned after = 0xffff);
    void remove(unsigned start, unsigned count = 0xffff);
    void get(cString& s,
             unsigned start = 1,
             unsigned count = 0xffff,
             const char delim = ' ');
    void sort(strList&);
    void reverse(strList&);
    strList& operator =(strList& sl);
    friend strList operator +(strList& sl1, strList& sl2);
    strList& operator +=(strList& sl);

    friend int operator ==(strList& sl1, strList& sl2);
};

#endif
```

There are four constructors for the `strList` class:

- The default constructor creates an empty list.
- The constructor with the `const char*` parameter creates a list with a single member, which is the argument for the parameter.
- The constructor with the `cString&` parameter creates a list with a single member, which is the argument of the `cString&` parameter.
- The constructor with the `strList&` parameter creates a list by copying the nodes of the argument. This constructor calls the `copyList` function to copy the list nodes.

The class destructor simply calls the `clear` function to remove the list nodes.

The `strList` class contains the `getListSize`, `clear`, and `insert` functions, which are needed to query and manipulate the strings in the class instances:

- The `getListSize` function simply returns the value of the `listSize` data member.
- The `clear` function deletes the nodes of the dynamic list. The deletion proceeds from front to back.
- The `insert` function enables you to insert a string after a list node specified by number. The `s` parameter specifies the inserted string. The `count` parameter indicates the number of the node after which string `s` is inserted. The list nodes are numbered from 1 and up. The default argument for the `after` parameter is `0xffff`. This value indicates that the string `s` is inserted at the tail of the list. There are several cases for inserting a new string:
    1. The list is empty. The string `s` is inserted as the new head of the list. The argument for parameter `after` is ignored.
    2. The argument for the `after` parameter exceeds the value stored in the `listSize` member. This case leads to inserting string `s` at the end of the list.
    3. The argument for the `after` parameter is in the range `[1..listSize]`. The string `s` is inserted in a node that is neither the head node nor the tail node.
    4. The argument for the `after` parameter is 0. The string `s` is inserted as the new head of the list. (It now should be apparent why list nodes are numbered from 1 and up, rather than 0 and up.)
- The `remove` function deletes one or more list nodes. The `start` parameter specifies the index of the first node to delete. The argument for the `start` parameter must be in the range `[1..listSize]`. The `count` parameter indicates the number of nodes to delete. The default argument for `count` is `0xffff`. This value indicates that the `remove` function deletes all nodes starting at index `start`. If the argument for the `start` parameter is `2` or greater, the `remove` function uses a `while` loop to traverse the list nodes until it reaches the first node to be deleted. The function then uses another `while` loop either to delete the specified number of nodes, or to delete nodes until the pointer to the next node is null.

- The `getList` function obtains one or more nodes from the list. The `s` parameter contains the extracted string. The `start` parameter indicates the index of the first node. The arguments for this parameter must be in the range `[1..listSize]`. The default argument is `1`. The `count` parameter indicates the number of nodes to copy in the `s` parameter. The default argument for this parameter is `0xffff`. This value indicates that the `getList` function should copy the rest of the list node to the `s` parameter. The `delim` parameter specifies the delimiter character that separates the various substrings. The default argument for this parameter is the space character. This character is suitable for extracting words.

  The `getList` function uses a `while` loop to locate the first node to be retrieved. The `getList` function then assigns a null string to the `s` parameter and uses a second `while` loop to concatenate the string in the current node together with the delimiter character. When the loop ends, the `getList` function deletes the last character of `s`. This character is an extra delimiter character.

- The `sort` function sorts the nodes of the list using a local array of `cString` instances. The `sort` function performs the following tasks:

  1. Creates a local dynamic array of multiple instances of `cString`.
  2. Copies the list nodes into the array.
  3. Sorts the array members using the new Combsort method. This method was developed by Richard Cox and Stephen Lacey; see their article on Combsort in the April 1991 issue of *BYTE* magazine. The Combsort method is somewhat similar to the Shell-Metzner method, but the Combsort method is two to three times faster for unordered arrays.
  4. Clears the list nodes.
  5. Inserts the ordered array members into the list.
  6. Deletes the local array of multiple instances of `cString`.

- The `reverseList` function copies the members of list `sl` to the targeted `strList` instance in the reverse order. The function first clears the targeted `strList` instance and then inserts the various nodes of list `sl`. The function accesses the nodes of list `sl` in reverse order and uses the `insert` function for the insertion. The argument for the `after` parameter, in the call to the `insert` function, always is 0. This value forces inserting the current node of `sl` into the head of the targeted `strList` instance.

- The assignment operator (=) assigns the nodes of the sl parameter to the targeted strList instance. The operator first deletes the previous nodes of the targeted list before copying the nodes of list sl.
- The concatenation operator (+) adds the nodes of the sl1 and sl2 parameters. The result is a separate list.
- The append operator (+=) appends the nodes of the list sl to the targeted strList instance.
- The equality operator (==) compares the sl1 and sl2 parameters. If these two lists have the same contents, the operator returns 1. Otherwise, the operator returns 0.

Listing 15.2. The source code for the STRLIST.CPP library file.

```
//////////////////////////////////////////////////////////////////////
//                                                                  //
//                       NCS String Library                         //
//                                                                  //
//            Copyright (c) 1992  Namir Clement Shammas             //
//                                                                  //
// Version 1.1.0                                           3/25/91 //
//                                             Last Update: 6/16/92 //
//                                                                  //
// Implements a class for maintaining a list of cString objects.   //
//                                                                  //
//////////////////////////////////////////////////////////////////////

#include "strlist.hpp"

/////////////////////////////////////////////////////////////////////
//
strList::strList()
//
// Purpose: the default constructor that creates an empty list.
//
{
    head = NULL;
    tail = NULL;
    listSize = 0;
}
```

```
////////////////////////////////////////////////////////////////////
//
strList::strList(const char* s)
//
// Purpose: the constructor that creates a list with a single
// member which stores the argument for parameter s.
//
// Parameters:
//
//    input: s - the initial list member.
//
{
    head = new strListNode;
    head->data = s;
    head->nextNode = NULL;
    tail = head;
    listSize = 1;
}

////////////////////////////////////////////////////////////////////
//
strList::strList(cString& s)
//
// Purpose: the constructor that creates a list with a single
// member which stores the argument for parameter s.
//
// Parameters:
//
//    input: s - the initial list member.
//
{
    head = new strListNode;
    head->data = s;
    head->nextNode = NULL;
    tail = head;
    listSize = 1;
}

////////////////////////////////////////////////////////////////////
//
```

continues

Listing 15.2. continued

```
strList::strList(strList& sl)
//
// Purpose: the constructor that creates a list using an existing
// list sl.
//
// Parameters:
//
//    input: sl - the source list object.
//
{
    head = NULL;
    tail = NULL;
    listSize = 0;
    // make a copy of list sl
    copyList(sl);
}

////////////////////////////////////////////////////////////////////
//
strList::~strList()
//
// Purpose: destroys the instances of strList.
//
{
    clear();
}

////////////////////////////////////////////////////////////////////
//
void strList::copyList(strList& sl)
//
// Purpose: appends the data of list sl into this list.  The
// previous list nodes ARE preserved.
//
// Parameters:
//
//    input: sl - the appended list.
//
{
    cString s;
```

```
    for (unsigned i = 1; i <= sl.listSize; i++) {
        sl.get(s, i, 1);
        insert(s);
    }
}

////////////////////////////////////////////////////////////////////
//
void strList::clear()
//
// Purpose: deletes the nodes of this list.
//
{
    strListNode* p = head;

    // loop to delete the nodes
    while (head) {
        head = p->nextNode;
        delete p;
        p = head;
    }
    tail = NULL;
    listSize = 0;
}

////////////////////////////////////////////////////////////////////
//
void strList::insert(const cString& s, unsigned after)
//
// Purpose: inserts a copy of string object s after
// the list node number 'after'.
//
// Parameters:
//
//    input: s - the inserted string object.
//           after - the insertion index.
//
{
    strListNode *p, *q, *r;
```

continues

Listing 15.2. continued

```
        if (head) {
            if (after > listSize) { // new tail
                // allocate new list node
                r = new strListNode;
                r->data = s;
                r->nextNode = NULL;
                // link old tail node to new one
                tail->nextNode = r;
                tail = r; // update tail pointer
            }
            else if (after > 0) { // insert inside the list
                p = head;
                q = NULL;
                // find the correct node
                while (after-- > 0 && p) {
                    q = p;
                    p = p->nextNode;
                }
                r = new strListNode;
                r->data = s;
                r->nextNode = p;
                q->nextNode = r;
            }
            else { // new head
                p = new strListNode;
                p->data = s;
                p->nextNode = head;
                head = p;
            }
        }
        else { // insert the first node in the list
            head = new strListNode;
            head->data = s;
            head->nextNode = NULL;
            tail = head;
        }
        listSize++;
    }
```

```
////////////////////////////////////////////////////////////////////
//
void strList::remove(unsigned start, unsigned count)
//
// Purpose: removes one or more list nodes.
//
// Parameters:
//
//    input: start - the index of the first list node to be deleted.
//           count - the number of nodes to remove.
//
{
    strListNode *p, *q, *r;

    if (start > 0 && start <= listSize) {
        if (start > 1) {
            p = head;
            r = NULL;
            while (start-- > 1 && p) {
                r = p;
                p = p->nextNode;
            }
            while (count-- > 0 && p) {
                q = p;
                p = p->nextNode;
                delete q;
                listSize--;
            }
            r->nextNode = p;
            if (!p)
                tail = q; // update tail pointer
        }
        else {
            while (count-- > 0 && head) {
                p = head;
                head = head->nextNode;
                delete p;
                listSize--;
            }
```

continues

Listing 15.2. continued

```
            if (!head) // is the entire list deleted?
                tail = NULL; // make tail point to NULL
        }
    }
}

////////////////////////////////////////////////////////////////////
//
void strList::get(cString& s,
                  unsigned start,
                  unsigned count,
                  const char delim)
//
// Purpose: obtains one or more string objects from the list.  The
// argument for parameter s returns the extracted strings delimited
// by character delim.
//
//
// Parameters:
//
//    input: start - the index of the first node whose string
//             is obtained.
//           count - the number of string objects to retrieve.
//           delim - the character that delimits the extracted
//             strings.
//
//    output: s  - the string that contains the extracted characters.
//
{
    strListNode *p;

    if (start > 0 && start <= listSize) {
        p = head;
        // find the start'th node
        while (start-- > 1)
            p = p->nextNode;
        s = "";
        while (count-- > 0 && p) {
            s = s + p->data + delim;
            p = p->nextNode;
        }
```

```
        s.trimright(delim); // delete the tail "delim" character
    }
    else
        s = ""; // return empty cString s
}

////////////////////////////////////////////////////////////////////
//
void strList::sort(strList& sl)
//
// Purpose: sorts the nodes of list sl using a local array and
// the new Combsort method.  The sorted list is assigned to this
// list.
//
// Parameters:
//
//    input: sl - the source list object.
//
{
    cString *p;
    cString s;
    unsigned i, j, offset, n = sl.listSize;
    boolean inorder;

    // there are "n" elements in the array of "cString".
    // element 0 is used to swap strings, while elements
    // 1..n are used to store the words
    p = new cString[n+1];
    for (i = 1; i <= n; i++) {
        sl.get(s, i, 1);
        *(p+i) = s;
    }
    // start Combsort method
    offset = n;
    do {
      offset = (8 * offset) / 11;
      offset = (offset == 0) ? 1 : offset;
      inorder = true;
      for (i = 1; i <= (n - offset); i++) {
        j = i + offset;
```

continues

Listing 15.2. continued

```
            if (*(p + i) > *(p + j)) {
              inorder = false;
              *p = *(p + i);
              *(p + i) = *(p + j);
              *(p + j) = *p;
            }
          }
        } while (!(inorder == true && offset == 1));
        clear(); // clear the current object
        // insert the sorted words
        for (i = 1; i <= n; i++)
            insert(*(p+i));
        delete [] p; // delete array of cStrings
}

////////////////////////////////////////////////////////////////////
//
void strList::reverse(strList& sl)
//
// Purpose: reverses the order of the nodes of list sl and stores
// the reversed nodes in this list.
//
// Parameters:
//
//    input: sl - the source list object.
//
{
    cString s;

    clear(); // clear this list
    for (unsigned i = 1; i <= sl.listSize; i++) {
        sl.get(s, i, 1);
        insert(s, 0); // insert as the new head
    }
}

////////////////////////////////////////////////////////////////////
//
strList& strList::operator =(strList& sl)
//
```

```
// Purpose: copies the list sl to this list.
//
// Parameters:
//
//    input: sl - the source list object.
//
{
    if (head)
        clear();
    copyList(sl);
    return *this;
}

////////////////////////////////////////////////////////////////////
//
strList operator +(strList& sl1, strList& sl2)
//
// Purpose: adds the lists sl1 and sl2.
//
// Parameters:
//
//    input: sl1 - the first operand.
//           sl2 - the second operand.
//
{
    strList result;

    result.copyList(sl1);
    result.copyList(sl2);
    return result;
}

////////////////////////////////////////////////////////////////////
//
strList& strList::operator +=(strList& sl)
//
// Purpose: appends the list sl to this list.
//
// Parameters:
//
//    input: sl - the appended list object.
```

continues

Listing 15.2. continued

```
//
{
    copyList(sl);
    return *this;
}

////////////////////////////////////////////////////////////////////
//
int operator ==(strList& sl1, strList& sl2)
//
// Purpose: compares the lists sl1 and sl2.  The function returns
// 1 if the two lists are equivalent.  Otherwise, the function
// yields 0.
//
// Parameters:
//
//    input: sl1, sl2 - the compared list objects.
//
{
    strListNode* p1;
    strListNode* p2;

    if (sl1.listSize != sl2.listSize)
        return 0;
    p1 = sl1.head;
    p2 = sl2.head;
    // compare each node
    while (p1 && p2) {
        if (p1->data != p2->data)
            return 0;
        p1 = p1->nextNode;
        p2 = p2->nextNode;
    }
    // lists are equivalent
    return 1;
}
```

Listing 15.3 contains the source code for the TSSTRLIS.CPP program, which tests the functions of the `strList` class. The program declares three instances of

`strList` class—`SL1`, `SL2`, and `SL3`—and two instances of the `cString` class—`s1` and `s2`. The test program performs the following tests:

1. Inserts the string `"One "` (with a trailing space) in list `SL1`.
2. Inserts the string `"Two "` (with a trailing space) in list `SL1`.
3. Inserts the string `"Three "` (with a trailing space) in list `SL1`.
4. Invokes the `get` function to access all the strings in list `SL1`. The argument for the resulting string is `s1`. The function call uses default arguments for the `start`, `count`, and `delim` parameters.
5. Displays the string `s1`, which contains the formatted image of list `SL1`.
6. Inserts string `Four` into list `SL2`.
7. Inserts string `Five` into list `SL2`.
8. Invokes the `get` function to access all the strings in list `SL2`. The argument for the resulting string is `s1`. The function call uses default arguments for the `start`, `count`, and `delim` parameters.
9. Displays the string `s1`, which contains the formatted image of list `SL2`.
10. Assigns list `SL1` to list `SL2` by using the assignment operator (`=`).
11. Uses the `get` function to obtain the strings of list `SL3` in a manner similar to obtaining the strings of lists `SL1` and `SL2`.
12. Displays the string `s1`, which stores the formatted image of list `SL3`.
13. Appends the strings of list `SL2` to list `SL3`. This task uses the append operator (`+=`).
14. Invokes the `get` function to access all the strings in list `SL3`. The argument for the resulting string is `s2`. Default arguments are used for the other parameters of the `get` function.
15. Displays the string `s2`, which contains the formatted image of list `SL3`.
16. Removes the second and third words from list `SL3`. This task calls the `remove` function.
17. Obtains the formatted image of list `SL3` using the `get` function and string `s1`.
18. Displays string `s1`.

The program output is as follows:

```
List #1 is: One  Two  Three
List #2 is: Four  Five
List #3 is: One Two Three
List #2 + List #3 is: One Two Three Four Five
After removing words 2 and 3, the above list is: One Four Five
```

Listing 15.3. The source code for the TSSTRLIS.CPP program.

```
// Test the strList class
#include "wordstr.hpp"
#include <iostream.h>

main()
{
    strList SL1, SL2, SL3;
    cString s1(40), s2(40);

    cout << "\n\n";
    SL1.insert("One ");
    SL1.insert("Two ");
    SL1.insert("Three ");
    SL1.get(s1);
    cout << "List #1 is: " << s1 << '\n';
    SL2.insert("Four ");
    SL2.insert("Five");
    SL2.get(s1);
    cout << "List #2 is: " << s1 << '\n';
    SL3 = SL1;
    SL3.get(s2);
    cout << "List #3 is: " << s2 << '\n';
    SL3 += SL2;
    SL3.get(s2);
    cout << "List #2 + List #3 is: " << s2 << '\n';
    SL3.remove(2, 2);
    SL3.get(s1);
    cout << "After removing words 2 and 3, the above list is: "
         << s1 << '\n';

    return 0;
}
```

The Class of Words

Managing words efficiently benefits from data structures such as lists, trees, and hash tables. Although binary trees and hash tables offer faster search capabilities, they have their operational costs. Binary trees can require significant stack space for recursive operations such as searching. Hash tables do not support ordered data. Singly linked lists are slower to search, but do not require as much overhead and computing effort as trees and hash tables when inserting and deleting data.

Listing 15.4 shows the source code for the wordstr.hpp header file. Listing 15.5 contains the source code for the WORDSTR.CPP library file. The wordstr.hpp header file contains the declarations for the `wordstr` class (the class of words), the `itemstr` class (the class of items), and the `tokenstr` class (the class of tokens). In this section I focus on the `wordstr` class. In the next sections I discuss the `itemstr` and `tokenstr` classes.

The `wordstr` class, a descendant of `strList`, declares the private copy function, five constructors, a destructor, a set of functions, and a friend function.

The default constructor builds an empty list of words by calling the default constructor of the `strList` class. The `wordstr(const char*)` constructor creates a list of words by parsing the list's string-typed argument. The constructor actually uses `cString` instances `s2` and `s3`, which copy the argument. The constructor first trims the leading and trailing spaces and removes any sequences of spaces that are imbedded in string `s2`. The constructor then uses the `cString::stringtok` and `strList::insert` functions and a `while` loop to extract the words from string `s2` and assign them to string `s3`.

The string `s3` is inserted in the list of words by each loop iteration. You might notice that string `s3` is created using the argument `s`. This form of initialization ensures that the string `s3` has the same size as argument `s`. This matching string size means that the string `s3` will not have to be resized later if string `s` is greater than the default size of `cString` instances. Moreover, if string `s` contains a single word (and no spaces), string `s3` is large enough to contain a copy of that single word without resizing.

The `wordstr(cString& s)` constructor creates a list of words using an instance of class `cString`. This constructor works like the default constructor.

The wordstr(strList&) constructor builds a list of words by copying the members of the list s1. The constructor *assumes* that the members of list s1 are void of spaces.

The wordstr(wordstr&) constructor creates a list of words using an existing instance of the wordstr class. The constructor merely calls the copy function to duplicate the list of words in its argument.

The class destructor clears the list of words by calling strList::clear.

The private copy function, as the name suggests, copies the nodes of the list w to the targeted instance of wordstr. This process involves dynamically allocating the nodes of the new list and copying the nodes.

The wordstr class declares a set of assignment (=) operators. These operators use the various class constructors and the copy function to parse the operator's argument and assign the parsed words to a wordstr instance.

Listing 15.4. The source code for the wordstr.hpp header file.

```
//////////////////////////////////////////////////////////////////////
//                                                                  //
//                        NCS String Library                        //
//                                                                  //
//              Copyright (c) 1992  Namir Clement Shammas           //
//                                                                  //
// Version 1.1.0                                            3/25/91 //
//                                            Last Update: 6/16/92 //
//                                                                  //
// Implements a class for maintaining a list of words.              //
//                                                                  //
//////////////////////////////////////////////////////////////////////


#ifndef _WORDSTR_HPP
#define _WORDSTR_HPP

#include <iostream.h>
extern "C" {
```

```
   #include <stdio.h>
   #include <conio.h>
   #include <string.h>
}

#include "string.hpp"
#include "strlist.hpp"

class wordstr : public strList
{

  private:
    wordstr& copy(wordstr& w);

  public:
    // constructors and destructors
    wordstr(const char*);
    wordstr(cString&);
    wordstr(strList&);
    wordstr(wordstr&);
    wordstr();
    ~wordstr();

    // assignment operator
    wordstr& operator =(const char);
    wordstr& operator =(const char*);
    wordstr& operator =(cString&);
    wordstr& operator =(wordstr&);

    // state manipulation member functions
    unsigned pos(wordstr& w,
                 unsigned first = 1,
                 unsigned last = 1,
                 unsigned start = 1,
                 boolean caseSense = true);
    void insert(wordstr& w,
                unsigned first = 1,
                unsigned last = 0xffff,
                unsigned after = 0xffff);
    void translate(wordstr& findword,
                   wordstr& replaceword,
```

continues

Listing 15.4. continued

```
                       unsigned& count,
                       unsigned start = 1,
                       unsigned freq = 0xffff,
                       boolean caseSense = true);
        // stream output
        friend ostream& operator <<(ostream&, wordstr&);
};

class itemstr : public wordstr
{

    private:
        itemstr& copy(itemstr& t);

    public:
        // constructors and destructors
        itemstr(const char* s);
        itemstr(cString&);
        itemstr(strList&);
        itemstr(itemstr&);
        itemstr();
        ~itemstr();
        // assignment operator
        itemstr& operator =(const char);
        itemstr& operator =(const char*);
        itemstr& operator =(cString&);
        itemstr& operator =(itemstr&);
        // stream output
        friend ostream& operator <<(ostream&, itemstr&);
};

class tokenstr : public wordstr
{

    private:
        tokenstr& copy(tokenstr& t);
    public:
        cString delimstring;
        // constructors and destructors
        tokenstr(const char* s, const char* delimstr);
```

```
    tokenstr(cString&, cString&);
    tokenstr(strList&, cString&);
    tokenstr(tokenstr&);
    tokenstr();
    ~tokenstr();
    // state manipulation member functions
    // assignment operator
    tokenstr& operator =(tokenstr&);
    tokenstr& assign(cString&, cString&);
    // stream output
    friend ostream& operator <<(ostream& , tokenstr&);
};

#endif
```

The `wordstr` class also declares the following functions:

- The `pos` function. This function searches the list of words for a specific word and returns the index of the list node that contains the matching word. The `w` parameter specifies the word to be searched. The `first` and `last` parameters specify the index of the words in the `w` parameter that are searched in a `wordstr` instance. The default argument for both the `first` and `last` parameter is `1`. This value enables you to search only the first word in the `w` parameter.

  The `start` parameter specifies the index of the first searched word in the targeted `wordstr` instance. The default argument for the `start` parameter is 1. This value indicates that the search begins at the first word. The Boolean `caseSense` parameter indicates whether the search is case-sensitive. The function returns the index of the first matching word, or yields 0 if no match is found.

  The `pos` function uses a method based on the algorithm applied by brute-force character matching. In this case, the `pos` function is matching words and not characters. The `do/while` loop allows the function to scan the words of the `w` parameter for a match in the targeted `wordstr` instance. The function uses the local variable `lastj` to avoid rereading the last word of the `w` parameter. This scheme bypasses unneeded calls to the `get` function, especially when `j` is `1`.

- The `insert` function inserts the words of an existing `wordstr` instance into the targeted `wordstr` instance. The `w` parameter provides the source list. The `first` and `last` parameters specify the first and last words of the `w` parameter to insert. The default arguments for these parameters are `1` and `0xffff`. These values enable you to insert all the words of the `w` parameter. The `after` parameter indicates where the insertion takes place. The `insert` function uses a downward-counting `for` loop to insert the words of the `w` parameter, starting with the last word.

- The `translate` function replaces words in a `wordstr` instance. The `findword` and `replaceword` parameters specify the search and replacement words. The reference parameter `count` returns the actual number of words translated. The `start` parameter indicates the index of the first word to be affected by the translation process. The default argument for this parameter is 1.

  The `freq` parameter specifies the maximum number of translations. The argument for this parameter is `0xffff`. The Boolean parameter `caseSense` signals whether or not the replacement of words is case-sensitive. The default argument for this parameter is `True`.

You may have noticed that the first two parameters of the `translate` function are instances of `wordstr`. Using this class instead of `cString` might surprise you at first. Using the `cString` class makes the arguments of these parameters susceptible to containing spaces. Consequently, such arguments for `findstr` do not find a match. Worse yet, similar arguments for `replaceword` store space-embedded words in the list nodes—a violation of the basic rules for maintaining the list of words.

The `translate` function performs the following tasks:

- Extracts the first word from the `findword` and `replaceword` parameters. These words are stored in the local `cString` instances `findstr` and `replacestr`.
- If the translation is case-insensitive, the function converts the characters of string `findstr` to uppercase.
- Searches for the start word using a `while` loop.
- Translates the words while the current list node is not null and while the value of the `freq` parameter is positive. Each loop iteration stores the current node's data in the local string `datastr`. If the translation is case-insensitive, the function converts the characters of string `datastr` to uppercase. The function then compares the strings `datastr` and `findstr`. If they match, the function assigns the string `replacestr` to the current node's data, decrements the `freq` parameter, and increments the reference parameter `count`.

The insertion operator (<<) writes a formatted list of words to a stream. The insertion operator calls `strList::get()` to obtain all the words in a list and stores them in the local `cString` instance `s`. The insertion operator then writes the string `s` to the output stream `os`. The words of `wordstr` instance `w` appear in a space-delimited form on the output stream.

The Class of Items

Listing 15.4 showed the declaration of the `itemstr` class. This class is a descendant of `wordstr` and models comma-delimited items. Because `itemstr` is a descendant of the `wordstr` and `strList` classes, it inherits a number of the required functions. Consequently, implementing the functions of class `itemstr` involves few new members. Listing 15.5 shows the implementation of the members of class `itemstr`.

The class `itemstr` declares five constructors, a destructor, a single private function, and a set of operators. There are no declared functions for inserting, retrieving, deleting, searching, and translating items; these operations are adequately supported by the inherited functions.

The default constructor creates an empty list of items by calling the default constructor of the parent class `wordstr`. You may recall that the default `wordstr` constructor calls the default `strList` class constructor.

The constructor `itemstr(const char*)` creates a list of items by parsing its argument. The constructor creates local `cString` instances `s2` and `s3`, which are copies of the argument. These `cString` instances are then modified by the constructor. The constructor performs the following tasks:

- If the first character of `s2` is a comma, the constructor prepends a space to the string `s2`. This task inserts a leading space character.
- If the last character of `s2` is a comma, the constructor appends a space to the string `s2`. This task inserts a trailing space character.
- The constructor replaces sequences of two commas (`,,`) with a comma, a space, and another comma (`, ,`). This task inserts space items. The approach of using a space to represent a null item makes coding easier, because it replaces null strings with single-space strings.
- The constructor extracts the first item using the `cString::stringtok` function. The string of delimiter is a comma (`,`).

- The constructor extracts the rest of the items using a `while` loop that iterates as long as the length of the last token is greater than zero. Here's one case of coding made easier by replacing null items with single spaces.

The `itemstr(cString&)` constructor creates a list of items by parsing its argument. This constructor works in a manner very similar to the `itemstr(const char*)` version.

The `itemstr(strList&)` constructor creates a list of items by using a `strList` instance. You must ensure that the nodes of the `strList` argument do not contain any commas. The constructor calls the `wordstr(StrList&)` constructor which then calls the `strList(strList)` constructor.

The `itemstr(itemstr&)` constructor creates a list of items by copying the items from an existing `itemstr` instance. The constructor merely calls the private copy function to perform the required task.

The class destructor clears the list of words by calling `strList::clear()`.

The private copy function, as the name suggests, copies the nodes of the list `w` to the targeted instance of `itemstr`. This process involves dynamically allocating the nodes of the new list and copying the nodes.

The `itemstr` class declares a set of assignment (=) operators. These operators use the various class constructors and the `copy` function to parse the operator's argument and assign the parsed items to an `itemstr` instance.

The insertion (<<) operator writes the items of the `itemstr` instance to the output stream `os`. The operator calls the `strList::get` function to obtain a comma-delimited string image of the item list. The call to the `get` function specifies the arguments of `start`, `count`, and `delim` as `1`, `0xffff`, and the comma character.

Listing 15.5. The source code for the WORDSTR.CPP library file.

```
//////////////////////////////////////////////////////////////////////
//                                                                  //
//                        NCS String Library                        //
//                                                                  //
```

```
//              Copyright (c) 1992  Namir Clement Shammas          //
//                                                                  //
// Version 1.1.0                                           3/25/91 //
//                                            Last Update: 6/16/92 //
//                                                                  //
// Implements a class for maintaining a list of words.             //
//                                                                  //
//////////////////////////////////////////////////////////////////////


#include <iostream.h>
extern "C" {
   #include <string.h>
}
#include "wordstr.hpp"

/////////////////////////////////////////////////////////////////////
///////////////////////// Class wordstr /////////////////////////
/////////////////////////////////////////////////////////////////////


/////////////////////////////////////////////////////////////////////
//
wordstr::wordstr(const char* s)
//
// Purpose: constructor that builds a list of words using the
// space-delimited parameter s.
//
// Parameters:
//
//    input: s - the string that contains one or more
//             space-delimited words
//
{
    cString s2(s), s3(s);

    head = NULL;
    listSize = 0;
    // trim leading, trailing and multiple internal spaces
    s2.trimends();
    s2.trimSequenceChars();
```

continues

Listing 15.5. continued

```
    s3.stringtok(s2, " ", true);
    // loop to extract the words from string s3
    while (s3.stringlen() > 0) {
        strList::insert(s3);
        s3.stringtok(s2, " ", false);
    }
}

//////////////////////////////////////////////////////////////////////
//
wordstr::wordstr(cString& s)
//
// Purpose: constructor that builds a list of words using the
// space-delimited parameter s.
//
// Parameters:
//
//    input: s - the string that contains one or more
//             space-delimited words
//
{
    cString s3(s);

    head = NULL;
    listSize = 0;
    // trim leading, trailing and multiple internal spaces
    s.trimends();
    s.trimSequenceChars();
    s3.stringtok(s, " ", true);
    // loop to extract words
    while (s3.stringlen() > 0) {
        strList::insert(s3);
        s3.stringtok(s, " ", false);
    }
}

//////////////////////////////////////////////////////////////////////
//
wordstr::wordstr(strList& sl) : strList(sl) {}
//
```

```
// Purpose: builds a list of words using the list sl.
//
// Parameters:
//
//    input: sl - the source list object.
//

//////////////////////////////////////////////////////////////////////
//
wordstr::wordstr() : strList() {}
//
// Purpose: default constructor.
//

//////////////////////////////////////////////////////////////////////
//
wordstr::wordstr(wordstr& w)
//
// Purpose: builds a list of words using an existing one.
//
// Parameters:
//
//    input: w - the source list of words.
//
{
    copy(w);
}

//////////////////////////////////////////////////////////////////////
//
wordstr::~wordstr()
//
// Purpose: deletes this list of words.
//
{
    clear();
}

//////////////////////////////////////////////////////////////////////
//
wordstr& wordstr::copy(wordstr& w)
```

continues

Listing 15.5. continued

```
//
// Purpose: copies the list of words w to this list.  The old list
// is first deleted.
//
// Parameters:
//
//    input: w - the source list of words.
//
{
    strListNode* p;
    strListNode* q;
    strListNode* r;

    if (head)
       clear();
    listSize = w.listSize;
    if (listSize == 0) {
       head = NULL;
       tail = NULL;
    }
    else {
       // create the head of the new list
       head = new strListNode;
       q = head;
       p = w.head;
       q->data = p->data;
       q->nextNode = NULL;
       p = p->nextNode;
       while (p) {
          r = new strListNode;
          r->data = p->data;
          r->nextNode = NULL;
          q->nextNode = r;
          q = q->nextNode;
          p = p->nextNode;
       }
       tail = q; // tail points to the last node
    }
    return *this;
}
```

```
/////////////////////////////////////////////////////////////////////
//
wordstr& wordstr::operator =(const char c)
//
// Purpose: overwrites a list of words with a single character.
//
// Parameters:
//
//    input: c - the source character.
//
{
    cString s(c);
    wordstr w(s);
    copy(w);
    return *this;
}

/////////////////////////////////////////////////////////////////////
//
wordstr& wordstr::operator =(const char* s)
//
// Purpose: overwrites a list of words with a single string s.
//
// Parameters:
//
//    input: s - the source string.
//
{
    wordstr w(s);
    copy(w);
    return *this;
}

/////////////////////////////////////////////////////////////////////
//
wordstr& wordstr::operator =(cString& s)
//
// Purpose: overwrites the word list with string object s.
//
// Parameters:
//
```

continues

Listing 15.5. continued

```
//    input: s - the source string.
//
{
    wordstr w(s);
    copy(w);
    return *this;
}

//////////////////////////////////////////////////////////////////
//
wordstr& wordstr::operator =(wordstr& w)
//
// Purpose: overwrites the word list with list w.
//
// Parameters:
//
//    input: w - the source list of words.
//
{
    copy(w);
    return *this;
}

//////////////////////////////////////////////////////////////////
//
unsigned wordstr::pos(wordstr& w,
                      unsigned first,
                      unsigned last,
                      unsigned start,
                      boolean caseSense)
//
// Purpose: searches for the word position of words first to last of
// w in this list of words, starting at word number start.  The
// function returns the index of the first matching word.
//
// Parameters:
//
//    input: w - the search word.
//           first - the first word in w to be searched.
//           last - the last word in w to be searched.
```

```
//          start - the index of the first searched word.
//          caseSense - the case-sensitivity mode.
//
{
    cString s1, s2;
    unsigned i, j, lastj = 0;

    if (start == 0       ||
        start > listSize ||
        w.listSize == 0  ||
        first > last     ||
        first > w.listSize)
        return 0;
    last = (last <= w.listSize) ? last : w.listSize;
    // initialize the search indices
    i = start; // search this list
    j = first; // search w
    do {
      // extract the word j from w.  Use lastj to avoid
      // extracting the same member (especially for j = 1)
      if (j != lastj) {
        w.get(s1, j, 1);
        lastj = j;
      }
      // extract the word i from this list
      get(s2, i, 1);
      // convert s1 and s2 to uppercase if search is case-insensitive
      if (!caseSense) {
        s1.stringupr();
        s2.stringupr();
      }
      if (s1 == s2) {
        i++;
        j++;
      }
      else {
        i += 2 - j;
        j = 1;
      }
    } while (!(j > last) || (i > listSize));
    // return match outcome
```

continues

Listing 15.5. continued

```
    return (j > last) ? i - last : i;
}

//////////////////////////////////////////////////////////////////////
//
void wordstr::insert(wordstr& w,
                     unsigned first,
                     unsigned last,
                     unsigned after)
//
// Purpose: inserts the list of words w after the specified word
// index.
//
// Parameters:
//
//    input: w - the inserted list of words.
//           first - the index of the first inserted word.
//           last - the index of the last inserted word.
//           after - the insertion word index.
//
{
   cString s;
   if (first <= last &&
       first <= w.listSize) {
     last = (last <= w.listSize) ? last : w.listSize;
     // process the words of w, starting with the last one
     for (unsigned i = last; i >= first; i--) {
        // get the next string of list w
        // and insert it in the list
        w.get(s, i, 1);
        strList::insert(s, after);
     }
   }
}

//////////////////////////////////////////////////////////////////////
//
void wordstr::translate(wordstr& findword,
                        wordstr& replaceword,
                        unsigned& count,
```

```
                        unsigned start,
                        unsigned freq,
                        boolean caseSense)
//
// Purpose: replaces the first word of list findword with the
// first word of list replaceword.
//
// Parameters:
//
//    input: findword - the search word.
//           replaceword - the replacement word.
//           start - the word index of the first searched word.
//           freq - the maximum number of word replacements.
//           caseSense - the case-sensitivity mode.
//
//    output: count - the actual number of word replacements.
//
// Comment: the function extracts the first word from both findword
// and replaceword.  Extra words in these parameters are ignored.
//
{
  strListNode* p;
  cString findstr, replacestr, datastr;

  count = 0;
  if (   start == 0
      || start > listSize
      || findword.listSize == 0
      || replaceword.listSize == 0)
    return;
  // extract the search string object
  findword.get(findstr, 1, 1);
  // convert to uppercase if search is case-insensitive
  if (!caseSense)
      findstr.stringupr();
  // extract the replacement string object
  replaceword.get(replacestr, 1, 1);
  p = head;
  // search for word number start
  while (p && start-- > 1)
    p = p->nextNode;
```

continues

Listing 15.5. continued

```
    while (p && freq > 0) {
       datastr = p->data;
       // convert to uppercase if search is case-insensitive
       if (!caseSense)
          datastr.stringupr();
       // current word matches the search string object?
       if (datastr == findstr) {
          // replace the current word
          p->data = replacestr;
          freq--;
          count++;
       }
       p = p->nextNode;
    }
}

////////////////////////////////////////////////////////////////////
//
ostream& operator <<(ostream& os, wordstr& w)
//
// Purpose: writes the list of words to a stream.
//
// Parameters:
//
//    input: w - the output list of word.
//
//    in/out: os - the output stream.
//
{
   cString s;
   // get all the words in the list
   w.get(s);
   os << s;
   return os;
}

////////////////////////////////////////////////////////////////////
/////////////////////////  Class itemstr /////////////////////////
////////////////////////////////////////////////////////////////////
```

```
//////////////////////////////////////////////////////////////////////
//
itemstr::itemstr(const char* s)
//
// Purpose: creates a list of comma-delimited items from the
// string s.
//
// Parameters:
//
//    input: s - the source string.
//
{
    // create local duplicates of string s that are
    // modified internally
    cString s2(s), s3(s);
    unsigned count;

    head = NULL;
    listSize = 0;
    // prepend a space to s2 if its first character is a comma
    if (s2[0] == ',')
       s2 = ' ' + s2;
    // append a space to s2 if its first character is a comma
    if (s2[s2.stringlen()] == ',')
        s2 += ' ';
    // replace ",," with ", ,"
    s2.replace(",,", ", ,", count);
    // extract the first item
    s3.stringtok(s2, ",", true);
    // loop while there is a extracted item
    while (s3.stringlen() > 0) {
        // insert the item in this list
        strList::insert(s3);
        // extract the next item
        s3.stringtok(s2, ",", false);
    }
}

//////////////////////////////////////////////////////////////////////
//
itemstr::itemstr(cString& s)
```

continues

Listing 15.5. continued

```
//
// Purpose: creates a list of comma-delimited items from the
// string object s.
//
// Parameters:
//
//    input: s - the source string.
//
{
    // create local duplicates of string s that are
    // modified internally
    cString s2(s), s3(s);
    unsigned count;

    head = NULL;
    listSize = 0;
    // prepend a space to s2 if its first character is a comma
    if (s2[0] == ',')
       s2 = ' ' + s2;
    // append a space to s2 if its first character is a comma
    if (s2[s2.stringlen()] == ',')
        s2 += ' ';
    // replace ",," with ", ,"
    s2.replace(",,", ", ,", count);
    // extract the first item
    s3.stringtok(s2, ",", true);
    // loop while there is a extracted item
    while (s3.stringlen() > 0) {
        // insert the item in this list
        strList::insert(s3);
        // extract the next item
        s3.stringtok(s2, ",", false);
    }
}

//////////////////////////////////////////////////////////////////
//
itemstr::itemstr(strList& sl) : wordstr(sl) {}
//
```

```
// Purpose: creates a list as a copy of the existing list sl.
//
// Parameters:
//
//    input: sl - the source list.
//

////////////////////////////////////////////////////////////////////
//
itemstr::itemstr() : wordstr() {}
//
// Purpose: the default constructor.
//

////////////////////////////////////////////////////////////////////
//
itemstr::itemstr(itemstr& t)
//
// Purpose: creates a list of items based on the existing list
// of items t.
//
// Parameters:
//
//    input: t - the source list of items.
//
{
    copy(t);
}

////////////////////////////////////////////////////////////////////
//
itemstr::~itemstr()
//
// Purpose: deletes the list of items and frees their dynamic
// space.
//
{
    clear();
}
```

continues

Listing 15.5. continued

```
/////////////////////////////////////////////////////////////////////
//
itemstr& itemstr::copy(itemstr& t)
//
// Purpose: copies the list of items t.
//
// Parameters:
//
//    input: t - the source list of items.
//
{
    strListNode* p;
    strListNode* q;
    strListNode* r;

    // clear this list if it is not empty
    if (head)
       clear();
    // update the list size
    listSize = t.listSize;
    // is list empty?
    if (listSize == 0) {
       head = NULL;
       tail = NULL;
    }
    else {
       // create the head of the new list
       head = new strListNode;
       q = head;
       p = t.head;
       q->data = p->data;
       q->nextNode = NULL;
       p = p->nextNode;
       // loop to copy the nodes
       while (p) {
          r = new strListNode;
          r->data = p->data;
          r->nextNode = NULL;
          q->nextNode = r;
          q = q->nextNode;
```

```
            p = p->nextNode;
        }
        tail = q; // tail points to the last node
    }
    return *this;
}

//////////////////////////////////////////////////////////////////////
//
itemstr& itemstr::operator =(const char c)
//
// Purpose: assigns the character c as the new item in this list.
// The current list items are deleted.
//
// Parameters:
//
//    input: c - the new and only list item.
//
{
    cString s(c);
    itemstr t(s);
    copy(t);
    return *this;
}

//////////////////////////////////////////////////////////////////////
//
itemstr& itemstr::operator =(const char* s)
//
// Purpose: assigns the string s as the new item in this list.
// The current list items are deleted.
//
// Parameters:
//
//    input: s - the new and only list item.
//
{
    strList s2(s);
    itemstr t(s2);
    copy(t);
    return *this;
}
```

continues

Listing 15.5. continued

```
////////////////////////////////////////////////////////////////////
//
itemstr& itemstr::operator =(cString& s)
//
// Purpose: assigns the string s as the new item in this list.
// The current list items are deleted.
//
// Parameters:
//
//    input: s - the new and only list item.
//
{
    itemstr t(s);
    copy(t);
    return *this;
}

////////////////////////////////////////////////////////////////////
//
itemstr& itemstr::operator =(itemstr& t)
//
// Purpose: assigns the list of items t to this list.  The current
// list items are deleted.
//
// Parameters:
//
//    input: t - the source list of items.
//
{
    copy(t);
    return *this;
}

////////////////////////////////////////////////////////////////////
//
ostream& operator <<(ostream& os, itemstr& t)
//
// Purpose: writes the list of items t to the output stream os.
//
// Parameters:
```

```
//
//    input: t - the output list of items.
//
//    in/out: os - the output stream.
//
{
   cString s;
   // obtain all of the items in the string s
   t.get(s, 1, 0xffff, ',');
   os << s;
   return os;
}

////////////////////////////////////////////////////////////////////
//////////////////////////  Class tokenstr //////////////////////////
////////////////////////////////////////////////////////////////////

////////////////////////////////////////////////////////////////////
//
tokenstr::tokenstr(const char* s, const char* delimstr)
//
// Purpose: creates a token list using the string s and the
// delimiter string delimstr.
//
// Parameters:
//
//    input: s - the source string.
//           delimstr - the string containing the delimiter
//             characters.
//
{
    cString s2(s), s3(s);

    // assign delimstr parameter to the delimstring member
    delimstring = delimstr;
    head = NULL;
    listSize = 0;
    // extract the first token
    s3.stringtok(s2, delimstr, true);
    // loop while there is an extracted token
    while (s3.stringlen() > 0) {
```

continues

Listing 15.5. continued

```
            // insert the token in the list
            strList::insert(s3);
            // extract the next token
            s3.stringtok(s2, delimstr, false);
        }
    }

////////////////////////////////////////////////////////////////////
//
tokenstr::tokenstr(cString& s, cString& delimstr)
//
// Purpose: creates a token list using the string s and the
// delimiter string delimstr.
//
// Parameters:
//
//    input: s - the source string.
//           delimstr - the string containing the delimiter
//             characters.
//
//
{
    cString s2(s), s3(s);

    // assign delimstr parameter to the delimstring member
    delimstring = delimstr;
    head = NULL;
    listSize = 0;
    // extract the first token
    s3.stringtok(s2, delimstr.getstr(), true);
    // loop while there is an extracted token
    while (s3.stringlen() > 0) {
        // insert the token in the list
        strList::insert(s3);
        // extract the next token
        s3.stringtok(s2, delimstr.getstr(), false);
    }
}
```

```
////////////////////////////////////////////////////////////////////
//
tokenstr::tokenstr(strList& sl, cString& delimstr) : wordstr(sl)
//
// Purpose: creates a list of tokens using an existing list of
// strings sl.  The number of items is determined by the number
// of comma-delimited substrings in the list sl.
//
// Parameters:
//
//    input: sl - the source list of strings.
//           delimstr - the string containing the delimiter
//             characters.
//
{
   delimstring = delimstr;
}

////////////////////////////////////////////////////////////////////
//
tokenstr::tokenstr() : wordstr()
//
// Purpose: the default constructor.
//
{
   delimstring = " ";
}

////////////////////////////////////////////////////////////////////
//
tokenstr::tokenstr(tokenstr& t)
//
// Purpose: creates a list of tokens using the existing list of
// tokens t.
//
// Parameters:
//
//    input: t - the source list of tokens.
//
{
    copy(t);
}
```

continues

Listing 15.5. continued

```
//////////////////////////////////////////////////////////////////////
//
tokenstr::~tokenstr()
//
// Purpose: deletes the list of tokens and frees its
// dynamic space.
//
{
    clear();
}

//////////////////////////////////////////////////////////////////////
//
tokenstr& tokenstr::copy(tokenstr& t)
//
// Purpose: copies the existing list of tokens t to this list.  The
// current list of tokens are first deleted.
//
// Parameters:
//
//    input: t - the source list of tokens.
//
//    output:
//
{
    strListNode* p;
    strListNode* q;
    strListNode* r;

    // clear this list if it is not empty
    if (head)
       clear();
    listSize = t.listSize;
    // is the new list empty?
    if (listSize == 0) {
       head = NULL;
       tail = NULL;
    }
    else {
       // create the head of the new list
```

```
        head = new strListNode;
        q - head;
        p = t.head;
        q->data = p->data;
        q->nextNode = NULL;
        p = p->nextNode;
        // loop to copy the nodes
        while (p) {
           r = new strListNode;
           r->data = p->data;
           r->nextNode = NULL;
           q->nextNode = r;
           q = q->nextNode;
           p = p->nextNode;
        }
        tail = q; // tail points to the last node
    }
    delimstring = t.delimstring;
    return *this;
}

//////////////////////////////////////////////////////////////////
//
tokenstr& tokenstr::operator =(tokenstr& t)
//
// Purpose: copies the existing list of tokens.
//
// Parameters:
//
//    input: t - the source list of tokens.
//
{
   copy(t);
   return *this;
}

//////////////////////////////////////////////////////////////////
//
tokenstr& tokenstr::assign(cString& s, cString& delimstr)
//
// Purpose: Uses the strings s and delimstr to build a list of
// tokens.
```

continues

Listing 15.5. continued

```
//
// Parameters:
//
//    input: s - the source string.
//           delimstr - the string containing the delimiter
//             characters.
//
{
   tokenstr t(s, delimstr);

   copy(t);
   return *this;
}

////////////////////////////////////////////////////////////////////
//
ostream& operator <<(ostream& os, tokenstr& t)
//
// Purpose: writes the list of tokens to an output stream.  The
// output appears delimited with the first character of member
// delimstring.
//
// Parameters:
//
//    input: t - the output stream.
//
//    in/out: os - the output stream.
//
{
   cString s;
   t.get(s, 1, 0xffff, t.delimstring[0]);
   os << s;
   return os;
}
```

The Class of Tokens

Listing 15.4 showed the declaration of the `tokenstr` class. This class is a descendant of `wordstr` and models tokens that are delimited with user-defined characters. Like `itemstr`, the `tokenstr` class is a descendant of the `wordstr` and `strList` classes. The class also inherits a number of functions. Listing 15.5 showed the implementation of the members of the `tokenstr` class.

The `tokenstr` class declares the `delimstr` data member, five constructors, a destructor, the private copy function, the `assign` function, and the assignment (=) and insertion (<<) operators. (The latter is a friend function.)

The `delimstring` member stores the delimiting characters. The value assigned to this member comes through the class constructor and the `assign` function. More about these routines next.

The default class constructor creates an empty list of tokens with the space character as the token delimiter. You may want to assign a different character or assign additional characters to the `delimstring` data member.

The constructor `tokenstr(const char* s, const char* delimstr)` creates a list of tokens by parsing the argument of the s parameter, using the delimiter characters specified by the argument of the `delimstr` parameter. The constructor assigns the argument for `delimstr` to the `delimstring` member and parses the different tokens using a `while` loop.

The code for the constructor `tokenstr(cString& s, cString& delimstr)` is similar to that of the `itemstr(const char*)` constructor. The difference is in the parameter types.

The constructor `tokenstr(strList& sl, cString& delimstr)` creates a list of tokens by copying the nodes of the `sl` parameter to the targeted `tokenstr` instance. The constructor assigns the argument of the `delimstr` parameter to the delimstring member. You are responsible for ensuring that the nodes of the `sl` parameter are parsed correctly according to the characters in string `delimstr`.

The `tokenstr(tokenstr&)` constructor creates a list of tokens using an existing instance of class `tokenstr`. The constructor simply calls the private function `copy` to duplicate the list nodes of the argument.

The class destructor removes the list of tokens by calling the inherited `strList::clear` function.

The `assign` function plays a special role in creating a new list of tokens that use a *different* set of delimiting characters. This means that the previous list of tokens is deleted. This is a logical step because changing the delimiter most likely will alter the parsed tokens. The `assign` member creates a local instance of class `tokenstr` and then copies that list to the targeted `tokenstr` instance.

The assignment operator (=) enables you to assign a list of tokens to a `tokenstr` instance without altering the delimiting characters. This operator has the same effect as using the `assign` function with the argument for `delimstr`, matching the current value in the `delimstring` member.

The insertion operator (<<) writes a list of tokens, `t`, to an output stream `os`. The first character in the `delimstring` member is used to delimit the tokens in the string image `s`. Admittedly, this is not a satisfactory solution. I suggest that you customize the code to suit your needs.

Testing Words, Items, and Tokens

Listing 15.6 contains the source code for the TSWORD.CPP program, which tests the classes `wordstr`, `itemstr`, and `tokenstr`. The test for the `wordstr` class involves the following tasks:

1. Declaring initialized instances of `wordstr` `w1`, `w2`, `w3`, `w4`, and `w`.
2. Assigning the string `Clement` to the instance `w`, inserting `w` in the instance `w4`, and repeating this task for other strings.
3. Displaying the instances `w1`, `w2`, `w3`, and `w4`.
4. Assigning the strings `Mimi` and `Bobbi` to the `wordstr` instances `w1` and `w2`, respectively.
5. Translating the words in instance `w4` by replacing the first word of `w1` with the first word of `w2`. The variable `count` contains the number of translations after the *translate* function is called.
6. Displaying the instance `w4` and the number of translations.
7. Assigning the string `clEmenT` to instance `w1`.
8. Displaying the word index of instance `w1` in instance `w4`. This task involves calling the `pos` function to perform a case-insensitive search.
9. Sorting the words in instance `w3` and then displaying that instance.
10. Reversing the order of the words in instance `w3` and then displaying that instance.
11. Removing the second, third, and fourth words from instance `w4` and then displaying that instance.
12. Assigning instance `w4` to `w3` and then comparing these instances using an `if` statement. This task tests the (==) operator.
13. Displaying the updated instance `w3`.
14. Assigning the string `General Patton` to instance `w3` and then displaying that instance.

The output of the preceding tasks is as follows:

```
Namir
Clement
Shammas
Namir Clement Mimi Shammas Mimi
Namir Clement Bobbi Shammas Bobbi
2 translation(s)
word index of 'clEmenT' = 2
Sorted words are: Bobbi Bobbi Clement Namir Shammas
```

```
Reverse sorted words are: Shammas Namir Clement Bobbi Bobbi
Shammas Bobbi
words w3 and w4 are the same
Shammas Bobbi
General Patton
press any key to continue ...
```

The program tests the `itemstr` class by performing the following tasks:

1. Creating the initialized instances of class `itemstr` `t1`, `t2`, `t3`, `t4`, and `t`.
2. Assigning the string `Clement` to the instance `t`, inserting `w` in the instance `t4`, then repeating this task for other strings.
3. Displaying the instances `t1`, `t2`, `t3`, and `t4`.
4. Assigning the strings `Mimi` and `Bobbi` to the `itemstr` instances `t1` and `t2`, respectively.
5. Translating the items in instance `t4` by replacing the first item of `t1` with the first item of `t2`. The variable count contains the number of translations after the `translate` function is called.
6. Displaying the instance `t4` and the number of translations.
7. Assigning the string `Clement` to instance `t1`.
8. Displaying the item index of instance `t1` in instance `t4`. This task involves calling the `pos` function to perform a case-sensitive search.
9. Sorting the items in instance `t3` and then displaying that instance.
10. Removing the second, third, and fourth items from instance `t4` and then displaying that instance.
11. Assigning instance `t4` to `t3`.
12. Displaying the updated instance `w3`.
13. Assigning the string `General Patton` to instance `t3` and then displaying that instance.

The output of the above tasks is as follows:

```
Namir
Clement
   Shammas
```

```
  Namir,Clement,Mimi,   Shammas,Mimi
  Namir,Clement,Bobbi,   Shammas,Bobbi
2 translation(s)
item index of Clement = 2
Sorted items are:    Shammas,  Namir,Bobbi,Bobbi,Clement
  Namir,Bobbi
  Namir,Bobbi
General,Patton
press any key to continue ...
```

The test program performs tests on the `tokenstr` class that are similar to those of the `itemstr` class discussed earlier. The test program creates instances of `tokenstr` class `tk1`, `tk2`, `tk3`, `tk4`, and `tk`. These instances are manipulated in a similar manner as the instances `t1`, `t2`, `t3`, `t4`, and `t`. The output of these tasks is as follows:

```
Namir
Clement
Shammas
Namir Clement Mimi Shammas Mimi
Namir Clement Bobbi Shammas Bobbi
2 translation(s)
token index of Clement = 2
Sorted tokens are: Bobbi Bobbi Clement Namir Shammas
Namir Bobbi
Namir Bobbi
General Patton

press any key to end the program ...
```

Listing 15.6. The source code for the TSWORD.CPP program.

```
#include "video.h"
#include "wordstr.hpp"

main()
{
    unsigned count;
    {
      // ------------------ test words ---------------
      wordstr w1("   Namir  "),
              w2("  Clement  "),
```

continues

Listing 15.6. continued

```
            w3("   Shammas   "),
            w4("Namir"),
            w("Any");
    clrscr();
    w = "Clement"; w4.insert(w);
    w = "Mimi";    w4.insert(w);
    w = "Shammas"; w4.insert(w);
    w = "Mimi";    w4.insert(w);
    cout << w1 << '\n';
    cout << w2 << '\n';
    cout << w3 << '\n';
    cout << w4 << '\n';
    w1 = "Mimi"; w2 = "Bobbi";
    w4.translate(w1, w2, count);
    cout << w4 << '\n';
    cout << count << " translation(s)" << '\n';
    w1 = "clEmenT";
    cout << "word index of '" << w1 << "' = "
         << w4.pos(w1, 1, 1, 1, false) << '\n';
    w3.sort(w4);
    cout << "Sorted words are: " << w3 << '\n';
    w4.reverse(w3);
    cout << "Reverse sorted words are: " << w4 << '\n';
    w4.remove(2, 3);
    cout << w4 << '\n';
    w3 = w4;
    if (w3==w4)
       cout << "words w3 and w4 are the same";
    else
       cout << "words w3 and w4 are NOT the same";
    cout << '\n';
    cout << w3 << '\n';
    w3 = "General Patton";
    cout << w3 << '\n';
    cout << "press any key to continue ...";
    getch();
  }
  {
    // -------------------- test items --------------------
```

```
  itemstr t1("Namir"),
          t2("Clement"),
          t3("   Shammas"),
          t4("  Namir"),
          t("Any");
  clrscr();
  t = "Clement"; t4.insert(t);
  t = "Mimi"; t4.insert(t);
  t = "   Shammas"; t4.insert(t);
  t = "Mimi"; t4.insert(t);
  cout << t1 << '\n';
  cout << t2 << '\n';
  cout << t3 << '\n';
  cout << t4 << '\n';
  t1 = "Mimi"; t2 = "Bobbi";
  t4.translate(t1, t2, count);
  cout << t4 << '\n';
  cout << count << " translation(s)" << '\n';
  t1 = "Clement";
  cout << "item index of Clement = "
       << t4.pos(t1) << '\n';
  t3.sort(t4);
  cout << "Sorted items are: " << t3 << '\n';
  t4.remove(2, 3);
  cout << t4 << '\n';
  t3 = t4;
  cout << t3 << '\n';
  t3 = "General,Patton";
  cout << t3 << '\n';
  cout << "press any key to continue ...";
  getch();
}
{
  // --------------------- test tokens -------------
  char delim[] = " ,¦";
  tokenstr tk1("Namir", delim),
           tk2("Clement", delim),
           tk3("Shammas", delim),
           tk4("Namir", delim),
           tk("Any", delim);
```

continues

Listing 15.6. continued

```
        clrscr();
        tk.assign("Clement", delim); tk4.insert(tk);
        tk.assign("Mimi", delim);    tk4.insert(tk);
        tk.assign("Shammas", delim); tk4.insert(tk);
        tk.assign("Mimi", delim);    tk4.insert(tk);
        cout << tk1 << '\n';
        cout << tk2 << '\n';
        cout << tk3 << '\n';
        cout << tk4 << '\n';
        tk1.assign("Mimi", delim);
        tk2.assign("Bobbi", delim);
        tk4.translate(tk1, tk2, count);
        cout << tk4 << '\n';
        cout << count << " translation(s)" << '\n';
        tk1.assign("Clement", delim);
        cout << "token index of Clement = "
             << tk4.pos(tk1) << '\n';
        tk3.sort(tk4);
        cout << "Sorted tokens are: " << tk3 << '\n';
        tk4.remove(2, 3);
        cout << tk4 << '\n';
        tk3 = tk4;
        cout << tk3 << '\n';
        tk3.assign("General,Patton", delim);
        cout << tk3 << '\n';
      }
      // ---------------- end of tests ----------------
      cout << '\n' << "press any key to end the program ...";
      getche();
      return 0;
}
```

Summary

This chapter presented classes that model lists of strings, words, items, and tokens. Using inheritance, these classes are constructed in an efficient way, sharing common functionality.

- The `strList` class, which models the list of strings, offers many operations that manipulate words, items, and tokens.
- The `wordstr` class, which models the class of words, provides a number of functions that handle substrings that are delimited with spaces.
- The classes `itemstr` and `tokestr` handle strings delimited by commas and user-defined delimiters, respectively. The functionality of class `wordstr` is inherited by these descendant classes. Inheritance and linked lists permit both shared functionality among these three classes and the elimination of redundant code.

If you plan to create C++ applications that process text, the classes presented in this chapter are versatile tools. These classes also provide good nuclei for descendants that offer more customized string manipulation, such as pattern search and data compression.

Sorting And Searching Arrays

Arrays are among the most commonly used data structures. Many programming languages such as C++, C, BASIC, and Pascal support arrays. The power of arrays comes from the capability to access their elements at random. Because of their flexibility, arrays are used to store and manipulate data in memory. Arrays also are ideal for small-scale databases that store and manage a variety of information. Managing arrays involves two important operations, sorting and searching. This chapter looks at a simple template class for arrays. The main focus of the chapter is not the `Array` class itself, but the searching and sorting operations.

The Array Class

Start by looking at the template class `Array`. Listing 16.1 shows the source code for the array.hpp header file, which contains the declaration of the `Array` class. This class models arrays that resemble C++ arrays. In other words, the lowest array index is 0, and you're responsible for tracking the portion of the array that contains meaningful data. You can modify the class and its member functions to support a *working size*—the number of leading array elements that contain meaningful data. Using the working size establishes a more formal partition between used array elements, which contain meaningful data, and unused array elements, which contain garbage data.

The header file declares two constants, `NO_ELEM_FOUND` and `DEFAULT_ARRAY_SIZE`. The various search functions of the `Array` class use `NO_ELEM_FOUND` to indicate that no match is found. The value of this constant indicates that the range of indices of an ar-ray is `0` to `0xfffe`. The second constant, `DEFAULT_ARRAYS_SIZE`, specifies the default size of an array.

The header file also declares the enumerated type `linearSearchMove`. This type declares the enumerated values used by the `LinearSearch` function. This chapter covers both topics later.

The template class `Array` declares the following data members. Most of them are protected, as expected.

- The `arrPtr` member is a pointer to the template class `T`, and it represents the dynamic space that stores the various array elements.
- The `size` member stores the current array size.
- The `badIndex` member is an instance of the template class `T`. This member is referenced by the access operator (`[]`) when the supplied index is equal to or greater than the data member `size`. To assign a value to the `badIndex` member, you must use a high index (for example, 0xffff).
- The `allocateError` member stores the state of the last dynamic allocation.

The public data member `isSorted` is a Boolean member that indicates whether the array has sorted elements. Why make `isSorted` public? The answer lies in the fact that most

> sorting functions enable you to sort a portion of the array. This means that you can exclude array elements that contain meaningful data when sorting.
>
> In fact, you can have several distinct groups of sorted elements in a single array! Consequently, an instance of the Array class may be completely ordered, partially ordered (with possible multiple groups of elements), or completely unordered. The access operator ([]) also adds to the problem. Because the operator works to store and recall data in the array, there's no way to tell whether an invocation of the access operator stores or recalls data.
>
> Although recalling data from an array element does not affect the array order, storing new information most likely will corrupt the order of that array. Combine the three array-order states with how the access operator works, and you quickly draw the conclusion that the `Array` class cannot easily maintain the array-order state.
>
> The solution to this problem is to provide a Boolean public member that your applications can set and clear to indicate some type of order. The `isSorted` member is set to true by the sorting functions to indicate that there is *some* level of order in the array. The searching functions don't use the value of `isSorted` because that value is not indicative of the extent of order. Therefore, your applications are responsible for manipulating the `isSorted` member and interpreting its value.

The `Array` class declares constructors, a destructor, functions, and operators. The functions fall into these categories:

- Instance (or state) query functions
- Instance (or state) manipulation functions and operators
- Sorting functions
- Searching functions

Some of the instance-query and instance-manipulation functions have in-line code that appears in the class declaration. Most of the previous functions are defined in the ARRAY.CPP library file. I present the contents of the ARRAY.CPP file in segments that appear in the following multiple listings.

Listing 16.1. The source code for the array.hpp header file.

```
//////////////////////////////////////////////////////////////////////
//                                                                  //
//                        Array Library                             //
//                                                                  //
//               Copyright  1992  Namir Clement Shammas             //
//                                                                  //
// Version 1.0.0                                           6/09/92 //
//                                                                  //
//                                                                  //
//  Implement a library of a simple template class of arrays        //
//  accompanied by a rich set of sorting and searching              //
//  functions.                                                      //
//                                                                  //
//////////////////////////////////////////////////////////////////////

#ifndef _ARRAY_HPP
#define _ARRAY_HPP

#include "comndata.h"

const unsigned NO_ELEM_FOUND = 0xffff;
const DEFAULT_ARRAY_SIZE = 10;

enum linearSearchMove
   { moveNot,      // do not move matching array element
     moveUp,       // move up matching array element by one position
     moveToFront, // move matching array element to front
     moveHalfWay  // move matching array element halfway
                   // to the front
   };

template<class T>
class Array
{

  protected:
    T* arrPtr;
    unsigned size;
    T badIndex;
    boolean allocateError;
```

```
  void copy(Array<T>& srcArray);
  void Qsort(unsigned first, unsigned last);

public:
  boolean isSorted;
  Array();
  Array(unsigned arraySize);
  Array(Array<T>& srcArray)
    { copy(srcArray); }
  ~Array()
    { delete [] arrPtr; }
  boolean expand(unsigned newSize);
  boolean getAllocateError() const
    { return allocateError; }
  unsigned getSize() const
    { return size; }
  T& operator[](unsigned index)
    { return (index < size) ? *(arrPtr + index) : badIndex; }
  Array<T>& operator =(Array<T>& array)
   {
     copy(array);
     return *this;
   }
  void fillArray(T fillValue)
   {
     for (unsigned i = 0; i < size; i++)
       *(arrPtr + i) = fillValue;
   }

  ////////////////////// Sort member functions ////////////////
  void ShellSort(unsigned last, unsigned first = 0);
  void CombSort(unsigned last, unsigned first = 0);
  void QuickSort(unsigned last, unsigned first = 0);
  void HeapSort(unsigned last);
  boolean MergeSortedArrays(Array<T>& Array1,
                            Array<T>& Array2,
                            unsigned last1,
                            unsigned last2,
                            unsigned first1 = 0,
                            unsigned first2 = 0,
                            unsigned start = 0);
```

continues

Listing 16.1. continued

```
    ////////////////////// Search member functions ////////////////
    unsigned LinearSearch(T& searchData,
                          unsigned last,
                          unsigned first = 0,
                          unsigned start = 0,
                          boolean searchForward = true,
                          linearSearchMove move = moveNot);
    unsigned StatisticalSearch(T& searchData,
                               unsigned last,
                               unsigned first = 0);
    unsigned StatLinearSearch(T& searchData,
                              unsigned last,
                              unsigned first = 0);
    unsigned BinarySearch(T& searchData,
                          unsigned last,
                          unsigned first = 0);
    unsigned ModifiedBinarySearch(T& searchData,
                                  unsigned last,
                                  unsigned first = 0,
                                  unsigned occurrence = 1);

    unsigned InterpolativeSearch(T& searchData,
                                 double searchValue,
                                 double* arrValues,
                                 unsigned last,
                                 unsigned first = 0);

    unsigned InterpBinSearch(T& searchData,
                             double searchValue,
                             double* arrValues,
                             unsigned last,
                             unsigned first = 0);

};

#endif
```

Listing 16.2. The constructors for the `Array` class.

```
//////////////////////////////////////////////////////////////////////
//                                                                  //
//                        Array Library                             //
//                                                                  //
//              Copyright (c) 1992  Namir Clement Shammas           //
//                                                                  //
// Version 1.0.0                                            6/09/92 //
//                                                                  //
//                                                                  //
//  Implement a library of a simple template class of arrays        //
//  accompanied by a rich set of sorting and searching              //
//  functions.                                                      //
//                                                                  //
//////////////////////////////////////////////////////////////////////

#include "array.hpp"

//////////////////////////////////////////////////////////////////////
//
template<class T>
Array<T>::Array()
//
// Purpose: the default constructor. Creates an array with a
// default size.
//
{
   arrPtr = new T[size = DEFAULT_ARRAY_SIZE];
   isSorted = false;
   allocateError = (arrPtr) ? false : true;
}

//////////////////////////////////////////////////////////////////////
//
template<class T>
Array<T>::Array(unsigned arraySize)
//
// Purpose: creates an array with a specified size.
//
```

continues

Listing 16.2. continued

```
//
//    input: arraySize - the array size.
//
{
   size = (arraySize == 0) ? 1 : arraySize;
   arrPtr = new T[size];
   isSorted = false;
   allocateError = (arrPtr) ? false : true;
}
```

The `Array` class declares three constructors: the default constructor, the `Array(unsigned)` constructor, and the `Array(Array<T>&)` constructor.

- The default constructor creates an empty array with `DEFAULT_ARRAY_SIZE` elements.
- The `Array(unsigned)` constructor creates an array with its size specified by the argument.
- The `Array(Array<T>&)` constructor creates an array that is a copy of the argument, an existing instance of `Array`. This constructor calls the protected function `copy` to create a duplicate of the argument.

The implementation of the first two constructors appears in Listing 16.2.

The class destructor recuperates the dynamic space accessed by the member `arrPtr`.

The `Array` class has the following functions, defined in the class declaration:

- The `getAllocateError` function. This function returns the value stored in the `allocateError` data member. Call the `getAllocateError` function to obtain the state of the last dynamic allocation.
- The `getSize` function. This function returns the current size of the array.
- The `fillArray` function. This function fills an instance of the `Array` class with the value of the parameter `fillValue`. This function initializes or resets the values of an `Array` instance.
- The access operator (`[]`). This operator returns the reference to the array member `index`. If the value of `index` is not less than the `size` member, the operator returns the reference to the `badIndex` data member.

- The assignment operator (=). This operator enables you to assign one instance of the Array class to another. These two instances must have the same type used in instantiating the template class Array.

The Array class has a single state-manipulating function, the expand function, defined in the ARRAY.CPP file. Listing 16.3 shows the expand function. This function expands the size of an Array instance to newSize. The function returns a value of True if the array is expanded and False if otherwise. The argument for newSize must exceed the value of the size data member; otherwise, the function returns a value of False. If the dynamic allocation for the new array fails, the function returns a value of False and sets the member allocateError to True. Therefore, you must check the values returned by this function and by getAllocateError to better determine the type of error.

Listing 16.3. The expand function.

```
/////////////////////////////////////////////////////////////////////
//
template<class T>
boolean Array<T>::expand(unsigned newSize)
//
// Purpose: expands the current array size to newSize. If the
// expansion fails due to an allocation error, the function assigns
// true to the allocateError data member.
//
// Parameters:
//
//    input: newSize - the new array size.
//
{
  T* p;

  allocateError = false;
  if (newSize > size) {
    // create the space for the expanded array
    p = new T[newSize];
    // allocation failed?
    if (!p) {
```

continues

Listing 16.3. continued

```
      allocateError = true;
      return false;
    }
    // if current array has data
    if (arrPtr) {
      // copy arrPtr in members
      for (unsigned i = 0; i < size; i++)
        *(p + i) = *(arrPtr + i);
      // remove the old array
      delete [] arrPtr;
    }
    // assign pointer p to pointer arrPtr
    arrPtr = p;
    // update the array size
    size = newSize;
    allocateError = false;
    return true;
  }
  else
    return false;
}
```

The source code for the protected `copy` function (mentioned earlier in regard to the `Array(Array<T>&)` constructor) appears in Listing 16.4. The `copy` function duplicates the array `scrArray` to the targeted `Array` instance. If the two arrays are of different sizes, the `copy` function deletes the dynamic space of the targeted array and reallocates a new space that matches that of `srcArray`. The function copies the elements of `scrArray` to the elements of the targeted array using a `for` loop. Each loop iteration copies a single array element. This approach relies on the assignment operator (=) of the `template` class to correctly copy the elements. This step-by-step copying is needed, especially when the instances of class `T` have dynamic data.

Listing 16.4. The copy function.

```
//////////////////////////////////////////////////////////////////////
//
template<class T>
```

```
void Array<T>::copy(Array<T>& srcArray)
//
// Purpose: copies the srcArray array to this instance.
//
// Parameters:
//
//    input: srcArray - the source array to be copied.
//
//
{
  T *p, *q;

  if (size != srcArray.size) {
    delete [] arrPtr;
    arrPtr = new T[size = srcArray.size];
  }
  isSorted = srcArray.isSorted;
  if (!arrPtr) {
    allocateError = true;
    return;
  }
  p = arrPtr;
  q = srcArray.arrPtr;
  for (unsigned i = 0; i < size; i++, p++, q++)
    *p = *q;
  allocateError = false;
}
```

Sorting Methods

In this section I present the various sorting functions and discuss the methods they use. The discussion assumes that you already are familiar with the algorithms for these functions.

Sorting operations include the Shell-Metzner method, the new Combsort method, the fast QuickSort method, and the Heapsort method. Most of the functions that implement these methods are coded to enable you to sort any portion of the array.

The Shell-Metzner Sort Method

The Shell-Metzner method (sometimes called the *diminishing increments* method) belongs to the category of *in-place exchange-sort methods* (methods that swap the array elements to order them without the need for extra array elements or additional arrays). The basic algorithm sorts an array in cycles. Each cycle compares array elements that are set apart by a certain offset. Initially, the offset ranges from about half or a third (depending on the implementation) of the array size. This initial offset value permits the comparison of distant array elements and supports a long-range swap. Such a swap quickly puts the array elements in the vicinity of their final location.

Each cycle in the Shell-Metzner method consists of multiple passes. These passes ensure that the array elements set apart by the current offset value are in order. This order is only partial. Once a cycle orders the targeted elements, the offset value is reduced and the previous process is repeated. The last cycle compares immediately neighboring elements. When the last pass of the last cycle is completed, the array is sorted.

The order of the Shell sort is, approximately, $O(n (\lg(n)2)$, where $\lg(n)$ is the base 2 logarithm of n, the number of the sorted elements, if the optimum sequence of offset values is used. The order also has been found by some researchers to be $O(n1.5)$.

The proposed sequence for the offset value, h(i), is

```
h(i+1) = (h(i) - 1) / 2
h(i+1) = (h(i) - 1) / 3
```

The value for h(0) usually is taken as the number of array elements to sort. In comparing the two sequences, the first sequence produces a faster sort for large arrays (about 500 elements or more). The second sequence is faster for smaller arrays. The second sequence was proposed by Knuth.

Listing 16.5 shows the `ShellSort` function. The parameters `last` and `first` define the index range for the elements to sort. The default argument for `first` is `0`, the most likely value. The `last` parameter has no default argument. This is why it appears before `first` in the parameter list.

The function exits if any of the following conditions is true:

- The `first` parameter is greater than or equal to the `last` parameter.
- The `first` parameter is greater than or equal to the data member `size`.
- The data member `size` is less than 2.

The ShellSort function uses Knuth's sequence of calculating the comparison offset. The while loop contains the code for the cycles used in sorting the array. The while loop contains the code that supports the passes used to order array elements that are offset members apart. The for loop compares the array elements for each pass. The function uses the isSorted data member to flag the order of the array elements being sorted. When the function successfully exits, the value of member isSorted is True. This value indicates that there are sorted array elements in the targeted instance of the Array class.

Listing 16.5. The ShellSort function.

```
//////////////////////////////////////////////////////////////////////
//
template<class T>
void Array<T>::ShellSort(unsigned last, unsigned first)
//
// Purpose: sorts the array elements in the range [first...last]
// using the Shell-Metzner sort method.
//
// Parameters:
//
//    input: first, last - the range of sorted array elements.
//
{
   unsigned i, j, offset, n;
   T swapElem;

   if (first >= last ||
       first >= size ||
       size < 2)
     return;

    // adjust the parameter last?
    last = (last >= size) ? size - 1 : last;
    n = last - first + 1;
    offset = n;
    while (offset > 1) {
      // update offset and make sure it never goes below 1
      offset = (offset - 1) / 3;
      offset = (offset == 0) ? 1 : offset;
```

continues

Listing 16.5. continued

```
        // order neighbors that are offset elements apart
        do {
          isSorted = true;
          // compare neighbors that are offset elements apart
          for (i = first; i <= (last - offset); i++) {
            j = i + offset;
            // need to swap?
            if (*(arrPtr + i) > *(arrPtr + j)) {
              // swap elements i and j
              isSorted = false;
              swapElem = *(arrPtr + i);
              *(arrPtr + i) = *(arrPtr + j);
              *(arrPtr + j) = swapElem;
            }
          }
        } while (!isSorted);
      }
}
```

The Combsort Method

The Combsort method is a relatively new sorting method. It also belongs to the category of in-place exchange methods. It was developed by Richard Box and Stephen Lacey (for more information, see their article on the Combsort method in the April 1991 issue of *Byte*).

The Combsort method is a clever and efficient modification of the Bubble (yes, Bubble) sort method. The enhancement in sorting presented by the Combsort method offers a quantum leap over the bubble sort method. The tests conducted by Box and Lacey show that the Combsort method is about 50 times faster than the bubble sort. Box and Lacey also found the Combsort method to be slightly faster than the Heapsort method, but twice as slow as the Quicksort method. My own tests show the speed ratio between the Combsort method and the Shell method to be between 1:2 and 1:2.5. Box and Lacey claim that the order of the Combsort method is $O(n\lg(n))$. This is the same order as that of the Heapsort and Quicksort methods.

Because the Combsort method is new, let's discuss details. Box and Lacey state that they observed two types of elements while studying the slow bubble method, *turtles* and *rabbits*. Turtles, as the name suggests, are the array elements that slowly move toward their appropriate location in the array. By contrast, rabbits are the array elements that reach their final destination quickly. Box and Lacey argued that, by comparing more-distant array elements, they can increase the number of rabbits and decrease the number of turtles in an array. They studied the best sequence of offset values (similar to the offset used in the Shell-Metzner method) and came up with the following sequence:

```
h(i+1) = 8 * h(i) / 11
```

An interesting aspect of the Combsort method is that it can be regarded as a common modification of the bubble and the Shell-Metzner sort methods. Box and Lacey prefer to think of the Combsort method as a superset modification of the Bubble sort. When I look at the Combsort method, I see a subset modification of the Shell-Metzner method that succeeds in outperforming the Shell-Metzner method. How, you might ask, is that possible?

Recall that the Shell-Metzner method sorts an array by using cycles of ordering elements at different offset distances from each other. Each cycle consists of multiple passes that ensure the order of the (initially) distant array elements. The last pass of each cycle compares these ordered elements (ordered with respect to the current offset distance). In other words, the Shell-Metzner method establishes several stages of ordering the array elements—from elements that are about halfway across the array to the immediate neighbors.

In contrast, the Combsort method seems to eliminate these intermediate stages of ordering array elements that aren't immediate neighbors. Instead, the Combsort method is more concerned with quickly moving array elements to the vicinity of their final location. The Combsort method thus uses single-pass cycles for moving distant neighbors and multiple-passes for

> ordering immediate neighbors. In other words, the Shell method performs extra work that slows down the sorting process. The reduction in effort seems to work in favor of the Combsort method.
>
> Compare the code of the `CombSort` and `ShellSort` functions. You should arrive at the same conclusions.

Listing 16.6 shows the `CombSort` function. The function has parameters similar to those of the `ShellSort` function. The `CombSort` function has an outer `do-while` loop and an inner `for` loop. The `do-while` loop performs the single-pass cycles that move the compared distant array elements. The same loop offers the multiple passes required to breathe order among the elements that are immediate neighbors.

Listing 16.6. The `CombSort` function.

```
////////////////////////////////////////////////////////////////////////
//
template<class T>
void Array<T>::CombSort(unsigned last, unsigned first)
//
// Purpose: sorts the array elements in the range [first...last]
// using the new Combsort method.
//
// Parameters:
//
//    input: first, last - the range of sorted array elements.
//
// Comments: The function exits if parameter first is greater than
// or equal to the member size, or the parameter first is greater
// than or equal to the parameter last. If the parameter last is
// greater than or equal to member size, the function assigns the
// expression size - 1 to the parameter last.
//
//
```

```
{
  unsigned i, j, n, offset;
  T swapElem;

  if (first >= size ||
      first >= last ||
      size < 2)
    return;

  // adjust the argument for the parameter last ?
  last = (last >= size) ? size - 1 : last;
  // get the initial offset which is also
  // the number of sorted array elements.
  offset = last - first + 1; // get the initial offset
  // start loop to sort the array elements in the
  // range [first...last]
  do {
    // update the offset, making sure that it
    // does not become less than 1
    offset = (offset * 8) / 11;
    offset = (offset == 0) ? 1 : offset;
    isSorted = true;
    // start comparing array elements that are
    // offset members apart
    for (i = first; i <= (last - offset); i++) {
      j = i + offset;
      // need to swap elements i and j?
      if (*(arrPtr + i) > *(arrPtr + j)) {
        // swap the elements i and j
        isSorted = false;
        swapElem = *(arrPtr + i);
        *(arrPtr + i) = *(arrPtr + j);
        *(arrPtr + j) = swapElem;
      }
    }
  } while (!(isSorted && offset == 1));
}
```

The Quicksort Method

This method needs no introduction; it's the king of the hill among sorting methods. This reputation stems from the speed of the QuickSort implementations under favorable conditions. The algorithm has its weaknesses, which slow it down—but do you hear anyone complaining? The optimum performance of the Quicksort method has an order of $O(n \lg(n))$, whereas the worst-case performance is $O(n2)$. The performance is affected by the median value used in creating the partitions.

Listing 16.7 shows the source code for the public `QuickSort` function and the private `Qsort` function. The `QuickSort` function acts as a shell that checks the parameters before invoking the recursive function `Qsort`. The workhorse is the protected function `Qsort`. The speed of the Quicksort method comes from the simplicity and speed of the `while` loops in the `Qsort` function. Although the analysis of the Quicksort and Heapsort algorithms show that they both have the order of $O(n \lg(n))$, the Quicksort method is the faster of the two. This superior speed is attributed to the fast `while` loops used by the `Qsort` function.

Listing 16.7. The `QuickSort` and `Qsort` functions.

```
/////////////////////////////////////////////////////////////////////
//
template<class T>
void Array<T>::QuickSort(unsigned last, unsigned first)
//
// Purpose: sorts the array elements in the range of [first...last]
// using the QuickSort method. This function calls the recursive
// (and protected) Qsort method to perform the actual sorting.
//
// Parameters:
//
//    input: first, last - the range of sorted array elements.
//
{
  if (first >= last ||
      first >= size ||
      size < 2)
      return;

  // adjust the parameter last?
  last = (last >= size) ? size - 1 : last;
```

```
  Qsort(first, last);
  isSorted = true;
}

//////////////////////////////////////////////////////////////////////
//
template<class T>
void Array<T>::Qsort(unsigned first, unsigned last)
//
// Purpose: sorts the array elements in the range [first...last].
//
// Parameters:
//
//    input: first, last - the range of sorted array elements.
//
{
  unsigned i, j;
  T swapElem, median;

  i = first;
  j = last;
  // get the median element
  median = *(arrPtr + (first + last) / 2);
  do {
    while (*(arrPtr + i++) < median); // empty loop
    i--; // adjust for the last test
    while (median < *(arrPtr + j--)); // empty loop
    j++; // adjust for the last test
    if (i <= j) {
      swapElem = *(arrPtr + i);
      *(arrPtr + i++) = *(arrPtr + j);
      *(arrPtr + j--) = swapElem;
    }
  } while (i <= j);

  if (first < j)
    Qsort(first, j);

  if (i < last)
    Qsort(i, last);
}
```

The Heapsort Method

The Heapsort method is among the fastest of the in-place sorting algorithms. The Heapsort method has an order of O(*n* lg(*n*)), and compares with the Quicksort method as follows:

- The Heapsort method has the same order as the Quicksort method.
- The Heapsort method performs in-place sorting and does not require additional stack space. (The recursive version of the Quicksort method does require additional stack space.)
- Both the best- and worst-case performances have the order of O(*n* lg(*n*)). In other words, the Heapsort method does not suffer from a decrease in efficiency for certain data patterns.

Listing 16.8 shows the `HeapSort` function. The parameter `last` specifies the index of the last sorted array element. The first array element always is taken as 0. Defining and using a `first` parameter, just like with the other sorting functions, adds more overhead to the code. The function performs two main tasks using `for` loops:

- The first `for` loop builds the heap.
- The second `for` loop sifts through the heap. This action takes the *root* of the current heap and moves it to the proper array element.

Typical performance of the Heapsort algorithm shows it to be half as fast as the Quicksort algorithm. The Heapsort method is not recommended to sort small arrays. The overhead for building the heap is significant for small arrays.

Listing 16.8. The `HeapSort` function.

```
//////////////////////////////////////////////////////////////////////
//
template<class T>
void Array<T>::HeapSort(unsigned last)
//
// Purpose: sorts the elements of this array in the range of
// [0..last] using the Heapsort method.
//
// Parameters:
//
```

```
//    input: last - the array index that defines the upper range
//              for the sorted elements.
//
{
  unsigned i, j, k;
  T elem;

  // exit if array is too small for sorting
  if (size < 2)
    return;

  // adjust the argument for the parameter last ?
  last = (last >= size) ? size - 1 : last;

  // construct the heap
  for (i = 1; i < last; i++) {
    elem = *(arrPtr + i);
    j = i;
    k = (j - 1) / 2;
    while (j > 0 && *(arrPtr + k) < elem) {
      *(arrPtr + j) = *(arrPtr + k);
      j = k;
      k = (j - 1) / 2;
    }
    *(arrPtr + j) = elem;
  }
  // sift the heap elements
  for (i = last - 1; i > 0; i--) {
    elem = *(arrPtr + i);
    *(arrPtr + i) = *(arrPtr + 0);
    k = 0;
    j = (i == 1) ? 0xffff : 1;
    j = (i > 2 &&
         *(arrPtr + 2) > *(arrPtr + 1)) ? 2 : j;
    while (j != 0xffff && elem < *(arrPtr + j)) {
      *(arrPtr + k) = *(arrPtr + j);
      k = j;
      j = 2 * k + 1;
      j = ((j + 1) <= (i - 1) &&
           *(arrPtr + j) < *(arrPtr + j + 1)) ? j + 1 : j;
```

continues

Listing 16.8. continued

```
    }
    *(arrPtr + k) = elem;
  }
}
```

Merging Sorted Arrays

You can merge sorted arrays to take advantage of the already existing order to quickly produce a larger, sorted array. Listing 16.9 shows the `MergeSortedArrays` function. This function merges the `first1` to `last1` elements of `Array1` with the `first2` to `last2` elements of `Array2`. The merged elements are copied to the targeted instance of `Array`. The parameter `start` specifies the index of the first merged array. The `last1`, `last2`, `first1`, `first2`, and `start` parameters permit flexibility in specifying the desired parts of the merged arrays and the storage location of the resulting array. The `first1`, `first2`, and `start` parameters all have default arguments of 0.

The `MergeSortedArrays` function uses the following simple steps:

1. Compare the elements of `Array1` and `Array2`, one at a time, and copy the smaller elements to the targeted instance of `Array`. This process continues until the elements of either `Array1` or `Array2` are completely copied to the target array.
2. Copy the elements of the remaining source array to the targeted array.

Listing 16.9. The `MergeSortedArrays` function.

```
//////////////////////////////////////////////////////////////////////
//
template<class T>
boolean Array<T>::MergeSortedArrays(Array<T>& Array1,
                                    Array<T>& Array2,
                                    unsigned last1,
                                    unsigned last2,
                                    unsigned first1,
                                    unsigned first2,
                                    unsigned start)
```

```
//
// Purpose: merges the ordered array Array1 and Array2. The
// function returns true if the arrays are merged. Otherwise, the
// function yields false.
//
// Parameters:
//
//    input: Array1, Array2 - the merged ordered arrays
//           first1, last1 - the range of Array1 elements to merge.
//           first2, last2 - the range of Array2 elements to merge.
//           start - the index of the first element in this array
//             to store the merged arrays.
//
{
  // check parameters
  if (Array1.size == 0 ¦¦ Array2.size == 0)
    return false;
  // adjust parameters first1, first2, last1, last2 , and start
  last1 = (last1 >= Array1.size) ? Array1.size : last1;
  last2 = (last2 >= Array2.size) ? Array2.size : last2;
  first1 = (first1 > last1) ? last1 : first1;
  first2 = (first2 > last2) ? last2 : first2;
  start = (start > size) ? 0 : start;

  // calculate the new size of this array
  unsigned newSize = last1 - first1 + last2 - first2 + 2 + start;
  // expand this array to make more needed room?
  if (newSize > size)
     if (!expand(newSize))
       return false; // exit if this array cannot be expanded

  unsigned i1 = first1;
  unsigned i2 = first2;
  unsigned i = start;
  // loop to copy from either arrays
  while (i1 <= last1 ¦¦ i2 <= last2) {
    if (*(Array1.arrPtr + i1) < *(Array2.arrPtr + i2))
      *(arrPtr + i++) = *(Array1.arrPtr + i1++);
    else
```

continues

Listing 16.9. continued

```
      *(arrPtr + i++) = *(Array2.arrPtr + i2++);
  }

  // are all of the elements of Array1 copied
  if (i1 > last1)
    // copy the elements of Array2
    while (i2 <= last2)
      *(arrPtr + i++) = *(Array2.arrPtr + i2++);
  else
    // copy the elements of Array1
    while (i1 <= last1)
      *(arrPtr + i++) = *(Array1.arrPtr + i1++);

  return true;
}
```

Searching Methods

In this section I present the various searching functions and discuss the methods they use. The discussion assumes that you already are familiar with the algorithms for these functions.

Searching methods include the following:

- A smart version of the linear-search method
- A statistical method
- A smart, statistical-linear method
- The basic binary-search method for sorted arrays
- The modified binary-search method that locates specific occurrences of data in sorted arrays
- The interpolative-search method for sorted arrays
- The interpolative binary-search method for sorted arrays

The Smart Linear Search Method

Just mention "linear search" to programmers and observe their loss of interest in the conversation. After all, most of us probably coded this search algorithm while learning to program. What can be interesting about a linear search? The answer is: not much! However, you can take the trivial linear-search algorithm and enhance it with circular search, forward or backward search, and heuristic (that is, capable of learning) movement of matching elements. Now we're talking about an enhanced linear-search method that's anything but trivial!

Let's look at the interrelated aspects of improving the basic linear-search method:

- Defining the search range. This aspect enables you to zoom in exclusively on an area you want to search. The worst-case number of searches in an array using the basic linear-search method is equal to the number of searched elements. The average number of searches is equal to half the number of searched array elements. If you know that an array element is in a specific region in the array, you can specify the lower and upper bounds of that region. Using such a range shortens the linear-search effort.

- Implementing forward or backward searching. In the basic search algorithm, it really makes no difference whether you search forward or backward. However, when you incorporate heuristic aspects in the linear search, the search direction becomes more significant in reducing the search effort.

- Implementing a circular search. Once you define a range of array elements to search, you can specify the location of the first searched element in the defined range, and the search direction. The location and search direction represent a heuristic guess based on past search results. This guess can decrease the effort in locating the matching element. What if the heuristic guess is wrong? Well, all's not lost yet—thanks to the circular search feature. This features ensures that the search resumes from the other end of the specified range and runs up to the initial search location.

- Moving the matching array elements. In many unordered arrays it makes no difference where the data is located in that array. Consequently, the array elements that match the search data can be moved upward. There are three heuristic schemes for such movements:

The *move-to-front scheme* places the matching array element as the new first array element. This movement is the most optimistic because it assumes that the same array very likely will be sought again soon. This method costs your program some of its speed by moving array elements to support such a far-ranging swap.

The *move-up scheme* swaps the matching array element with its leading neighbor. This movement is rather pessimistic because it assumes that a matching element will not be called soon. The movement allows the matching array element to bubble to the front when it is sought repeatedly. As for movement overhead, this method has none other than swapping the neighboring array elements.

The *move-halfway scheme* swaps the matching array element halfway to the front of the array. This scheme is conservative because it uses a wait-and-see approach. There's an overhead for moving the matching array element, but it's half that of the move-to-front scheme.

Using forward or backward searching adds more to the preceding heuristic schemes. The forward search enforces the optimism that the matching array elements will be sought again, and soon. The backward search assumes that these elements have had their day, so to speak, and won't be sought again soon. Consequently, moving them to the front actually puts them in a low-priority location.

Listing 16.10 contains the `LinearSearch` function. The `searchData` parameter specifies the search data. The parameters `last` and `first` define the range of array elements to search. The `start` parameter indicates the first array element to search. The Boolean `searchForward` parameter indicates whether the search is forward or backward. The `move` parameter specifies how to move the matching array element, if at all.

The `LinearSearch` function conducts a circular search when either of the following conditions is true:

- When the value of the `searchForward` parameter is `True` and the `start` parameter is greater than the `first` parameter.
- When the value of the `searchForward` parameter is `False` and the `start` parameter is less than the `last` parameter.

The power of the `LinearSearch` function comes from the fact that you can fine-tune and adapt its operation through its parameters. For example, you can toggle or alter the heuristic mode (which moves the matching array element), change search direction, and narrow or widen the search range. Optimum use of the `LinearSearch` function can produce a rewarding search speed.

When a search function finds an array element that matches the search data, it assigns the matching element to the `searchData` argument. This argument is passed by reference. This assignment allows the `searchData` parameter to retrieve data members in the matching element that are not involved in the relational operators of the template class `T`. All the search functions of the `Array` class share this feature.

Listing 16.10. The `LinearSearch` function.

```
////////////////////////////////////////////////////////////////////////
//
template<class T>
unsigned Array<T>::LinearSearch(T& searchData,
                                unsigned last,
                                unsigned first,
                                unsigned start,
                                boolean searchForward,
                                linearSearchMove move)
//
// Purpose: performs a smart linear search in the range of [first
// ...last]. The search begins at index start and may be carried
// out in either forward or backward direction. The search also
// can be conducted in a circular fashion when:
//
// 1. The searchForward is true and start > first.
//
// 2. The searchForward is false and start < last.
//
// The function returns the index of the first
// array member that matches the searchData. If no match is found,
// the function yields NO_ELEM_FOUND.
//
```

continues

Listing 16.10. continued

```
// Parameters
//
//    input: searchData - the data to search.
//           first, last - the range of indices to search.
//           start - the index of the first searched elements.
//           searchForward - search direction flag.
//           move - mode of moving the matching array element.
//
{
   boolean circularSearch;
   boolean notFound = true;
   unsigned i;

   // check the arguments
   if (start >= size ||
       first >= size ||
       first > last ||
       start < first)
     return NO_ELEM_FOUND;

   // adjust the argument for parameter last
   last = (last < size) ? last : size - 1;
   // is search in the forward direction?
   if (searchForward) {
     circularSearch = (start > first) ? true : false;
     i = start;
     // search from start to last
     while (i <= last && notFound)
       if (*(arrPtr + i) != searchData)
         i++;
       else
         notFound = false;

     // not match found and the search is circular?
     if (notFound && circularSearch) {
       // if no match is found search from first to start - 1
       i = first;
       while (i < start && notFound)
```

```
      if (*(arrPtr + i) != searchData)
        i++;
      else
        notFound = false;
  }
}
else {
// search direction is backward
  circularSearch = (start < last) ? true : false;
  // search from start to first
  i = start;
  while (i >= first && notFound)
    if (*(arrPtr + i) != searchData)
      i = (i > 0) ? i - 1 : 0;
    else
      notFound = false;

  // not match found and the search is circular?
  if (notFound && circularSearch) {
    // if no match is found search from last to start + 1
    i = last;
    while (i > start && notFound)
     if (*(arrPtr + i) != searchData)
       i--;
     else
       notFound = false;
  }
}

// found a match ?
if (!notFound) {
  T swapElem;
  // copy the data from the matching member to searchData.
  // This step is relevant when class T has members that are
  // not used in the relational operators.
  searchData = *(arrPtr + i);
  switch (move) {
    case moveNot:
       break;
```

continues

Listing 16.10. continued

```
    case moveUp:
      if (i > first) {
        // swap the matching element with its leading neighbor
        swapElem = *(arrPtr + i);
        *(arrPtr + i) = *(arrPtr + i - 1);
        *(arrPtr + i - 1) = swapElem;
        i--;
      }
      break;

    case moveToFront:
      if (i > first) {
        // store the matching array element in swapElem
        swapElem = *(arrPtr + i);
        // move up the elements in the range start...i-1
        for (unsigned j = i; j > first; j--)
          *(arrPtr + j) = *(arrPtr + j - 1);
        // assign the matching element as the new first element
        // in the range first...last
        *(arrPtr + first) = swapElem;
        i = first;
      }
      break;

    case moveHalfWay:
      if (i > (first + 1)) {
        unsigned n;
        // store the matching array element in swapElem
        swapElem = *(arrPtr + i);
        n = (first + i) / 2;
        // move up the elements in the range n...i-1
        for (unsigned j = i; j > n; j--)
          *(arrPtr + j) = *(arrPtr + j - 1);
        *(arrPtr + n) = swapElem;
        i = n;
      }
      break;
  }
  // return (possibly adjusted) index of
```

```
      // the matching array element
      return i;
    }
    else
      return NO_ELEM_FOUND;
}
```

The Statistical-Linear Search Method

The basic linear-search algorithm (used in either forward or backward searching) has an elementary flaw that contradicts basic statistics. Assuming that the array elements are sought with equal probability, basic statistics indicate the following:

- The average most-likely location for a matching element is the median of the search-range size.
- The standard deviation for finding a match is 0.288 times the search-range size.

Therefore, a smart, nonheuristic, linear-search algorithm should start in the middle of the search range and continue by alternating above and below the median. The first and last array elements in the search range would be the last elements examined.

Listing 16.11 shows the `StatisticalSearch` function. The `searchData` parameter specifies the search data. The `last` and `first` parameters define the range of array elements to search. The function has no start element; the search systematically begins at the median value of the search range.

The implementation of the function is simple:

1. If the number of searched array elements is odd, the function first examines the median element. If that element matches the search data, the function returns the median index.
2. If the number of searched elements is even or if the median of an odd-number range does not match `searchData`, the function searches the array using a `while` loop. Each loop iteration searches the next array element above and below the median by a certain offset value. If the range is an even number, the first loop iteration examines the median array element. Each iteration increments the offset value used.

3. The loop uses the local Boolean variable `notFound` to stop the search and avoid searching below the median if `searchData` matches the element above the median. The function is coded such that the `while` loop can search an equal number of array elements above and below the median element.

Listing 16.11. The `StatisticalSearch` function.

```
//////////////////////////////////////////////////////////////////////
//
template<class T>
unsigned Array<T>::StatisticalSearch(T& searchData,
                                      unsigned last,
                                      unsigned first)
//
// Purpose: performs a linear search that starts at the median
// array element and resumes toward the first and last members.
// The function returns the index of the first array member that
// matches the searchData. If no match is found, the function
// yields NO_ELEM_FOUND.
//
// Parameters:
//
//    input: searchData - the search data.
//           first, last - the range of indices to search.
//
{
  unsigned n, m, i, j, k, count, shift;
  boolean notFound = true;

  if (first > last ||
      first >= size)
    return NO_ELEM_FOUND;

  n = last - first + 1;
  m = n / 2;
  count = m;
  // is n an odd number?
  if ((n % 2) > 0) {
    // examine the median of an odd-number range
    if (*(arrPtr + m) == searchData) {
```

```
      searchData = *(arrPtr + m);
      return m;
    }
    shift = 1;
  }
  else
    shift = 0;
  k = 2 * m + shift;
  // search around the median value
  while (notFound && count > 0) {
    // search above the median
    j = k - count;
    // array[j] match search data ?
    if (*(arrPtr + j) == searchData) {
       k = j; // save matching index in k
       notFound = false;
    }

    // still not found a match
    if (notFound) {
      // search below the median and also
      // decrement count
      i = count-- - 1;
      // array[i] match search data ?
      if (*(arrPtr + i) == searchData) {
        k = i; // save matching index in k
        notFound = false;
      }
    }
  }

  // copy the data from the matching member to searchData.
  // This step is relevant when class T has members that are
  // not used in the relational operators.
  if (!notFound) {
    searchData = *(arrPtr + k);
    return k;
  }
  else
    return NO_ELEM_FOUND;
}
```

The Adaptive Statistical Linear-Search Method

The statistical-linear method presented in the last section works fine as long as the underlying assumptions hold true. Although it is based on simple statistical concepts, the statistical-linear method is not adaptive. An adaptive statistical method stores the index of the matching elements to obtain an average matching index value. This value can be used, for example, in deciding whether to conduct a forward or backward linear search. If the average is greater than 0.5, backward searching is favored to reduce the number of searches. Otherwise, the method prescribes forward searching.

Listing 16.12 contains the `StatLinearSearch` function. The parameters `searchData`, `last`, and `first` are similar to those described under earlier search functions. The `StatLinearSearch` function uses the following static variables to maintain data between function calls:

- The `numPoints` variable stores the number of matches.
- The `sumIndex` variable stores the sum of the matching indices.
- The `oldFirst` variable stores the most recently updated argument for the `first` parameter.
- The `oldLast` variable stores the most recently updated argument for the `last` parameter.

The last two variables require clarification. The maintained, basic statistics for the matching array elements are relevant for a specific range. Changing the range makes the statistics unreliable, if not wrong. Therefore, the function needs to store the last different arguments for the `first` and `last` parameters. The function compares these values with the current arguments for `first` and `last` to determine whether the search range is the same as the last time the function was called. If the range is different, the function resets the `numPoints` and `sumIndex` variables and updates the `oldFirst` and `oldLast` variables.

The `StatLinearSearch` function calls the `LinearSearch` function when the value of `numPoints` variable is less than 2. In this case, the `StatLinearSearch` function is the phase of building the basic statistics to a minimum required level.

If the value of the numPoints variable exceeds 1, the function calculates the average index for the matching array elements. When that average is greater than 0.5, the function searches the array backward. Otherwise, the function searches the array forward. If the array contains an element that matches the searchData parameter, the function increments the numPoints variable and updates the sumIndex variable with the index of the matching element.

Listing 16.12. The StatLinearSearch function.

```
//////////////////////////////////////////////////////////////////////////
//
template<class T>
unsigned Array<T>::StatLinearSearch(T& searchData,
                                    unsigned last,
                                    unsigned first)
//
// Purpose: searches for an array member that matches the searchData
// parameter. The parameters first and last specify the search range.
// The function uses local static variables to maintain the average
// value for the matching indices. If that average is greater than
// 0.5, the function searches the array starting with the member at
// index last. Otherwise, the function searches the array starting
// with the member at the index first. The function also keeps track
// of the arguments for first and last using local static variables.
// If you supply different arguments for first or last in successive
// calls to this function, the function resets the variables that
// store the statistics for the matching indices. This approach
// ensures that the available statistics are for a certain range.
// The function returns the index of the first array member that
// matches the searchData. If no match is found, the function
// yields NO_ELEM_FOUND.
//
// Parameters:
//
//    input: searchData - the search data.
//           first, last - the range of searched indices.
//
{
  static unsigned numPoints = 0;
  static double sumIndex = 0;
```

continues

Listing 16.12. continued

```
static unsigned oldFirst = 0;
static unsigned oldLast = 0;
boolean notFound;
unsigned i;

if (first > last ||
    first >= size)
  return NO_ELEM_FOUND;

// adjust the parameter last?
last = (last >= size) ? size - 1 : last;

// handle a new range?
if (first != oldFirst || last != oldLast) {
   numPoints = 0;
   sumIndex = 0;
   oldFirst = first;
   oldLast = last;
}

if (numPoints < 2) {
   i = LinearSearch(searchData, last, first, first);
   if (i != NO_ELEM_FOUND) {
      numPoints++;
      sumIndex += (double)i;
   }
   return i;
}
else {
  if (sumIndex / numPoints > 0.5) {
    // search the array starting from the last member
    i = last;
    notFound = true;
    while (notFound && i >= first)
      if (*(arrPtr + i) != searchData)
        i = (i > 0) ? i-1 : i;
      else
        notFound = false;
  }
  else {
```

```
      // search the array starting from the first member
      i = first;
      notFound = true;
      while (notFound && i <= last)
        if (*(arrPtr + i) != searchData)
          i++;
        else
          notFound = false;
    }
  }

  // copy the data from the matching member to searchData.
  // This step is relevant when class T has members that are
  // not used in the relational operators.
  if (!notFound) {
    searchData = *(arrPtr + i);
    numPoints++;
    sumIndex += (double) i;
  }

  // return the index of the matching array member
  return (notFound) ? NO_ELEM_FOUND : i;

}
```

The Binary-Search Method

The binary-search method is the most efficient general-purpose search algorithm for sorted arrays. Usually, the algorithm is implemented for arrays that are sorted in an ascending order. The binary search tolerates duplicate data and makes no assumption about the distribution of the data in the array. The worst-case number of searches is in the order O(lg(n)). Doubling the array size requires, in the worst case, only an additional comparison. The algorithm searches the median element of the current range in an iterative fashion. Each iteration reduces the search range by half until one of the following occurs:

- A match is found.
- A search range of one element lacks the search data.

Listing 16.13 shows the `BinarySearch` function. The `searchData`, `last`, and `first` parameters are similar to those described under earlier search functions. The `BinarySearch` function uses a `do-while` loop to obtain the median element and reduce the search range by half. The loop stops iterating when either a match is found or the value of parameter `first` exceeds that of parameter `last`. The function returns the index of the matching array element or yields `NO_ELEM_FOUND` when there is no match.

The binary-search algorithm and its implementation, the `BinarySearch` function, search one item at a time. In a case where you can collect the search data and store them in a sorted array, you can improve the efficiency of `BinarySearch` data. The method involved uses the index of the last matching array element as the argument for the parameter first in the next call to the `BinarySearch` function. This shortens the range of the binary-search algorithm. The following sample code fragment demonstrates this technique:

```
// declare searchArray, targetArray and indexArray as
// instances of Array with specific data
unsigned j, first = 0;
unsigned numMatch = 0;
unsigned last = targetArray.getSize();
for (unsigned i = 0; i < searchArray.getSize(); i++) {
     j = targetArray.BinarySearch(searchArray[i], last, first);
     if (j != NO_ELEM_FOUND) {
          first = j;
          indexArray[numMatch++] = j;
     }
}
```

When an array contains elements with duplicate data (at least the same template class members used by the relational operators), the basic binary-search algorithm finds any one of these duplicates. To obtain a specific occurrence requires a backward linear search. This search attempts to locate the first occurrence of an array element that matches the search data. Once that element is found, you can determine whether the occurrence you seek exists.

Listing 16.14 contains the `ModifiedBinarySearch` function. The parameters of the function are `searchData`, `last`, `first`, and `occurrence`. The `occurrence` parameter specifies the sought occurrence of the search data. The function returns the index of the specified occurrence or yields `NO_ELEM_FOUND` if that occurrence does not exist. The

ModifiedBinarySearch function calls the BinarySearch function to locate an occurrence of the search data. If the result of the BinarySearch function indicates a match, the ModifiedBinarySearch function uses a while loop to perform a backward linear search and locate the first occurrence of the search data. The ModifiedBinarySearch function stores the index of the first occurrence in the local variable i. The function then compares the array element at the i+occurrence-1 index with the search data. If the two items match, the function returns the index of the targeted occurrence; otherwise, the function yields NO_ELEM_FOUND.

Listing 16.13. The BinarySearch function.

```
//////////////////////////////////////////////////////////////////////
//
template<class T>
unsigned Array<T>::BinarySearch(T& searchData,
                                unsigned last,
                                unsigned first)
//
// Purpose: performs a simple binary search on the ordered elements
// of an array. You are responsible for ensuring that the array elements
// in the range [first...last] are ordered.
//
// Parameters:
//
//    input: searchData - the search data.
//           first, last - the range of searched indices.
//
{
  T median;
  unsigned m = (first + last) / 2;

  do {
    m = (first + last) / 2;
    if (searchData < *(arrPtr + m))
      last = m - 1;
    else
      first = m + 1;
  } while (!(searchData == *(arrPtr + m) || first > last));
```

continues

Listing 16.13. continued

```
    // found a match
    if (searchData == *(arrPtr + m)) {
      searchData = *(arrPtr + m);
      return m;
    }
    else
      return NO_ELEM_FOUND;
  }
```

Listing 16.14. The `ModifiedBinarySearch` function.

```
//////////////////////////////////////////////////////////////////
//
template<class T>
unsigned Array<T>::ModifiedBinarySearch(T& searchData,
                                        unsigned last,
                                        unsigned first,
                                        unsigned occurrence)
//
// Purpose: searches for a specific occurrence of searchData in this
// array. You are responsible for ensuring that the array elements
// in the range [first...last] are ordered. The function returns the
// index of the specified occurrence or yields NO_ELEM_FOUND if
// that occurrence does not exist.
//
// Parameters:
//
//    input: searchData - the search data.
//           first, last - the range of searched indices.
//           occurrence - the sought occurrence of searchData.
//
{
  unsigned i, j;
  boolean resumeSearch = true;

  if (first > last ||
      first >= size)
     return NO_ELEM_FOUND;
```

```
    // adjust parameter last?
    last = (last >= size) ? size - 1 : last;
    occurrence = (occurrence == 0) ? 1 : occurrence;

    // find the index of any occurrence of searchData
    i = BinarySearch(searchData, last, first);
    // found a match?
    if (i != NO_ELEM_FOUND) {
      while (i > 0 && resumeSearch) {
        if (*(arrPtr + i) != *(arrPtr + i - 1))
          resumeSearch = false;
        else
          i--;
      }
      // the first occurrence is at index i (at least
      // in the range [first...last])
      j = i + occurrence - 1;
      if (*(arrPtr + j) == searchData) {
        searchData = *(arrPtr + j);
        return j;
      }
      else
        return NO_ELEM_FOUND;
    }
    else
      return i;
}
```

The Interpolative-Search Method

The binary-search algorithm performs an efficient and systematic halving of the search range in order to search for data. The method makes no attempt to zoom in on the possible matching element. The interpolative search can perform a smarter search, zooming in on the array element that matches the search string. However, the sorted array must have the following properties:

- You can obtain a numerical value from the search-related members of the `T` template class. This value is either an integer or a floating-point number.

- The data in the array is uniformly distributed.
- The array contains few duplicates.

The interpolative-search method uses mathematical linear interpolation to calculate the guess for the index of the matching array element. This guess is based on the value at each end of the current range of indices. If the obtained index does not lead to a match, the method reduces the interval and obtains a new guess. When the searched array fulfills the previous conditions, the interpolative search is faster than the binary method.

Listing 16.15 shows the `InterpolativeSearch` function. The `searchData`, `last`, and `first` parameters are similar to those described under earlier search functions. The double-typed `searchValue` parameter specifies the numeric equivalent of the search data. The `arrValues` parameter is a pointer to an array of doubles that stores the numeric equivalent of the data in the searched array. I chose to use the double type rather than an integer type because floating-point numbers are more flexible and have a wide range of values. Obtaining the arguments for the `searchValue` and `arrValues` parameters is easy when the targeted array stores integers or floating-point numbers. When the array stores strings, you can calculate the numerical equivalent by using the first few characters of each array element.

The `InterpolativeSearch` function uses a `while` loop to search for an array element that matches the `searchData` parameter. The loop performs the following tasks:

1. Calculates the interpolated index as a double type, using the numeric equivalents of the search data and the array elements at the `first` and `last` indices.
2. Converts the interpolated index to an integer value, `i`, if that index is in the range of `first` to `last`. Otherwise, the loop obtains the median value of parameters `first` and `last`. This task ensures that nonuniformity in the array data does not yield out-of-range indices.
3. Compares the search data with the array element at the `i` index. The outcome of the comparison determines how the search range is reduced.

When the `while` loop stops iterating, the function compares the search data with the array element at the `first` index to determine whether there's a match. The function returns the current value of `first` if there is a match. Otherwise, the function yields `NO_ELEM_FOUND`.

Listing 16.15. The InterpolativeSearch function.

```
//////////////////////////////////////////////////////////////////////
//
template<class T>
unsigned Array<T>::InterpolativeSearch(T& searchData,
                                       double searchValue,
                                       double* arrValues,
                                       unsigned last,
                                       unsigned first)
//
// Purpose: searches for an array element that contains searchData
// in the index range [first...last]. The function uses a floating-
// point interpolative technique to obtain the index of the matching
// array element. The function returns NO_ELEM_FOUND if no match
// is found.
//
// Parameters:
//
//    input: searchData - the search data.
//           searchValue - the double-typed value of searchData.
//           arrValues - an array of doubles that stores the
//             "values" for this array.
//           first, last - the range of array elements to search.
//
{
   unsigned i;
   double x;

   if (first >= last || first >= size)
     return NO_ELEM_FOUND;

  // adjust parameter last?
  last = (last >= size) ? size - 1 : last;

   while (*(arrPtr + last) >= searchData &&
          *(arrPtr + first) < searchData) {
     // calculate the interpolated index
     x = (searchValue - *(arrValues + first)) /
         (*(arrValues + last) - *(arrValues + first)) *
         (last - first) + first;
```

continues

Listing 16.15. continued

```
        // is index within [first...last] range?
        if (x >= first && x <= last)
          // yes. Convert x to i
          i = x;
        else
          // no. Use median value instead
          i = (first + last) / 2;
        if (searchData > *(arrPtr + i))
          first = i + 1;
        else if (searchData < *(arrPtr + i))
          last = i - 1;
        else
          first = i;
      }

      if (*(arrPtr + first) == searchData) {
         searchData = *(arrPtr + first);
         return first;
      }
      else
         return NO_ELEM_FOUND;

   }
```

The Interpolative Binary-Search Method

The interpolative method works well with uniformly distributed data that has a low number of duplicate data elements. In a case in which the array elements do not contain uniform data, the binary-search method works better. It's possible to combine both interpolative and binary-search methods such that the interpolative method provides the starting search index. Subsequent searches use the binary-search method. This dual-method approach can help you zoom in on the area of the array in which the match is most likely to occur. If the interpolative step gives a somewhat erroneous initial guess, the binary-search method performs just as well as if it were the only search method used.

Listing 16.16 shows the `InterpBinSearch` function. This function has the same parameters as the `InterpolativeSearch` function. The code of the function is a modified version of the `InterpolativeSearch` function. The modifications allow the interpolative search to be conducted once, followed by calls to the `BinarySearch` function.

Listing 16.16. The `InterpBinSearch` function.

```
////////////////////////////////////////////////////////////////////
//
template<class T>
unsigned Array<T>::InterpBinSearch(T& searchData,
                                   double searchValue,
                                   double* arrValues,
                                   unsigned last,
                                   unsigned first)
//
// Purpose: searches for an array element that contains searchData
// in the index range [first...last]. The function uses interpolation
// to zoom in on the area around the possible matching array element.
// The function then uses the binary search to locate that element
// in the narrowed-down range of indices. The function returns
// NO_ELEM_FOUND if no match is found.
//
// Parameters:
//
//    input: searchData - the search data.
//           searchValue - the double-typed value of searchData.
//           arrValues - an array of doubles that stores the
//             "values" for this array.
//           first, last - the range of array elements to search.
//
{
   unsigned i;
   double x;

   if (first >= last || first >= size)
     return NO_ELEM_FOUND;
```

continues

Listing 16.16. continued

```
    // adjust parameter last?
    last = (last >= size) ? size - 1 : last;

    if (*(arrPtr + last) >= searchData &&
           *(arrPtr + first) < searchData) {
      // calculate the interpolated index
      x = (searchValue - *(arrValues + first)) /
          (*(arrValues + last) - *(arrValues + first)) *
          (last - first) + first;
      // is index within [first...last] range?
      if (x >= first && x <= last)
        // yes. Convert x to i
        i = x;
      else
        // no. Use median value instead
        i = (first + last) / 2;
      if (searchData > *(arrPtr + i))
        first = BinarySearch(searchData, last, i + 1);
      else if (searchData < *(arrPtr + i)) {
        last = i - 1;
        first = BinarySearch(searchData, last, first);
      }
      else
        // found match!
        first = i;
    }

    if (*(arrPtr + first) == searchData) {
       searchData = *(arrPtr + first);
       return first;
    }
    else
       return NO_ELEM_FOUND;

}
```

Function Testing

The next sections in this chapter test various functions of the template class `Array`. These sections present three test programs:

- The first program tests the sorting functions.
- The second program tests various aspects of the `LinearSearch` function.
- The third program tests the remaining search functions.

Testing the Sort Functions

Listing 16.17 contains the source code for the TSARR1.CPP program, which tests the sort functions using arrays of integers. The program listing includes the VIDEO.H header file, which contains functions that support the screen cursor and the `getch()` function. The program declares the `ARRAY_SIZE` constant to specify the size of the tested arrays.

The program declares the following functions:

- The `displayArray` function. This function displays a selection of array elements. The `msg` parameter specifies the text that accompanies the displayed array elements. The `arr` parameter specifies the array to be displayed. The `first` and `last` parameters indicate the range of elements in `arr` to display.
- The `displayArray2` function. This function displays a selection of array elements in a manner similar to the `displayArray` function. The difference is that this function displays the following additional strings at the array indices specified by the `low` and `hi` parameters:

  Displays the string `"<— first sorted element"` after displaying the data of element `low`.

  Displays the string `"<— last sorted element"` after displaying the data of element `hi`.

Incorporating the `main` function gives the following results:

1. `main` declares three instances of `Array<int>`—`ar1`, `ar2`, and `ar3`. The function initializes `ar1` with random integers ranging from 100 to 999.

2. The program first displays the unsorted array by calling the `displayArray` function and passing the `ar1` array as the argument for the `arr` parameter.
3. The program starts the first testing phase, during which it sorts the entire `ARRAY_SIZE` elements using the `CombSort`, `ShellSort`, `QuickSort`, and `HeapSort` functions. Each time, the program assigns the elements of the unsorted `ar1` array to `ar2` before calling a sorting function.
4. Once sorted, the program displays the `ar2` array using the `displayArray` function.
5. The second phase of the testing sorts array elements (*n*/4) to (3**n*/4), where *n* is equal to `ARRAY_SIZE-1`. The program performs steps similar to those in phase one, except that the range of sorted array elements is different. The program calls the `displayArray2` function to display the partially sorted array elements and visually indicate these elements.

Listing 16.17. The source code for the TSARR1.CPP program.

```
// Test class of Array<T>

#include <stdlib.h>
#include "video.h"
#include <iostream.h>
#include "array.cpp"

const unsigned ARRAY_SIZE = 17;

void displayArray(const char* msg,
                  Array<int>& arr,
                  unsigned first,
                  unsigned last)
{

  clrscr();
  cout << msg << "\n\n";
  for (unsigned i = first; i < last; i++)
    cout << arr[i] << '\n';
  cout <<"\n\npress any key to continue...";
  getch();
}
```

```
void displayArray2(const char* msg,
                   Array<int>& arr,
                   unsigned first, unsigned last,
                   unsigned low, unsigned hi)
{

  clrscr();
  cout << msg << "\n\n";
  for (unsigned i = first; i < last; i++) {
    cout << arr[i];
    if (i == low)
      cout << "  <--- first sorted element";
    else if (i == hi)
      cout << "  <--- last sorted element";
    cout << '\n';
  }
  cout <<"\n\npress any key to continue...";
  getch();
}

main()
{
  Array<int> ar1(ARRAY_SIZE), ar2(ARRAY_SIZE), ar3(10);
  unsigned i, n = ARRAY_SIZE - 1;
  unsigned low = n / 4;
  unsigned hi = (3 * n) / 4;

  srand(17);
  // initialize the array ar1 with random integers in the
  // range of 100 to 999.
  for (i = 0; i < ARRAY_SIZE; i++)
    ar1[i] = 100 + rand() % 900;


  displayArray("Unsorted array is:", ar1, 0, n);

  ////////////////////////////////////////////////////////////////////
  ////////////////// Test sorting an entire array ////////////////////
  ////////////////////////////////////////////////////////////////////
```

continues

Listing 16.17. continued

```
ar2 = ar1;
// test the CombSort method
ar2.CombSort(n);
displayArray("Array sorted using Combsort is:", ar2, 0, n);

ar2 = ar1;
// test the ShellSort method
ar2.ShellSort(n);
displayArray("Array sorted using Shellsort is:", ar2, 0, n);

ar2 = ar1;
// test the HeapSort method
ar2.HeapSort(n);
displayArray("Array sorted using HeapSort is:", ar2, 0, n);

ar2 = ar1;
// test the QuickSort method
ar2.QuickSort(n);
displayArray("Array sorted using QuickSort is:", ar2, 0, n);

/////////////////////////////////////////////////////////////////
////////////////// Test sorting part of an array /////////////////
/////////////////////////////////////////////////////////////////

ar2 = ar1;
// test the CombSort method
ar2.CombSort(hi, low);
displayArray2("Array partially sorted using Combsort is:",
              ar2, 0, n, low, hi);

ar2 = ar1;
// test the QuickSort method
ar2.QuickSort(hi, low);
displayArray2("Array partially sorted using QuickSort is:",
              ar2, 0, n, low, hi);

/////////////////////////////////////////////////////////////////
/////////////////// Test merging sorted arrays //////////////////
/////////////////////////////////////////////////////////////////
```

```
  srand(17);
  // initialize the array arl with random integers in the
  // range of 100 to 999.
  for (i = 0; < ARRAY_SIZE / 2; i++) {
    ar1[i] = 100 + rand() % 900;
    ar2[i] = 100 + rand() % 900;
  }
  n = ARRAY_SIZE / 2;
  ar1. CombSort(n);
  ar2. CombSort(n);
  displayArray("First sorted array is:", ar1, 0, n);
  displayArray("Second sorted array is:", ar2, 0, n);
  if (ar3.MergeSortedArrays(ar1, ar2, n, n))
    displayArray("Merged arrays are:", ar3, 0, 2 * n - 1);
  else {
    cout << "Error in merging the arrays";
    cout << "\n\nPress any key ...";
    getch();
  }

  return 0;
}
```

Testing the LinearSearch Function

The second test program illustrates the `LinearSearch` function. Listing 16.18 contains the source code for the TSARR2.CPP program. This test program includes the VIDEO.H header file and declares the `ARRAY_SIZE` global constant to specify the size of the tested arrays. The listing includes the following functions:

- The `showArray` function. This function is similar to the `displayArray` function, which appears in TSARRA2.CPP. The difference is that `showArray` returns the number of the row in which the first array element appears.
- The `searchElem` function. This function streamlines the testing of the `LinearSearch` function. The `searchData` parameter specifies the search data. The `arr` reference parameter specifies the array to search. The `first` and `last` parameters define the range of array elements to search. The `move` parameter indicates how to move the matching array element.

The `searchElem` function uses the `move` parameter in a `switch` statement to assign the appropriate string describing the current testing. The function then displays the search value at the bottom of the screen and waits for you to press a key. Once you press a key, the function calls the `LinearSearch` function to perform a case-sensitive linear search in the range of `[first...last]`. The function examines the result of the `LinearSearch` function to determine the success or failure of the search. If the search is successful, the function calls the `showArray` function to redisplay the array elements and places an asterisk to the left of the matching number. If no match is found, the `searchElem` function displays a message to that effect at the bottom of the screen.

The `main` function declares three instances of `Array<int>`—`ar1`, `ar2`, and `ar3`. The program assigns random numbers, ranging from 100 to 999, to the elements of the `ar1` array. The program then displays the unsorted elements of the `ar1` array. To search the unsorted elements of the `ar1` array in a nonsequential manner, the program assigns the data of the `ar1` array to the `ar2` array and then sorts the latter. The program performs the following tests on the `LinearSearch` function:

1. A simple invocation of the `LinearSearch` function. The program uses a `for` loop to locate the elements of the `ar2` array in the `ar1` array. The call to the `LinearSearch` function uses all of the default arguments. Consequently, the case-sensitive search is conducted over all of the array elements. In addition, matching elements are not moved. The program informs you of the search data and then displays an asterisk to the left of the matching array element. The program prompts you to press a key to search for another value or to move on to the next test.
2. Moving up the matching elements. This test searches for the `ar2[0]` element four consecutive times. The program calls the `searchElem` function and passes the enumerated `moveUp` argument to the `move` parameter. Because the `searchElem` function updates the displayed array elements, you can watch the matching array element move up by one location. The program then searches three consecutive times for the `ar2[n]` element, where `n` is equal to `ARRAY_SIZE-1`, in the `ar1` array. The visual effect is similar to searching for `ar2[0]`. The program prompts you to press a key to search for another value or to move on to the next test.
3. Moving the matching elements to the front. This test searches for the `ar2[1]` element three consecutive times. The program calls the `searchElem` function and passes the enumerated `moveToFront` argument to the `move` parameter.

Because the searchElem function updates the displayed array elements, you can watch the matching array element move to the first array element. The program then searches ar1 two consecutive times for the ar2[n-1] element, where n is equal to ARRAY_SIZE-1. The visual effect is similar to that of searching for ar2[1]. The program prompts you to press a key to search for another value or to move on to the next test.

4. Moving the matching elements halfway to the front. This test searches three consecutive times for the element ar2[2]. The program calls the searchElem function and passes the enumerated moveHalfWay argument to the move parameter. Because the searchElem function updates the displayed array elements, you can watch the matching array element gradually move halfway to the first array element. The program then searches for the ar2[n/2] element in the ar1 array for two consecutive times. The visual effect is similar to that of searching for ar2[2]. The program prompts you to press a key to search for another value or to move on to the next test.

Listing 16.18. The source code for the TSARR2.CPP program.

```
// Test class of Array<T>

#include <stdlib.h>
#include <string.h>
#include "video.h"
#include <iostream.h>
#include "array.cpp"

const unsigned ARRAY_SIZE = 9;

unsigned showArray(const char* msg,
                   Array<int>& arr,
                   unsigned first,
                   unsigned last)
{
  unsigned y;

  clrscr();
  cout << msg << "\n\n";
  y = wherey();
  for (unsigned i = first; i <= last; i++)
```

continues

Listing 16.18. continued

```
    cout << "  " << arr[i] << '\n';
  return y;
}

void searchElem(int searchData, Array<int>& arr,
                unsigned first, unsigned last,
                linearSearchMove move)
{
  char s[81];
  unsigned y, j;

  switch (move) {
    case moveUp:
      strcpy(s, "Testing moving up matching elements");
      break;

    case moveToFront:
      strcpy(s, "Testing moving to front matching elements");
      break;

    case moveHalfWay:
      strcpy(s,
             "Testing moving halfway to front matching elements");
      break;
  }

  gotoxy(1, 23);
  cout << "To search for " << searchData << " press any key";
  getch();
  j = arr.LinearSearch(searchData, last, first, 0, true, move);
  if (j != NO_ELEM_FOUND) {
    y = showArray(s, arr, 0, last);
    gotoxy(1, y + j);
    cout << '*';
  }
  else {
    gotoxy(1, 23);
    clreol();
```

```
    cout << "No match found. Press any key to continue...";
    getch();
  }
}

main()
{
  Array<int> ar1(ARRAY_SIZE), ar2(ARRAY_SIZE), ar3(10);
  unsigned i, j, y;
  unsigned n = ARRAY_SIZE - 1;

  srand(17);
  // initialize the array ar1 with random integers in the
  // range of 100 to 999.
  for (i = 0; i < ARRAY_SIZE; i++)
    ar1[i] = 100 + rand() % 900;

  y = showArray("Unsorted array is:", ar1, 0, n);
  ar2 = ar1;
  ar2.CombSort(n);

  // test the LinearSearch function
  for (i = 0; i < ARRAY_SIZE; i++) {
    gotoxy(1, 23);
    clreol();
    cout << "To search for " << ar2[i] << " press any key...";
    getch();
    j = ar1.LinearSearch(ar2[i], n);
    if (j != NO_ELEM_FOUND) {
      gotoxy(1, y + j);
      cout << '*';
    }
  }
  gotoxy(1, 23);
  clreol();
  cout << "Press any key to continue...";
  getch();
  // Test for successful matches by moving up the array elements
  showArray("Testing moving up matching elements",
             ar1, 0, n);
  // search for ar2[0] in array ar1
```

continues

Listing 16.18. continued

```
searchElem(ar2[0], ar1, 0, n, moveUp);
searchElem(ar2[0], ar1, 0, n, moveUp);
searchElem(ar2[0], ar1, 0, n, moveUp);
searchElem(ar2[0], ar1, 0, n, moveUp);
// search for ar2[n] in array ar1
searchElem(ar2[n], ar1, 0, n, moveUp);
searchElem(ar2[n], ar1, 0, n, moveUp);
searchElem(ar2[n], ar1, 0, n, moveUp);
gotoxy(1, 23);
clreol();
cout << "Press any key to continue...";
getch();
// Test moving to front the array elements that are
// successful matches
showArray("Testing moving to front matching elements",
           ar1, 0, n);
// search for ar2[1] in array ar1
searchElem(ar2[1], ar1, 0, n, moveToFront);
searchElem(ar2[1], ar1, 0, n, moveToFront);
searchElem(ar2[1], ar1, 0, n, moveToFront);
// search for ar2[n-1] in array ar1
searchElem(ar2[n-1], ar1, 0, n, moveToFront);
searchElem(ar2[n-1], ar1, 0, n, moveToFront);
gotoxy(1, 23);
clreol();
cout << "Press any key to continue...";
getch();
// Test moving halfway to front the array elements
// that are successful matches
showArray("Testing moving halfway to front matching elements",
           ar1, 0, n);
// search for ar2[2] in array ar1
searchElem(ar2[2], ar1, 0, n, moveHalfWay);
searchElem(ar2[2], ar1, 0, n, moveHalfWay);
searchElem(ar2[2], ar1, 0, n, moveHalfWay);
// search for ar2[n/2] in array ar1
searchElem(ar2[n/2], ar1, 0, n, moveHalfWay);
searchElem(ar2[n/2], ar1, 0, n, moveHalfWay);
getch();
```

```
  gotoxy(1, 23);
  cout << "Press any key to end the program...";
  getch();

  return 0;
}
```

Testing the Remaining Search Functions

The third program, TSARR3.CPP, shown in Listing 16.19, tests the remaining search functions. The program contains the `showArray` function, introduced in TSARR2.CPP (shown in Listing 16.18). The program creates three instances of `Array<int>`—`ar1`, `ar2`, and `ar3`. The test program assigns random integers to the elements of `ar1`, copies `ar1` to `ar2`, and then sorts `ar2`. The elements of `ar2` are used to search for matching `ar1` elements in linear-search functions. Conversely, the elements of `ar1` are used to search for matching `ar3` elements in binary and interpolative-search functions.

To get a better insight on how the search functions work, use a debugger to single-step through the execution of these functions.

The program performs the following tests:

1. Tests the `StatisticalSearch` function. The program first displays the elements of `ar1` in a single column. Then, the program uses a `for` loop to search for the elements of ordered `ar2` in the unordered `ar1`. Each loop iteration displays the search data at the bottom of the screen and places an asterisk to the left of the matching array element. The program prompts you to press a key to search for another value or to move on to the next test.
2. Tests `StatLinearSearch`. The program first displays the elements of `ar1` in a single column. The program then uses a `for` loop to search three consecutive times for the first element of `ar2` in `ar1`. Using a debugger will help you get a better feel for how the tested function works. Each loop iteration displays the

value of the search data at the bottom of the screen and places an asterisk to the left of the matching array element. The program prompts you to press a key to search for the value of `ar2[0]` again or to move on to the next phase of this test. In the second phase, the program uses a second `for` loop to search for the remaining elements of `ar2` in `ar1`. The screen output and user-interaction is similar to the first phase of testing the `StatLinearSearch` function.

3. Tests the `BinarySearch` function. The program first displays the elements of `ar2` in a single column. The program then uses a `for` loop to search for the elements of unordered `ar1` in the ordered `ar2`. Each loop iteration displays the search data at the bottom of the screen and places an asterisk to the left of the matching array element. The program prompts you to press a key to search for another value or to move on to the next test.

4. Tests the `ModifiedBinarySearch` function. The program first copies the elements of `ar2` into `ar3`. The program then copies the value of `ar3[3]` into `ar3[1]` and `ar3[2]` to create the duplicate data in `ar3`. Next, the program displays the elements of `ar3` in a single column. Then, the program uses a `for` loop to search for the elements of unordered `ar1` in the ordered `ar3`. Each loop iteration displays the search data at the bottom of the screen and places an asterisk to the left of the matching array element.

   Two elements in `ar1` do not have a match in `ar3`. This is due to the data-duplication step, which overwrote two data elements in `ar3`. The program prompts you to press a key to search for another value or to move to the next phase of this test. In the second phase of testing the `ModifiedBinarySearch` function, the program searches for the second and third occurrence of the duplicate data in `ar3`. The program uses a `for` loop and employs the loop-control variable as the argument for the sought occurrence. The loop-control variable, `i`, thus appears as the last argument for the `ModifiedBinarySearch` function call. The screen output and user-interaction is the similar to the first phase of testing the `ModifiedBinarySearch` function.

5. Tests the `InterpolativeSearch` function. The program uses a `for` loop to convert the integers of `ar2` to double-typed values stored in the `searchValues` array. The program then displays the elements of `ar2` in a single column. Next, the program uses a `for` loop to search for the elements of unordered `ar1` in the ordered `ar2`. Each loop iteration displays the search data at the bottom of the screen and places an asterisk to the left of the matching array element. Notice

that the argument for the `searchValue` parameter is the expression `(double)ar1[i]`. The program prompts you to press a key to search for another value or to move on to the next test.

6. Tests the `InterBinarySearch` function. The steps involved in testing this function are similar to those that test the `InterpolativeSearch` function.

Listing 16.19. The source code for the TSARR3.CPP program.

```
// Test class of Array<T>
#include <stdlib.h>
#include <string.h>
#include "video.h"
#include <iostream.h>
#include "array.cpp"

const unsigned ARRAY_SIZE = 9;

unsigned showArray(const char* msg,
                   Array<int>& arr,
                   unsigned first,
                   unsigned last)
{
  unsigned y;

  clrscr();
  cout << msg << "\n\n";
  y = wherey();
  for (unsigned i = first; i <= last; i++)
    cout << "  " << arr[i] << '\n';
  return y;
}

main()
{
  Array<int> ar1(ARRAY_SIZE), ar2(ARRAY_SIZE), ar3(ARRAY_SIZE);
  double searchValues[ARRAY_SIZE];
  unsigned i, j, y;
  unsigned n = ARRAY_SIZE - 1;
```

continues

Listing 16.19. continued

```
srand(17);
// initialize the array ar1 with random integers in the
// range of 100 to 999.
for (i = 0; i < ARRAY_SIZE; i++)
  ar1[i] = 100 + rand() % 900;

y = showArray("*** Testing StatisticalSearch function ***",
              ar1, 0, n);
ar2 = ar1;
ar2.CombSort(n);

// test the StatisticalSearch function
for (i = 0; i < ARRAY_SIZE; i++) {
  gotoxy(1, 23);
  clreol();
  cout << "To search for " << ar2[i] << " press any key...";
  getch();
  j = ar1.StatisticalSearch(ar2[i], n);
  if (j != NO_ELEM_FOUND) {
    gotoxy(1, y + j);
    cout << '*';
  }
}
gotoxy(1, 23);
clreol();
cout << "Press any key to continue...";
getch();

y = showArray("*** Testing StatLinearSearch function ***",
              ar1, 0, n);
// test the StatLinearSearch function
for (i = 1; i <= 3; i++) {
  gotoxy(1, 23);
  clreol();
  cout << "To search for " << ar2[0] << " press any key...";
  getch();
  j = ar1.StatLinearSearch(ar2[0], n);
  if (j != NO_ELEM_FOUND) {
    gotoxy(1, y + j);
```

```
      cout << '*';
    }
  }
  for (i = 1; i < ARRAY_SIZE; i++) {
    gotoxy(1, 23);
    clreol();
    cout << "To search for " << ar2[i] << " press any key...";
    getch();
    j = ar1.StatLinearSearch(ar2[i], n);
    if (j != NO_ELEM_FOUND) {
      gotoxy(1, y + j);
      cout << '*';
    }
  }
  y = showArray("*** Testing BinarySearch function ***",
                ar2, 0, n);
  // test the BinarySearch function
  for (i = 0; i < ARRAY_SIZE; i++) {
    gotoxy(1, 23);
    clreol();
    cout << "To search for " << ar1[i] << " press any key...";
    getch();
    j = ar2.BinarySearch(ar1[i], n);
    if (j != NO_ELEM_FOUND) {
      gotoxy(1, y + j);
      cout << '*';
    }
  }
  gotoxy(1, 23);
  clreol();
  cout << "Press any key to continue...";
  getch();

  // copy sorted array ar2 into ar3
  ar3 = ar2;
  // duplicate a few array elements in array ar3
  ar3[1] = ar3[3];
  ar3[2] = ar3[3];
  y = showArray("*** Testing ModfiedBinarySearch function ***",
                ar3, 0, n);
```

continues

Listing 16.19. continued

```
// test the ModifiedBinarySearch function
for (i = 0; i < ARRAY_SIZE; i++) {
  gotoxy(1, 23);
  clreol();
  cout << "To search for " << ar1[i] << " press any key...";
  getch();
  j = ar3.ModifiedBinarySearch(ar1[i], n);
  if (j != NO_ELEM_FOUND) {
    gotoxy(1, y + j);
    cout << '*';
  }
}
// search for the second and third occurrences
// of array element 1 (which are found at index 2 and 3)
for (i = 2; i < 4; i++) {
  gotoxy(1, 23);
  clreol();
  cout << "To search for " << ar3[1] << " press any key...";
  getch();
  j = ar3.ModifiedBinarySearch(ar3[1], n, 0, i);
  if (j != NO_ELEM_FOUND) {
    gotoxy(1, y + j);
    cout << '*';
  }
}

gotoxy(1, 23);
clreol();
cout << "Press any key to continue...";
getch();

y = showArray("*** Testing InterpolativeSearch function ***",
              ar2, 0, n);
for (i = 0; i < ARRAY_SIZE; i++)
  searchValues[i] = (double)(ar2[i]);

// test the InterpolativeSearch function
for (i = 0; i < ARRAY_SIZE; i++) {
  gotoxy(1, 23);
```

```
    clreol();
    cout << "To search for " << ar1[i] << " press any key...";
    getch();
    j = ar2.InterpolativeSearch(ar1[i], (double)ar1[i],
                                searchValues, n);
    if (j != NO_ELEM_FOUND) {
      gotoxy(1, y + j);
      cout << '*';
    }
  }
  gotoxy(1, 23);
  clreol();
  cout << "Press any key to continue...";
  getch();

  y = showArray("*** Testing InterpBinSearch function ***",
                ar2, 0, n);
  for (i = 0; i < ARRAY_SIZE; i++)
    searchValues[i] = (double)(ar2[i]);

  // test the InterpBinSearch function
  for (i = 0; i < ARRAY_SIZE; i++) {
    gotoxy(1, 23);
    clreol();
    cout << "To search for " << ar1[i] << " press any key...";
    getch();
    j = ar2.InterpBinSearch(ar1[i], (double)ar1[i],
                            searchValues, n);
    if (j != NO_ELEM_FOUND) {
      gotoxy(1, y + j);
      cout << '*';
    }
  }
  gotoxy(1, 23);
  clreol();
  cout << "Press any key to end the program...";
  getch();

  return 0;
}
```

Summary

This chapter presented the `Array` template class, which models arrays similar to those supported in C++. Instances of the `Array` class are dynamic and expandable, and they include several sorting and searching functions. The sorting functions implement the following algorithms:

- The Shell-Metzner in-place sorting method
- The new Combsort in-place sorting method
- The recursive Quicksort method
- The Heapsort in-place method

The search functions implement the following algorithms:

- A smart version of the linear-search method. This includes limiting the search range, bidirectional search, circular search, and heuristic movement of matching arrays.
- A statistical method, which starts searching in the middle of the search range and expands the search outward.
- A smart statistical-linear method, which keeps track of the average matching index. The method uses this statistic to determine whether to search forward or backward.
- The basic binary-search method for sorted arrays.
- The modified binary-search method, which locates specific occurrences of data in sorted arrays.
- The interpolative-search method for sorted arrays.
- The interpolative binary-search method for sorted arrays.

Lists

Lists are data structures suitable for storing data items when the number of items to be stored is not known ahead of time. Typically, lists are made up of nodes, which are allocated dynamically. Lists use pointers to link nodes. Single-linked and double-linked lists are the most popular dynamic list structures. Single-linked lists, as the name suggests, link any two consecutive list nodes with a single pointer. Consequently, you can traverse the single-linked list in one direction only: head-to-tail. In addition, list traversal is irreversible.

By contrast, double-linked lists link any two consecutive nodes with two pointers. These pointers support bidirectional traversal of lists. Such traversal includes the capability to move back and forth between the list nodes. Linked lists also are classified according to the order of the list nodes. Ordered linked lists maintain the nodes in a sorted order; unordered lists do not. The way you order data in a list affects the effort of searching for data in that list.

This chapter presents a template of a double-linked list class. The double-linked list is more versatile than the single-linked list. You can easily modify the code to create a single-linked version by removing the declarations and statements that include the backward pointer.

The List Operations

The class of double-linked lists presented here implements the following popular operations:

- *Searching data.* For unordered lists, this operation involves a linear search. The worst-case search examines the entire list. By contrast, searching in an ordered list is more efficient because it generally reduces the number of searched nodes.
- *Inserting data.* For ordered lists, this means inserting the information in the appropriate location in order to maintain a sorted list. For unordered lists, insertion means putting the new data at the tail of the list.
- *Deleting data.* This operation involves locating the target node and deleting it.
- *Clearing the list.* This operation sequentially removes the nodes of a linked list and recuperates the dynamic space of these nodes.
- *List node traversal.* Traversing the nodes of double-linked lists can occur in either sequential or random fashion.

> The last item requires clarification. The sequential traversal of the nodes in a list starts with visiting either the head node (for forward traversal) or the tail node (for backward traversal). Subsequent sequential traversal visits the other nonterminal nodes, with the option of altering the traversal direction. Random traversal of the node works like accessing the element of an array. You access the data in a list node by specifying the index of the target node.

The List Classes

Listing 17.1 shows the source code for the list.hpp header file. The class `DoubleList` models unordered lists; the class `SortedDoubleList` models ordered lists. The `SortedDoubleList` class is a descendant of `DoubleList`. Inheritance plays a major role in sharing many data members and functions between the two classes.

Listing 17.1. The source code for the list.hpp header file.

```
////////////////////////////////////////////////////////////////////
//                                                                //
//              Copyright (c) 1992   Namir Clement Shammas       //
//                                                                //
//  Version:  1.0.0                                DATE 5/5/92  //
//                                                                //
//  Purpose: implements a class of double-linked lists with      //
//           the following operations and features:              //
//                                                                //
//             + insert new node.                                 //
//             + search for a node with a specific occurrence    //
//               of a key.                                        //
//             + delete a node with a specific occurrence of a   //
//               key.                                             //
//             + traverse the nodes of the lists.                 //
//                                                                //
////////////////////////////////////////////////////////////////////

#include "comndata.h"
#include <string.h>

#ifndef _LIST_HPP
#define _LIST_HPP

template<class T>
class DoubleList
{
  protected:
    struct ListNode {
       T listNodeData;
       ListNode *prevNode;
       ListNode *nextNode;
    };

    ListNode *thisPtr,  // search node pointer
             *nodePtr,  // node-visitation pointer
             *tailPtr,  // pointer to the tailPtr of list
             *headPtr;  // pointer to headPtr of list
    unsigned nodeCount;      // number of nodes
    string80 errMsg;  // error message
```

continues

Listing 17.1. continued

```
        DoubleList<T>& copy(DoubleList<T>&);

    public:
        // ************** state manipulation methods **************
        DoubleList();
        DoubleList(DoubleList<T>& dl)
          { headPtr = NULL; copy(dl); }
        ~DoubleList()
          { clear(); }

        // ****************** state query methods *****************
        boolean isListEmpty() const
          { return (nodeCount == 0) ? true : false; }
        unsigned getNodeCount() const
          { return nodeCount; }
        char* getErrMsg();

        // ************** object manipulation methods *************
        virtual boolean insert(T&);
        virtual boolean remove(T& x, unsigned occur = 1);
        virtual boolean search(T& x, unsigned occur = 1);
        virtual boolean getFirstNode(T& x);
        boolean getPrevNode(T& x);
        virtual boolean getNextNode(T& x);
        boolean getLastNode(T& x);
        boolean getData(T& x,
                        unsigned index = 0;
                        boolean updateNodePtr = false);
        virtual void clear();
        DoubleList<T>& operator =(DoubleList<T>& dl)
          { copy(dl); return *this; }
};

template<class T>
class SortedDoubleList  : public DoubleList<T>
{
    public:
        // ************** state manipulation methods **************
        SortedDoubleList () : DoubleList<T>() {}
```

```
    SortedDoubleList (SortedDoubleList <T>& dl)
      { headPtr = NULL; copy(dl); }

    // ************** object manipulation methods *************
    virtual boolean insert(T&);
    virtual boolean search(T& x, unsigned occur = 1);

    SortedDoubleList <T>& operator =(SortedDoubleList <T>& dl)
      { copy(dl); return *this; }
};

#endif
```

The `DoubleList` class declares the nested structure `ListNode`. The members of this structure are typical of double-linked list nodes. They include an instance of the template class to store data and pointers to the next and previous list nodes.

The `DoubleList` class declares the following data members:

- The member `thisPtr`, a pointer used mainly in searching nodes.
- The member `nodePtr`, a pointer to a list node. This member tracks the current node when sequentially traversing a list node.
- The `tailPtr` and `headPtr` members, pointers to the head and tail nodes of the list.
- The `nodeCount` member, which stores the current number of list nodes.
- The `errMsg` member, which stores the text for any error messages emitted by a function.

The `DoubleList` class declares constructors and functions, some of which are defined within the class declaration. These functions include the following:

- The copy constructor, which creates an instance of class `DoubleList` by copying the data from an existing instance. This constructor calls the protected function `copy` to duplicate the data of instance `sl`.
- The class destructor, which calls the `clear` function to delete all dynamically allocated list nodes.
- The Boolean function `isEmpty`, which returns true when the `nodeCount` data member is `0` or false when otherwise.

- The getNodeCount function, which returns the value stored in the data member nodeCount.
- The assignment operator (=), which copies the data of the parameter dl into the targeted instance of class DoubleList. This operator also calls the protected function copy to perform the required task.

The SortedDoubleList list inherits the ListNode structure, the data members, and many functions from its parent class DoubleList. The SortedDoubleList class declares two constructors, two functions, and one operator. The first constructor is the default constructor, which simply invokes the default constructor of the parent class, DoubleList. The second constructor is the copy constructor. This constructor also calls the inherited function copy. The assignment operator (=) also calls the copy function to copy the data in the parameter dl to the targeted instance of SortedDoubleList.

Listing 17.2 contains the source code for the LIST.CPP library file.

Listing 17.2. The source code for the LIST.CPP library file.

```
////////////////////////////////////////////////////////////////////
//                                                                //
//              Copyright (c) 1992   Namir Clement Shammas        //
//                                                                //
//  Version:  1.0.0                                DATE 5/5/92    //
//                                                                //
//  Purpose: implements a class of double-linked lists with       //
//           the following operations and features:               //
//                                                                //
//             + insert new node.                                 //
//             + search for a node with a specific occurrence     //
//               of a key.                                        //
//             + delete a node with a specific occurrence of a    //
//               key.                                             //
//             + traverse the nodes of the lists.                 //
//                                                                //
////////////////////////////////////////////////////////////////////

#include "list.hpp"

/////////////////////////////////////////////////////////////////// /
//
template<class T>
```

```
DoubleList<T>::DoubleList()
//
// Purpose: initializes a linked list object.
//
{
    nodeCount = 0;
    nodePtr = NULL;
    headPtr = NULL;
    tailPtr = NULL;
    errMsg[0] = '\0';
}

////////////////////////////////////////////////////////////////////////
//
template<class T>
DoubleList<T>& DoubleList<T>::copy(DoubleList<T>&  dl)
//
// Purpose: copies a double-linked list.
//
// Parameters:
//
//    input: dl - the list to be copied.
//
{
    ListNode *p, *q, *r;

    if (headPtr)
        clear();
    nodeCount = dl.nodeCount;
    nodePtr = NULL;
    headPtr = NULL;
    tailPtr = NULL;
    errMsg[0] = '\0';
    if (!dl.headPtr)
        return *this;
    headPtr = new ListNode;
    if (!headPtr) {
        strcpy(errMsg, ALLOCATE_ERROR);
        return *this;
    }
    headPtr->listNodeData = dl.headPtr->listNodeData;
    headPtr->nextNode = NULL;
```

continues

Listing 17.2. continued

```
        headPtr->prevNode = NULL;
        tailPtr = headPtr;
        p = headPtr;
        r = NULL;
        q = dl.headPtr->nextNode;
        while (q) {
            r = new ListNode;
            if (!r) {
                strcpy(errMsg, ALLOCATE_ERROR);
                return *this;
            }
            r->listNodeData = q->listNodeData;
            r->nextNode = NULL;
            r->prevNode = p;
            p->nextNode = r;
            tailPtr = r;
            p = p->nextNode;
            q = q->nextNode;
        }
        return *this;
    }
    //////////////////////////////////////////////////////////////////////
    //
    template<class T>
    char* DoubleList<T>::getErrMsg()
    //
    // Purpose: returns the contents of the errMsg data member and
    // assigns a null string to the errMsg member.
    //
    {
       string80 s;

       strcpy(s, errMsg);
       errMsg[0] = '\0';
       return s;
    }

    //////////////////////////////////////////////////////////////////////
    //
    template<class T>
```

```
boolean DoubleList<T>::insert(T& x)
//
// Purpose: performs unordered list insertion. Each new
// element becomes the last one in the list.
//
// Parameters:
//
//    input: x - the data item inserted in the list.
//
{
    errMsg[0] = '\0';
    if (!headPtr) {
        headPtr = new ListNode;
        if (!headPtr) {
          strcpy(errMsg, ALLOCATE_ERROR);
          return false;
        }
        headPtr->listNodeData = x;
        headPtr->nextNode = NULL;
        headPtr->prevNode = NULL;
        tailPtr = headPtr;
    }
    else {
        thisPtr = new ListNode;
        if (!thisPtr) {
          strcpy(errMsg, ALLOCATE_ERROR);
          return false;
        }
        thisPtr->listNodeData = x;
        thisPtr->prevNode = tailPtr;
        thisPtr->nextNode = NULL;
        tailPtr->nextNode = thisPtr;
        tailPtr = thisPtr;
    }
    nodeCount++;
    return true;
}

////////////////////////////////////////////////////////////////////
//
template<class T>
```

continues

Listing 17.2. continued

```
boolean DoubleList<T>::search(T& x, unsigned occur)
//
// Purpose: searches for x in the unordered list starting at the
// head of the list. The pointer to the current node is returned
// in the argument list. The complete datum of the matching node
// is accessed by parameter x. (This is relevant only for structure
// data.)
//
// Parameters:
//
//    input: x - the sought data element.
//           occur - the sought occurrence of a search key.
//
//    output: thisPtr - the pointer to the sought list element.
//
{

    occur = (occur > 0) ? occur : 1;
    thisPtr = headPtr;

    while (thisPtr && occur > 0) {
        if (x == thisPtr->listNodeData)
            occur--;
        if (occur > 0)
            thisPtr = thisPtr->nextNode;
    }

    if (occur == 0) // copy data to pointer x
        x = thisPtr->listNodeData;

    return (occur == 0) ? true : false;
}

//////////////////////////////////////////////////////////////////////
//
template<class T>
boolean DoubleList<T>::remove(T& x, unsigned occur)
//
// Purpose: attempts to delete an item from an ordered list.
// The boolean function result confirms the deletion process.
```

```
//
// Parameters:
//
//    input: x - the data element to be deleted from the list.
//           occur - the sought occurrence of a search key.
//
{
    ListNode *p;
    boolean match;

    occur = (occur > 0) ? occur : 1;
    // search for item to delete
    match = search(x, occur);

    if (match) {
        if (nodeCount == 1) {
            delete headPtr;
            headPtr = NULL;
            tailPtr = NULL;
        }
        else if (!thisPtr->nextNode) {
            // delete the last list member
            p = thisPtr->prevNode;
            p->nextNode = NULL;
            delete tailPtr;
            // link tailPtr pointer with new last element
            tailPtr = p;
        }
        else if (!thisPtr->prevNode) {
            // delete the list headPtr
            p = thisPtr->nextNode;
            p->prevNode = NULL;
            delete headPtr;
            headPtr = p; // link headPtr with new first element
        }
        else {
            thisPtr->prevNode->nextNode = thisPtr->nextNode;
            thisPtr->nextNode->prevNode = thisPtr->prevNode;
            delete thisPtr;
        }
        nodeCount--;
    }
```

continues

Listing 17.2. continued

```
    return match; // return function value
}

/////////////////////////////////////////////////////////////////////// /
//
template<class T>
boolean DoubleList<T>::getFirstNode(T& x)
//
// Purpose: visits the first node of the generic linked list. The
// function returns true if the list is not empty. Otherwise, it
// returns false.
//
// Parameters:
//
//    output: x - the data obtained from the first list node.
//
{
    if (headPtr) {
        x = headPtr->listNodeData;
        nodePtr = headPtr;
        return true;
    }
    else
        return false;
}

///////////////////////////////////////////////////////////////////////
//
template<class T>
boolean DoubleList<T>::getLastNode(T& x)
//
// Purpose: visits the tail of the linked list. The function returns
// true if the list is not empty. Otherwise, the function returns
// false.
//
// Parameters:
//
//    output: x - the obtained from the last list node.
//
{
```

```
    if (tailPtr) {
        x = tailPtr->listNodeData;
        nodePtr = tailPtr;
        return true;
    }
    else
        return false;
}

//////////////////////////////////////////////////////////////////////
//
template<class T>
boolean DoubleList<T>::getNextNode(T& x)
//
// Purpose: visits the next node in the generic list. The function
// returns false if an attempt is made to read beyond the tail of
// the list. Otherwise, the function returns true.
//
// Parameters:
//
//    output: x - the data obtained from the next list node.
//
{
    if (nodePtr && nodePtr->nextNode) {
        nodePtr = nodePtr->nextNode;
        x = nodePtr->listNodeData;
        return true;
    }
    else
        return false;
}

//////////////////////////////////////////////////////////////////////
//
template<class T>
boolean DoubleList<T>::getPrevNode(T& x)
//
// Purpose: visits the previous node in the generic list. The
// function returns false if an attempt is made to read beyond
// the tail of the list. Otherwise, returns true.
//
// Parameters:
```

continues

Listing 17.2. continued

```
//
//    output: x - the data obtained from the previous list node.
//
{
    if (nodePtr && nodePtr->prevNode) {
        nodePtr = nodePtr->prevNode;
        x = nodePtr->listNodeData;
        return true;
    }
    else
        return false;
}

//////////////////////////////////////////////////////////////////////
//
template<class T>
boolean DoubleList<T>::getData(T& x,
                              unsigned index,
                              boolean updateNodePtr)
//
// Purpose: obtains the data at node number index. The function
// returns true if index is less than the nodeCount member.
//
// Parameters:
//
//    input: index - the index of the sought node
//           updateNodePtr - flag to update nodePtr member.
//
//    output: x - the data obtained from the targeted list node.
//
{
  ListNode *p;

  if (index >= nodeCount)
    return false;

  p = headPtr;
  // search for the node number index
  while (index > 0) {
    p = p->nextNode;
```

```
    index--;
  }
  x = p->listNodeData;
  nodePtr = (updateNodePtr) ? p : nodePtr;
  return true;
}

//////////////////////////////////////////////////////////////////////
//
template<class T>
void DoubleList<T>::clear()
//
// Purpose: clears the linked list.
//
{
    ListNode* p;

    while (headPtr) {
        p = headPtr;
        headPtr = headPtr->nextNode;
        delete p;
        nodeCount--;
    }
    tailPtr = NULL;
    nodePtr = NULL;
}

//////////////////////////////////////////////////////////////////////
//
template<class T>
boolean SortedDoubleList <T>::search(T& x, unsigned occur)
//
// Purpose: searches for x in the sorted list starting at the
// head of the list. The complete datum of the matching node
// is accessed by parameter x. (This is relevant only for structured
// data.) The function returns true if the search data is located
// in the list; otherwise, it returns false.
//
// Parameters:
//
//    input: x - the sought data element.
//           occur - the sought occurrence of a search key.
```

continues

Listing 17.2. continued

```
//
{
    errMsg[0] = '\0';
    occur = (occur > 0) ? occur : 1;
    thisPtr = headPtr;

    while (thisPtr && occur > 0) {
        // element might be in the list ?
        if (x <= thisPtr->listNodeData)
            occur--;
        if (occur > 0)
            thisPtr = thisPtr->nextNode;
    }

    if (x == thisPtr->listNodeData)
        // copy data to x
        x = thisPtr->listNodeData;

    // return function value
    return (x == thisPtr->listNodeData) ? true : false;

}

//////////////////////////////////////////////////////////////////////
//
template<class T>
boolean SortedDoubleList <T>::insert(T& x)
//
// Purpose: performs ordered list insertion. The function returns
// true if the insertion has taken place.
//
// Parameters:
//
//    input: x - the reference to the data item inserted in the list.
//
{
    ListNode *p;
    boolean match;

    T buffer = x;
    match = search(buffer, 1);
```

```
if (!thisPtr) {
    // new item inserted at the tailPtr of the list
    p = new ListNode;
    if (!p) {
        strcpy(errMsg, ALLOCATE_ERROR);
        return false;
    }
    // assign key and other members
    p->listNodeData = x;
    if (headPtr) {
        tailPtr->nextNode = p;
        p->prevNode = tailPtr;
        p->nextNode = NULL;
        tailPtr = p;
    }
    else {
        headPtr = p;
        headPtr->nextNode = NULL;
        headPtr->prevNode = NULL;
        tailPtr = p;
    }
}
else if (!thisPtr->prevNode) {
    // new item is the new list headPtr
    p = new ListNode;
    if (!p) {
        strcpy(errMsg, ALLOCATE_ERROR);
        return false;
    }
    // assign key and other members
    p->nextNode = headPtr;
    p->prevNode = NULL;
    headPtr->prevNode = p;
    p->listNodeData = x;
    headPtr = p; // assign new pointer to the headPtr of the list
}
else {
    // insert new item inside the list or at its tailPtr
    p = new ListNode;
    if (!p) {
        strcpy(errMsg, ALLOCATE_ERROR);
        return false;
```

continues

Listing 17.2. continued

```
        }
        // link the head with the "current" node
        p->nextNode = thisPtr;
        // link back with the "previous" node
        p->prevNode = thisPtr->prevNode;
        thisPtr->prevNode->nextNode = p;
        thisPtr->prevNode = p;
        // assign key and other members
        p->listNodeData = x;
    }
    nodeCount++;
    errMsg[0] = '\0';
    return true; // return function value
}
```

Now let's take a closer look at the functions of class `DoubleList`:

- The default class constructor initializes the instances. The constructor allocates no dynamic data. Instead, it assigns `NULL` to the `headPtr`, `tailPtr`, and `nodePtr` pointers and `0` to the `nodeCount` and `errMsg` members.
- The `copy` function copies the data of an instance. The `copy` function first deletes any existing data in the list before copying the data in the nodes of parameter `dl`. The process of copying data begins with the first node, which is accessed by the `headPtr` member. The `copy` function uses a `while` loop to allocate the dynamic data for the new nodes and copy their data from the list `dl`. The function copies information in the `listNodeData` member using the assignment operator (=) of the template class `T`. If the dynamic allocation fails at any stage, the `copy` function assigns an error message to the `errMsg` member and exits. Your application should call the `getErrMsg` function when you want to trap dynamic allocation errors.
- The `getErrMsg` function returns the contents of the `errMsg` member and assigns an empty string to that member.
- The `insert` function inserts data in the list. Because the class `DoubleList` does not maintain ordered data, the insertion process merely appends new data to the tail of the list. The `insert` function first checks whether the `headPtr` is `NULL` in order to determine whether the function is inserting data in an empty

list—which requires special setup—or simply adding more data. Inserting data in an empty list requires that `headPtr` be involved in the process. Inserting at the tail of the list requires only adjustments to the `tailPtr` member.

To avoid inserting duplicate data in an instance of `DoubleList`, you first must call the `search` function (presented next) to ensure that the data does not already exist in the list.

- The `search` function searches for a specific occurrence of parameter `x` (designated by parameter `occur`). The default argument for the `occur` parameter is `1`, the most commonly used value. The `search` function uses a `while` loop to locate the occurrence of parameter `x`. If the function finds a match, it copies the data of the matching node to the reference parameter `x`. This action is relevant when the template class `T` has members that are not involved in the relational operators. The `search` function returns true when the sought occurrence of parameter `x` is found. Otherwise, the function returns false.
- The `remove` function deletes a specific occurrence of parameter `x` (indicated by parameter `occur`). The default argument for the `occur` parameter is `1`, the most commonly used value. The `remove` function first calls the `search` function to locate the sought node. If the search is successful, the function proceeds with the deletion. There are four cases in which a node is deleted:

  The last list node is deleted. This type of deletion requires assigning nulls to the `headPtr` and `tailPtr` members.

  The last node is deleted.

  The first node is deleted.

  A nonterminal node is deleted in a list that still contains data after the deletion.

  The remove function returns true if the sought occurrence of parameter `x` is deleted. Otherwise, the function returns false.
- The Boolean functions `getFirstNode` and `getLastNode` visit the head and tail list nodes, respectively. Either function must first be used to initiate a list traversal. These functions return true if the list is not empty or false when the

list is empty. The reference parameter x contains the data in the visited node. The getFirstNode and getLastNode functions assign the address of the visited node to the nodePtr data member.

- The Boolean getNextNode and getPrevNode functions visit the next and previous nodes, respectively. These functions return true if the targeted node is visited or false if the head or tail of the list was reached. The reference parameter x contains the data in the visited node. The getNextNode and getPrevNode functions assign the address of the visited node to the nodePtr data member.
- The Boolean getData function visits the list node specified by the parameter index. The Boolean parameter updateNodePtr indicates whether to assign the address of the accessed node to member nodePtr. The default arguments for parameters index and updateNodePtr are 0 and false, respectively. The getData function returns true if the specified index is within valid range [0...nodeCount - 1]; otherwise, the function returns false. The reference parameter returns the data of the sought node when the argument for parameter index is valid. The default argument for the parameter updateNodePtr enables you to use the getData function without disturbing the sequential list traversal performed by other getxxxxx functions. On the other hand, when you pass the argument true to the updateNodePtr parameter, you can resume list traversal, in either direction, in the vicinity of the node number index.
- The clear function sequentially deletes the dynamic list nodes. This process uses a while loop to destructively traverse the list.

The SortedDoubleList class defines its own versions of the search and insert functions:

- The search function inspects the list nodes for the specified occurrence of parameter x. The occur parameter indicates the sought occurrence. The default argument for this parameter is 1. The search function is more efficient than the DoubleList<T>::search function because it takes advantage of the sorted list nodes to reduce the search effort. If the search function finds a match, it copies the data of the matching node to the reference parameter x. This action is relevant when the template class T has members that are not involved in the relational operators. The function returns true when the sought occurrence of parameter x is found. Otherwise, the function returns false.

The search function serves two purposes: it searches for matching data, and it determines the appropriate insertion point for new data. To accomplish the latter purpose, the search function uses the member thisPtr as the pointer involved in the search. (There's more about the role of member thisPtr in the next item.)

- The insert function inserts the argument of the reference parameter x in the list. The insert function first calls the search function to determine the appropriate insertion point. This information is provided by the member thisPtr, which is used by search as the search pointer. The insert function uses a series of if statements to handle different cases of inserting data, including inserting at the head of the list, inserting at the tail of the list, and inserting at a nonterminal list node. The function returns true if the insertion is successful or false if a dynamic allocation error occurs.

Testing The List Classes

Now, look at a simple program that tests the DoubleList and SortedDoubleList classes. Listing 17.3 contains the source code for the TSLIST.CPP test program. The program tests lists of cString classes and declares two functions: viewList and main.

Listing 17.3. The source code for the TSLIST.CPP test program.

```
#include <iostream.h>
#include "video.h"
#include <string.h>
#include "string.hpp"
#include "list.cpp"

void viewList(DoubleList<cString>& list,
                         cString message,
                         boolean endOfProgram)
{
    boolean ok;
```

continues

Listing 17.3. continued

```
    unsigned i = 0;
    cString string;

    clrscr();
    cout << message.getstr() << '\n';
    ok = list.getFirstNode(string);
    while (ok) {
        cout << ++i << "  " << string.getstr() << '\n';
        ok = list.getNextNode(string);
    }
    if (!endOfProgram)
      cout << "\n\nPress any key . . . ";
    else
      cout << "\n\nPress any key to end the program ...";
    getch();
}

main()
{
    SortedDoubleList<cString> sortedList;
    SortedDoubleList<cString> sortedList2;
    DoubleList<cString> chronoList;
    cString message;
    cString country[] = { "France", "England", "Spain", "Italy",
                          "Ireland", "Poland", "Greece", "Germany"};

    unsigned arraySize = sizeof(country) / sizeof(cString);
    for (unsigned i = 0; i < arraySize ; i++)
        sortedList.insert(country[i]);
    sortedList2 = sortedList;
    viewList(sortedList, "Sorted list is:", false);

    for (i = 0; i < (arraySize / 2); i++) {
        sortedList.remove(country[i], 1);
        message = "After removing " + country[i];
        viewList(sortedList, message, false);
    }

    viewList(sortedList, "New list is:", false);
    viewList(sortedList2, "Original list was:", false);
```

```
    for (i = 0; i < arraySize ; i++)
        chronoList.insert(country[i]);

    viewList(chronoList, "Unsorted list is:", false);

    for (i = 0; i < (arraySize / 2); i++) {
        chronoList.remove(country[i], 1);
        message = "After removing " + country[i];
        viewList(chronoList, message, false);
    }

    viewList(chronoList, "New list is:", true);

    return 0;
}
```

The `viewList` function displays the data in the parameter `list` in a single column and waits for you to press a key. The reference parameter `list` specifies the instantiated class `DoubleList<cString>`. Because the template class `DoubleList` is the parent of the template class `SortedDoubleList`, the `viewList` function also can display instances of `SortedDoubleList<cString>`. The parameter `message` displays text at the top of the screen. The Boolean parameter `endOfProgram` indicates whether this is the last call to the `viewList` function in the program. The Boolean value of parameter `endOfProgram` determines the text of the prompting string that appears below the list nodes.

The `viewList` function calls the `getFirstNode` and `getNextNode` functions to traverse the nodes of parameter `list`. The local Boolean variable `ok` stores the results of the `getFirstNode` and `getNextNode` functions. The `viewList` function examines the value of variable `ok` in a `while` loop to determine when to stop iterating.

The `main` function declares the following relevant instances:

- Two instances of `SortedDoubleList<cString>`: `sortedList` and `sortedList2`.
- A single instance of `DoubleList<cString>` called `chronoList`.
- An array of `cString` instances, called `country`, that stores the names of European countries.

The `main` function carries out the following steps to manipulate the linked lists:

1. Uses a `for` loop to insert the elements of array `country` in the `sortedList` instance. Each loop iteration calls the `SortedDoubleList<T>::insert` function to introduce a string in the list.

2. Copies the data of instance `sortedList` to `sortedList2`. This step uses the `SortedDoubleList<T>::operator, =`.
3. Views the strings in the list `sortedList` by calling the `viewList` function.
4. Uses a `for` loop to remove half of the strings stored in the instance `sortedList`. Each loop iteration invokes the `remove` function and then calls the `viewList` function to display the updated list.
5. Displays the trimmed list and then displays the original list (stored in instance `sortedList2`).
6. Uses a `for` loop to insert the names of the countries in the unordered list `chronoList`. This step calls the `DoubleList<T>::insert` function.
7. Displays the entire list `chronoList` by calling the `viewList` function.
8. Uses a `for` loop to remove half of the strings stored in the instance `chronoList`. Each loop iteration calls the `remove` function and then invokes the `viewList` function to display the updated list.
9. Displays the trimmed list `chronoList`.

Summary

This chapter presented classes that model unordered and ordered template classes for double-linked lists. You learned about basic list operations, which include

- searching for data in the list nodes
- inserting data in the lists
- deleting data from the lists
- clearing a list
- list node traversal

This chapter also presented the classes `DoubleList` and `SortedDoubleList`, which implement double-linked lists. You learned about the data structures, data members, and functions involved in supporting these two classes. This chapter also presented a straightforward test program to illustrate using these classes.

Basic and Advanced Binary Trees

Trees are structures that offer more efficient search capabilities than linked lists offer. Trees link each node with two or more *child* nodes. This one-to-many link accelerates the search in a tree.

Tree structures typically are dynamic and maintain their data in an ordered fashion. The simplest type of tree is the *binary tree.* Computer scientists have come up with a number of variations on the basic binary tree to improve its performance. Popular examples are the AVL tree and the red-black tree. This chapter presents a template class that supports binary, AVL, and red-black trees. In addition, it discusses a special class that models binary trees using dynamic arrays, and it explains why and when such an unusual implementation of binary trees is feasible and advantageous.

Basic Binary Trees

As the name suggests, each node in a binary tree can be linked to two child nodes: the *left child node* and the *right child node.* A binary tree has a *root node* (where the search begins), *terminal* (or *leaf*) *nodes,* and *nonterminal nodes.* The distribution of the nodes in a binary tree directly affects search efficiency. A perfectly balanced tree can be searched most efficiently, comparable to the efficiency of a binary search in a sorted array. As the binary tree becomes less balanced, the search efficiency decreases. The worst-case scenario is a binary tree into which ordered data has been inserted. This type of binary tree essentially is a linked list. Binary trees thus are vulnerable to inserting ordered data. Conversely, binary trees work better with random data. The more random the inserted data is, the more balanced the binary tree.

The basic operations for a binary tree include

- *Node searching.* There are several reasons to search for data in a tree:

  1. To determine whether the data exists in the tree at all.
  2. To retrieve additional information from a matching node.
  3. To locate a node for deletion.
  4. To determine the insertion location for a new node.

- *Node insertion.*
- *Node deletion.*
- *Tree deletion.* This operation systematically deletes the nodes of the entire binary tree and frees its dynamic space.
- *Tree traversal.* This operation enables you to visit the nodes of the binary tree. The most popular type of tree traversal is the *in-order traversal,* which is a recursive process. In this process you visit the left child node, the target node, and the right child node, in that order.

  Any tree-traversal method is recursive and intermittent, and each traversal step locates the next unvisited node. There are several ways to implement tree traversal. For example, you might use an additional structure, such as an array or a stack, to obtain a sorted copy of the binary tree nodes. The cost of more-efficient data access is the additional memory space, but such a go-between structure is justified because it's easier to examine that structure's data without recursion.

Figure 18.1 shows a typical binary tree.

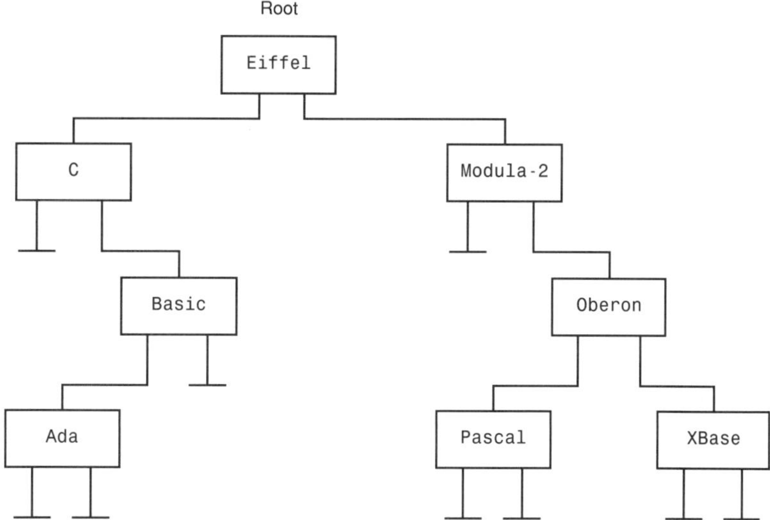

Figure 18.1. A typical binary tree.

The BinaryTree Class

This section presents the template class `BinaryTree`, which models binary trees. Listing 18.1 shows the source code for the bintree.hpp header file. The header file also declares the template structure `Binstruct`, which models the individual node of a binary tree.

Examine the declaration of structure `Binstruct`: you'll find that it declares not two, but three node pointers. The members `leftPtr` and `rightPtr` are the typical left-child and right-child node pointers, respectively. The member `parentPtr` points to the parent node. This third pointer is the main reason I included the implementation of a binary-tree class in this book: by using an additional node pointer, the implementation of the binary-tree class becomes easier and shorter than typical binary-tree code. The `Binstruct` structure also declares the `dataNode` member and `marked` data members. The `dataNode` member stores the node's data. The Boolean `marked` member is a node-traversal flag. This member tells recursive tree-traversal routines whether the node's data has been accessed.

The template `BinaryTree` class declares a set of data members and member functions. The declaration includes protected and public members. The `BinaryTree` class declares the following data members as protected:

- The `numNodes` member, which stores the number of nodes in a binary tree.
- The `errMsg` member, which stores the error text returned by the various functions.
- The `nodePtr` member, which stores the currently visited node.
- The `root` member, which stores the pointer to the root of the AVL tree.
- The `buffer` member, which is an internal buffer.
- The Boolean `seekNode` member, which is used in the traversal of a binary tree.

The `BinaryTree` class also declares the following data members as public:

- The class destructor, which invokes the clear function to deallocate the dynamic space of the binary-tree nodes.
- The `getNodeCount` function, which returns the value stored in the `numNodes` data member.
- The `setBuffer` function, which assigns a special value to the internal buffer. The parameter `newBuffer` assigns special data to critical members of the `buffer` data member.
- The `search` function, which searches for the specified occurrence of a tree node. The reference parameter `x` specifies the search data. The `occur` parameter indicates the sought occurrence. The default argument for this parameter is `1`. The `search` function returns `true` if the sought information is located, `false` if not. When the search is successful, the function assigns a copy of the matching node's data to the argument of parameter `x`. This assignment allows the function to retrieve nonsearch data members of the template class `T`. The `search` function invokes the protected `searchBinaryTree` function.
- The `clear` function deletes an instance of class `BinaryTree` by invoking the protected function `clearNode` and supplying it with the argument `root`.

Listing 18.1. The source code for the bintree.hpp header file.

```
////////////////////////////////////////////////////////////////////////
//                                                                    //
//                Copyright (c) 1992 Namir Clement Shammas            //
//                                                                    //
//  Version: 1.0.0                                    Date 7/9/92     //
//                                                                    //
//  Purpose: implements class of binary trees that have the           //
//           following functionality:                                 //
//                                                                    //
//             + insert data.                                         //
//             + search for data.                                     //
//             + delete data.                                         //
//             + nodes with duplicate keys are optional.              //
//                                                                    //
//                                                                    //
////////////////////////////////////////////////////////////////////


#include "comndata.h"

#ifndef _BINTREE_HPP
#define _BINTREE_HPP

template<class T>
struct Binstruct {
    T              dataNode;  // node data
    Binstruct<T>  *parentPtr, // pointer to parent node
                  *leftPtr,   // left child pointer
                  *rightPtr;  // right child pointer
    boolean        marked;    // visit flag
};


template<class T>
class BinaryTree
{

  protected:
    unsigned   numNodes;     // number of nodes
```

continues

Listing 18.1. continued

```
    string80   errMsg;        // error message
    Binstruct<T> *nodePtr,
                 *root;     // pointer to the heap
    T            buffer;    // data buffer
    boolean seekNode;

    Binstruct<T>* searchBinaryTree(T& x, unsigned occur = 1);
    void clearNode(Binstruct<T>* &rootPtr);
    Binstruct<T>* getSuccessor(Binstruct<T>* &p);
    void clearMarks(Binstruct<T>* rootPtr);
    void visitTree(Binstruct<T>* rootPtr,
                   Binstruct<T>* &node);

  public:
    // ************** state manipulation methods **************
    BinaryTree();
    ~BinaryTree()
      { if (root) clear(); }

    char* getErrorMessage();
    unsigned getNodeCount() const
      { return numNodes; }

    // ************** object manipulation methods *************
    void setBuffer(T& newBuffer)
      { buffer = newBuffer; }
    virtual void insert(T& x);
    virtual boolean search(T& x, unsigned occur = 1)
    {
       return (searchBinaryTree(x, occur)) ? true : false;
    }
    virtual boolean remove(T& x, unsigned occur = 1);
    virtual boolean getFirstNode(T& x);
    virtual boolean getNextNode(T& x);
    virtual void clear()
      { clearNode(root); }
    boolean probeParent(T& x);
    boolean probeLeftChild(T& x);
    boolean probeRightChild(T& x);
```

```
};

#endif
```

The other functions of the `BinaryTree` class are defined in Listing 18.2. This listing contains the source code for the BINTREE.CPP library file. The class members in Listing 18.2 are as follows:

- The default (and only) class constructor. This constructor initializes instances of `BinaryTree`, including assigning nulls and zero to the members `errMsg`, `numNodes`, and `root`. The constructor allocates no dynamic member.
- The `getErrorMessage` function, which retrieves the contents of the `errMsg` member and assigns a null string to that member.
- The `insert` function, which inserts the argument of parameter `x` into the binary tree. The `insert` function uses a `while` loop to search for the proper insertion location. Once this location is found, the `insert` function establishes the links with the parent and child nodes.
- The protected `searchBinaryTree` function, which searches for a specific occurrence of a data item in the binary tree. The parameters of this function are identical to those of the search function mentioned earlier. The `searchBinaryTree` function performs a nonrecursive search and returns the pointer of the matching binary-tree node, or `NULL` if no match is found.
- The protected `clearNode` function, which performs node deletion using a recursive, in-order traversal.
- The `remove` function, which deletes the specified occurrence of the searched data. The parameter `x` specifies the search data. The `occur` parameter indicates the occurrence to delete. The default argument for this parameter is `1`. This Boolean function returns `true` when the sought node is deleted, or `false` if not.
- The protected `clearMarks` function, which recursively prepares for the tree traversal. The `clearMarks` function sets the `marked` member of each binary-tree node to `false`.
- The protected `visitTree` function, which recursively visits the nodes of a binary tree. When the next node to visit is found, this function sets the `marked` member of that node to `true`. This value enables the traversal functions to skip the node in future calls to the `visitTree` function.

- The getFirstNode function, which visits the first—that is, the first ranking—node in a binary tree. This function calls the protected clearMarks function to prepare for a new round of tree traversal. The getFirstNode function then calls the protected visitTree function to find the first node. The getFirstNode function returns true if the binary tree is not empty. The reference parameter x supplies the data in the first visited node. The getFirstNode function must be called before invoking the getNextNode function.
- The getNextNode function, which visits a subsequent binary-tree node. This Boolean function returns true when it finds a node to visit, or false when all binary-tree nodes have been visited. The getNextNode function calls the protected visitTree function to locate the next node. The reference parameter x supplies the data in the next visited node.
- The Boolean probeLeftChild, probeRightChild, and probeParent functions allow you to peek at the data stored in the left, right, and parent nodes, respectively. The probeLeftChild, probeRightChild, and probeParent functions work in a similar manner: each function returns true if the node it seeks exists. The reference parameter x returns the data in the node.
- The protected getSuccessor function, which returns the pointer to the successor node.

Listing 18.2. The source code for the BINTREE.CPP library file.

```
//////////////////////////////////////////////////////////////////////
//                                                                  //
//               Copyright (c) 1992 Namir Clement Shammas          //
//                                                                  //
//  Version: 1.0.0                                  Date 7/9/92    //
//                                                                  //
//  Purpose: implements class of binary trees that have the        //
//           following functionality:                               //
//                                                                  //
//             + insert data.                                       //
//             + search for data.                                   //
//             + delete data.                                       //
//             + visit the tree nodes.                              //
//                                                                  //
//                                                                  //
//////////////////////////////////////////////////////////////////////
```

```
#include <string.h>
#include "bintree.hpp"

////////////////////////////////////////////////////////////////////
//
template<class T>
BinaryTree<T>::BinaryTree()
//
// Purpose: initializes the instances of an binary tree.
//
//
{
    errMsg[0] = '\0';
    numNodes = 0;
    root = NULL;
}

////////////////////////////////////////////////////////////////////
//
template<class T>
char* BinaryTree<T>::getErrorMessage()
//
// Purpose: returns the contents of the errMsg data member
// and assigns an empty string to that member.
//
//
{
    string80 s;

    strcpy(s, errMsg);
    strcpy(errMsg, "");
    return s;
};

////////////////////////////////////////////////////////////////////
//
template<class T>
void BinaryTree<T>::insert(T& x)
//
// Purpose: performs node insertion in an binary tree.
//
//  Parameters:
```

continues

Listing 18.2. continued

```
//
//    in/out: x - the inserted data.
//
{
  Binstruct<T> *p = new Binstruct<T>;
  Binstruct<T> *q = root, *t = NULL;

  if (!p) {
    strcpy(errMsg, ALLOCATE_ERROR);
    return;
  }
  numNodes++;
  // assign initial data to new node
  p->dataNode = x;
  p->leftPtr = NULL;
  p->rightPtr = NULL;
  p->parentPtr = NULL;


  // find the insertion location
  while (q) {
    t = q;
    q = (p->dataNode <= q->dataNode) ? q->leftPtr : q->rightPtr;
  }

  p->parentPtr = t;
  if (!t)
    root = p;
  else {
    if (p->dataNode <= t->dataNode)
      t->leftPtr = p;
    else
      t->rightPtr = p;
  }
}

/////////////////////////////////////////////////////////////////////
//
template<class T>
Binstruct<T>* BinaryTree<T>::searchBinaryTree(T& x, unsigned occur)
```

```
//
// Purpose: searches for a specific occurrence of a key. The
// function returns a pointer to the sought node, or NULL if
// no match was found.
//
//  Parameters:
//
//   input: x - the search key data.
//          occur - the sought occurrence.
//
{
    // initialize count for actual occurrence of x
    unsigned count = 0;
    Binstruct<T>* p;

    // assign 1 to occur if tree has no node with duplicate keys
    occur = (occur == 0) ? 1 : occur;
    if (occur > numNodes)
        // data is impossible to find
        return NULL;

    p = root;
    while (p && count < occur) {
      if (x > p->dataNode)
          p = p->rightPtr;
      else if (x < p->dataNode)
          p = p->leftPtr;
      else { // match is found
          count++;
          if (count < occur)
              p = p->leftPtr;
      }
    }

    if (p)
        x = p->dataNode;

    return p;
}

////////////////////////////////////////////////////////////////////
//
```

continues

Listing 18.2. continued

```
template<class T>
boolean BinaryTree<T>::remove(T& x, unsigned occur)
//
//
// Purpose: performs node deletion.
//
//  Parameters:
//
//    input: x - the data to be removed
//           occur - the occurrence of key data for the deleted node.
//
{
    Binstruct<T> *p, *q, *t;

    occur = (occur == 0) ? 1 : occur;
    if (occur > numNodes)
        return false;

    buffer = x;
    // locate sought node
    p = searchBinaryTree(buffer, occur);
    // found matching node?
    if (p) {
      if (!p->leftPtr || !p->rightPtr)
        t = p;
      else
        t = getSuccessor(p);

      q = (t->leftPtr) ? t->leftPtr : t->rightPtr;

      q->parentPtr = (q) ? t->parentPtr : q->parentPtr;

      if (!t->parentPtr)
        root = q;
      else {
        if (t == t->parentPtr->leftPtr)
          t->parentPtr->leftPtr = q;
        else
          t->parentPtr->rightPtr = q;
      }
```

```
        if (t != p)
          p->dataNode = t->dataNode;
        // remove node
        delete t;
        return true;
      }
      return false;
}

//////////////////////////////////////////////////////////////////////
//
template<class T>
Binstruct<T>* BinaryTree<T>::getSuccessor(Binstruct<T>* &p)
//
// Purpose: returns a pointer to the successor node.
//
// Parameters:
//
//     input: p - the pointer to the node whose successor is sought
//
//     output:
//
{
   Binstruct<T> *q, *t;

   if (p->rightPtr) {
      // find the minimum node attached to the
      // right child node of p.
      q = p->rightPtr;
      while (q->leftPtr)
        q = q->leftPtr;
      return q;
   }

   t = q->parentPtr;
   while (t && q == t->rightPtr) {
     q = t;
     t = t->parentPtr;
   }
   return t;
}
```

continues

Listing 18.2. continued

```
//////////////////////////////////////////////////////////////////////
//
template<class T>
void BinaryTree<T>::clearMarks(Binstruct<T>* rootPtr)
//
// Purpose: recursive function used to traverse the
// binary tree and set the marked flags to false.
//
//  Parameters:
//
//    input: rootPtr - pointer to the root of the binary tree.
//
{
    if (rootPtr) {
        clearMarks(rootPtr->leftPtr);
        rootPtr->marked = false;
        clearMarks(rootPtr->rightPtr);
    }
}

//////////////////////////////////////////////////////////////////////
//
template<class T>
void BinaryTree<T>::visitTree(Binstruct<T>* rootPtr,
                              Binstruct<T>* &node)
//
// Purpose: recursive function used to traverse the binary tree.
//
//  Parameters:
//
//    input: rootPtr - pointer to the root of the binary tree.
//
//    output: node - the pointer to the next node visited.
//
{
    if (seekNode && rootPtr) {
        visitTree(rootPtr->leftPtr, node);
        if (seekNode && !rootPtr->marked) {
            seekNode = false;
            rootPtr->marked = true;
            node = rootPtr;
```

```
                return;
            }
            visitTree(rootPtr->rightPtr, node);
        }
}

//////////////////////////////////////////////////////////////////////
//
template<class T>
void BinaryTree<T>::clearNode(Binstruct<T>* &rootPtr)
//
// Purpose: recursive function to delete subtrees.
//
// Parameters:
//
//    input: rootPtr - the pointer of the node to delete
//
{
    if (rootPtr) {
        clearNode(rootPtr->leftPtr);
        clearNode(rootPtr->rightPtr);
        delete rootPtr;
    }
}

//////////////////////////////////////////////////////////////////////
//
template<class T>
boolean BinaryTree<T>::getFirstNode(T& x)
//
// Purpose: visits the root of the binary tree. The function
// returns true if the binary tree object has a root.
//
//  Parameters:
//
//   input: x - the pointer to the data associated with the root of
//          the binary tree.
{
    if (root) {
        seekNode = true;
        clearMarks(root);
        visitTree(root, nodePtr);
```

continues

Listing 18.2. continued

```
        x = nodePtr->dataNode;
    }
    return (root) ? true : false;
}

//////////////////////////////////////////////////////////////////////
//
template<class T>
boolean BinaryTree<T>::getNextNode(T& x)
//
// Purpose: visits the next node in the binary tree. The function
// returns true if there was a next node to visit.
//
//  Parameters:
//
//    input: x - the pointer to the data associated with the visited
//              node.
//
{
    seekNode = true;
    if (root) {
        visitTree(root, nodePtr);
        if (!seekNode)
            x = nodePtr->dataNode;
    }
    return (!seekNode) ? true : false;
}

//////////////////////////////////////////////////////////////////////
//
template<class T>
boolean BinaryTree<T>::probeParent(T& x)
//
// Purpose: visits the parent of the current node. The function
// returns true if the current node has a parent. This is true of
// all nodes, except the root of the binary tree.
//
//  Parameters:
//
//    input: x - the data associated with the parent node.
{
```

```
    if (nodePtr && nodePtr->parentPtr) {
        x = nodePtr->parentPtr->dataNode;
        return true;
    }
    else
        return false;
}

//////////////////////////////////////////////////////////////////////
//
template<class T>
boolean BinaryTree<T>::probeLeftChild(T& x)
//
// Purpose: visits the left child of the current node. The function
// returns true if the current node has a left child.
//
//  Parameters:
//
//    input: x - the data associated with the left child node.
{
    if (nodePtr && nodePtr->leftPtr) {
        x = nodePtr->leftPtr->dataNode;
        return true;
    }
    else
        return false;
}

//////////////////////////////////////////////////////////////////////
//
template<class T>
boolean BinaryTree<T>::probeRightChild(T& x)
//
// Purpose: visits the right child of the current node. The
// function returns true if the current node has right child.
//
//  Parameters:
//
//   input: x - the data associated with the right child node.
//
{
    if (nodePtr && nodePtr->rightPtr) {
```

continues

Listing 18.2. continued

```
            x = nodePtr->rightPtr->dataNode;
            return true;
        }
        else
            return false;
}
```

Testing the BinaryTree Class

Let's looks at a simple program to test the `BinaryTree` class. Listing 18.3 shows the source code for the TSBINTRE.CPP test program. This test program manipulates instances of `BinaryTree` instantiated using the `cString` class. The program declares the functions `showTree`, `searchNode`, and `main`:

- The `showTree` function displays the strings stored in an instance of `BinaryTree<cString>` in a single column. The parameter `t` specifies the binary tree. The parameter `msg` passes the commenting text that appears at the top of the screen. The `showTree` function uses the local Boolean variable `ok` to traverse the binary tree `t`. The `showTree` function initializes the variable `ok` with the Boolean result of `t.getFirstNode`. The routine uses a `while` loop to examine the value of variable `ok`. Each iteration displays the contents of variable `str`, a local instance of class `cString`. In addition, each loop iteration calls the `getNextNode` function to visit the next node and assigns the Boolean result to the variable `ok`.

- The `searchNode` function searches for a specific data element in a binary tree. The parameter `t` specifies the searched binary tree. The parameter `s` passes the search string. The `searchNode` function assumes that the nodes of tree `t` have been displayed by the `showTree` function. The `searchNode` function calls the `BinaryTree::search` function to look for the argument of parameter `s` in the argument of `t`. The `searchNode` function displays text that reflects the search outcome.

- The `main` function declares the object `tree`, an instance of `BinaryTree` instantiated with the class `cString`. The `main` function also declares `country`, an array of `cString` instances, and initializes the array with the names of European countries. The array `country` supplies the data to the tested binary tree. To test

for existing and nonexisting data in the `BinaryTree` instance, the `main` function stores all members of the array `country` in the binary tree (except the last two members, Greece and Denmark).

The `main` function tests the binary tree as follows:

1. Inserts the members of array `country` (except the last two members) using a `for` loop. Each loop iteration calls the `BinaryTree::insert` function to insert a `cString` instance.
2. Displays the data in the object `tree` by calling the `showTree` function. The `showTree` function displays the sorted names of the countries in a single column and waits for you to press any key.
3. Searches for the elements of array `country` in the object `tree`. This step uses a `for` loop that calls the `searchNode` function. The loop iterates over all the elements of array `country`, including Greece and Denmark. Therefore, the last two iterations should result in a no-match message displayed by the `searchNode` function.
4. Removes half the nodes in object `tree`. The `main` function uses a `for` loop to call the `BinaryTree::remove` function. The arguments for the `remove` function are the elements of array `country`.
5. Repeats steps 2 and 3 with the trimmed binary tree.

Listing 18.3. The source code for the TSBINTRE.CPP test program.

```
#include <iostream.h>
#include "video.h"
#include "string.hpp"
#include "bintree.cpp"

void showTree(BinaryTree<cString>& t, cString msg)
{
  cString str;
  boolean ok = t.getFirstNode(str);

  clrscr();
  cout << msg << "\n\n";
  while (ok) {
    cout << str << '\n';
    ok = t.getNextNode(str);
```

continues

Listing 18.3. continued

```
  }
  gotoxy(1, 23);
  cout << "Press any key ... ";
  getch();
}

void searchNode(BinaryTree<cString>& t, cString& s)
{
  gotoxy(1, 23);
  clreol();
  gotoxy(1, 22);
  cout << "Press any key to search for " << s;
  getch();
  gotoxy(1, 22);
  clreol();
  if (t.search(s))
    cout << "Found " << s << " in tree\n";
  else
    cout << "No match for " << s << '\n';
  cout << "Press any key to continue ... ";
  getch();
}

main()
{
  BinaryTree<cString> tree;
  cString country[] = { "France",
                        "Germany",
                        "Sweden",
                        "Ireland",
                        "Italy",
                        "Spain",
                        "Portugal",
                        "Switzerland",
                        "Belgium",
                        "England",
                        "Greece",   // not inserted in tree
                        "Denmark"   // not inserted in tree
                      };
  unsigned count = sizeof(country) / sizeof(cString);
  unsigned testSize = count - 2;
```

```
  // insert the names of the countries
  for (unsigned i - 0; i < testSize; i++)
    tree.insert(country[i]);

  // display binary tree
  showTree(tree, "Complete binary tree is:");

  for (i = 0; i < count; i++)
    searchNode(tree, country[i]);

  for (i = 0; i < count / 2; i++)
    tree.remove(country[i]);

   // display binary tree
  showTree(tree, "Trimmed binary tree is:");

  for (i = 0; i < count; i++)
    searchNode(tree, country[i]);

  gotoxy(1, 22); clreol();
  gotoxy(1, 23); clreol();

  return 0;
}
```

AVL Trees

The AVL tree (named after G.M. Adel'son-Vel'skii and E.M. Landis, the Russian mathematicians who invented it) solves the problem of balancing a binary tree. Each node of an AVL tree has a *tilt data field* that ensures a balanced, or near-balanced, state of the tree. Nodes can be left-tilted, right-tilted, or neutral:

- The left-tilt balanced state indicates that the left subtree has one more node level than the right subtree.
- The right-tilt balanced state indicates that the right subtree has one more node level than the left subtree.
- The neutral-balanced state indicates an equal number of subtree nodes attached to both left and right child nodes.

The AVL tree requires the rebalancing of nodes if one subtree of a node is two or more levels deeper than the other subtree of the same node. Figure 18.2 shows a typical AVL tree.

The ability of AVL trees to guard against tree imbalance makes them superior to the basic binary tree. As expected, this superior performance comes at the cost of some overhead. This overhead occurs in two areas:

- The nodes of an AVL tree must have a node-balanced data field.
- The insertion and deletion operations of an AVL tree are more elaborate than those of a simple binary tree. Thus, the AVL tree requires more code (longer functions and additional functions to support tree rebalancing).

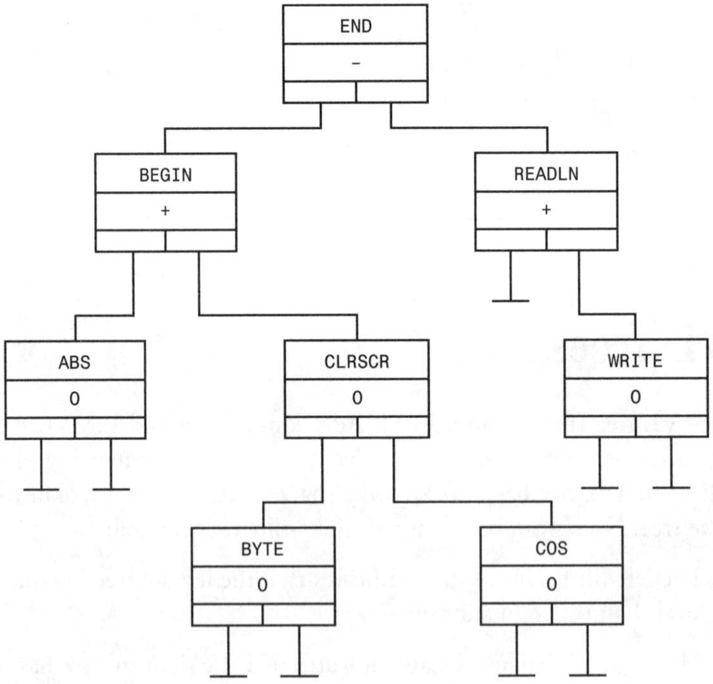

Figure 18.2. A typical AVL tree.

The AVLtree Class

Let's look at the C++ code that implements a template AVL tree class. Listing 18.4 shows the source code for the avl.hpp header file. Notice that the header file declares an enumerated type for the state of balance in an AVL tree. The enumerated values are `leftTilt`, `noTilt`, and `rightTilt`.

The header file also declares the template structure `AVLstruct`. This structure models the individual node of an AVL tree. The members of the `AVLstruct` structure are as follows:

- The `dataNode` member, which stores the data in an AVL tree.
- The `balance` member, which stores the state of balance in an AVL tree node.
- The `leftPtr` and `rightPtr` members, which are pointers to the left and right child nodes, respectively.
- The Boolean `marked` member, which is a special node-traversal flag. This flag is used by the AVL tree class functions to intermittently and recursively visit the nodes of an AVL tree in sequence.

The template `AVLtree` class declares a rich number of data members and functions. The declaration includes private, protected, and public members. The private members deal with the inner working of AVL tree operations. These operations include insertion, deletion, node rotation, node balance, and tree traversal.

I've declared these members private because, due to the vital roles they play, descendants of AVL trees should not override them. If you do not share my view, you certainly can modify the code and make these functions protected.

The `AVLtree` class declares the following data members as protected:

- The `numNodes` member, which stores the number of nodes in an AVL tree.
- The `errMsg` member, which stores the error text returned by a function.
- The `nodePtr` member, which stores the currently visited node.
- The `root` member, which stores the pointer to the root of the AVL tree.
- The `buffer` member, which is an internal buffer.

The `AVLtree` class defines the following members as public (the other members are defined in the AVLTREE.CPP file):

- The class destructor, which invokes the `clear` function to deallocate the dynamic space of the AVL tree nodes.
- The `getNodeCount` function, which returns the value stored in the `numNodes` data member.
- The `setBuffer` function, which assigns a special value to the internal buffer. The parameter `newBuffer` assigns special data to critical members of the data member `buffer`.
- The `search` function, which locates the specified occurrence of a tree node. The reference parameter `x` specifies the search data, while the `occur` parameter indicates the sought occurrence. The default argument for the `occur` parameter is `1`. The `search` function returns `true` if the sought information is located, or `false` when otherwise. When the search is successful, the function assigns a copy of the matching node's data to the argument of reference parameter `x`. This assignment allows the function to retrieve nonsearch data members of the template class `T`. The `search` function invokes the private `searchAVLtree` function.
- The `clear` function deletes the instance of `AVLtree` by invoking the private function `delSubTree` and supplying it with the argument `root`.

Listing 18.4. The source code for the avl.hpp header file.

```
//////////////////////////////////////////////////////////////////////
//                                                                  //
//                Copyright (c) 1992 Namir Clement Shammas          //
//                                                                  //
//  Version: 1.0.0                                 Date 7/6/92      //
//                                                                  //
//  Purpose: implements class of AVL trees that have the            //
//           following functionality:                               //
//                                                                  //
//             + insert data.                                       //
//             + search for data.                                   //
//             + delete data.                                       //
//             + visit tree nodes.                                  //
//                                                                  //
//                                                                  //
//////////////////////////////////////////////////////////////////////
```

```
#include "comndata.h"

#ifndef _AVL_HPP
#define _AVL_HPP

enum balanceState { leftTilt, noTilt, rightTilt };

template<class T>
struct AVLstruct {
    T               dataNode;   // node data
    balanceState    balance;    // node balance
    AVLstruct<T>   *leftPtr,    // left child pointer
                   *rightPtr;   // right child pointer
    boolean         marked;     // visit flag
};
template<class T>
class AVLtree
{
  private:
    boolean insertedOk, // insertion flag
            seekNode;
    AVLstruct<T> *nodeMarker; // special node pointer used in deletion

    void rightRotate(AVLstruct<T>* &rootPtr);
    void leftRotate(AVLstruct<T>* &rootPtr);
    void rightBalance(AVLstruct<T>* &rootPtr, boolean& delok);
    void leftBalance(AVLstruct<T>* &rootPtr, boolean& delok);
    void deleteBothChildren(AVLstruct<T>* &rootPtr,
                            AVLstruct<T>* &ptr,
                            boolean& delok);
    void clearMarks(AVLstruct<T>* rootPtr);
    void insertNode(AVLstruct<T>* &rootPtr);
    void removeNode(AVLstruct<T>* &rootPtr,
                    unsigned &occur,
                    boolean& delok);
    void visitTree(AVLstruct<T>* rootPtr,
                   AVLstruct<T>* &node);
    AVLstruct<T>* searchAVLtree(T& x, unsigned occur = 1);
    boolean delSubTree(AVLstruct<T>* &rootPtr);

  protected:
    unsigned   numNodes;     // number of nodes
```

continues

Listing 18.4. The source code for the avl.hpp header file.

```
    string80    errMsg;         // error message
    AVLstruct<T> *nodePtr,
                 *root;         // pointer to the heap
    T            buffer;        // data buffer

  public:
    // ************** state manipulation methods **************
    AVLtree();
    ~AVLtree()
      { if (root) clear(); }

    char* getErrorMessage();
    unsigned getNodeCount() const
      { return numNodes; }

    // ************** object manipulation methods *************
    void setBuffer(T& newBuffer)
      { buffer = newBuffer; }
    virtual void insert(T& x);
    virtual boolean search(T& x, unsigned occur = 1)
    {
        return (searchAVLtree(x, occur)) ? true : false;
    }
    virtual boolean remove(T& x, unsigned occur = 1);
    virtual boolean getFirstNode(T& x);
    virtual boolean getNextNode(T& x);
    virtual void clear()
      { delSubTree(root); }
    boolean probeLeftChild(T& x);
    boolean probeRightChild(T& x);

};

#endif
```

The other functions of the `AVLtree` class are defined in Listing 18.5. This listing contains the source code for the AVL.CPP library file. The class members in Listing 18.5 are as follows:

- The default (and only) class constructor. This constructor initializes the instances of `AVLtree`. This includes assigning nulls and zero to the members `errMsg`, `numNodes`, and `root`. The constructor allocates no dynamic member.
- The `getErrorMessage` function, which retrieves the contents of the `errMsg` member and assigns a null string to that member.
- The private `rightRotate` and `leftRotate` functions, which rotate the tree nodes to the right and left, respectively. These rotations are required to maintain the state of near-balance in the nodes of an AVL tree.
- The private `insertNode` function, which is the workhorse recursive routine. This function is used to carry out node insertions in an AVL tree. The insertion includes the necessary rotation of nodes to maintain the state of near-balance in the AVL tree.
- The `insert` function, which inserts the argument of parameter `x` in the AVL tree. The `insert` function relies on the private `insertNode` function to perform the insertion and subsequent node balance. Before calling the `insertNode` function, the `insert` function performs some simple initialization required for the recursive insertion process.
- The private `searchAVLtree` function, which searches for a specific occurrence of a data item in the AVL tree. The parameters of this function are identical to those of the `search` function mentioned earlier. The `searchAVLtree` function performs a nonrecursive search, and returns the pointer of the matching AVL tree node, or `NULL` if no match is found.
- The private `rightBalance` and `leftBalance` functions, which restore the near-balanced state of an AVL tree by rebalancing the right and left subtrees, respectively.
- The private `deleteBothChildren` function, which removes AVL tree leaf nodes.
- The private `removeNode` function, which performs node deletion recursively. The `removeNode` function also updates the balance of the AVL tree after the deletion.
- The `remove` function, which deletes the specified occurrence of the searched data. The parameter `x` specifies the search data. The `occur` parameter indicates the occurrence to delete. The default argument for this parameter is `1`. This Boolean function returns `true` if the sought node is deleted, or `false` when otherwise.

- The private `delSubTree` function, which recursively removes a subtree in an AVL tree. The `delSubTree` function returns a Boolean result relevant only for the recursive calls.
- The private `clearMarks` function, which recursively prepares for the tree traversal. The `clearMarks` function sets the `marked` member of each AVL tree node to `false`.
- The private `visitTree` function, which recursively visits the nodes of an AVL tree. When the next node to visit is found, the `visitTree` function sets the `marked` member of that node to `true`. This value enables the traversal functions to skip the node in future calls to the `visitTree` function.
- The `getFirstNode` function, which visits the first—that is, the first ranking—node in an AVL tree. The `getFirstNode` function calls the private function `clearMarks` to prepare for a new round of tree traversal. The function then calls the private `visitTree` function to find the first node. The function returns `true` if the AVL tree is not empty. The reference parameter `x` supplies the data in the first visited node. The function `getFirstNode` must be called before invoking the `getNextNode` function.
- The `getNextNode` function, which visits a subsequent AVL tree node. This Boolean function returns `true` when it finds a node to visit, or `false` when all AVL tree nodes have been visited. The `getNextNode` function calls the private `visitTree` function to locate the next node. The reference parameter `x` supplies the data in the next visited node.
- The Boolean `probeLeftChild` and `probeRightChild` function, which allow you to peek at the data stored in the left and right nodes, respectively. The `probeLeftChild` and `probeRightChild` functions work in a similar manner: each function returns `true` if the node it seeks exists. The reference parameter `x` returns the data of the node.

Listing 18.5. The source code for the AVL.CPP library file.

```
//////////////////////////////////////////////////////////////////////
//                                                                  //
//             Copyright (c) 1992 Namir Clement Shammas             //
//                                                                  //
//  Version: 1.0.0                                   Date 7/6/92    //
//                                                                  //
//  Purpose: implements class of AVL trees that have the            //
```

```
//           following functionality:                              //
//                                                                 //
//             + insert data.                                      //
//             + search for data.                                  //
//             + delete data.                                      //
//             + visit the tree nodes.                             //
//                                                                 //
//                                                                 //
/////////////////////////////////////////////////////////////////////

#include <string.h>
#include "avl.hpp";

////////////////////////////////////////////////////////////////////
//
template<class T>
AVLtree<T>::AVLtree()
//
// Purpose: initializes the instances of an AVL tree.
//
//
{
    errMsg[0] = '\0';
    numNodes = 0;
    root = NULL;
}

////////////////////////////////////////////////////////////////////
//
template<class T>
char* AVLtree<T>::getErrorMessage()
//
// Purpose: returns the contents of the errMsg data member
// and assigns an empty string to that member.
//
//
{
    string80 s;
    strcpy(s, errMsg);
    strcpy(errMsg, "");
    return s;
};
```

continues

Listing 18.5. continued

```
//////////////////////////////////////////////////////////////////////
//
template<class T>
void AVLtree<T>::rightRotate(AVLstruct<T>* &rootPtr)
//
// Purpose: rearranges the tree nodes by rotating them to the
// right.
//
//  Parameters:
//
//    in/out: rootPtr - pointer to a node of the AVL tree.
//
{
    AVLstruct<T> *ptr2, *ptr3;

    ptr2 = rootPtr->rightPtr;
    if (ptr2->balance == rightTilt) { // rotate once
        rootPtr->rightPtr = ptr2->leftPtr;
        ptr2->leftPtr = rootPtr;
        rootPtr->balance = noTilt;
        rootPtr = ptr2;
    }
    else { // rotate twice
        ptr3 = ptr2->leftPtr;
        ptr2->leftPtr = ptr3->rightPtr;
        ptr3->rightPtr = ptr2;
        rootPtr->rightPtr = ptr3->leftPtr;
        ptr3->leftPtr = rootPtr;
        ptr2->balance = (ptr3->balance == leftTilt) ? rightTilt
                                                    : noTilt;
        rootPtr->balance = (ptr3->balance == rightTilt) ? leftTilt
                                                        : noTilt;
        rootPtr = ptr3;
    }
    rootPtr->balance = noTilt;
}

//////////////////////////////////////////////////////////////////////
//
template<class T>
void AVLtree<T>::leftRotate(AVLstruct<T>* &rootPtr)
```

```
//
// Purpose: rearranges the tree nodes by rotating them to the
// left.
//
//  Parameters:
//
//    in/out: rootPtr - pointer to the node of the AVL tree.
//
{
    AVLstruct<T> *ptr2, *ptr3;

    ptr2 = rootPtr->leftPtr;
    if (ptr2->balance == leftTilt) { // rotate once
        rootPtr->leftPtr = ptr2->rightPtr;
        ptr2->rightPtr = rootPtr;
        rootPtr->balance = noTilt;
        rootPtr = ptr2;
    }
    else { // rotate twice
        ptr3 = ptr2->rightPtr;
        ptr2->rightPtr = ptr3->leftPtr;
        ptr3->leftPtr = ptr2;
        rootPtr->leftPtr = ptr3->rightPtr;
        ptr3->rightPtr = rootPtr;
        ptr2->balance = (ptr3->balance == rightTilt) ? leftTilt
                                                     : noTilt;
        rootPtr->balance = (ptr3->balance == leftTilt) ? rightTilt
                                                       : noTilt;
        rootPtr = ptr3;
    }
    rootPtr->balance = noTilt;
}

////////////////////////////////////////////////////////////////////
//
template<class T>
void AVLtree<T>::insertNode(AVLstruct<T>* &rootPtr)
//
// Purpose: workhorse recursive routine to perform node insertion
// in an AVL tree.
//
//  Parameters:
//
```

continues

Listing 18.5. continued

```
//    in/out: rootPtr - pointer to a node of the AVL tree.
//
{
    if (!rootPtr) {
        rootPtr = new AVLstruct<T>; // create new memory space
        if (!rootPtr) {
            strcpy(errMsg, ALLOCATE_ERROR);
            return;
        }
        // copy data
        rootPtr->dataNode = buffer;
        rootPtr->leftPtr = NULL;
        rootPtr->rightPtr = NULL;
        rootPtr->balance = noTilt;
        rootPtr->marked = false;
        numNodes++;
        insertedOk = true;
     }
     else if (buffer <= rootPtr->dataNode) {
             insertNode(rootPtr->leftPtr);
             if (insertedOk) {
                 switch (rootPtr->balance) {
                     case leftTilt :
                         leftRotate(rootPtr);
                         insertedOk = false;
                         break;

                     case noTilt :
                         rootPtr->balance = leftTilt;
                         break;

                     case rightTilt :
                         rootPtr->balance = noTilt;
                         insertedOk = false;
                         break;
                 }
             }
     }
     else {
             insertNode(rootPtr->rightPtr);
```

```
            if (insertedOk) {
                switch (rootPtr->balance) {
                    case leftTilt :
                        rootPtr->balance = noTilt;
                        insertedOk = false;
                        break;

                    case noTilt :
                        rootPtr->balance = rightTilt;
                        break;

                    case rightTilt :
                        rightRotate(rootPtr);
                        insertedOk = false;
                        break;
                }
            }
    }
}

////////////////////////////////////////////////////////////////////
//
template<class T>
void AVLtree<T>::insert(T& x)
//
// Purpose: performs node insertion in an AVL tree.
//
//  Parameters:
//
//    in/out: x - the inserted data.
//
{
    insertedOk = false;
    buffer = x;
    insertNode(root);
}

////////////////////////////////////////////////////////////////////
//
template<class T>
AVLstruct<T>* AVLtree<T>::searchAVLtree(T& x, unsigned occur)
//
```

continues

Listing 18.5. continued

```
// Purpose: searches for a specific occurrence of a key. The
// function returns a pointer to the sought node, or NULL if
// no match was found.
//
//  Parameters:
//
//   input: x - the search key data.
//          occur - the sought occurrence.
//
{
    // initialize count for actual occurrence of x
    unsigned count = 0;
    AVLstruct<T>* p;

    // assign 1 to occur if tree has no node with duplicate keys
    occur = (occur == 0) ? 1 : occur;
    if (occur > numNodes)
        // data is impossible to find
        return NULL;

    p = root;
    while (p && count < occur) {
      if (x > p->dataNode)
          p = p->rightPtr;
      else if (x < p->dataNode)
          p = p->leftPtr;
      else { // match is found
          count++;
          if (count < occur)
              p = p->leftPtr;
      }
    }

    if (p)
        x = p->dataNode;

    return p;
}

//////////////////////////////////////////////////////////////////////
//
template<class T>
```

```
void AVLtree<T>::rightBalance(AVLstruct<T>* &rootPtr,
                              boolean& delOk)

//
// Purpose: restores the balanced or near-balanced state of an
// AVL tree by rebalancing a right subtree.
//
//  Parameters:
//
//    in/out: rootPtr - pointer to the root of the AVL subtree.
//            delOk - boolean flag used in verifying the deletion.
//
{
    AVLstruct<T> *ptr2, *ptr3;
    balanceState balance, balnc3;

    switch (rootPtr->balance) {
        case leftTilt :
            rootPtr->balance = noTilt;
            break;

        case noTilt :
            rootPtr->balance = rightTilt;
            delOk = false;
            break;

        case rightTilt :
            ptr2 = rootPtr->rightPtr;
            balance = ptr2->balance;
            if (balance != leftTilt) {
                rootPtr->rightPtr = ptr2->leftPtr;
                ptr2->leftPtr = rootPtr;
                if (balance == noTilt) {
                    rootPtr->balance = rightTilt;
                    ptr2->balance = leftTilt;
                    delOk = false;
                }
                else {
                    rootPtr->balance = noTilt;
                    ptr2->balance = noTilt;
                }
                rootPtr = ptr2;
            }
```

continues

Listing 18.5. continued

```
            else {
                ptr3 = ptr2->leftPtr;
                balnc3 = ptr3->balance;
                ptr2->leftPtr = ptr3->rightPtr;
                ptr3->rightPtr = ptr2;
                rootPtr->rightPtr = ptr3->leftPtr;
                ptr3->leftPtr = rootPtr;
                ptr2->balance = (balnc3 == leftTilt) ? rightTilt
                                                     : noTilt;
                rootPtr->balance = (balnc3 == rightTilt) ? leftTilt
                                                         : noTilt;
                rootPtr = ptr3;
                ptr3->balance = noTilt;
            }
            break;
    }
}

/////////////////////////////////////////////////////////////////////
//
template<class T>
void AVLtree<T>::leftBalance(AVLstruct<T>* &rootPtr,
                             boolean& delOk)

//
// Purpose: restores the balanced or near-balanced state of an
// AVL tree by rebalancing a left subtree.
//
//  Parameters:
//
//  in/out: rootPtr - pointer to the root of the AVL subtree.
//          delOk - boolean flag used in verifying the deletion.
//
{
    AVLstruct<T> *ptr2, *ptr3;
    balanceState balance, balnc3;

    switch (rootPtr->balance) {
        case rightTilt :
            rootPtr->balance = noTilt;
            break;
```

```
            case noTilt :
                rootPtr->balance = leftTilt;
                delOk = false;
                break;

            case leftTilt :
                ptr2 = rootPtr->leftPtr;
                balance = ptr2->balance;
                if (balance != rightTilt) {
                    rootPtr->leftPtr = ptr2->rightPtr;
                    ptr2->rightPtr = rootPtr;
                    if (balance == noTilt) {
                        rootPtr->balance = leftTilt;
                        ptr2->balance = rightTilt;
                        delOk = false;
                    }
                    else {
                        rootPtr->balance = noTilt;
                        ptr2->balance = noTilt;
                    }
                    rootPtr = ptr2;
                }
                else {
                    ptr3 = ptr2->rightPtr;
                    balnc3 = ptr3->balance;
                    ptr2->rightPtr = ptr3->leftPtr;
                    ptr3->leftPtr = ptr2;
                    rootPtr->leftPtr = ptr3->rightPtr;
                    ptr3->rightPtr = rootPtr;
                    ptr2->balance = (balnc3 == rightTilt) ? leftTilt
                                                          : noTilt;
                    rootPtr->balance = (balnc3 == leftTilt) ? rightTilt
                                                            : noTilt;
                    rootPtr = ptr3;
                    ptr3->balance = noTilt;
                }
                break;
        }
}

////////////////////////////////////////////////////////////////////
//
template<class T>
```

continues

Listing 18.5. continued

```
void AVLtree<T>::deleteBothChildren(AVLstruct<T>* &rootPtr,
                                    AVLstruct<T>* &ptr,
                                    boolean& delOk)

//
// Purpose: routine used to delete a node with two empty
// subtrees.
//
//  Parameters:
//
//    in/out: rootPtr - pointer to the root of the AVL subtree.
//            ptr - shared pointer.
//            delOk - boolean flag used in verifying the deletion.
//
{
    if (!ptr->rightPtr) {
        rootPtr->dataNode = ptr->dataNode;
        nodeMarker = ptr;
        ptr = ptr->leftPtr;
        delOk = true;
    }
    else {
        deleteBothChildren(rootPtr, ptr->rightPtr, delOk);
        if (delOk)
            leftBalance(ptr, delOk);
    }
}

//////////////////////////////////////////////////////////////////
//
template<class T>
void AVLtree<T>::removeNode(AVLstruct<T>* &rootPtr,
                            unsigned &occur,
                            boolean& delOk)

//
// Purpose: recursive function to perform node deletion.
// the balance of the AVL tree is also monitored and adjusted,
// if need be.
//
//  Parameters:
```

```
//
//    in/out: rootPtr - pointer to a node of the AVL tree.
//            occur - the occurrence of key data for the deleted node.
//            delOk - boolean flag used in verifying the deletion.
//
{
    AVLstruct<T>* p;

    if (!rootPtr)
        delOk = false;
    else {
        if (buffer == rootPtr->dataNode)
            occur--;
        if (occur > 0 && buffer <= rootPtr->dataNode) {
            removeNode(rootPtr->leftPtr, occur, delOk);
            if (delOk)
                rightBalance(rootPtr, delOk);
        }
        else if (buffer > rootPtr->dataNode) {
            removeNode(rootPtr->rightPtr, occur, delOk);
            if (delOk)
                leftBalance(rootPtr, delOk);
        }
        else {
            p = rootPtr;
            if (!rootPtr->rightPtr) {
                rootPtr = rootPtr->leftPtr;
                delOk = true;
                delete p;
                p = NULL;
            }
            else if (!rootPtr->leftPtr) {
                rootPtr = rootPtr->rightPtr;
                delOk = true;
                delete p;
                p = NULL;
            }
            else {
                deleteBothChildren(rootPtr, rootPtr->leftPtr, delOk);
                if (delOk)
                    rightBalance(rootPtr, delOk);
                //delete nodeMarker->dataNode;
```

continues

Listing 18.5. continued

```
                    delete nodeMarker;
                }
                numNodes--;
            }
        }
    }

    ////////////////////////////////////////////////////////////////////
    //
    template<class T>
    boolean AVLtree<T>::remove(T& x, unsigned occur)
    //
    //
    // Purpose: performs node deletion.
    //
    //  Parameters:
    //
    //    input: x - the data to be removed
    //           occur - the occurrence of key data for the deleted node.
    //
    {
        unsigned oldCount = numNodes;
        boolean deleteOk = false;

        occur = (occur == 0) ? 1 : occur;
        if (occur > numNodes)
            return false;

        buffer = x;
        removeNode(root, occur, deleteOk);
        return (oldCount > numNodes) ? true : false;
    }

    ////////////////////////////////////////////////////////////////////
    //
    template<class T>
    boolean AVLtree<T>::delSubTree(AVLstruct<T>* &rootPtr)
    //
    // Purpose: recursive function to prune the tree or subtree
    // starting at node rootPtr. The function result is relevant
    // only in recursive calls.
```

```
//
//  Parameters:
//
//    input: rootPtr - the pointer to the (sub)tree root to be
//               deleted.
//
{
    boolean deleteThisNode = false;

    if (!rootPtr->leftPtr && !rootPtr->rightPtr)
       deleteThisNode = true; // remove leaf node with no links
    else {
       if (rootPtr->leftPtr) // has leftPtr branch
            if (delSubTree(rootPtr->leftPtr)) {
                delete rootPtr->leftPtr;
                rootPtr->leftPtr = NULL;
            }

        if (rootPtr->rightPtr) // has rightPtr branch
            if (delSubTree(rootPtr->rightPtr)) {
                delete rootPtr->rightPtr;
                rootPtr->rightPtr = NULL;
            }

         deleteThisNode = (!rootPtr->leftPtr &&
                           !rootPtr->rightPtr) ? true : false;
    }
    return (deleteThisNode) ? true : false;
}

////////////////////////////////////////////////////////////////////
//
template<class T>
void AVLtree<T>::clearMarks(AVLstruct<T>* rootPtr)
//
// Purpose: recursive function used to traverse the
// AVL tree and set the marked flags to false.
//
//  Parameters:
//
//    input: rootPtr - pointer to the root of the AVL tree.
//
```

continues

Listing 18.5. continued

```
{
    if (rootPtr) {
        clearMarks(rootPtr->leftPtr);
        rootPtr->marked = false;
        clearMarks(rootPtr->rightPtr);
    }
}

//////////////////////////////////////////////////////////////////////
//
template<class T>
void AVLtree<T>::visitTree(AVLstruct<T>* rootPtr,
                           AVLstruct<T>* &node)
//
// Purpose: recursive function used to traverse the AVL tree.
//
//  Parameters:
//
//    input: rootPtr - pointer to the root of the AVL tree.
//
//    output: node - the pointer to the next node visited.
//
{
    if (seekNode && rootPtr) {
        visitTree(rootPtr->leftPtr, node);
        if (seekNode && !rootPtr->marked) {
            seekNode = false;
            rootPtr->marked = true;
            node = rootPtr;
            return;
        }
        visitTree(rootPtr->rightPtr, node);
    }
}

//////////////////////////////////////////////////////////////////////
//
template<class T>
boolean AVLtree<T>::getFirstNode(T& x)
//
// Purpose: visits the root of the AVL tree. The function
```

```
// returns true if the AVL tree object has a root.
//
//  Parameters:
//
//   input: x - the pointer to the data associated with the root of
//           the AVL tree.
{
    if (root) {
        seekNode = true;
        clearMarks(root);
        visitTree(root, nodePtr);
        x = nodePtr->dataNode;
    }
    return (root) ? true : false;
}

//////////////////////////////////////////////////////////////////////
//
template<class T>
boolean AVLtree<T>::getNextNode(T& x)
//
// Purpose: visits the next node in the AVL tree. The function
// returns true if there was a next node to visit.
//
//  Parameters:
//
//    input: x - the pointer to the data associated with the visited
//             node.
//
{
    seekNode = true;
    if (root) {
        visitTree(root, nodePtr);
        if (!seekNode)
            x = nodePtr->dataNode;
    }
    return (!seekNode) ? true : false;
}

//////////////////////////////////////////////////////////////////////
//
template<class T>
```

continues

Listing 18.5. continued

```
boolean AVLtree<T>::probeLeftChild(T& x)
//
// Purpose: visits the left child of the current node. The function
// returns true if the current node has a left child.
//
//  Parameters:
//
//    input: x - the data associated with the left child node.
{
    if (nodePtr && nodePtr->leftPtr) {
        x = nodePtr->leftPtr->dataNode;
        return true;
    }
    else
        return false;
}

//////////////////////////////////////////////////////////////////////
//
template<class T>
boolean AVLtree<T>::probeRightChild(T& x)
//
// Purpose: visits the right child of the current node. The
// function returns true if the current node has right child.
//
//  Parameters:
//
//   input: x - the data associated with the right child node.
//
{
    if (nodePtr && nodePtr->rightPtr) {
        x = nodePtr->rightPtr->dataNode;
        return true;
    }
    else
        return false;
}
```

Testing the AVLtree Class

Let's looks at a simple program to test the `AVLtree` class. Listing 18.6 shows the source code for the TSAVL.CPP test program. The test program manipulates instances of class `AVLtree` instantiated using the `cString` class. The program declares the functions `showTree`, `searchNode`, and `main`.

- The `showTree` function displays the strings stored in an instance of `AVLtree<cString>` in a single column. The parameter `t` specifies the AVL tree. The parameter `msg` passes the commenting text that appears at the top of the screen. The `showTree` function uses the local Boolean variable `ok` to traverse the AVL tree `t`. The `showTree` function initializes the variable `ok` with the Boolean result of `t.getFirstNode`. The routine uses a `while` loop to examine the value of variable `ok`. Each iteration displays the contents of variable `str`, a local instance of class `cString`. In addition, the loop iteration calls the `getNextNode` function to visit the next node and assigns the Boolean result to the variable `ok`.
- The `searchNode` function searches for a specific data element in an AVL tree. The parameter `t` specifies the searched AVL tree. The parameter `s` passes the search string. The `searchNode` function assumes that the nodes of tree `t` have been displayed by the `showTree` function. The `searchNode` function calls the `AVLtree::search` function to look for the argument of parameter `s` in the argument of `t`. The function displays text that reflects the search outcome.
- The `main` function declares the object `tree`, an instance of `AVLtree` instantiated with the class `cString`. The `main` function also declares `country`, an array of `cString` instances, and initializes the array with the names of European countries. The array `country` supplies the data to the tested AVL tree. To test for existing and nonexisting data in the instance of `AVLtree`, the `main` function stores all members of the array `country` in the AVL tree except the last two members, Greece and Denmark. This approach enables the program to test searching for data that is not in the AVL tree.

The `main` function tests the AVL tree by doing the following things:

1. Inserting the members of array `country` (except the last two) using a `for` loop. Each loop iteration calls the `AVLtree::insert` function to insert a `cString` instance.
2. Displaying the data in the object `tree` by calling the `showTree` function. The `showTree` function displays the sorted names of the countries in a single column and waits for you to press any key.

3. Searching for the elements of array `country` in the object `tree`. This step uses a `for` loop that calls the `searchNode` function. The loop iterates over all the elements of array `country`, including Greece and Denmark. The last two iterations, therefore, should result in a no-match message displayed by the `searchNode` function.
4. Removing half the nodes in object `tree`. The `main` function uses a `for` loop to call the `AVLtree::remove` function. The arguments for the `remove` function are the elements of array `country`.
5. Repeating steps 2 and 3 with the trimmed AVL tree.

Listing 18.6. The source code for the TSAVL.CPP test program.

```
#include <iostream.h>
#include "video.h"
#include "string.hpp"
#include "avl.cpp"

void showTree(AVLtree<cString>& t, cString msg)
{
  cString str;
  boolean ok = t.getFirstNode(str);

  clrscr();
  cout << msg << "\n\n";
  while (ok) {
    cout << str << '\n';
    ok = t.getNextNode(str);
  }
  gotoxy(1, 23);
  cout << "Press any key ... ";
  getch();
}

void searchNode(AVLtree<cString>& t, cString& s)
{
  gotoxy(1, 23);
  clreol();
  gotoxy(1, 22);
  cout << "Press any key to search for " << s;
```

```
  getch();
  gotoxy(1, 22);
  clreol();
  if (t.search(s))
    cout << "Found " << s << " in tree\n";
  else
    cout << "No match for " << s << '\n';
  cout << "Press any key to continue ... ";
  getch();
}

main()
{
  AVLtree<cString> tree;
  cString country[] = { "France",
                        "Germany",
                        "Sweden",
                        "Ireland",
                        "Italy",
                        "Spain",
                        "Portugal",
                        "Switzerland",
                        "Belgium",
                        "England",
                        "Greece",   // not inserted in tree
                        "Denmark"   // not inserted in tree
                      };
  unsigned count = sizeof(country) / sizeof(cString);
  unsigned testSize = count - 2;

  // insert the names of the countries
  for (unsigned i = 0; i < testSize; i++)
    tree.insert(country[i]);

  // display AVL tree
  showTree(tree, "Complete AVL tree is:");

  for (i = 0; i < count; i++)
    searchNode(tree, country[i]);

  for (i = 0; i < count / 2; i++)
```

continues

Listing 18.6. continued

```
    tree.remove(country[i]);

   // display AVL tree
  showTree(tree, "Trimmed AVL tree is:");

  for (i = 0; i < count; i++)
    searchNode(tree, country[i]);

  gotoxy(1, 22); clreol();
  gotoxy(1, 23); clreol();

  return 0;
}
```

Red-Black Trees

The AVL tree supports the near-balance of a binary tree by monitoring the tilt in the tree nodes after each insertion and deletion. However, the near-balance of a binary tree can be obtained by another scheme. Bayer—better known for inventing the B-tree structure—first introduced the concept behind the red-black binary tree. Tree "coloration" emerged as the result of an extensive study of this new type of tree by Guibas and Sedgewick. Figure 18.3 shows a typical red-black tree.

The idea behind a red-black binary tree is simple. The near-balance of the binary tree is maintained by adding a red- or black-colored member to each node in the binary tree. The properties of a red-black binary tree are as follows:

- A node is colored either red or black.
- The root node is black.
- Every leaf is black. In the case of the red-black tree, the leaf nodes are special null nodes.
- Every simple path from a node to a descendant leaf contains the same number of black nodes.

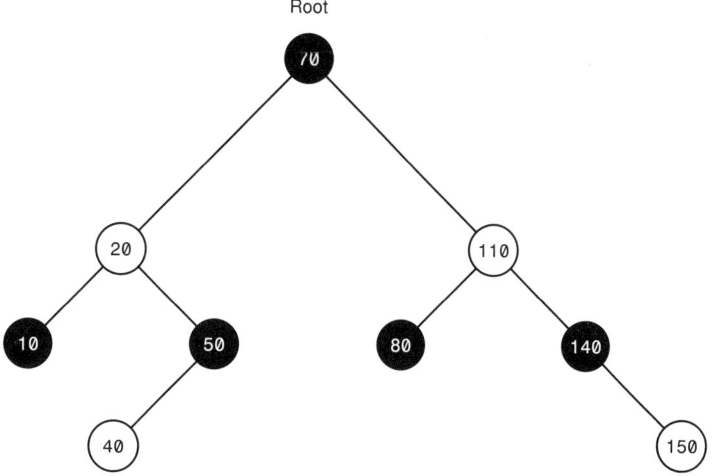

Figure 18.3. A typical red-black tree.

The RBtree Class

Let's look at the C++ code that implements a template class for the red-black tree. Listing 18.7 shows the source code for the rbtree.hpp header file. The header file declares the template structures `RBstruct` and `RBframe`. The `RBstruct` structure models the individual red-black tree node, whereas the `RBframe` models the rotated tree nodes. The members of the `RBstruct` structure are as follows:

- The `dataNode` member, which stores the data in a red-black tree.
- The Boolean `isRed` member, which stores the color of the node. When this member is `true`, the node is red. Otherwise, the node is black.
- The `leftPtr` and `rightPtr` members, which are pointers to the left and right child nodes, respectively.
- The Boolean `marked` member, which is a special node-traversal flag. This flag is used by the red-black tree class functions to intermittently and recursively visit the nodes of a red-black tree in sequence.

The template structure `RBframe` models the data needed to balance the nodes. The members of the `RBframe` structure are as follows:

- The Boolean `isLeftChild` member, which tells a node whether it is the left or right child of its parent node.
- The `ptr` member, which is a pointer to the `RBstruct` structure.

The template `RBtree` class declares a number of data members and functions. The declaration includes private, protected, and public members. The `RBtree` class declares the following data members as protected:

- The `numNodes` member, which stores the number of nodes in a red-black tree.
- The `errMsg` member, which stores the error text returned by the various functions.
- The `nodePtr` member, which stores the currently visited node.
- The `head` member, which stores the pointer to the actual root of the red-black tree. The scheme I use has the working root node as the right child of the node accessed by member `head`. More about this later in this section.
- The `buffer` member, which is an internal buffer.
- The Boolean member `seekNode`, a flag used in traversing the nodes of a red-black tree.
- The member `node`, which is a four-element array of structure `RBframe`. This array is used in balancing the nodes of a red-black tree around an inserted node.

The `RBtree` class declares a number of private, protected, and public members. The following members are defined in the class declaration (the file RBTREE.CPP contains the definition of the other member functions that contain multiple statements):

- The private `colorRed` function, which colors a node red. The `colorRed` function sets the `isRed` data member of its parameter `p` to `true`.
- The private `colorBlack` function, which colors a node black. The `colorBlack` function sets the `isRed` data member of its parameter `p` to `false`.
- The private Boolean `isLeaf` function returns `true` if the node `p` is a leaf node. The `isLeaf` function returns `true` if the left child pointer of parameter `p` points back to `p`. I explain this scheme later in this section.
- The class destructor, which invokes the `clear` function to deallocate the dynamic space of the red-black tree nodes.

- The `getNodeCount` function, which returns the value stored in the `numNodes` data member.
- The `setBuffer` function assigns a special value to the internal buffer. The parameter `newBuffer` is provided to assign special data to critical members of the `buffer` data member.
- The `clear` function, which deletes the instance of `RBtree` by invoking the protected function `clearNode` and supplying it with the argument `head`.

Listing 18.7. The source code for the rbtree.hpp header file.

```
//////////////////////////////////////////////////////////////////////
//                                                                  //
//                  Copyright (c) 1992 Namir Clement Shammas        //
//                                                                  //
//  Version: 1.0.0                                  Date 7/9/92     //
//                                                                  //
//  Purpose: implements class of red-black trees that have the      //
//           following functionality:                               //
//                                                                  //
//             + insert data.                                       //
//             + search for data.                                   //
//             + traverse the nodes in the tree                     //
//                                                                  //
//////////////////////////////////////////////////////////////////////


#include "comndata.h"

#ifndef _RBTREE_HPP
#define _RBTREE_HPP

template<class T>
struct RBstruct {
    T              dataNode;   // node data
    RBstruct<T>    *leftPtr,   // left child pointer
                   *rightPtr;  // right child pointer
    boolean        isRed;      // color of a red-black tree node
    boolean        marked;     // visit flag
};
```

continues

Listing 18.7. continued

```
template<class T>
struct RBframe {
  boolean isLeftChild;
  RBstruct<T> *ptr;
};

template<class T>
class RBtree
{

  protected:
    unsigned   numNodes;      // number of nodes
    string80   errMsg;        // error message
    RBstruct<T>   *nodePtr,
                  *head;
    T             buffer;     // data buffer
    boolean seekNode;
    RBframe<T> node[4];

    void clearNode(RBstruct<T>* &rootPtr);
    void clearMarks(RBstruct<T>* rootPtr);
    void visitTree(RBstruct<T>* rootPtr,
                   RBstruct<T>* &node);

    RBstruct<T>* makeNode(RBstruct<T>* node1,
                          RBstruct<T>* node2);
    RBstruct<T>* makeLeaf(T x);
    void singleRotate(int i);
    void rotate(int i);
    int flipColor(int i);

  private:

    void colorRed(RBstruct<T>* p)
      { p->isRed = true; }

    void colorBlack(RBstruct<T>* p)
      { p->isRed = false; }

    boolean isLeaf(RBstruct<T>* p)
      { return (p->leftPtr == p) ? true : false; }
```

```
  public:
    // ************** state manipulation methods **************
    RBtree(T Smallest, T Largest);
    ~RBtree()
      { clear(); }

    char* getErrorMessage();
    unsigned getNodeCount() const
      { return numNodes; }

    // ************** object manipulation methods *************
    void setBuffer(T& newBuffer)
      { buffer = newBuffer; }
    virtual boolean insert(T& x);
    virtual boolean search(T& x);
    virtual boolean getFirstNode(T& x);
    virtual boolean getNextNode(T& x);
    virtual void clear()
      { clearNode(head); }
    boolean probeLeftChild(T& x);
    boolean probeRightChild(T& x);
};

#endif
```

The other functions of the `RBtree` class, which contain multiple statements, are defined in Listing 18.8. This listing contains the source code for the RBTREE.CPP library file. The class members in Listing 18.8 are as follows:

- The class constructor. This constructor initializes the instances of `RBtree` by creating a three-node tree that contains a head node attached to two child nodes (one a left child, the other a right child). The left and child nodes contain extreme values. The right node is the working root of the red-black tree.

  The parameters of the constructor are the instances of the template class `Smallest` and `Largest`. These parameters represent the smallest and largest values in the range of data inserted in the red-black tree.

To clarify this a bit, think of a red-black tree that stores information whose key data are doubles. In this case, the key data for the argument of parameter `Smallest` is a negative number with the highest possible exponent—as close as you can get to minus infinity. Similarly, the key data for the argument of the parameter `Largest` is a positive number with the highest possible exponent—as close as you can get to plus infinity.

The working root for this implementation of the red-black tree is the right child of the node accessed by pointer head `head->rightPtr`.

- The `getErrorMessage` function, which retrieves the contents of the `errMsg` member and assigns a null string to that member.
- The protected `makeNode` function, which creates a node that is the parent of two nodes. These two nodes are represented by the parameters `node1` and `node2`. The `makeNode` function returns the pointer to the newly created node. The new node is attached to child nodes as follows:

   1. If the value of `node1`'s data is less than or equal to the value of `node2`'s data, `node1` and `node2` become the left and right child nodes of the new node.
   2. If the value of `node1`'s data is greater than the value of `node2`'s data, `node1` and `node2` become the right and left child nodes of the new node.

The `makeNode` function does not rotate or color tree nodes. The `makeNode` function assigns the data of the left child node to the data of the new node.

- The protected `makeLeaf` function creates a leaf node using the data item `x`. The `makeLeaf` function returns the pointer to the new leaf node. The function assigns the item `x` to the `dataNode` member of the newly created leaf node.

The implementation of the red-black tree makes the left and right child pointers of a leaf node point to the leaf node itself. This uncommon, *self-pointing* assignment is used for a couple of reasons:

- Red-black trees regard the left and right pointers of a leaf node as pointing to imaginary null nodes that have the same color as the leaf nodes.

> - This pointer assignment scheme works better with the code than if leaf nodes had null pointers.
>
> In all cases, keep in mind that you may not compare a leaf node with NULL.

- The protected `singleRotate` and `rotate` functions, which rotate the nodes of a red-black tree. The `singleRotate` function performs a single node rotation to the left or the right. The `singleRotate` function uses the node array-member in accessing a tree node and its parents. The `rotate` function performs a single or double rotation by invoking the `singleRotate` function either once or twice.
- The `flipColor` function toggles the colors of a node and its left and right child nodes and fixes any imbalance due to violation of the coloring rule. This fix involves calling the `rotate` function.
- The `insert` function inserts the argument of parameter `x` in the red-black tree. The `insert` function returns `true` if the item `x` is inserted in the red-black tree. If the item `x` is already in the red-black tree, the function returns `false` and exits without inserting data.

> Preventing nodes with duplicates of key data simplifies the search. Otherwise, the rotation of nodes complicates the search for the correct location of specific occurrences of data in the red-black tree.

The `insert` function uses a `do-while` loop to search for the proper insertion location. Once the insertion point is located, the `insert` function establishes the links with the parent and child nodes. The function then proceeds to update the colors of the nodes and deal with any violation of the red-black tree features. This process may involve flipping node colors and rotating nodes.

- The `search` function searches for the data item `x` in a red-black tree. The `search` function returns `true` if item `x` is in the searched tree, or `false` when otherwise. The search function uses a `while` loop to locate the node whose key data matches the key data of item `x`. Examine the condition of the `while` loop.

It is made up of ANDing two Boolean local variables: `notFound` and `iterate`. The `notFound` variable indicates whether a match has been found yet. The `iterate` variable indicates whether the loop should continue to iterate. These two local Boolean variables are initialized as `true`. The `search` function assigns `false` to the `iterate` variable when either one of the following conditions is true:

1. The item `x` is less than the data in the currently examined node *and* the right pointer of that node points to the node itself.
2. The item `x` is greater than the data in the currently examined node *and* the left pointer of that node points to the node itself.

   The iteration thus stops when the pointer of the next child node points back to the currently searched node. When the `search` function finds a match, it copies the `dataNode` member of the matching node to the reference parameter `x`.

- The protected `clearMarks` function, which recursively prepares for the tree traversal. The `clearMarks` function sets the `marked` member of each red-black tree node to `false`.

Notice the tests for terminal nodes in the `clearMarks` and subsequent functions. The pointers to the nodes are compared with the left or right child pointers to determine if the node is a leaf.

- The protected `visitTree` function, which recursively visits the nodes of a red-black tree. When the next node to visit is found, the `visitTree` function sets the `marked` member of that node to `true`. This value enables the traversal functions to skip the node in future calls to function `visitTree`.
- The `getFirstNode` function, which visits the first—that is, the first ranking—node in a red-black tree. The `getFirstNode` function calls the protected function `clearMarks` to prepare for a new round of tree traversal. The function then calls the protected `visitTree` function to find the first node. The function returns `true` if the red-black tree is not empty. The reference parameter `x` supplies the data in the first visited node. The `getFirstNode` function must be called before invoking the `getNextNode` function.

- The `getNextNode` function visits subsequent red-black tree nodes. This Boolean function returns `true` when it finds a node to visit, or `false` when all red-black tree nodes have been visited. The `getNextNode` function calls the protected `visitTree` function to locate the next node. The reference parameter `x` supplies the data in the next visited node.
- The Boolean `probeLeftChild` and `probeRightChild` functions enable you to peek at the data stored in the left and right nodes, respectively. The `probeLeftChild` and `probeRightChild` functions work in a similar manner: each function returns `true` if the node it seeks exists. The reference parameter `x` returns the data of the node.

Listing 18.8. The source code for the RBTREE.CPP library file.

```
//////////////////////////////////////////////////////////////////////
//                                                                  //
//                 Copyright (c) 1992 Namir Clement Shammas         //
//                                                                  //
//  Version: 1.0.0                                 Date 7/9/92      //
//                                                                  //
//  Purpose: implements class of red-black trees that have the      //
//           following functionality:                               //
//                                                                  //
//             + insert data.                                       //
//             + search for data.                                   //
//             + visit the tree nodes.                              //
//                                                                  //
//                                                                  //
//////////////////////////////////////////////////////////////////////

#include <string.h>
#include "rbtree.hpp"

/////////////////////////////////////////////////////////////////////
//
template<class T>
RBtree<T>::RBtree(T Smallest, T Largest)
//
// Purpose: initializes the instances of a red-black tree.  The
// constructor allocates space for the head, the smallest, and the
// largest values.
```

continues

Listing 18.8. continued

```
//
// Parameters:
//
//     input: Smallest - smallest value possible.
//            Largest - largest value possible.
{
    T temp;

    // swap limits if needed
    if (Smallest > Largest) {
      temp = Smallest;
      Smallest = Largest;
      Largest = temp;
    }

    errMsg[0] = '\0';
    numNodes = 0;
    head = makeNode(makeLeaf(Smallest), makeLeaf(Largest));

}

////////////////////////////////////////////////////////////////////
//
template<class T>
char* RBtree<T>::getErrorMessage()
//
// Purpose: returns the contents of the errMsg data member
// and assigns an empty string to that member.
//
//
{
    string80 s;

    strcpy(s, errMsg);
    strcpy(errMsg, "");
    return s;
};

////////////////////////////////////////////////////////////////////
//
template<class T>
```

```
RBstruct<T>* RBtree<T>::makeNode(RBstruct<T>* node1,
                                  RBstruct<T>* node2)
//
// Purpose: creates a node that becomes the new parent of nodes
// node1 and node2.  The function returns a pointer to the new
// parent node.
//
// Parameters:
//
//    input: node1, node2 - the children nodes.
//
{
  // exit if either nodes is NULL
  if (!(node1 && node2))
    return NULL;

  // create new node
  RBstruct<T>* p = new RBstruct<T>;

  if (!p) {
    strcpy(errMsg, ALLOCATE_ERROR);
    return NULL;
  }

  colorBlack(p);

  if (node1->dataNode <= node2->dataNode) {
    p->leftPtr = node1;
    p->rightPtr = node2;
  }
  else {
    p->leftPtr = node2;
    p->rightPtr = node1;
  }
  p->dataNode = p->leftPtr->dataNode;
  return p;
}

////////////////////////////////////////////////////////////////////
//
template<class T>
RBstruct<T>* RBtree<T>::makeLeaf(T x)
```

continues

Listing 18.8. continued

```
//
// Purpose: creates a new leaf node.  The function returns the
// pointer to the new node.
//
// Parameters:
//
//    input: x - the data that is inserted in a new leaf node.
//
{
  RBstruct<T>* p = new RBstruct<T>;

  if (!p) {
    strcpy(errMsg, ALLOCATE_ERROR);
    return NULL;
  }

  colorBlack(p);
  p->dataNode = x;
  // make the leaf node child pointers point to the node itself
  p->leftPtr = p;
  p->rightPtr = p;
  return p;
}

//////////////////////////////////////////////////////////////////////
//
template<class T>
void RBtree<T>::singleRotate(int i)
//
// Purpose: rotates the node at level i.
//
// Parameters:
//
//    input: i - the level of the rotated node.
//
{
  int j = i % 4;
  int j1 = (i + 1) % 4;
  int j2 = (i + 2) % 4;

  if (node[j2].isLeftChild)
```

```
    node[j1].ptr->leftPtr = node[j2].ptr->rightPtr;
  else
    node[j1].ptr->rightPtr = node[j2].ptr->leftPtr;

  if (node[j2].isLeftChild)
    node[j2].ptr->rightPtr = node[j1].ptr;
  else
    node[j2].ptr->leftPtr = node[j1].ptr;

  if (node[j1].isLeftChild)
    node[j].ptr->leftPtr = node[j2].ptr;
  else
    node[j].ptr->rightPtr = node[j2].ptr;

  node[j1].ptr = node[j2].ptr;
}

////////////////////////////////////////////////////////////////////
//
template<class T>
void RBtree<T>::rotate(int i)
//
// Purpose: rotate the nodes once or twice, as required.
//
// Parameters:
//
//    input: i - the node level.
//
{
  if (node[(i+3)%4].isLeftChild != node[(i+2)%4].isLeftChild)
    // require double rotation
    singleRotate(i+1);
  singleRotate(i);
}

////////////////////////////////////////////////////////////////////
//
template<class T>
int RBtree<T>::flipColor(int i)
//
// Purpose: flips and fixes the colors of tree nodes.
//
```

continues

Listing 18.8. continued

```
// Parameters:
//
//    input: i - the node level.
//
{
  colorRed(node[i%4].ptr);
  colorBlack(node[i%4].ptr->leftPtr);
  colorBlack(node[i%4].ptr->rightPtr);
  if (node[(i-1)%4].ptr->isRed) {
    colorRed(node[(i-2)%4].ptr);
    rotate(i - 3);
    colorBlack(node[(i-2)%4].ptr);
    i -= 3;
  }
  return i;
}

//////////////////////////////////////////////////////////////////////
//
template<class T>
boolean RBtree<T>::insert(T& x)
//
// Purpose: performs node insertion in an red-black tree.
//
//  Parameters:
//
//    in/out: x - the inserted data.
//
{
  int i = 0;

  // return false and exit if the item x is already in the
  // red-black tree.
  if (search(x))
    return false;

  node[0].ptr = head;
  do {
    node[(i+1)%4].isLeftChild = (x <= node[i%4].ptr->dataNode) ?
                                          true : false;
    node[(i+1)%4].ptr = (node[(i+1)%4].isLeftChild) ?
```

```
                              node[i%4].ptr->leftPtr :
                              node[i%4].ptr->rightPtr;
      i++;
      if (node[i%4].ptr->leftPtr->isRed &&
          node[i%4].ptr->rightPtr->isRed)
          i = flipColor(i);
    } while (!isLeaf(node[i%4].ptr));

    if (node[i%4].isLeftChild) {
      node[(i-1)%4].ptr->leftPtr = makeNode(node[i%4].ptr,
                                            makeLeaf(x));
      node[i%4].ptr = node[(i-1)%4].ptr->leftPtr;
    }
    else {
      node[(i-1)%4].ptr->rightPtr = makeNode(node[i%4].ptr,
                                             makeLeaf(x));
      node[i%4].ptr = node[(i-1)%4].ptr->rightPtr;
    }
    flipColor(i);
    // make root black
    colorBlack(head->rightPtr);
    numNodes++;
    return true;
}

//////////////////////////////////////////////////////////////////////
//
template<class T>
boolean RBtree<T>::search(T& x)
//
// Purpose: searches for a key.  The function returns a true if
// item x exists in the red-black tree, and yields false when
// no match was found.
//
//  Parameters:
//
//   input: x - the search key data.
//
{
    boolean notFound = true;
    boolean iterate = true;
    RBstruct<T>* p;
```

continues

Listing 18.8. continued

```
    if (numNodes == 0)
      return false;

    p = head->rightPtr;
    while (notFound && iterate) {
      if (x > p->dataNode)  {
          if (p != p->rightPtr)
            p = p->rightPtr;
          else
            iterate = false;
      }
      else if (x < p->dataNode) {
          if (p != p->leftPtr)
            p = p->leftPtr;
          else
            iterate = false;
      }
      else  // match is found
          notFound = false;
    }

    // found a match?
    if (notFound)
      return false;
    else {
      x = p->dataNode;
      return true;
    }
}

//////////////////////////////////////////////////////////////////////
//
template<class T>
void RBtree<T>::clearMarks(RBstruct<T>* rootPtr)
//
// Purpose: recursive function used to traverse the
// red-black tree and set the marked flags to false.
//
//  Parameters:
//
//    input: rootPtr - pointer to the root of the red-black tree.
```

```
//
{
    // does the node have a left child?
    if (rootPtr != rootPtr->leftPtr)
        clearMarks(rootPtr->leftPtr);
    rootPtr->marked = false;
     // does the node have a right child?
    if (rootPtr != rootPtr->rightPtr)
        clearMarks(rootPtr->rightPtr);
}

//////////////////////////////////////////////////////////////////////
//
template<class T>
void RBtree<T>::visitTree(RBstruct<T>* rootPtr,
                          RBstruct<T>* &node)
//
// Purpose: recursive function used to traverse the red-black tree.
//
//  Parameters:
//
//    input: rootPtr - pointer to the root of the red-black tree.
//
//    output: node - the pointer to the next node visited.
//
{
    if (seekNode && rootPtr != rootPtr->leftPtr) {
        visitTree(rootPtr->leftPtr, node);
        if (seekNode && !rootPtr->marked) {
            seekNode = false;
            rootPtr->marked = true;
            node = rootPtr;
            return;
        }
        visitTree(rootPtr->rightPtr, node);
    }
}

//////////////////////////////////////////////////////////////////////
//
template<class T>
void RBtree<T>::clearNode(RBstruct<T>* &rootPtr)
```

continues

Listing 18.8. continued

```
//
// Purpose: recursive function to delete subtrees.
//
// Parameters:
//
//    input: rootPtr - the pointer of the node to delete
//
{
    if (rootPtr != rootPtr->leftPtr)
        clearNode(rootPtr->leftPtr);
    if (rootPtr != rootPtr->rightPtr)
        clearNode(rootPtr->rightPtr);
    delete rootPtr;
}

//////////////////////////////////////////////////////////////////////
//
template<class T>
boolean RBtree<T>::getFirstNode(T& x)
//
// Purpose: visits the root of the red-black tree.  The function
// returns true if the red-black tree object has a root.
//
//  Parameters:
//
//   input: x - the pointer to the data associated with the root of
//           the red-black tree.
{

    if (!head->rightPtr)
      return false;
    else {
      seekNode = true;
      clearMarks(head->rightPtr);
      visitTree(head->rightPtr, nodePtr);
      x = nodePtr->dataNode;
      return true;
    }
}

//////////////////////////////////////////////////////////////////////
```

```
//
template<class T>
boolean RBtree<T>::getNextNode(T& x)
//
// Purpose: visits the next node in the red-black tree.  The function
// returns true if there was a next node to visit.
//
//  Parameters:
//
//    input: x - the pointer to the data associated with the visited
//              node.
//
{
    seekNode = true;
    if (!isLeaf(head->rightPtr)) {
        visitTree(head->rightPtr, nodePtr);
        if (!seekNode)
            x = nodePtr->dataNode;
    }
    return (!seekNode) ? true : false;
}

///////////////////////////////////////////////////////////////////
//
template<class T>
boolean RBtree<T>::probeLeftChild(T& x)
//
// Purpose: visits the left child of the current node.  The function
// returns true if the current node has a left child.
//
//  Parameters:
//
//    input: x - the data associated with the left child node.
{
    if (nodePtr != nodePtr->leftPtr) {
        x = nodePtr->leftPtr->dataNode;
        return true;
    }
    else
        return false;
}
```

continues

Listing 18.8. continued

```
//////////////////////////////////////////////////////////////////////
//
template<class T>
boolean RBtree<T>::probeRightChild(T& x)
//
// Purpose: visits the right child of the current node.  The
// function returns true if the current node has right child.
//
//  Parameters:
//
//   input: x - the data associated with the right child node.
//
{
    if (nodePtr != nodePtr->rightPtr) {
        x = nodePtr->rightPtr->dataNode;
        return true;
    }
    else
        return false;
}
```

Testing the RBTree Class

Let's look at a simple program to test the `RBtree` class. Listing 18.9 shows the source code for the TSRBTREE.CPP test program. The test program manipulates instances of `RBtree` instantiated using the `cString` class. The program declares the functions `showTree`, `searchNode`, and `main`.

- The `showTree` function displays the strings stored in an instance of `RBtree<cString>` in a single column. The parameter `t` specifies the red-black tree. The parameter `msg` passes the commenting text that appears at the top of the screen. The `showTree` function uses the local Boolean variable `ok` to traverse the red-black tree `t`. The function initializes the variable `ok` with the Boolean result of `t.getFirstNode`. The routine uses a `while` loop to examine the value of variable `ok`. Each iteration displays the contents of variable `str`, a local instance of class cString. In addition, the loop iteration calls the function getNextNode to visit the next node and return the Boolean result to the variable ok.

- The searchNode function searches for a specific data in a red-black tree. The parameter t specifies the searched red-black tree. The parameter s passes the search string. The searchNode function assumes that the nodes of tree t have been displayed by the showTree function. The searchNode function calls the RBtree::search function to look for the argument of parameter s in the argument of t. The searchNode function displays text that reflects the search outcome.
- The main function declares the object tree, an instance of RBtree instantiated with the class cString. The main function also declares country, an array of cString instances, and initializes the array with the names of European countries. The array country supplies the data to the tested red-black tree. To test for existing and nonexisting data in the instance of RBtree, the main function stores all members of the array country in the red-black tree except the last two members, Greece and Denmark.

The main function tests the red-black tree as follows:

1. Inserts the members of array country (expect the last two) using a for loop. Each loop iteration calls the RBtree::insert function to insert a cString instance.
2. Displays the data in the object tree by calling the showTree function. The function displays the sorted names of the countries in a single column and waits for you to press any key.
3. Searches for the elements of array country in the object tree. This step uses a for loop that calls the searchNode function. The loop iterates over all the elements of array country, including Greece and Denmark. The last two iterations, therefore, should result in a no-match message displayed by the searchNode function.

Listing 18.9. The source code for the tsrbtree.hpp test program.

```
#include <iostream.h>
#include "video.h"
#include "string.hpp"
#include "rbtree.cpp"
```

continues

Listing 18.9. continued

```
void showTree(RBtree<cString>& t, cString msg)
{
  cString str;
  boolean ok = t.getFirstNode(str);

  clrscr();
  cout << msg << "\n\n";
  while (ok) {
    cout << str << '\n';
    ok = t.getNextNode(str);
  }
  gotoxy(1, 23);
  cout << "Press any key ... ";
  getch();
}

void searchNode(RBtree<cString>& t, cString& s)
{
  gotoxy(1, 23);
  clreol();
  gotoxy(1, 22);
  cout << "Press any key to search for " << s;
  getch();
  gotoxy(1, 22);
  clreol();
  if (t.search(s))
    cout << "Found " << s << " in tree\n";
  else
    cout << "No match for " << s << '\n';
  cout << "Press any key to continue ... ";
  getch();
}

main()
{
  RBtree<cString> tree("A", "ZZZZZZZZZZZZZZZZ");
  cString country[] = { "France" ,
                        "Germany",
                        "Sweden",
                        "Ireland",
```

```
                        "Italy",
                        "Spain",
                        "Portugal",
                        "Switzerland",
                        "Belgium",
                        "England",
                        "Greece",   // not inserted in tree
                        "Denmark"   // not inserted in tree
                       };
  unsigned count = sizeof(country) / sizeof(cString);
  unsigned testSize = count - 2;

  // insert the names of the countries
  for (unsigned i = 0; i < testSize; i++)
    tree.insert(country[i]);

  // display red-black tree
  showTree(tree, "Complete red-black tree is:");

  for (i = 0; i < count; i++)
    searchNode(tree, country[i]);

  gotoxy(1, 22); clreol();
  gotoxy(1, 23); clreol();

  return 0;
}
```

Array-Based Binary Trees

Internal trees typically are dynamic structures that use pointers to allocate and deallocate dynamic space for nodes as needed. It's possible to build internal trees using arrays. When and why should you use this rather unusual approach for implementing trees? Array-based trees are suitable for trees that experience heavy data traffic, where a large amount of random data is inserted and then deleted soon afterward. In addition, array-based trees are suitable when the total number of data items remains within a known bound.

Heavy data traffic may cause typically constructed trees to fragment the heap or free store. Array-based trees combat the heap fragmentation problem by reserving a block of dynamic space. Array-based trees thus replace typical node allocation and deallocation with simple data assignment. In addition, array-based trees use indices and pointers to access specific tree nodes.

The next sections present a C++ class that models an array-based binary tree. I also discuss the basics of implementing such a binary tree. Because binary trees work well with random data, using an array-based version also should maintain good balance and an efficient search speed.

The basic method for implementing array-based binary trees is simple. The array-based binary tree needs at least three distinct arrays to represent a node. The first array stores the data; the second and third arrays store the pointers (or indices, if you prefer) to the other nodes. These distinct arrays easily can be replaced by the single array of a suitable structure. This structure models an array-based binary-tree node.

The basic design of the array-based binary tree must take node deletion into consideration. The initial design might consider three types of nodes: vacant, occupied, and deleted. This approach turns out to be complicated because of the need to separately track the deleted nodes. Tracking deleted nodes requires an additional array of indices.

To solve the problem and improve the node management, I consider binary-tree nodes to be either occupied or deleted. This reduction in node categories formally eliminates vacant nodes by considering them to be deleted nodes; the nodes of a newly created array-based binary tree all are deleted!

You still may wonder about how to track deleted nodes. The answer lies in using the right (or the left) pointers of a deleted node. Such pointers track the chain of deleted nodes. Additional array indices are needed to indicate the location of the first and last deleted node.

The ArrayBinTree Class

Let me present the `ArrayBinTree` class, which models array-based binary trees. Listing 18.10 shows the source code for the arbntree.hpp header file. The header file declares the following constants:

- The `NIL` constant, which is similar to the null pointer address. I chose to use the nil value with the array indices and assign it the high value of `0xffff`.

- The `LEFT` constant is an index that specifies the left subtree.
- The `RIGHT` constant is an index that specifies the right subtree.
- The `MIN_ARRAY_SIZE` constant, which indicates the minimum size of the array-based binary tree.

The header file also contains the declaration of the template structure `ArBinstruct`. This structure models the node of the binary tree. The members of the `ArBinstruct` structure are as follows:

- The `dataNode` member, which stores a data item in a node.
- The `leftPtr` and `rightPtr` members, which are indices to the left and right child nodes, respectively. The `rightPtr` member also is used to link deleted nodes.
- The Boolean `marked` member, which is a node-visitation flag.

The `ArrayBinTree` class declares a number of data members, protected functions, and public functions. The data members of the class are as follows:

- The `errMsg` member, which stores the error message returned by the various functions.
- The `arrSize` member, which stores the size of the dynamic array supporting the binary tree.
- The `numNodes` member, which stores the current number of nodes in an instance of `ArrayBinTree`.
- The `root` member, which stores the index to the array element containing the root node. Initially, the value stored in the `root` member is `NIL`.
- The `first` and `last` members, which store the indices of the array elements that contain the first and last deleted (or vacant) nodes, respectively.
- The `nodePtr` member, which is an index used in traversing the nodes of the binary tree.
- The `nodes` member, which is a pointer to the dynamic array of structure `ArBinstruct<T>`.
- The `emptyElem` member, which is an instance of the template class `T` used to clear the binary-tree nodes.
- The Boolean `seekNode` member, which is a flag used in traversing the nodes of the binary tree.

The ArrayBinTree class defines the constructor and the getNumNodes function in the class declaration. All other functions are defined in the ARBNTREE.CPP library file, shown in Listing 18.11.

I simplified the implementation of class ArrayBinTree by not implementing either features that track multiple occurrences of the same data or members that involve relational operators of the template class.

Listing 18.10. The source code for the arbntree.hpp header file.

```
//////////////////////////////////////////////////////////////////////
//                                                                  //
//                Copyright (c) 1992 Namir Clement Shammas          //
//                                                                  //
//  Version: 1.0.0                                  Date 8/9/92     //
//                                                                  //
//  Purpose: implements class of array-based binary trees that      //
//           have the following functionality:                      //
//                                                                  //
//             + insert data.                                       //
//             + search for data.                                   //
//             + delete data.                                       //
//             + nodes with duplicate keys are optional.            //
//                                                                  //
//                                                                  //
//////////////////////////////////////////////////////////////////////


#include "comndata.h"

#ifndef _ARBNTREE_HPP
#define _ARBNTREE_HPP

#define NIL 0xffff
#define LEFT 0
#define RIGHT 1
#define MIN_ARRAY_SIZE 20
```

```
template<class T>
struct ArBinstruct {
    T               dataNode;  // node data
    unsigned        leftPtr,   // left child index
                    rightPtr;  // right child index
    boolean         marked;    // visit flag
};

template<class T>
class ArrayBinTree
{

  protected:
    string80   errMsg;       // error message
    unsigned   arrSize,
               numNodes,      // number of nodes
               root,          // index to root
               first,         // first available vacant member
               last,          // last available vacant member
               nodePtr;
    ArBinstruct<T> *nodes;
    T emptyElem;
    boolean seekNode;

    void clearMarks();
    void visitTree(unsigned rootPtr,
                   unsigned &node);

  public:
    // ************** state manipulation methods **************
    ArrayBinTree(unsigned arraySize,
                 T emptyElement);
    ~ArrayBinTree()
      { clear();
        delete [] nodes;
      }

    char* getErrorMessage();
    unsigned getNodeCount() const
      { return numNodes; }

    // ************** object manipulation methods *************
```

continues

Listing 18.10. continued

```
    virtual boolean insert(T& x);
    virtual boolean search(T& x);
    virtual boolean remove(T& x);
    virtual boolean getFirstNode(T& x);
    virtual boolean getNextNode(T& x);
    virtual void clear();
    boolean probeLeftChild(T& x);
    boolean probeRightChild(T& x);

};

#endif
```

The `ArrayBinTree` class declares a single constructor, which takes the following parameters:

- The `arraySize` parameter, which specifies the number of elements in the array supporting the binary tree.

I implemented the class without a function that expands the supporting array. If you want to implement an `expand` function, remember to set the additional nodes as deleted nodes.

- The `emptyElement` parameter, which is an instance of the template class `T`. The argument for this parameter is assigned to the `emptyElem` data member.

The constructor performs the following tasks:

- Assigns a validated array size to the `arrSize` member.
- Allocates the dynamic space for the supporting array. This task involves the `nodes` pointer member. If the allocation fails, the constructor assigns an error message to the `errMsg` member and then exits.
- Assigns an empty string to the `errMsg` member.
- Assigns `0` to the `numNodes` member.

- Assigns NIL to the root member.
- Uses a for loop statement to use the right indices for the setup of the chain of deleted nodes. The loop iterates from the second node to the one before last.
- Assigns NIL to the right index of the last node.
- Assigns 0 and arrSize-1 to the members first and last, respectively. These values indicate the location of the first and last deleted nodes. This information, together with the right indices, permits the management of deleted nodes.
- Assigns the parameter emptyElement to the data member emptyElem.

The ArrayBinTree class declares the following functions, which are relevant to the binary-tree operations:

- The insert function inserts the data item x in an instance of class ArrayBinTree. The insert function returns false if the binary tree is full. Otherwise, the function performs the following tasks:
  1. Uses a while loop to locate the index for inserting the new data. The loop also updates the value in member first. The new value is the index of the next vacant node.
  2. Assigns the item x at the array element index.
  3. Assigns nil values to the left and right indices of the array element index.
  4. Increments the numNodes member.
  5. Returns true.
- The Boolean search function determines whether item x is in the binary tree. The search function returns true if x is located, or false otherwise. The search function uses a while loop to traverse the tree nodes and search for the item x. This search locates only the first occurrence of item x in the binary tree. If you want the ArrayBinTree class to support multiple occurrences, you must modify the search function. If item x is in the tree, the search function assigns the matching node to the reference parameter x. This assignment allows you to retrieve non-key data members in the template class T.
- The Boolean remove function deletes the first occurrence of the item x. The function returns true if x is deleted, or false if otherwise. The function promptly exits, returning false, if the binary tree is empty.

The `remove` function performs the following tasks to delete the node that contains the item `x`:

1. Uses a `while` loop to locate the node that matches the item `x`. The loop iterations update the local variables `lastIndex` and `direction`. These variables track both the parent node and the parent node link that lead to the currently examined node.
2. Exits, returning `false`, if the function finds no match for item `x`.
3. Starts deleting the node that matches item `x`. The first step assigns the value of `emptyElem` to the `dataNode` member of the targeted array element. This is a null or empty value for the instances of the template class `T`. If the class `T` accesses dynamic data, the `emptyElem` instance represents an instance that consumes less dynamic memory.
4. Uses an `if` statement to reconnect the nodes around the deleted node and maintain the chain of deleted nodes.
5. Assigns the deleted node index to the right index of the deleted node.
6. Assigns the deleted node index to the member `last`.
7. Decrements the `numNodes` member.
8. Returns `true` to signal the successful deletion of the targeted node.

- The `clearMarks` function, which clears the `marked` members of each binary-tree node. Since class `ArrayBinTree` uses an array, the code for the `clearMarks` class uses a simple `for` loop and avoids recursion altogether. The loop systematically assigns `false` to the marked members of all tree nodes. It makes no difference whether the node is deleted.
- The `visitTree` function, which is a recursive function that traverses the nodes of a binary tree. The arguments of this version of `visitTree` are unsigned integers, compared to pointers in the versions of `visitTree` presented earlier in this chapter. The code for `ArrayBinTree::visitTree` is similar to that of `BinaryTree::visitTree`. The difference is that the testing for null pointers is replaced here with comparison indices with nil values.
- The `clear` function, which clears the binary tree and assigns a new root. The `clear` function does not deallocate dynamic data. Instead, it reinitializes the array-based binary tree. This process is similar to the initialization performed by the class constructor.

- The `getFirstNode` and `getNextNode` functions are similar to these functions as presented in other tree-modeling classes. These functions enable you to traverse the nodes of a binary tree and use the index `nodePtr` to track the currently visited nodes.
- The `probeLeftChild` and `probeRightChild` functions are similar to these functions as implemented in other tree-modeling classes. These functions allow you to probe the data of child nodes when traversing a binary tree using `getFirstNode` and `getLastNode`.

Listing 18.11. The source code for the ARBNTREE.CPP library file.

```
//////////////////////////////////////////////////////////////////////
//                                                                  //
//               Copyright (c) 1992 Namir Clement Shammas           //
//                                                                  //
//  Version: 1.0.0                                   Date 8/9/92    //
//                                                                  //
//  Purpose: implements class of array-based binary trees that      //
//           have the following functionality:                      //
//                                                                  //
//             + insert data.                                       //
//             + search for data.                                   //
//             + delete data.                                       //
//             + visit the tree nodes.                              //
//                                                                  //
//                                                                  //
//////////////////////////////////////////////////////////////////////

#include <string.h>
#include "arbntree.hpp"

/////////////////////////////////////////////////////////////////////
//
template<class T>
ArrayBinTree<T>::ArrayBinTree(unsigned arraySize,
                              T emptyElement)
//
// Purpose: initializes the instances of a binary tree.
//
// Parameters:
```

continues

Listing 18.11. continued

```
//
//     input: arraySize - the maximum number of nodes in the binary
//             tree
//            emptyElement - an instance of the template class T
//             that represents an empty or null element.
//
{
    unsigned i, n;

    arrSize = (arraySize < MIN_ARRAY_SIZE) ? MIN_ARRAY_SIZE :
                                             arraySize;
    nodes = new ArBinstruct<T>[arrSize];
    numNodes = 0;

    if (!nodes) {
      strcpy(errMsg, ALLOCATE_ERROR);
      return;
    }

    errMsg[0] = '\0';
    numNodes = 1;
    root = NIL;
    // initialize the right pointers to set the chain
    // of vacant elements
    for (i = 0; i < (arrSize - 1); i++) {
      nodes[i].rightPtr = i + 1;
    }
    nodes[arrSize - 1].rightPtr = NIL;
    first = 0; // first available vacant element
    last = arrSize - 1; // last available vacant element
    emptyElem = emptyElement;
}

//////////////////////////////////////////////////////////////////////
//
template<class T>
char* ArrayBinTree<T>::getErrorMessage()
//
// Purpose: returns the contents of the errMsg data member
// and assigns an empty string to that member.
```

```
//
//
{
    string80 s;

    strcpy(s, errMsg);
    strcpy(errMsg, "");
    return s;
};
////////////////////////////////////////////////////////////////////
//
template<class T>
boolean ArrayBinTree<T>::insert(T& x)
//
// Purpose: performs node insertion in a binary tree.
//
//  Parameters:
//
//    input: x - the inserted data.
//
{
  unsigned index = root, nextPtr;
  boolean notFound = true;

  // is tree full?
  if (numNodes == arrSize)
    return false;

  // insert first element
  if (root == NIL) {
    // initialize data for inserting the first node
    root = 0;
    notFound = false;
    index = 0;
    first = 1;
  }

  // start searching for the insertion location
  while (notFound) {
    if (nodes[index].dataNode < x) {
      if (nodes[index].rightPtr != NIL)
        index = nodes[index].rightPtr;
```

continues

Listing 18.11. continued

```
      else {
        nextPtr = nodes[first].rightPtr;
        nodes[index].rightPtr = first;
        index = first;
        first = nextPtr;
        notFound = false;
      }
    }
    else {
      if (nodes[index].leftPtr != NIL)
        index = nodes[index].leftPtr;
      else {
        nextPtr = nodes[first].rightPtr;
        nodes[index].leftPtr = first;
        index = first;
        first = nextPtr;
        notFound = false;
      }
    }
  }
  nodes[index].dataNode = x;
  nodes[index].rightPtr = NIL;
  nodes[index].leftPtr = NIL;
  numNodes++;
  return true;
}

//////////////////////////////////////////////////////////////////////
//
template<class T>
boolean ArrayBinTree<T>::search(T& x)
//
// Purpose: searches for a specific key in the binary tree. The
// function returns true if item x is in the tree, or false if
// no match is found.
//
//  Parameters:
//
//    input: x - the search key data.
//
```

```
{
  boolean found = false;
  unsigned index = root;

  if (numNodes == 0)
    return false;

  while (index != NIL && !found) {
    if (nodes[index].dataNode < x)
      index = nodes[index].rightPtr;
    if (nodes[index].dataNode > x)
      index = nodes[index].leftPtr;
    else if (nodes[index].dataNode == x)
      found = true;
   }

   if (found)
     x = nodes[index].dataNode;
   return found;
}

////////////////////////////////////////////////////////////////////
//
template<class T>
boolean ArrayBinTree<T>::remove(T& x)
//
//
// Purpose: performs node deletion.
//
//  Parameters:
//
//    input: x - the data to be removed
//
{
   unsigned index = root;
   unsigned lastIndex = NIL;
   unsigned direction = NIL;
   unsigned nextPtr;
   boolean found = false;

   // does tree have one node?
   if (numNodes == 0)
```

continues

Listing 18.11. continued

```
    return false;

  while (index != NIL && !found) {
    if (nodes[index].dataNode == x)
      found = true;
    else {
      if (nodes[index].dataNode < x) {
        lastIndex = index;
        direction = RIGHT;
        index = nodes[index].rightPtr;
      }
      else {
        lastIndex = index;
        direction = LEFT;
        index = nodes[index].leftPtr;
      }
    }
  }

  if (!found)
    return false;

  // delete matching item
  nodes[index].dataNode = emptyElem;
  // reconnect left subtree?
  if (nodes[index].rightPtr == NIL) {
    if (lastIndex != NIL) { // delete nonroot node
      if (direction == LEFT)
        nodes[lastIndex].leftPtr = nodes[index].leftPtr;
      else
        nodes[lastIndex].rightPtr = nodes[index].leftPtr;
    }
    else // delete the root
      root = nodes[index].leftPtr;
    nodes[index].leftPtr = NIL;
  }
  // reconnect right sub-tree?
  else if (nodes[index].leftPtr == NIL) {
    if (lastIndex != NIL) { // delete nonroot node
      if (direction == LEFT)
```

```
        nodes[lastIndex].leftPtr = nodes[index].rightPtr;
      else
        nodes[lastIndex].rightPtr = nodes[index].rightPtr;
    }
    else // delete the root
      root = nodes[index].rightPtr;
    nodes[index].rightPtr = NIL;
  }
  else {
    nextPtr = nodes[index].rightPtr;
    while (nodes[nextPtr].leftPtr != NIL)
      nextPtr = nodes[nextPtr].leftPtr;
    nodes[nextPtr].leftPtr = nodes[index].leftPtr;
    if (lastIndex != NIL) { // delete nonroot node
      if (direction == LEFT)
        nodes[lastIndex].leftPtr = nodes[index].rightPtr;
      else
        nodes[lastIndex].rightPtr = nodes[index].rightPtr;
    }
    else // delete the root
      root = nodes[index].rightPtr;
    nodes[index].leftPtr = NIL;
    nodes[index].rightPtr = NIL;
  }
  nodes[last].rightPtr = index;
  last = index;
  numNodes--;
  if (numNodes == 0) {
    first = 0;
    root = NIL;
  }
  return true;
}

/////////////////////////////////////////////////////////////////////
//
template<class T>
void ArrayBinTree<T>::clearMarks()
//
// Purpose: clears the marked members of each binary tree node.
//
{
```

continues

Listing 18.11. continued

```
    for (unsigned i = 0; i < arrSize; i++)
      nodes[i].marked = false;
}
//////////////////////////////////////////////////////////////////////
//
template<class T>
void ArrayBinTree<T>::visitTree(unsigned rootPtr,
                                unsigned &node)
//
// Purpose: recursive function used to traverse the binary tree.
//
//  Parameters:
//
//    input: rootPtr - index to the root of the binary tree.
//
//    output: node - the index to the next node visited.
//
{
    if (seekNode && rootPtr != NIL) {
        visitTree(nodes[rootPtr].leftPtr, node);
        if (seekNode && !nodes[rootPtr].marked) {
            seekNode = false;
            nodes[rootPtr].marked = true;
            node = rootPtr;
            return;
        }
        visitTree(nodes[rootPtr].rightPtr, node);
    }
}

//////////////////////////////////////////////////////////////////////
//
template<class T>
void ArrayBinTree<T>::clear()
//
// Purpose: clears the binary tree.
//
// Parameters:
//
//     input: firstItem - the first item inserted in the binary tree
//
```

```
{
    for (unsigned i = 0; i < arrSize; i++) {
      nodes[i].marked = false;
      nodes[i].dataNode = emptyElem;
   }
   root = NIL;
   numNodes = 0;
   first = 0;
   errMsg[0] = '\0';
   // initialize the right pointers to set the chain
   // of vacant elements
   for (i = 1; i < (arrSize - 1); i++) {
     nodes[i].rightPtr = i + 1;
   }
   nodes[arrSize - 1].rightPtr = NIL;
   last = arrSize - 1; // last available vacant element
}

////////////////////////////////////////////////////////////////////
//
template<class T>
boolean ArrayBinTree<T>::getFirstNode(T& x)
//
// Purpose: visits the root of the binary tree. The function
// returns true if the binary tree object has a root.
//
//  Parameters:
//
//   input: x - the pointer to the data associated with the root of
//            the binary tree.
{
    if (numNodes > 0) {
        seekNode = true;
        clearMarks();
        visitTree(root, nodePtr);
        x = nodes[nodePtr].dataNode;
    }
    return (numNodes > 0) ? true : false;
}

////////////////////////////////////////////////////////////////////
//
```

continues

Listing 18.11. continued

```
template<class T>
boolean ArrayBinTree<T>::getNextNode(T& x)
//
// Purpose: visits the next node in the binary tree. The function
// returns true if there was a next node to visit.
//
//  Parameters:
//
//    input: x - the pointer to the data associated with the visited
//              node.
//
{
    seekNode = true;
    nodePtr = NIL;
    if (numNodes > 0) {
        visitTree(root, nodePtr);
        if (!seekNode)
            x = nodes[nodePtr].dataNode;
    }
    return (!seekNode) ? true : false;
}

//////////////////////////////////////////////////////////////////////
//
template<class T>
boolean ArrayBinTree<T>::probeLeftChild(T& x)
//
// Purpose: visits the left child of the current node. The function
// returns true if the current node has a left child.
//
//  Parameters:
//
//    input: x - the data associated with the left child node.
{
    unsigned n;

    if (nodePtr != NIL && nodes[nodePtr].leftPtr != NIL) {
        n = nodes[nodePtr].leftPtr;
        x = nodes[n].dataNode;
        return true;
    }
```

```
    else
        return false;
}

//////////////////////////////////////////////////////////////////////
//
template<class T>
boolean ArrayBinTree<T>::probeRightChild(T& x)
//
// Purpose: visits the right child of the current node. The
// function returns true if the current node has right child.
//
//  Parameters:
//
//   input: x - the data associated with the right child node.
//
{
    unsigned n;

    if (nodePtr != NIL && nodes[nodePtr].rightPtr != NIL) {
        n = nodes[nodePtr].rightPtr;
        x = nodes[n].dataNode;
        return true;
    }
    else
        return false;
}
```

Testing the ArrayBinTree Class

Let's look at a program to test the `ArrayBinTree` class. Listing 18.12 shows the source code for the TSARBIN.CPP test program. I derived this program from the TSBINTRE.CPP. The similarity between the two programs allows you to spot the few differences in using the two forms of binary trees. As expected, the TSARBIN.CPP uses a different tree header file and tree class. In addition, this test program declares the instance of `ArrayBinTree`, `tree`, using two arguments: `25` and `!`. The argument `25` specifies that the maximum number of nodes in the binary-tree instance is `25`. The string `"!"` represents the argument for the empty element. TSARBIN.CPP performs tasks in testing the `ArrayBinTree` class that are parallel to the tasks used by TSBINTRE.CPP in testing the `BinaryTree` class.

Listing 18.12. The source code for the TSARBIN.CPP test program.

```
#include <iostream.h>
#include "video.h"
#include "string.hpp"
#include "arbntree.cpp"

void showTree(ArrayBinTree<cString>& t, cString msg)
{
  cString str;
  boolean ok = t.getFirstNode(str);

  clrscr();
  cout << msg << "\n\n";
  while (ok) {
    cout << str << '\n';
    ok = t.getNextNode(str);
  }
  gotoxy(1, 23);
  cout << "Press any key ... ";
  getch();
}

void searchNode(ArrayBinTree<cString>& t, cString& s)
{
  gotoxy(1, 23);
  clreol();
  gotoxy(1, 22);
  cout << "Press any key to search for " << s;
  getch();
  gotoxy(1, 22);
  clreol();
  if (t.search(s))
    cout << "Found " << s << " in tree\n";
  else
    cout << "No match for " << s << '\n';
  cout << "Press any key to continue ... ";
  getch();
}

main()
{
```

```
  ArrayBinTree<cString> tree(25, "!");
  cString country[] = { "France",
                        "Germany",
                        "Sweden",
                        "Ireland",
                        "Italy",
                        "Spain",
                        "Portugal",
                        "Switzerland",
                        "Belgium",
                        "England",
                        "Greece",   // not inserted in tree
                        "Denmark"   // not inserted in tree
                      };
  unsigned count = sizeof(country) / sizeof(cString);
  unsigned testSize = count - 2;

  // insert the names of the countries
  for (unsigned i = 0; i < testSize; i++)
    tree.insert(country[i]);

  // display AVL tree
  showTree(tree, "Complete binary tree is:");

  for (i = 0; i < count; i++)
    searchNode(tree, country[i]);

  for (i = 0; i < count / 2; i++)
    tree.remove(country[i]);

   // display AVL tree
  showTree(tree, "Trimmed binary tree is:");

  for (i = 0; i < count; i++)
    searchNode(tree, country[i]);

  gotoxy(1, 22); clreol();
  gotoxy(1, 23); clreol();

  return 0;
}
```

Summary

This chapter presented C++ classes that model the simple binary tree and its variants, the AVL tree, the red-black tree, and the array-based binary tree. Simple binary trees store their data in a manner such that each node is connected to two other nodes. The chapter covered the following aspects of binary trees:

- The basic operations of the simple binary tree.
- The conditions that make binary trees susceptible to subtree tilts, which decrease the efficiency of a search through a binary tree.
- The template structure `Binstruct`, which models the node of a binary tree. This structure is noted for maintaining a pointer to the parent nodes. Using such a pointer allows the code manipulating the binary tree to be easier and shorter than in implementations that do not have pointers to the parent nodes.
- The C++ class template `BinaryTree`, which models the binary tree. Operations supported by this class include adding nodes, deleting nodes, searching for data, traversing the nodes of a binary tree, and peeking at parent and child nodes.

The AVL tree improves the search efficiency of the binary tree by maintaining a balanced or near-balanced state. This chapter covered the following topics:

- Although the search method of an AVL tree matches that of a simple binary tree, all other operations on AVL trees are more complex. This is due to the rotation of nodes performed to maintain the near-balanced state of an AVL tree.
- AVL tree nodes have three tilt states: left, right, and neutral.
- The template `AVLstruct` models the node of an AVL tree. This structure includes a member to maintain the tilt of a node.
- The C++ `AVLtree` class models the AVL tree. The operations supported by this class include adding nodes, deleting nodes, searching for data, rotating nodes, rebalancing subtrees, traversing the AVL tree, and peeking at child nodes.

The red-black tree is another version of the binary tree that maintains near-balanced state. This chapter covered the following topics:

- Using node coloring of red and black to track the near-balance of the red-black tree.

- The rules of maintaining a red-black tree.
- The template `RBstruct`, which models the node of a red-black tree. This structure includes a member to maintain the node color.
- The template `RBframe` structure, used to represent data involved in rotating nodes.
- The C++ `RBtree` class, which models the red-black tree. The operations supported by this class include adding nodes, deleting nodes, searching for data, rotating nodes, traversing the red-black tree, and peeking at child nodes.

The chapter also presented a version of the simple binary tree that uses a dynamic array as a supporting data structure. This type of binary tree works for cases in which random data are inserted and then deleted shortly afterward. The maximum number of nodes in this type of binary tree is bound by a predetermined limit. The advantage of such a binary tree is the minimization of heap fragmentation and reserving the required space for the tree nodes. This chapter covered the following topics:

- The basic design for using dynamic arrays to maintain the nodes of a binary tree. The design is influenced by the management of deleted nodes.
- The template structure `ArBinstruct`, which models the node of an array-based binary tree.
- The C++ class template `ArrayBinaryTree`, which models the binary tree. Operations supported by this class include adding nodes, deleting nodes, searching for data, traversing the nodes of a binary tree, and peeking at parent and child nodes.

The Character Set Class

Character sets are suitable in applications that scan text. Such applications include compilers, interpreters, and text-pattern scanners. This chapter presents a class that models character sets and supports various operations for manipulating such sets. With these sets, you can easily and efficiently scan characters.

The CharSet Class

Listing 19.1 shows the source code for the charset.hpp header file, which contains the declaration of the `CharSet` class. This class stores the 128 standard ASCII characters and the 128 extended ASCII characters as bits of a 32-member array of bytes. The class declares member functions that are private, protected, and public. The functions of the `CharSet` class perform the following operations:

- Bit query and manipulation.
- Construction of class instances.

- Adding, removing, counting, and searching for character members in a character set.
- Creating new sets by the union, intersection, and difference of other character sets. These operations basically are general set operations applied to the `CharSet` class.
- Creating special character sets, such as lowercase, uppercase, and alphanumeric character sets.

Listing 19.1. The source code for the charset.hpp header file.

```
//////////////////////////////////////////////////////////////////////
//                                                                  //
//                        Character Set Library                     //
//                                                                  //
//              Copyright (c) 1992  Namir Clement Shammas           //
//                                                                  //
// Version 1.0.0                                            3/25/91 //
//                                                                  //
// Implements a class for a character set that stores each member  //
// in a bit. Each instance uses 32 bytes of storage for the         //
// character set.                                                   //
//                                                                  //
//////////////////////////////////////////////////////////////////////

#ifndef _CharSet_HPP
#define _CharSet_HPP

#include "comndata.h"
#include <string.h>
#include "string.hpp"
#include <iostream.h>

const unsigned CHAR_SIZE = 8;
const unsigned CHAR_ARRAY_SIZE = 256 / CHAR_SIZE;

class CharSet
{
   private:
     unsigned char bitVal[CHAR_SIZE];
```

```
  void initbitVal();
  void setbit(unsigned char bitnum);
  void clearbit(unsigned char bitnum);
  boolean testbit(unsigned char bitnum);

protected:
  unsigned char cset[CHAR_ARRAY_SIZE];
  unsigned char setSize;
  unsigned char xmitstr[3];

  char* xlat(unsigned char c);

public:
  CharSet();
  CharSet(unsigned char first, unsigned char last);
  CharSet(cString& s);
  CharSet(CharSet& cs);
  unsigned char getSetSize() const { return setSize; }
  CharSet& clear();
  boolean ismember(unsigned char c) { return testbit(c); }
  boolean ismember(unsigned char first, unsigned char last);
  boolean ismember(cString& s);
  boolean ismember(CharSet& cs);
  CharSet& add(unsigned char c);
  CharSet& add(unsigned char first, unsigned char last);
  CharSet& add(cString& s);
  CharSet& add(CharSet& cs);
  CharSet& remove(unsigned char c);
  CharSet& remove(unsigned char first, unsigned char last);
  CharSet& remove(cString& s);
  CharSet& remove(CharSet& cs);
  CharSet& intersect(CharSet& cs);
  CharSet& reverse();
  // special sets
  CharSet& mkupcase();
  CharSet& mklocase();
  CharSet& mkdigit();
  CharSet& mkletter();
  CharSet& mkalphanumeric();
```

continues

Listing 19.1. continued

```
        // operators and friend operators
        CharSet& operator =(CharSet& cs);
        CharSet& operator +=(CharSet& cs);
        CharSet& operator -=(CharSet& cs);
        CharSet& operator /=(CharSet& cs);
        friend CharSet operator +(CharSet& cs1, CharSet& cs2);
        friend CharSet operator -(CharSet& cs1, CharSet& cs2);
        friend CharSet operator /(CharSet& cs1, CharSet& cs2);
        friend int operator ==(CharSet& cs1, CharSet& cs2);
        friend ostream& operator <<(ostream& o, CharSet& cs);
};

#endif
```

The Class Implementation

Listing 19.2 shows the source code for the CHARSET.CPP library file. The `CharSet` class declares the following data members:

- The private `bitVal` member, which is an array that stores the values of the bits `0` to `7`.
- The `cset` member, which is a 32-element array that stores the bits for a character set.
- The `setSize` member, which stores the number of members in the character sets.
- The `xmitstr` member, which is a 3-element array used in the output of a character set.

I am using the word *members* in this chapter to indicate set membership.

The basic bit-manipulation functions are the following private functions:

- The `initbitVal` function, which initializes the elements of the private array `bitVal`.
- The `setbit` function, which sets the bit with a number that represents the ASCII code of a character. Because the bits of a `CharSet` instance are stored in 8-bit bytes, the expression

  ```
  (bitnum / CHAR_SIZE)
  ```

  provides the index of the manipulated `cset` element. The expression

  ```
  (bitVal[bitNum % CHAR_SIZE])
  ```

  provides the value that is set as a bitwise `OR` with the target `cset` element.
- The `clearbit` function, which clears the bit with a number that represents the ASCII code of a character. The expression

  ```
  bitVal[bitNum % CHAR_SIZE]
  ```

  provides the value that is set as a bitwise `XOR` with the `cset` element at index `(bitnum / CHAR_SIZE)`.
- The Boolean `testbit` function, which tests whether a bit, containing a number that represents the ASCII code of a character, is set. The function returns `true` if the tested bit is set or `false` if that bit is clear. The `testbit` function obtains its result by taking the bitwise `AND` of the expressions

  ```
  (cset[bitnum / CHAR_SIZE]
  ```

  and

  ```
  bitVal[bitnum % CHAR_SIZE].
  ```
- The `xlat` function, which translates its character argument to a formatted form. Control characters are translated to the `^char` form.

The `CharSet` class contains the following four constructors:

- The default constructor, which creates an empty character set.
- The `CharSet(CharSet& cs)` constructor, which creates an instance of `CharSet` using another existing instance. The argument of the `cs` parameter provides the source instance.

- The `CharSet(unsigned char first, unsigned char last)` constructor, which builds a class instance using a range of characters `first` and `last`. The `first` parameter need not be equal to or greater than the `last` parameter. The function swaps the values of `first` and `last` if `first` is greater than `last`.
- The `CharSet(cString& s)` constructor, which builds a class instance by using the characters of the `s` parameter. The function can detect duplicate characters in the `s` string. For example, if `s` is `A ZA`, a three-member character set is created that contains the letter A, the letter Z, and the space character.

The `CharSet` class contains the following functions for manipulating members of a character set:

- The `getSetSize` function, which returns the number of characters in an instance of `CharSet`.
- The `clear` function, which clears a character set.
- The overloaded Boolean `ismember` functions, which query the existence of one or more characters in an instance of `CharSet`. The overloaded functions are:
    - The `ismember(unsigned char c)` function tests the member of the single character `c`. The function returns the result of the private function `testbit`.
    - The `ismember(unsigned char first, unsigned char last)` function, which tests whether the character set contains a range of characters defined by `first` and `last`. The function returns `true` if the character range is in the set; otherwise, it returns `false`.
    - The `ismember(cString& s)` function, which tests whether all characters in string `s` are members in this character set. The function returns `true` if all the characters of `s` are members; otherwise, it returns `false`.
    - The `ismember(CharSet& cs)` function, which tests whether the `cs` set is equal to or is a subset of the targeted character set. The function returns `true` if this condition is true; otherwise, it returns `false`.
- The overloaded `add` functions, which add one or more characters in an instance of `CharSet`. These overloaded functions are as follows:
    - The `add(unsigned char c)` function, which adds the character `c` to the targeted character set. The function first tests whether the argument already is a member in the targeted character set. If not, the function

includes the character in the set and increments the `setSize` data member.

- The `add(unsigned char first, unsigned char last)` function, which adds a range of characters defined by the `first` and `last` parameters. The function swaps the arguments of these parameters if `first` is greater than `last`. The `add` function uses a loop to test the set membership of each character. If a character is not already a set member, the function inserts it in the set by calling the `setbit` function. The function then increments the `setSize` data member.

- The `add(cString& s)` function, which adds the characters of string `s` to the targeted character set. The function uses a loop to insert the various characters of the `s` string. Each iteration performs a membership test and insertion, similar to `add(unsigned char first, unsigned char last)`, described in the previous item.

- The `add(CharSet& cs)` function, which adds the characters of the `cs` set to the targeted character set. If the `cs` set is empty, the function exits. Otherwise, the function proceeds with adding the characters of the `cs` set. This process involves two `For` loops, both of which iterate over the entire range of characters. The first loop performs a bitwise `OR` operation on the bits of the `cs` set and the targeted set. The second loop obtains the new set size by counting the number of bits set in the targeted set.

- The overloaded `remove` functions, which remove one or more characters from an instance of `CharSet`. The overloaded remove functions are as follows:

  - The `remove(unsigned char c)` function, which deletes the character `c` from the targeted set. The function first tests for the membership of `c` in the targeted character set. If `c` is a member, the function calls the `clearbit` function and then decrements the `setSize` data member.

  - The `remove(unsigned char first, unsigned char last)` function, which removes the characters, defined by the range `first` to `last`, from this set. The function swaps the arguments of `first` and `last` if `first` is greater than `last`. The function uses a `For` loop statement to test the set membership of each character in the range `first` to `last` before that character is deleted. When a character is removed from the set, the function decrements the `setSize` data member.

  - The `remove(cString& s)` function, which removes the characters of the `s` string. The function uses a `for` loop statement to test the set membership of each character in the `s` string before that character is deleted. When a character is removed from the set, the function decrements the `setSize` data member.
  - The `remove(CharSet& cs)` function, which removes the characters in the `cs` set that also are members of this set. This process involves two `For` loops, both of which iterate over the entire range of characters. The first loop performs a bitwise `XOR` operation on the bits of the `cs` set and the targeted set. The second loop obtains the new set size by counting the number of bits that are set in the targeted set.
- The `intersect` function, which creates a new set containing the characters common to both the targeted set and the `cs` character set. The function discards the characters in the `cs` set but not in the original targeted set. This process involves two `For` loops, both of which iterate over the entire range of characters. The first loop performs a bitwise `AND` operation on the bits of the `cs` set and the targeted set. The second loop obtains the new set size by counting the number of bits that are set in the targeted set.
- The `reverse` function, which toggles the membership of a character set. The function simply applies a bitwise `NOT` operator to all the elements of the `cset` array.

The `CharSet` class declares the following operators and friend operators:

- The assignment operator (`=`), which copies the members of the `cs` set to the targeted character set. This process involves copying the `setSize` and `cset` members from the `cs` source set to the targeted character set.
- The append operator (`+=`), which adds the members of the `cs` character set to the targeted character set. The operator simply calls the `add(CharSet& cs)` function and returns this object.
- The delete-first operator (`-=`), which removes the members of the `cs` character set from the targeted character set. The operator simply calls the `remove(CharSet& cs)` function and returns the targeted object.
- The truncate-first operator (`/=`), which intersects the members of the `cs` character set with the targeted character set. The operator simply calls the `intersect(CharSet& cs)` function and returns the targeted object.

- The friend operators: the concatenation operator (+), the deletion operator (-), and the truncation operator (/), which offer convenient forms for adding, removing, and intersecting sets. The operators involve the `add`, `remove`, and `intersect` functions.
- The operator (==), which tests the equality of two character sets. The function returns 1 if the two set match; otherwise, the function yields 0.
- The insertion operator (<<), which sends the formatted output of a character set to an output stream. The formatted set is enclosed in brackets and has the following features:
  - A contiguous range of characters, which appears in the general form of first to last.
  - Control characters, which appear with a caret (^) symbol to the left.
  - Individual characters, which appear as single characters.

The `CharSet` class contains the following functions, which create common sets of characters:

- The `mkupcase` function, which creates a set of uppercase letters.
- The `mklocase` function, which creates a set of lowercase letters.
- The `mkdigit` function, which creates a set of digits.
- The `mkletter` function, which creates a set of letters.
- The `mkalphanumeric` function, which creates a set of letters and digits.

Listing 19.2. The source code for the CharSet.CPP library file.

```
//////////////////////////////////////////////////////////////////////
//                                                                  //
//                       Character Set Library                      //
//                                                                  //
//              Copyright (c) 1992  Namir Clement Shammas           //
//                                                                  //
// Version 1.0.0                                           3/25/91 //
//                                                                  //
// Implements a class for the character set that stores each member//
// in a bit. Each instance uses 32 bytes of storage for the        //
```

continues

Listing 19.2. continued

```
// character set.                                                    //
//                                                                   //
///////////////////////////////////////////////////////////////////////

#include "charset.hpp"

//////////////////////////////////////////////////////////////////////
//
void CharSet::initbitVal()
//
// Purpose: assigns power of 2 values to the elements of array bitVal:
//
//              bitVal[i] = 2 ^ i, for i = 0, 1, ..., 7
//
{
   bitVal[0] = 1;
   for (unsigned char i = 1; i < CHAR_SIZE; i++)
      bitVal[i] = 2 * bitVal[i-1];
}

//////////////////////////////////////////////////////////////////////
//
CharSet& CharSet::clear()
//
// Purpose: clears the CHAR_ARRAY_SIZE bytes of array cset and
// assign zero to the setSize data member.
//
{
   for (unsigned char i = 0; i < CHAR_ARRAY_SIZE; i++)
      cset[i] = 0;
   setSize = 0;
   return *this;
}

void CharSet::setbit(unsigned char bitnum)
//
// Purpose: sets bit number bitnum.
//
```

```
// Parameters:
//
//    input: bitnum - the bit to set.
//
{
    cset[bitnum / CHAR_SIZE] |= bitVal[bitnum % CHAR_SIZE];
}

//////////////////////////////////////////////////////////////////
//
void CharSet::clearbit(unsigned char bitnum)
//
// Purpose: clears bit number bitnum.
//
// Parameters:
//
//    input: bitnum - the bit to clear.
//
{
    cset[bitnum / CHAR_SIZE] ^= bitVal[bitnum % CHAR_SIZE];
}

//////////////////////////////////////////////////////////////////
//
boolean CharSet::testbit(unsigned char bitnum)
//
// Purpose: tests if bit number bitnum is set or clear. The
// function returns true if bit is set or false if bit is clear.
//
// Parameters:
//
//    input: bitnum - the number of the tested bit.
//
{
    return ((cset[bitnum / CHAR_SIZE] &
             bitVal[bitnum % CHAR_SIZE]) > 0) ? true : false;
}

//----------------- class constructors ---------------
```

continues

Listing 19.2. continued

```
////////////////////////////////////////////////////////////////////
//
CharSet::CharSet()
//
//  Purpose: constructs an empty character set.
//
{
    clear();
    initbitVal();
}

////////////////////////////////////////////////////////////////////
//
CharSet::CharSet(CharSet& cs)
//
//  Purpose: constructs a character set that duplicates the cs set.
//
// Parameters:
//
//    input: cs - the source character set.
//
{
    setSize = cs.setSize;
    memcpy(cset, cs.cset, CHAR_ARRAY_SIZE);
    initbitVal();
}

////////////////////////////////////////////////////////////////////
//
CharSet::CharSet(unsigned char first, unsigned char last)
//
//  Purpose: constructs a character set using a range of
//  characters first and last. The first parameter may be
//  equal to, greater than, or less than the last parameter.
//  The function swaps the values of first and last if first
//  is greater than last.
//
// Parameters:
//
```

```
//    input: first - the lower limit of the specified character
//             range.
//           last - the higher limit of the specified character
//             range.
//
{
    unsigned char c;
    initbitVal();
    clear();
    // need to swap parameters first and last?
    if (first > last) {
       c = first;
       first = last;
       last = c;
    }
    setSize = last - first + 1;
    for (c = first; c <= last; c++)
        setbit(c);
}

///////////////////////////////////////////////////////////////////
//
CharSet::CharSet(cString& s)
//
//  Purpose: constructs a character set using the characters
//  of the s parameter. The function can detect duplicate
//  characters in the s string. For example, if s is "   ", a single
//  character set, containing the space character, is created.
//
// Parameters:
//
//    input: s - the source string.
//
{
   char c;

   clear();
   initbitVal();
   setSize = 0;
   for (unsigned i = 0; i < s.stringlen(); i++) {
```

continues

Listing 19.2. continued

```
        // get the next character of string s
        c = s[i];
        // is c not already in the character set?
        if (!testbit(c)) {
            // set the bit for character c
            setbit(c);
            // increment the set size
            setSize++;
        }
    }
}

//////////////////////////////////////////////////////////////////
//
boolean CharSet::ismember(unsigned char first, unsigned char last)
//
//  Purpose: tests whether the character set contains a range of
//  characters defined by first and last. The function returns
//  true if the character range is in the set; otherwise, it
//  returns false.
//
// Parameters:
//
//    input: first - the lower limit for the tested character range.
//           last  - the upper limit for the tested character range.
//
{
    unsigned c;

    // need to swap parameters first and last?
    if (first > last) {
       c = first;
       first = last;
       last = c;
    }

    c = first;
    // loop to test more characters
    while (c <= last)
```

```
        // is c not a member of this character set?
        if (!testbit(c++))
           return false; // exit
     // all tested characters are in the set
     return true;
}

/////////////////////////////////////////////////////////////////////
//
boolean CharSet::ismember(cString& s)
//
//  Purpose: tests if all the characters in the s string are members
//  in this character set. The function returns true if all the
//  characters of s are members and false otherwise.
//
// Parameters:
//
//    input: s - the string that contains the set of characters to
//              be tested for their membership in this character set.
//

{
   unsigned len = s.stringlen();
   unsigned i = 0;

   // return 0 if the string s is empty
   if (len == 0)
      return false;

   // loop to test the characters of string s
   while (i < len)
      // is the next character not a set member?
      if(!testbit(s[i++]))
         // exit: at least one character in string s is not a member
         return false;
   // all characters of s are members in this set
   return true;
}
/////////////////////////////////////////////////////////////////////
//
```

continues

Listing 19.2. continued

```
boolean CharSet::ismember(CharSet& cs)
//
//  Purpose: tests if the cs set is equal to or is a subset of the
//  current set. Function returns true if the previous condition is
//  true, and returns false if otherwise.
//
// Parameters:
//
//    input: cs - the tested character set.
//
{
   int i;
   unsigned bit = 0;
   // loop to test the members of cs
   do {
      // is character ASCII "bit" a member of cs
      i = cs.testbit((unsigned char)bit);
      if (i) {
         // is member of cs not a member of this set?
         if (!testbit((unsigned char)bit))
            // cs is not equivalent or a subset of this set
            return false;
      }
      bit++;
   } while (bit < CHAR_ARRAY_SIZE);
   // Every member of cs is also a member of this set
   return true;
}

///////////////////////////////////////////////////////////////////
//
CharSet& CharSet::add(unsigned char c)
//
//  Purpose: adds the character c to this set. The function tests
//  if the argument already is a member.
//
// Parameters:
//
//    input: c - the character added to this set.
```

```
//
{
   // is c not a member of this set?
   if (!testbit(c)) {
      setbit(c); // add to set
      setSize++; // increment set size
   }
   return *this;
}
//////////////////////////////////////////////////////////////////////
//
CharSet& CharSet::add(unsigned char first, unsigned char last)
//
// Purpose: adds a range of characters defined by the first and last
// parameters. The functions swaps the arguments of these parameters
// if first is greater than last.
//
// Parameters:
//
//    input: first - the lower limit of the added character set.
//           last - the upper limit of the added character set.
//
{
    unsigned char c;

    // need to swap first and last?
    if (first > last) {
       c = first;
       first = last;
       last = c;
    }

    // loop to process the range of characters defined
    // by the parameters first and last
    for (c = first; c <= last; c++)
       // is c not a member of this set?
       if (!testbit(c)) {
          setbit(c); // add c to this set
          setSize++;  // increment the set size
       }
```

continues

Listing 19.2. continued

```
   return *this;
}

//////////////////////////////////////////////////////////////////////
//
CharSet& CharSet::add(cString& s)
//
// Purpose: adds the characters of the s string to this set.
//
// Parameters:
//
//    input: s - the string that contains the added characters.
//
{
    unsigned len = s.stringlen();

    // exit if string s is empty
    if (len == 0)
        return *this;
    // loop for each string character
    for (unsigned i = 0; i < len; i++)
       // is the current character not a set member?
       if (!testbit(s[i])) {
          setbit(s[i]); // add character to this set
          setSize++;    // increment the set size
       }
    return *this;
}

//////////////////////////////////////////////////////////////////////
//
CharSet& CharSet::add(CharSet& cs)
//
// Purpose: adds the characters of the cs set to this set.
//
// Parameters:
//
//    input: cs - the set with characters that are added to this set.
//
```

```
{
    // exit if set cs is empty
    if (cs.setSize == 0)
        return *this;
    // bitwise OR the cset members of this set and set cs
    for (unsigned i = 0; i < CHAR_ARRAY_SIZE; i++)
       cset[i] |= cs.cset[i];
    // reset the set size
    setSize = 0;
    // scan the members of this set to recalculate setSize
    for (i = 0; i < CHAR_ARRAY_SIZE; i++)
       // is ASCII i a member of this set?
       if (testbit((unsigned char)i))
         setSize++; // increment the set size
    return *this;
}

//////////////////////////////////////////////////////////////////////
//
CharSet& CharSet::remove(unsigned char c)
//
// Purpose: deletes the character c from this set.
//
// Parameters:
//
//    input: c - the deleted character.
//
{
   // is character c a member of this set?
   if (testbit(c)) {
      // delete the character from this set
      clearbit(c);
      // decrement the set size
      setSize--;
   }
   return *this;
}

//////////////////////////////////////////////////////////////////////
//
```

continues

Listing 19.2. continued

```
CharSet& CharSet::remove(unsigned char first, unsigned char last)
//
// Purpose: deletes the characters, defined by the range first to
// last, from this set. The function swaps the arguments of first
// and last if first is greater than last.
//
// Parameters:
//
//    input: first - the lower limited of the deleted character
//               range.
//           last  - the lower limited of the deleted character
//               range.
//
{
    unsigned char c;

    // need to swap first and last?
    if (first > last) {
       c = first;
       first = last;
       last = c;
    }

    // loop for the range defined by first and last
    for (c = first; c <= last; c++)
       // is character c a member of this set?
       if (testbit(c)) {
          // delete the character from this set
          clearbit(c);
          // decrement the set size
          setSize--;
       }
    return *this;
}

/////////////////////////////////////////////////////////////////
//
CharSet& CharSet::remove(cString& s)
//
```

```
// Purpose: deletes the characters of the s string that are members
// of this set.
//
// Parameters:
//
//    input: s - the string containing the characters to delete
//              from this set.
//
{
    unsigned len = s.stringlen();

    // exit if string s is empty
    if (len==0)
        return *this;

    // examine the characters of string s
    for (unsigned i = 0; i < len; i++)
       // is character number i a member of this set?
       if (testbit(s[i])) {
          // delete the character from this set
          clearbit(s[i]);
          // decrement the set size
          setSize--;
       }
    return *this;
}

//////////////////////////////////////////////////////////////////////
//
CharSet& CharSet::remove(CharSet& cs)
//
// Purpose: deletes the characters in the cs set that are members
// of this set.
//
// Parameters:
//
//    input: cs - the set of characters to delete from this set.
//
{
    // exit if the set cs is empty
```

continues

Listing 19.2. continued

```
    if (cs.setSize == 0)
        return *this;

    // bitwise XOR to clear members of this set
    // that are also in set cs
    for (unsigned i = 0; i < CHAR_ARRAY_SIZE; i++)
       cset[i] ^= cs.cset[i];
    // reset the set size
    setSize = 0;
    // scan the bits of this set to recalculate the new set size
    for (i = 0; i < CHAR_ARRAY_SIZE; i++)
       if (testbit((unsigned char)i))
         setSize++;
    return *this;
}

////////////////////////////////////////////////////////////////////
//
CharSet& CharSet::intersect(CharSet& cs)
//
// Purpose: intersect the cs set with this set. This function adds
// the members of cs set that already are in this set.
//
// Parameters:
//
//    input: cs - the intersected set.
//
{
    // exit if set cs is empty
    if (cs.setSize == 0)
        return *this;

    // bitwise AND the members of set cs with this set
    for (unsigned i = 0; i < CHAR_ARRAY_SIZE; i++)
       cset[i] &= cs.cset[i];
    // reset the set size
    setSize = 0;
    // scan the bits of this set to recalculate the new set size
    for (i = 0; i < CHAR_ARRAY_SIZE; i++)
```

```
        if (testbit((unsigned char)i))
          setSize++;
    return *this;
}

//////////////////////////////////////////////////////////////////////
//
CharSet& CharSet::reverse()
//
// Purpose: toggles the membership of this set. The characters that
// were not members of this set become members and vice versa.
//
{
    // bitwise NOT the set members
    for (unsigned char i = 0; i < CHAR_ARRAY_SIZE; i++)
       cset[i] = ~cset[i];
    // update the set size
    setSize = ~setSize;
    return *this;
}

//////////////////////////////////////////////////////////////////////
//
CharSet& CharSet::mkupcase()
//
// Purpose: makes this set contain members that are uppercase
// characters. The previous set members are cleared.
//
{
   clear();
   add('A', 'Z');
   return *this;
}

//////////////////////////////////////////////////////////////////////
//
CharSet& CharSet::mklocase()
//
// Purpose: makes this set contain members that are lowercase
// characters. The previous set members are cleared.
```

continues

Listing 19.2. continued

```
//
{
   clear();
   add('a', 'z');
   return *this;
}

//////////////////////////////////////////////////////////////////////
//
CharSet& CharSet::mkdigit()
//
// Purpose: makes this set contain members that are digits. The
// previous set members are cleared.
//
{
   clear();
   add('0', '9');
   return *this;
}

//////////////////////////////////////////////////////////////////////
//
CharSet& CharSet::mkletter()
//
// Purpose: makes this set contain members that are letters.
// The previous set members are cleared.
//
{
   clear();
   add('A', 'Z');
   add('a', 'z');
   return *this;
}

//////////////////////////////////////////////////////////////////////
//
CharSet& CharSet::mkalphanumeric()
//
// Purpose: makes this set contain members that are letters and
// digits. The previous set members are cleared.
```

```
//
{
   clear();
   add('0', '9');
   add('A', 'Z');
   add('a', 'z');
   return *this;
}

///////////////////////////////////////////////////////////////////
//
CharSet& CharSet::operator =(CharSet& cs)
//
// Purpose: assigns the cs character set to this set.
//
// Parameters:
//
//    input: cs - the source character set.
//
{
   setSize = cs.setSize;
   memcpy(cset, cs.cset, CHAR_ARRAY_SIZE);
   return *this;
}

///////////////////////////////////////////////////////////////////
//
CharSet& CharSet::operator +=(CharSet& cs)
//
// Purpose: adds the members of the cs character set to this set.
//
// Parameters:
//
//    input: cs - the added character set.
//
{
   add(cs);
   return *this;
}
```

continues

Listing 19.2. continued

```
//////////////////////////////////////////////////////////////////////
//
CharSet& CharSet::operator -=(CharSet& cs)
//
// Purpose: deletes the members of the cs character set from this set.
//
// Parameters:
//
//    input: cs - the set of characters to delete.
//
{
   remove(cs);
   return *this;
}

//////////////////////////////////////////////////////////////////////
//
CharSet& CharSet::operator /=(CharSet& cs)
//
// Purpose: intersects the members of the cs set with this set.
//
// Parameters:
//
//    input: cs - the intersected character set.
//
{
   intersect(cs);
   return *this;
}

//////////////////////////////////////////////////////////////////////
//
CharSet operator +(CharSet& cs1, CharSet& cs2)
//
// Purpose: adds the cs1 and cs2 character sets.
//
// Parameters:
//
//    input: cs1 - the first operand.
```

```
//            cs2 - the second operand.
//
{
   CharSet result(cs1);
   result.add(cs2);
   return result;
}

/////////////////////////////////////////////////////////////////////
//
CharSet operator -(CharSet& cs1, CharSet& cs2)
//
// Purpose: deletes the cs2 set from the cs1 set.
//
// Parameters:
//
//    input: cs1 - the first operand.
//           cs2 - the second operand.
//
{
   CharSet result(cs1);
   result.remove(cs2);
   return result;
}

/////////////////////////////////////////////////////////////////////
//
CharSet operator /(CharSet& cs1, CharSet& cs2)
//
// Purpose:  intersects cs1 and cs2.
//
// Parameters:
//
//    input: cs1 - the first operand.
//           cs2 - the second operand.
//
{
   CharSet result(cs1);
   result.intersect(cs2);
   return result;
}
```

continues

Listing 19.2. continued

```
///////////////////////////////////////////////////////////////////
//
int operator ==(CharSet& cs1, CharSet& cs2)
//
// Purpose: compares cs1 and cs2. The function returns 1 if
// the two set match; otherwise, the function yields 0.
//
// Parameters:
//
//    input: cs1 - the first operand.
//           cs2 - the second operand.
//
{
   for (unsigned i = 0; i < CHAR_ARRAY_SIZE; i++)
      // compare byte number i
      if (cs1.cset[i] != cs2.cset[i])
         return 0; // sets do not match
   // sets match
   return 1;
}

///////////////////////////////////////////////////////////////////
//
char* CharSet::xlat(unsigned char c)
//
// Purpose: translates the character c to a formatted form.
// Control characters are translated to ^char form.
//
// Parameters:
//
//    input: c - the input character.
//
{
   if (c < 26 ¦¦ c == '[' ¦¦ c == ']' ¦¦ c == '^' ¦¦ c == '-') {
     xmitstr[0] = '^';
     xmitstr[1] = (c < 26) ? ('A' + (int)c) : c;
     xmitstr[2] = '\0';
   }
   else {
```

```
      xmitstr[0] = c;
      xmitstr[1] = '\0';
    }
    return xmitstr;
}

////////////////////////////////////////////////////////////////////
//
ostream& operator <<(ostream& os, CharSet& cs)
//
// Purpose: writes a formatted output of the cs set to the stream os.
//
// Parameters:
//
//     input: cs - the output set.
//
//     in/out: os - the output stream.
//
{
    unsigned char qsize = 0;
    unsigned char c, lastc;

    os << '[';
    for (unsigned i = 0, count = 0;
         i < 256 && count <= cs.setSize;
         i++) {
      c = (unsigned char)i;
      if (cs.ismember(c)) {
        count++;
        if (qsize == 0) {
          lastc =c;
          qsize = 1;
          os << cs.xlat(c);
        }
        else {
          if ((c - lastc) == 1) {
            lastc = c;
            qsize++;
          }
          else {
```

continues

Listing 19.2. continued

```
            if (qsize == 1) {
              lastc = c;
              qsize = 1;
              os << cs.xlat(c);
            }
            else if (qsize == 2) {
              os << cs.xlat(lastc);
              lastc = c;
              qsize = 1;
              os << cs.xlat(c);
            }
            else {
              os << '-' << cs.xlat(lastc);
              lastc = c;
              qsize = 1;
              os << cs.xlat(c);
            }
          }
        }
      }
    }
    if (qsize > 1) {
      if (qsize > 2)
         os << '-';
      os << cs.xlat(lastc);
    }
    os << ']';
    return os;
}
```

Testing The CharSet Class

Now examine a program to test the `CharSet` class. Listing 19.3 shows the source code for the TSCHARSE.CPP test program. The program declares the following objects:

- The `cs1` character set, which contains the uppercase letters A to Z.

- The `CS2` character set, which contains the control characters with an ASCII code range from 0 to 25.
- The `cString` instances that contain the caret (`^`) and minus (`-`) characters.
- The `CS3` character set, which contains characters of object `s`.

The test program performs the following tasks:

1. Displays the `CS1` and `CS2` sets. The output is as follows:

   ```
   Set CS1 is [A-Z]
   Set CS2 is [^A-^Z]
   ```

2. Clears the `CS1` set and displays it. The output is as follows:

   ```
   Set CS1 is []
   ```

3. Calls the `mkalphanumeric` function to create a set of letters and digits in `CS1` set. The output is as follows:

   ```
   Set CS1 is [0-9A-Za-z]
   ```

4. Removes the lowercase characters from `CS1` set and adds the letters y and z. The output is as follows:

   ```
   Set CS1 is [0-9A-Zyz]
   ```

5. Adds the characters of `CS2` to `CS1` and then displays `CS1`. This addition involves the append operator (+=). The output is as follows:

   ```
   Set CS1 is [^A-^Z0-9A-Zyz]
   ```

6. Assigns `CS1` to `CS2`, using the assignment operator (=), and then displays `CS2`. The output is as follows:

   ```
   Set CS2 is [^A-^Z0-9A-Zyz]
   ```

7. Removes the characters with ASCII codes that are `1`, `2`, `3`, and `4` from `CS2`.

8. Adds the characters of `CS3` to `CS2` and displays `CS2`. The output is as follows:

   ```
   Set CS2 is [^A^F-^Z^-0-9A-Z^^yz]
   ```

   Notice that the characters `-` and `^` appear as `^-` and `^^` in the previously displayed set.

Listing 19.3. The source code for the TSCHARSE.CPP test program.

```
#include "video.h"
#include "string.hpp"
#include "charset.hpp"

main()
{
   CharSet CS1('A','Z'), CS2(0, 25);
   cString s("^-");
   CharSet CS3(s);

   clrscr();
   cout << "Set CS1 is " << CS1 << '\n';
   cout << "Set CS2 is " << CS2 << '\n';
   CS1.clear();
   cout << "Set CS1 is " << CS1 << '\n';
   CS1.mkalphanumeric();
   cout << "Set CS1 is " << CS1 << '\n';
   CS1.remove('a', 'z').add('y', 'z');
   cout << "Set CS1 is " << CS1 << '\n';
   CS1 += CS2;
   cout << "Set CS1 is " << CS1 << '\n';
   CS2 = CS1;
   cout << "Set CS2 is " << CS2 << '\n';
   CS2.remove(1, 4);
   CS2 += CS3;
   cout << "Set CS2 is " << CS2 << '\n';
   cout << "Press any key to end the program ...";
   getch();
   return 0;
}
```

Summary

Character sets are structures useful in text-scanning applications. This chapter presented the `CharSet` class, which models the set of 128 ASCII characters and 128 extended ASCII characters. The `CharSet` class supports the following character set operations:

- Bit manipulation and testing.
- Adding characters to a character set object.
- Removing characters from a character set object.
- Inverting the members of a character set object.
- Performing set operations on character sets, such as intersection and union.
- Creating popular character sets, such as sets for digits, lowercase, uppercase, and alphanumeric characters.

Internal and External Search Tables

Search tables are data structures that specialize in fast data retrieval. You can use sorted arrays, such as those discussed in Chapter 15, "Words, Items, and Tokens," as search tables. Such an array is suitable for use as a search table when the number of its elements is relatively small. As the number of elements increase, the speed of the search also increases. Maintaining faster search speeds becomes more significant when extensive searches are conducted.

An alternative kind of search table is a *hash table.* Hash tables have gained popularity among the developers of compilers, interpreters, and other applications that require fast data access.

This chapter examines both internal and external hash tables. Internal hash tables use dynamic memory to store and access their data. External hash tables use the random-access stream functions `seekg`, `write`, and `read`.

The Basics of Hashing

Hash tables are basically arrays that convert some or all of the data into an *array index.* The term frequently used for an array index is *hash address.* A *hash function* performs the conversion of data into a hash address. Typically, hash functions generate random numbers in the range of 0 to the hash-table size minus 1. Hash tables, therefore, offer fast data access using rather chaotic random numbers instead of ordered arrays. Consequently, hash tables do not support accessing data in ascending or descending order. This lack of order is not critical for many applications, such as compilers and interpreters; these applications are more concerned with determining the existence of an identifier and accessing its data.

The choice of hash function is another important issue in operating hash tables. Hash functions should generate unique numbers for each possible data member. Sometimes, hash functions yield the same address for at least two different sets of data. This occurrence is called *collision.* Two main factors cause this to occur:

- The first factor leading to collision is the size of the hash table itself. If, at any given time, you have more data than the size of the hash table, you're overloading your hash table. No matter how wonderful the applied hash function is, it still yields the same address for two sets of data. Therefore, making the hash table reasonably large helps minimize collision.
- Notice that I said minimize, not eliminate. The second factor is that hash functions invariably yield the same address for two sets of data, regardless of the hash-table size.

The conclusion to draw is that collisions always occur, and that you must handle them with the operations of the hash tables.

Knuth has suggested that the size of the hash table should be a prime number because the modulo operation that involves a prime number yields a more randomized number. The basic form for the hash function is therefore

```
h(x) = x mod tableSize
```

a simple but nontrivial form of hash function is

```
h(x) = (k1 + x * k2) mod tableSize
```

where `k1` and `k2` are small, prime numbers, such as 11, 13, or 17.

Internal Hash Tables

Internal hash tables reside in memory and enable quick data searches for small sets of data. Computer scientists have proposed a variety of methods for dealing with the collisions of internal hash tables. Discussing all of these is beyond the scope of this book, but my favorite method is called *chaining.* This method views the hash table as an array of linked lists. Each linked list stores hash-table entries at a specific hash-table address. To resolve the collision problem, the hash table inserts the colliding data in linked lists.

Figure 20.1 shows a typical hash table that uses linked lists for chaining colliding data. You can use either ordered or unordered linked lists. If you're using an efficient hash function and an adequately sized hash table, the number of colliding elements should be small. In this case, an unordered linked list is adequate. By contrast, if you determine that your data produces long linked lists, you might consider using ordered linked lists to speed up the search process.

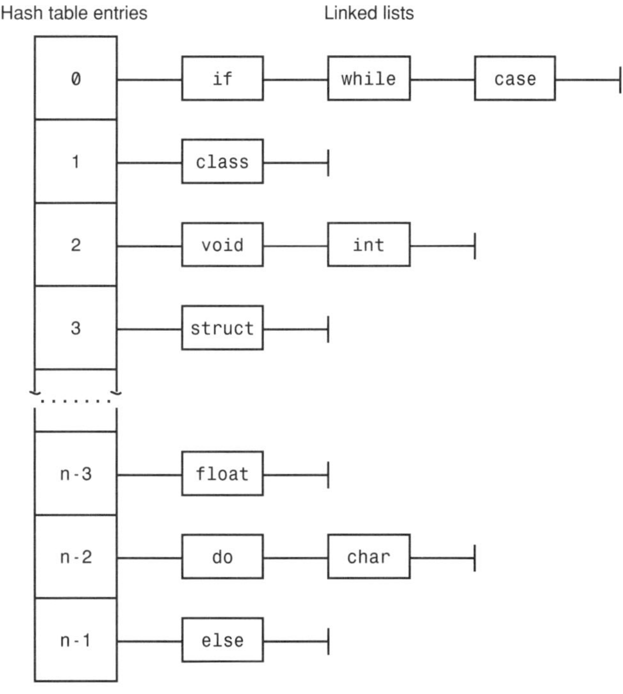

Figure 20.1. A typical hash table that uses linked lists for chaining colliding data.

As an alternative to linked lists, apply AVL trees. (AVL trees are discussed in Chapter 17, "Lists.") Many programmers may regard this approach as overkill. Using AVL trees, you transform the hash table into an array of pointers to AVL trees. Operations to search for, insert, and delete data are performed quickly in such a hash table. Figure 20.2 shows a hash table that uses AVL trees for chaining colliding data.

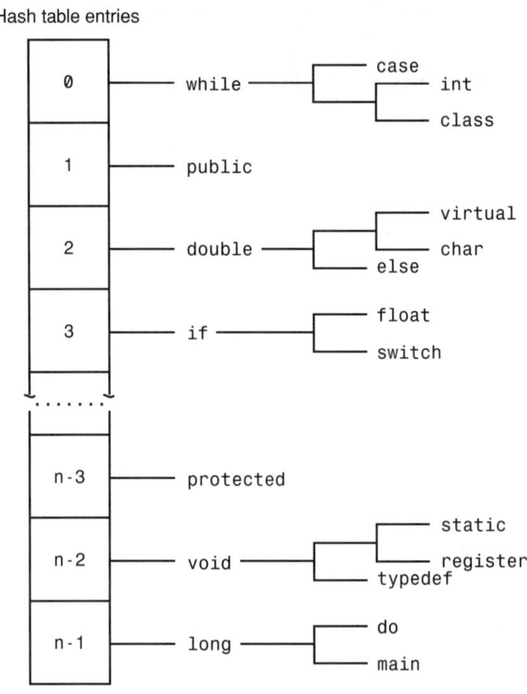

Figure 20.2. A hash table that uses AVL trees for chaining colliding data.

External Hash Tables

External hash tables are stored in mass-storage devices. Hash-table entries are organized in buckets. Each *bucket* contains one or more hash-table entries that share the same hash-table address. Because nothing guarantees that all colliding data will fit in a single bucket, it's necessary to chain buckets. A hash table thus uses two types of buckets, primary and secondary. *Primary* (also called *main*) *buckets* are allocated when the hash table is initialized. The number of primary buckets is equal to the size of an external hash table. *Secondary* (also called *overflow*) *buckets* are created as needed. Initially, no secondary buckets exist. Figure 20.3 shows a typical external hash table with primary and secondary buckets. The hash table has `n` primary buckets and (`m - n`) secondary buckets.

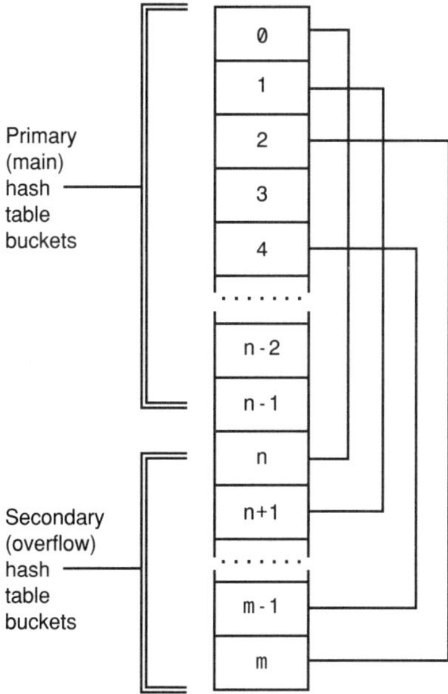

Figure 20.3. The external hash table.

Figure 20.4 shows the bucket of an external hash table and illustrates that each bucket contains the following items:

- The current number of hash-table entries in the bucket. When a primary bucket is created, this value is 0. When a secondary bucket is created, this value is 1.
- The number, or index, of chained buckets.
- Hash-table entries.
- Optional blank data.

Each bucket (primary and secondary) carries an index used to chain it to other buckets. When a bucket is first created, its overflow index is set to a terminal value. I suggest the value of 0 as suitable because bucket number 0 is the first primary bucket in the hash table. As colliding data fill a bucket, that bucket overflows and requires the creation of a new secondary bucket. The index of the overflowing bucket is set to the new secondary bucket.

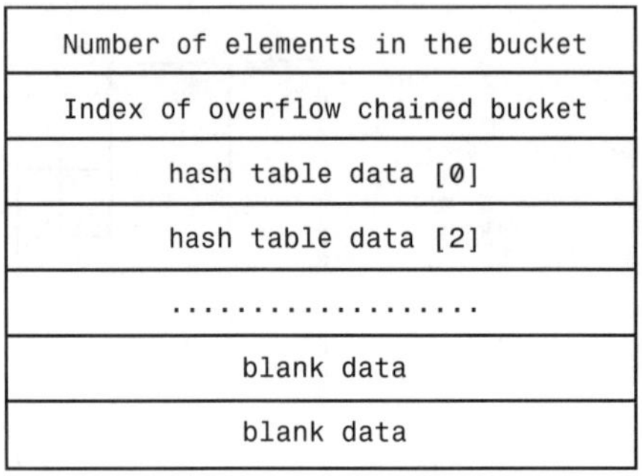

Number of elements in the bucket
Index of overflow chained bucket
hash table data [0]
hash table data [2]
....
blank data
blank data

Figure 20.4. The bucket of the external hash table.

The Internal HashTable Class

This section presents a C++ class that models the internal hash table. Listing 20.1 contains the source code for the hashtabl.hpp header file, which declares the `HashTable` class. This class uses AVL trees to store the colliding data of the hash-table entries. The class declares the following data members:

- The `hashTableSize` member, which stores the size of the hash table.
- The `workSize` member, which stores the current number of entries in the hash tables. Initially, the `workSize` member contains 0 and may exceed the value in the `hashTableSize` member.
- The `tableIndex` member, which is used to track the currently visited AVL tree.
- The `hfunc` member, which is a pointer to the hash function.
- The `errMsg` member, which stores the error message sent by the various functions.
- The `table` member, which is the double pointer to the `AVLtree` class. This member is used to create an array of pointers to the `AVLtree` class. (See Chapter 17 for more on the `AVLtree` class.)

The `HashTable` class declares several protected and public functions. Among these functions, only the `getWorkSize` function is defined in the class declaration. The `getWorkSize` function returns the value stored in the `workSize` data member.

It's worth noting that the `HashTable` class relies on the `AVLtree` class to perform basic data search, insertion, and deletion. This is why the `HashTable` class contains no low-level (protected or private) functions that perform these basic operations.

Listing 20.1. The source code for the hashtbl.hpp header file.

```
//////////////////////////////////////////////////////////////////////
//                                                                  //
//              Copyright (c) 1992 Namir Clement Shammas            //
//                                                                  //
//  Version: 1.0                                   Date 7/9/1992    //
//                                                                  //
//  Purpose: implements a template class of hash tables.            //
//           The following operations are implemented:              //
//                                                                  //
//           + insertion                                            //
//           + search                                               //
//           + deletion                                             //
//           + sequential visit to the hash-table entries           //
//                                                                  //
//////////////////////////////////////////////////////////////////////

#include "comndata.h"
#include "avl.cpp"
#include <string.h>

#ifndef _HASHTABL_HPP
#define _HASHTABL_HPP

template<class T>
class HashTable {
```

continues

Listing 20.1. continued

```
  protected:
    unsigned hashTableSize,           // size of hash table
             workSize,                // number of entries
             tableIndex;              // visited entry index
    unsigned (*hfunc)(T&, unsigned); // hash function
    string80 errMsg;                  // error message
    AVLtree<T> **table;               // pointer to hash table

 public:
    // ************** state manipulation methods **************
    HashTable(unsigned maxHashTableSize,
              unsigned (*aHashFunc)(T&, unsigned)),
    ~HashTable();
    char* getErrorMessage();
    unsigned getWorkSize() const { return workSize; }

    // ************** object manipulation methods *************
    virtual boolean insertItem(T&);
    virtual boolean search(T&);
    virtual boolean remove(T&);
    virtual boolean getFirstNode(T&);
    virtual boolean getNextNode(T&, boolean&);
    boolean setTableIndex(unsigned);
};

#endif
```

The `HashTable` class declares the following constructor, destructor, and member functions:

- The class constructor, which creates instances of `HashTable` given the size of the hash table and the hash function. The constructor creates an array of pointers to `AVLtree` class instances, which are accessed by the `table` data member. The constructor then uses a `for` loop to assign nulls to the members of the pointer array. As long as a hash-table entry is empty, its corresponding pointer is null.
- The class destructor, which deletes the array of pointer, the member `table`, and recuperates its dynamic space.

- The `getErrorMessage` function, which returns the string stored in the `errMsg` data member and also assigns an empty string to that member.
- The `insertItem` function, which inserts a data item in the hash table. The function calculates the hash address for the inserted data by calling the hash function accessed by the `hfunc` data member. The `insertItem` function then uses the calculated address to access the corresponding pointer to the `AVLtree` class instance using the local `AVLtree` pointer `p`. If the targeted hash-table entry is not empty, the `insertItem` function performs the following tasks:
  1. Invokes the `AVLtree::search` function to determine whether the inserted `x` item already exists in the hash table.
  2. If the item is not in the hash table, the function calls the `AVLtree::insert` function to perform the insertion. The function increments the `workSize` member and returns `true` if the insertion proceeds without any error.
  3. If the `x` item is already in the hash table, the function returns `false`.If the targeted hash-table entry is empty, the `insertItem` function performs the following tasks:
     1. Creates a new instance of the `AVLtree` class. This instance is accessed by the local pointer `p`.
     2. Calls the `AVLtree::insert` function to insert the `x` item in the new AVL tree.
     3. Verifies that the AVL tree insertion has proceeded without error. If so, the function increments the `workSize` member and updates the pointer table.
- The `search` function, which searches the hash table for the `x` item. The function obtains the hash address from the search data and uses that address to access the corresponding pointer in the array of AVL tree pointers. If the targeted pointer is not null, the function invokes the `AVLtree::search` function to search the targeted AVL tree. The `search` function returns the value of the `AVLtree::search` function. If the targeted AVL tree pointer is null, the `search` function returns `false`.
- The `remove` function, which deletes an item from the hash table. If the `workSize` member is 0, the function returns `false`. Otherwise, the function performs the following tasks:

1. Obtains the hash address using the search data.
2. Sets the local AVL tree pointer `p` to the hash-table entry that corresponds to the calculated hash-table address.
3. Returns `false` if the `p` pointer is null when the targeted hash-table entry is empty.
4. Invokes the `AVLtree::remove` function to remove the `x` item from the targeted `AVLtree` instance. The `ok` local variable stores the Boolean value returned by the `AVLtree::remove` function.
5. Examines whether the targeted AVL tree is empty. If so, the AVL tree is deleted, and the table pointer is adjusted.
6. Decrements the `workSize` member.
7. Returns the value stored in the `ok` local variable.

- The `getFirstNode` function, which visits the first entry in the hash table. The function returns `true` if the hash table is not empty. The `x` reference parameter yields the data of the visited hash-table entry. The `getFirstNode` function performs the following tasks:

1. Sets the `tableIndex` member to 0, the index of the first hash-table entry.
2. Uses a `while` loop to locate the first hash-table entry that contains data.
3. If an occupied hash-table entry is located, the function `getFirstNode` assigns the corresponding AVL tree's pointer to the local pointer `p`. The function then invokes and returns the value of the `AVLtree::getFirstNode` function for the targeted AVL tree.
4. If no occupied hash-table entry is located, the function returns `false`.

- The `getNextNode` function, which visits the next hash-table entry. The visited entry, if it exists, is either a colliding item in the same AVL tree (the one currently being visited) or the first element in a subsequent AVL tree. The function returns `true` if successful; otherwise, it returns `false`. The `x` reference parameter returns the data of the visited hash-table entry. The reference boolean parameter, `firstEntry`, indicates whether the visited item is the first entry—that is, the smallest value of an AVL tree—in a hash table. The `getNextNode` function carries out the following tasks:

1. Assigns `false` to the `firstEntry` parameter.
2. Returns `false` if the value in the `tableIndex` member is equal to or greater than the `hashTableSize` member.
3. Assigns the pointer to the targeted AVL tree to the local pointer `p`.
4. Invokes the `AVLtree::getNextNode` function. If this function returns `true`, the `getNextNode` function returns `true` as well.
5. Increments the `tableIndex` member to visit the next hash-table entry.
6. Uses a loop to locate the occupied hash-table entry.
7. If the `getNextNode` function finds an occupied hash-table entry, it assigns `true` to `firstEntry` and returns the value of the `AVLtree::getFirstNode` invoked for the current AVL tree.
8. If no occupied hash-table entry is located, the `getNextNode` function returns `false`.

- The `setTableIndex` function, with which you can assign a new value for the `tableIndex` data member to redirect the action of the `getNextNode` function. The function returns `true` if a `newTableIndex` is in the range `[0..hashTableSize-1]`; otherwise, it returns `false`. An out-of-range value for `newTableIndex` leaves the `tableIndex` data member unchanged.

Listing 20.2 contains the source code for the HASHTABL.CPP library file.

Listing 20.2. The source code for the HASHTABL.CPP library file.

```
//////////////////////////////////////////////////////////////////////
//                                                                  //
//              Copyright (c) 1992 Namir Clement Shammas            //
//                                                                  //
//  Version: 1.0                                  Date 7/9/1992     //
//                                                                  //
//  Purpose: implements a template class of hash tables.            //
//           The following operations are implemented:              //
//                                                                  //
//           + insertion                                            //
//           + search                                               //
```

continues

Listing 20.2. continued

```
//          + deletion                                               //
//          + sequential visit to the hash-table entries             //
//                                                                   //
///////////////////////////////////////////////////////////////////////

#include "hashtabl.hpp"

//////////////////////////////////////////////////////////////////////
//
template<class T>
HashTable<T>::HashTable(unsigned maxHashTableSize,
                        unsigned (*aHashFunc)(T&, unsigned))
//
// Purpose: initializes a hash table.
//
// Parameters:
//
//   input: maxHashTableSize - the size of the hash table.
//          aHashFunc - the hash function.
//
{
    hashTableSize = maxHashTableSize;
    workSize = 0;
    hfunc = aHashFunc;
    table = new AVLtree<T>*[hashTableSize * sizeof(AVLtree<T>*)];
    if (!table) {
        strcpy(errMsg, ALLOCATE_ERROR);
        return;
    }
    else
        errMsg[0] = '\0';
    // assign nulls to the has table pointers
    for(unsigned i = 0; i < hashTableSize; i++)
        *(table + i) = NULL;
}
```

```
//////////////////////////////////////////////////////////////////////
//
template<class T>
HashTable<T>::~HashTable()
//
// Purpose: removes a hash-table object.
//
{
    delete [] table;
}

//////////////////////////////////////////////////////////////////////
//
template<class T>
char* HashTable<T>::getErrorMessage()
//
// Purpose: returns the string stored in member errMsg and
// clears the string in that member.
//
{
    string80 s;

    strcpy(s, errMsg);
    errMsg[0] = '\0';
    return s;
}

//////////////////////////////////////////////////////////////////////
//
template<class T>
boolean HashTable<T>::insertItem(T& x)
//
// Purpose: builds a hash table by inserting a single item.
// You should call this routine several times to build
// a complete hash table. The function returns true if the
// x item is inserted; otherwise, the function returns false.
//
// Parameters:
//
//   input: x - the data inserted in the hash table.
//
```

continues

Listing 20.2. continued

```
{
    unsigned hashAddress;
    AVLtree<T>* p;
    boolean notfound;

    errMsg[0] = '\0';

    // get the has table address
    hashAddress = (*hfunc)(x, hashTableSize);
    p = *(table + hashAddress);

    // is the table entry not empty?
    if (p) {
      // is x not in the hash table?
      if (!p->search(x)) {
        // insert data in the AVL tree accessed by pointer p
        p->insert(x);
        // copy error message reported by the function
        // AVLtree::getErrorMessage
        strcpy(errMsg, p->getErrorMessage());
        // increment workSize if no error occurred
        if (errMsg[0] == '\0')
          workSize++;
        return (errMsg[0] == '\0') ? true : false;
      }
      else
         return false;
    }
    else {
      // create new table entry
      p = new AVLtree<T>;
      if (p) {
        // insert data in the AVL tree accessed by pointer p
        p->insert(x);
        // copy error message reported by the function
        // AVLtree::getErrorMessage
        strcpy(errMsg, p->getErrorMessage());
        // increment workSize if no error occurred
        if (errMsg[0] == '\0') {
          workSize++;
```

```
          // assign pointer p to a hash-table entry
          *(table + hashAddress) = p;
          return true;
        }
        else
          return false;
      }
      else {
        strcpy(errMsg, ALLOCATE_ERROR);
        return false;
      }
    }
}

//////////////////////////////////////////////////////////////////////
//
template<class T>
boolean HashTable<T>::search(T& x)
//
// Purpose: searches hash table for a specific key. The
// x parameter returns the nonkey data for the matching
// hash-table member. The function returns true if a
// matching element exists or false if no match is found.
//
// Parameters:
//
//   input: x - the sought data.
//
{
    unsigned hashAddress;
    AVLtree<T>* p;
    hashAddress = (*hfunc)(x, hashTableSize);
    p = *(table + hashAddress);
    if (p)
      return p->search(x);
    else
      return false;
}
```

continues

Listing 20.2. continued

```
//////////////////////////////////////////////////////////////////////
//
template<class T>
boolean HashTable<T>::remove(T& x)
//
// Purpose: deletes a specific entry from the hash table. The
// function returns true if a matching element exists or
// false if no match is found.
//
// Parameters:
//
//   input: x - the reference to the search data.
//
{
    boolean ok;
    unsigned hashAddress;
    AVLtree<T> *p;

    // is hash table empty ?
    if (workSize == 0)
        return false;

    // get the hash-table address
    hashAddress = (*hfunc)(x, hashTableSize);
    p = *(table + hashAddress);
    // return false if hash-table entry is empty
    if (!p)
      return false;
    // remove sought data
    ok = p->remove(x);
    // was the last hash-table entry removed?
    if (ok && p->getNodeCount() == 0) {
      // delete AVLtree instance
      delete p;
      // assign NULL to hash-table entry at hashAddress
      *(table + hashAddress) = NULL;
    }
    if (ok)
      workSize--;
    return ok;
}
```

```
/////////////////////////////////////////////////////////////////////
//
template<class T>
boolean HashTable<T>::getFirstNode(T& x)
//
// Purpose: visits the first entry in the hash table. The function
// returns true if the hash table is not empty; otherwise, it
// returns false.
//
// Parameters:
//
//   output: x - the reference to the data in the first entry.
//
{
    AVLtree<T>* p;

    tableIndex = 0;
    // search for first entry in hash table
    while (tableIndex < hashTableSize && !*(table + tableIndex))
        tableIndex++;

    // found a hash-table entry?
    if (tableIndex < hashTableSize) {
       p = *(table + tableIndex);
       // invoke member function AVLtree::getFirstNode
       return p->getFirstNode(x);
    }
    else
        return false;
}

/////////////////////////////////////////////////////////////////////
//
template<class T>
boolean HashTable<T>::getNextNode(T& x,
                                  boolean& firstEntry)
//
// Purpose: visits the next entry in the hash table. The function
// returns true if the next entry was found.
//
```

continues

Listing 20.2. continued

```
// Parameters:
//
//   output: x - the data in the next entry.
//           firstEntry - true if visited data is at the head of
//            the linked list attached to an entry. The returned
//            value is significant only if the function value is true.
//
{
    AVLtree<T> *p;

    firstEntry = false; // default assignment
    if (tableIndex >= hashTableSize)
      return false;
    else
      p = *(table + tableIndex);

    // was the last node visitation successful?
    if (p->getNextNode(x))
        return true;

    // search for next entry in hash table
    tableIndex++;
    while (tableIndex < hashTableSize && !*(table + tableIndex))
        tableIndex++;

    // found a hash-table entry?
    if (tableIndex < hashTableSize) {
       firstEntry = true;
       p = *(table + tableIndex);
       // invoke member function AVLtree::getFirstNode
       return p->getFirstNode(x);
    }
    else
        return false;
}

//////////////////////////////////////////////////////////////////////
//
template<class T>
boolean HashTable<T>::setTableIndex(unsigned newTableIndex)
```

```
//
// Purpose: assigns a new value for the tableIndex data member
// to redirect the action of function getNextNode. The function
// returns true if a newTableIndex is in the range
// [0..hashTableSize-1]; otherwise, it returns false. An out-of-range
// value for newTableIndex leaves the data member tableIndex
// unchanged.
//
// Parameters:
//
//   input: newTableIndex - the new value for tableIndex.
//
{
    if (newTableIndex < hashTableSize) {
        tableIndex = newTableIndex;
        return true;
    }
    else
        return false;
}
```

Testing the HashTable Class

Let's look at two programs to test the `HashTable` class. The first program manipulates a hash table containing instances of the `cString` class. Listing 20.3 contains the source code for the TSHASH1.CPP test program, which declares the `hashFunction` function to provide the `HashTable` class with the required hash function.

The `main` function creates the `h` hash table with 23 entries and specifies that the `hashFunction` function is the hash function for the instances of `cString`. The program also creates the `cString` instance `s` used to insert, search, remove, and visit data in the `h` hash table.

The program tests the `HashTable` instance `h` by carrying out the following tasks:

1. Inserts 20 instances of `cString` in `h`. The program uses a `for` loop statement to insert the strings `AAAAA` to `TAAAA`. Each iteration alters the `s` string and then inserts it in the hash table by calling the `insertItem` function.

2. Searches for the strings AAAAA to TAAAA in h. The program uses a for loop to search for each string by calling the search function. If the search function returns true, the program displays the index of the matching string and the matching string itself; otherwise, the program displays a line informing you that the searched string is absent in the hash table. The outcome of each iteration appears on a separate line. When the results of all iterations are displayed, the program waits for you to press a key.
3. Visits the hash-table entries using the getFirstNode and getNextNode functions. The output shows you a map of the hash-table entries. Colliding entries are displayed on the same line and separated with two dashes. The program first calls the getFirstNode function and assigns its result to the ok Boolean variable. The program then uses a while loop to iterate as long as the ok variable is true. Each iteration performs the following tasks:
    1. Displays the string of the last visited hash-table entry.
    2. Calls the getNextNode function and assigns the function result to the ok variable.
    3. Sends a new line if the isfirst variable is true; otherwise, sends two dashes when ok is true.
    4. Once the strings are displayed, the program waits for you to press a key.
4. Deletes the strings EAAAA through OAAAA. The program uses a for loop to delete the targeted strings by calling the remove function. If the remove function returns false, the program displays a warning message that the sought string was not removed because it was not found.
5. Repeats step 2 to search for strings AAAAA to TAAAA. This time, the strings deleted (EAAAA through OAAAA) in the previous steps are not found. The program informs you that these strings are not in the hash table.
6. Repeats step 3 to display the hash table map for the trimmed hash table.

Listing 20.3. The source code for the TSHASH1.CPP test program.

```
#include <iostream.h>
#include "video.h"
#include "string.hpp"
#include "hashtabl.cpp"
```

```
unsigned hashFunction(cString& s, unsigned modulo)
{
  return s.hash(modulo);
}

main()
{
    char akey;
    HashTable<cString> h(23, hashFunction);
    cString s("AAAA");
    unsigned i;
    boolean ok, isfirst;

    clrscr();
    // insert 20 elements
    for(i = 1; i < 21; i++) {
        s[0] = char(64 + i);
        h.insertItem(s);
    }
    // search for the elements
    for(i = 1; i < 21; i++) {
        s[0] = char(64 + i);
        cout.width(2);
        if (h.search(s))
            cout << i << "   " << s.getstr() << '\n';
        else
            cout << "no match for " << s.getstr() << '\n';
    }
    cout << "\npress any key to visit and map hash nodes ";
    getch();
    cout << '\n';
    clrscr();
    ok = h.getFirstNode(s); // visit first node
    while (ok) {
        cout << s.getstr();
        ok = h.getNextNode(s, isfirst);
        if (isfirst)
            cout << '\n';
        else {
            if (ok)
                cout << "--";
```

continues

Listing 20.3. continued

```
        }
    }
    cout << "\n\npress any key to delete elements 5 through 14";
    getch(); clrscr();
    clrscr();
    // delete members 5 through 14
    s = "AAAA";
    for(i = 5; i < 15; i++) {
        s[0] = char(64 + i);
        ok = h.remove(s);
        if (!ok)
            cout << "did not delete " << s.getstr() << '\n';
    }
    if (! ok) {
        cout << "press any key ";
        getch(); cout << '\n';
    }
    // view set of strings
    for(i = 1; i < 21; i++) {
        s = "AAAA";
        s[0] = char(64 + i);;
        cout.width(2);
        if (h.search(s))
            cout << i << "   " <<
                    s.getstr() << " was found\n";
        else
            cout << i << "   " <<
                    s.getstr() << " was NOT found\n";
    }
    cout << '\n';
    cout << "press any key to visit and map hash table";
    getch(); clrscr();
    // visit hash-table node
    ok = h.getFirstNode(s);
    while (ok) {
        cout << s.getstr();
        ok = h.getNextNode(s, isfirst);
        if (isfirst)
            cout << '\n';
```

```
        else {
            if (ok)
                cout << "--";
        }
    }
    cout << "\n\npress any key to end the program... ";
    getch();

    return 0;
}
```

Let's look at the second test program, which involves the user-defined `chemElem` class. Listing 20.4 shows the source code for the TSHASH2.CPP test program. The class models the basic information of chemical elements. The data members of the `chemElem` class are as follows:

- The `name` member, which is an instance of `cString` that stores the name of an element.
- The `symbol` member, which is an instance of `cString` that stores the symbol of an element. Symbols of chemical elements are either one or two characters. The first character always is an uppercase letter. The second character (if used) always is a lowercase letter.
- The `atomicNumber` member, which stores the atomic number of an element. The atomic number is to chemical elements what social security numbers are to people.
- The `atomicWeight` member, which stores the atomic weight of an element.

Of the previous data members, only the `name` member is used in determining the hash address of a `chemElem` instance. The remaining members are considered secondary members. The program demonstrates the following:

- The use of certain data members to obtain the hash address
- The retrieval of secondary members using the `HashTable::search` function

The `chemElem` class defines a minimal set of functions that include:

- A default class constructor.
- The `assign` function, with which you can assign values to the data members of a `chemElem` class instance.

- The `display` function, which displays the members of the class.
- The `hashNames` friend function, which is the hash function required by the `HashTable` class.
- The set of relational operators.
- The stream insertion operator (<<).

The `main` function in the test program creates the following instances of various classes:

- The instance `h` of the `HashTable` class. This object is the tested hash table that contains 23 entries and uses the `hashNames` hash function.
- The array of the `chemElem` class, `b`. This array stores up to ten instances of `chemElem`.
- The instance `c` of `chemElem`. The program uses this instance to assemble the data for the instances of `chemElem` and then stores them in the `b` array.

The test program performs the following tasks:

1. Initializes the array of `chemElem` instances, `b`. The process involves calling the `chemElem::assign` function to assign data to `c`, an instance of `chemElem`. The program then uses the `Array::operator[]` and the `chemElem::operator=` to assign the `c` object to an element of the `b` array.
2. Inserts the elements of the `b` array in the `h` hash table. This task uses a `for` loop statement. Each loop iteration calls the `HashTable::insertItem` function and supplies it with the `b[i]` argument.
3. Searches for the elements of the `b` array in the `h` hash table. The program uses a decrementing `for` loop to search for the elements of `b`, starting with the last element at index 9. Each iteration displays the name of the sought chemical element at the bottom of the screen and then pauses. The pause slows down the test program and prevents it from promptly displaying the entire output.

   The program assigns the `name` member of the searched array member, `b[i]`, to the `name` element of the `c` object. The other data members, which are secondary members, are assigned dummy values. The dummy value enables you to verify that the `HashTable::search` function is really accessing the values of the secondary members.

The function calls the `HashTable::search` function. If the result of that function is `true`, the program displays the data members of the `c` object. Otherwise, the program displays a message reflecting that the `c` object is not in the hash table. This search occurs using a time-delay function (the program uses the delay function which is prototyped in the dos.h header file), preventing the need to press any key while the search is in progress. Figure 20.5 shows the output at this stage. Once the search is complete, you must press any key to view the hash-table map of the `h` object.

```
9:    Copper  (Cu)  has an atomic number = 29 and an atomic wt.  = 63.5
8:      Iron  (Fe)  has an atomic number = 26 and an atomic wt.  = 55.8
7: Magnesium  (Mg)  has an atomic number = 12 and an atomic wt.  = 24.3
6:   Calcium  (Ca)  has an atomic number = 20 and an atomic wt.  = 40
5:   Bromine  (Br)  has an atomic number = 35 and an atomic wt.  = 79.9
4:  Chlorine  (Cl)  has an atomic number = 17 and an atomic wt.  = 35.5
3:   Silicon  (Si)  has an atomic number = 14 and an atomic wt.  = 28.1
2:    Sodium  (Na)  has an atomic number = 11 and an atomic wt.  = 23
1:    Nickel  (Ni)  has an atomic number = 28 and an atomic wt.  = 58.7
0:      Neon  (Ne)  has an atomic number = 10 and an atomic wt.  = 20.1

press any key to visit and may hash nodes

searching for Neon
```

Figure 20.5. The output of the search for the various elements in the hash table of program TSHASH2.CPP.

4. Visits the hash-table entries using the `getFirstNode` and `getNextNode` functions. The output shows you a map of the hash-table entries. Colliding entries are displayed on the same line and separated by two dashes. The program first calls the `getFirstNode` function and assigns its result to the `ok` Boolean variable. The program then uses a `while` loop to iterate as long as the `ok` variable is `true`. Each iteration performs the following:

   1. Displays the name of a chemical obtained at the last visited hash-table entry.

   2. Calls the `getNextNode` function and assigns the function result to the `ok` variable.

   3. Sends a new line if the `isfirst` variable is `true`. Otherwise, emits two dashes when `ok` is `true`.

Figure 20.6 shows the hash-table map produced by this task. Once the strings are displayed, the program waits for you to press a key in order to end the test program.

```
 Chlorine
   Copper   -->   Iron
Magnesium
   Nickel
  Silicon
     Neon
  Bromine   -->   Sodium
  Calcium

press any key to end the program...
```

Figure 20.6. The hash-table map for the TSHASH2.CPP test program.

Listing 20.4. The source code for the TSHASH2.CPP test program.

```
/*
  Program to test the hash table with a user-defined class.
*/

#include <iostream.h>
#include "video.h"
#include <dos.h>
#include "string.hpp"
#include "array.cpp"
#include "hashtabl.cpp"

const unsigned wait = 2000;

class chemElem
{
   public:
     cString name;
     cString symbol;
     int atomicNumber;
     double atomicWeight;

     chemElem() { }
     void assign(cString aName,
                 cString aSymbol,
                 int atomicNum,
                 double atomicWt);
     void display();
```

```
    friend unsigned hashNames(chemElem& aChemElem,
                              unsigned tableSize)
      { return aChemElem.name.hash(tableSize); }
    chemElem& operator =(chemElem& aChemElem);
    int operator <(chemElem& aChemElem)
      { return name < aChemElem.name; }
    int operator <=(chemElem& aChemElem)
      { return name <= aChemElem.name; }
    int operator >(chemElem& aChemElem)
      { return name > aChemElem.name; }
    int operator >=(chemElem& aChemElem)
      { return name >= aChemElem.name; }
    int operator ==(chemElem& aChemElem)
      { return name == aChemElem.name; }
    int operator !=(chemElem& aChemElem)
      { return name != aChemElem.name; }
    friend ostream& operator <<(ostream& os, chemElem& aChemElem);
};

void chemElem::assign(cString aName,
                      cString aSymbol,
                      int atomicNum,
                      double atomicWt)
{
    name = aName;
    symbol = aSymbol;
    atomicNumber = atomicNum;
    atomicWeight = atomicWt;
}

chemElem& chemElem::operator =(chemElem& aChemElem)
{
    name = aChemElem.name;
    symbol = aChemElem.symbol;
    atomicNumber = aChemElem.atomicNumber;
    atomicWeight = aChemElem.atomicWeight;
    return *this;
}

void chemElem::display()
```

continues

Listing 20.4. continued

```
{
    cout.width(10);
    cout << name.getstr() << " (" << symbol.getstr() << ") ";
    cout.width(3);
    cout << "has an atomic number = " << atomicNumber;
    cout.width(5);
    cout << " and an atomic wt. = " << atomicWeight;
}

ostream& operator <<(ostream& os, chemElem& aChemElem)
{
  os << aChemElem.atomicNumber << " "
     << aChemElem.atomicWeight
     << aChemElem.symbol << " "
     << aChemElem.name;
  return os;
}

main()
{
    HashTable<chemElem> h(23, hashNames);
    Array<chemElem> b(10);
    chemElem c;
    int posy;
    boolean ok, isfirst;

    clrscr();

    // initialize the array b
    c.assign("Neon",      "Ne",  10,  20.1); b[0] = c;
    c.assign("Nickel",    "Ni",  28,  58.7); b[1] = c;
    c.assign("Sodium",    "Na",  11,  23.0); b[2] = c;
    c.assign("Silicon",   "Si",  14,  28.1); b[3] = c;
    c.assign("Chlorine",  "Cl",  17,  35.5); b[4] = c;
    c.assign("Bromine",   "Br",  35,  79.9); b[5] = c;
    c.assign("Calcium",   "Ca",  20,  40.0); b[6] = c;
    c.assign("Magnesium", "Mg",  12,  24.3); b[7] = c;
    c.assign("Iron",      "Fe",  26,  55.8); b[8] = c;
    c.assign("Copper",    "Cu",  29,  63.5); b[9] = c;
```

```
// insert 10 elements
for(int i = 0; i < 10; i++)
    h.insertItem(b[i]);

// search for the elements
for(i = 9; i >= 0; i--) {
    posy = wherey();
    gotoxy(1, 24);
    clreol();
    cout << "searching for " << b[i].name.getstr();
    delay(wait);
    gotoxy(1, posy);
    c.name = b[i].name;
    c.symbol = "";
    c.atomicNumber = 0;
    c.atomicWeight = 0.0;
    if (h.search(c)) {
        cout.width(2);
        cout << i << " : ";
        c.display();
        cout << '\n';
    }
    else
        cout << "no match for " <<  c.symbol.getstr() << '\n';
    delay(wait);
}
cout << "\npress any key to visit and map hash nodes ";
getch(); cout << '\n';
clrscr();
ok = h.getFirstNode(c); // visit first node
while (ok) {
    cout.width(10);
    cout << c.name.getstr();
    ok = h.getNextNode(c, isfirst);
    if (isfirst)
        cout << '\n';
    else {
        if (ok)
            cout << " --> ";
    }
}
```

continues

Listing 20.4. continued

```
    cout << "\n\npress any key to end the program...";
    getch();
    return 0;
}
```

The External Hash Table Class

External hash tables store their data in streams and come in two general types:

- The first type accommodates dynamic data and uses variable-length stream blocks to store the data.
- The second type uses random-access streams and fixed-length stream blocks.

This section presents a class that models the second type of external hash table. This approach simplifies the external hash table class because it does not contain pointers that access dynamic data. As a penalty for this simplification, the client template classes must not contain data members that are pointers. All information you want to store in an external hash table must be contained by the various data members of the client classes. Because the most suitable type of client class is the one that models the fixed-size records of a database, using external hash tables with fixed-size stream blocks is still practical.

Listing 20.5 contains the source code for the VMHSHTBL.HPP header file, which declares the `VmHashTable` class. The header file also contains the declaration of the `NO_HAS_ELEM_FOUND` constant, which is used to flag a no-match value in search operations that look for data in a hash-table bucket.

The `VmHashTable` class declares the following data members:

- The `VmHashTableSize` member, which stores the number of primary (or main) buckets in an external hash table.
- The `workSize` member, which stores the total number of entries in an external hash table.
- The `tableIndex`, `visitIndex`, and `entryIndex` members, which track the visited hash-table entries. The `tableIndex` member is the index of the currently

or most recently visited primary bucket. The `visitIndex` member is the index of the currently visited secondary bucket. The `entryIndex` member is the index of the last visited data in a primary or secondary bucket.

Maintaining two indices for the hash-table buckets is dictated by the fact that there are two types of buckets. When a primary bucket has one or more secondary buckets chained to it, you visit the data in the primary bucket first and then proceed to the data in secondary buckets. When you're finished with the secondary buckets, you must go on to the next primary bucket. This type of resumption requires the use of the `tableIndex` member.

- The `bucketSize` member, which stores the total byte size of each hash-table bucket. Bucket number `N` is located at an offset of `(bucketSize * N)` bytes from the beginning of the stream.
- The `elemsPerBucket` and `elemsInBucket` members, which store the maximum and current number of data items in a bucket.
- The `overflowIndex` member, which is the index of the chained bucket.
- The `maxBuckets` member, which stores the index of the last bucket. When an external hash table is first created, the `maxBuckets` member stores the value `VmHashTableSize - 1`.
- The `hfunc` member, which is the pointer to the hash function.
- The `errMsg` member, which stores the error message sent by the various functions.
- The `bucketArray` member, which is a pointer to the `T` template class. This member is used to create a dynamic array containing `elemsPerBucket` elements. The hashed data is read and written to the stream using the `bucketArray` member.
- The `f` data member, which supports the stream I/O operations for an external hash table.

The `VmHashTable` class declares a constructor, a destructor, and several protected and public functions. The functions of the `VmHashTable` class are a superset of the functions of the `HashTable` class. Although the two classes have functions that share the same name, these functions operate quite differently.

Listing 20.5. The source code for the vmhshtbl.hpp header file.

```
//////////////////////////////////////////////////////////////////////
//                                                                  //
//            Copyright (c) 1992 Namir Clement Shammas              //
//                                                                  //
//  Version: 1.0                                   Date 7/9/1992    //
//                                                                  //
//  Purpose: implements a template class of virtual hash tables.    //
//           The following operations are implemented:              //
//                                                                  //
//           + insertion                                            //
//           + search                                               //
//           + deletion                                             //
//           + sequential visit to the hash-table entries           //
//                                                                  //
//////////////////////////////////////////////////////////////////////

#include "comndata.h"
#include <string.h>
#include <fstream.h>

#ifndef _VMHSHTBL_HPP
#define _VMHSHTBL_HPP

const unsigned NO_HASH_ELEM_FOUND = 0xffff;

template<class T>
class VmHashTable
{

  protected:
    unsigned VmHashTableSize, // size of hash table
             workSize,        // number of entries
             tableIndex,      // visited primary-bucket index
             visitIndex,      // visit secondary-bucket index
             entryIndex,      // visited entry index
             bucketSize,      // byte size of a bucket
             elemsPerBucket,  // maximum number of elements
                              // per bucket
             elemsInBucket,   // actual number of elements
                              // in a bucket
```

```
              overflowIndex,    // index of chained bucket
              maxBuckets;       // index of the last bucket
     unsigned (*hfunc)(T&, unsigned); // hash function
     string80 errMsg;           // error message

     T blankElem;               // blank element
     T* bucketArray;            // array of elements in a bucket
     fstream f;                 // supporting stream

     void readBucket(unsigned bucketNumber);
     void writeBucket(unsigned bucketNumber,
                      boolean writeAll);
     unsigned linSearch(T& x);

  public:
     // ************** state manipulation methods **************
     VmHashTable() {};
     VmHashTable(
          unsigned maxVmHashTableSize,
          const char* HashFilename,
          unsigned theElemsPerBucket,
          T& emptyElem,
          unsigned (*aHashFunc)(T&, unsigned));
     ~VmHashTable();
     char* getErrorMessage();
     unsigned getWorkSize() const { return workSize; }

     // ************** object manipulation methods *************
     virtual boolean insertItem(T&);
     virtual boolean search(T&);
     virtual boolean remove(T&);
     virtual boolean getFirstNode(T&);
     virtual boolean getNextNode(T&, boolean&);
     boolean setTableIndex(unsigned);
};

#endif
```

Listing 20.6 shows the source code for the VMHSHTBL.CPP library file. The `VmHashTable` class declares a constructor that initializes the class instances. The parameter list of the constructor includes the following parameters:

- The `maxVmHashTableSize` parameter, which specifies the number of primary (or main) buckets.
- The `HashFilename` parameter, which specifies the name of the file opened as the input/output stream.
- The `theElemsPerBucket` parameter, which specifies the maximum number of elements in a bucket.
- The `emptyElem` parameter, which is an instance of the template class. This parameter specifies the empty or blank element. With blank elements in the output streams you can more easily examine the stream file using a text editor. The class constructor assigns the argument of `emptyElem` to the data member `blankElem`.
- The `aHashFunc` parameter, which specifies the hash function.

The class constructor performs the following tasks:

1. Assigns the arguments for the parameters to their corresponding data members. The constructor validates the arguments for the `maxVmHashTableSize` and `theElemsPerBucket` parameters before assigning them to their corresponding data members. The argument for the `HashFilename` parameter is not assigned to any data member. Instead, this parameter is used only in opening the random-access stream.
2. Initializes other data members, such as `workSize`, `maxBuckets`, `bucketSize`, and `blankElem`.
3. Allocates the dynamic space for the in-memory bucket. The `bucketArray` member is the pointer used to access the in-memory bucket array. The constructor creates an array of the `T` class with `elemsPerBucket` elements. If the allocation fails, the constructor assigns an error message to the `errMsg` member and exits.
4. Initializes the array accessed by `bucketArray` using the `emptyElem` data member.
5. Initializes the `overflowIndex` and `elemsInBucket` data members. Each bucket stores the values of `overflowIndex`, `elemsInBucket`, and the in-memory bucket array accessed by the `bucketArray` pointer.
6. Opens the stream for binary input and output. The constructor verifies that the stream is opened. If the stream is not opened, the constructor assigns an error message to the `errMsg` member and exits.

7. Fills the primary buckets with empty data. This task involves the `writeBucket` function.

The class destructor performs two simple tasks:

1. It deallocates the dynamic space for the in-memory bucket array.
2. It closes the input/output stream.

The `VmHashTable` class declares the following functions, which are relevant to the operations of external hash tables:

- The protected `readBucket` function, which reads a primary or secondary bucket. The function's single parameter specifies the bucket number, or index. When the `readBucket` function is called to read a primary bucket, the `bucketNumber` parameter represents a hash address. When the `readBucket` function is called to read a secondary bucket, the `bucketNumber` parameter represents an overflow index. The `readBucket` function first calls the `seekg` function to position the stream pointer at the proper bucket. The function then reads the `elemsInBucket` and `overflowIndex` data members and the in-memory bucket array.

- The protected `writeBucket` function, which writes data to a primary or secondary bucket. The function has two parameters, `bucketNumber` and `writeAll`. The `bucketNumber` parameter specifies the index of the bucket read. This index also is a hash-table address when writing a primary bucket. The `writeAll` parameter tells the `writeBucket` function whether to output blank elements. Passing a `true` argument for `writeAll` is required when writing a new bucket. The `writeBucket` function first calls the `seekg` function to position the stream pointer at the proper bucket. The function then writes the `elemsInBucket` and `overflowIndex` data members and the in-memory bucket array. When the `writeAll` parameter is `false`, the function writes only the first `elemsInBucket` elements of the in-memory bucket array.

- The protected `linSearch` function, which performs a simple linear search to look for the argument of the `x` parameter in the array accessed by the `bucketArray` pointer. The function returns the index of the matching array element, or `NO_HASH_ELEM_FOUND` when no match is found. If you have an in-memory bucket array with a relatively large number of elements, you might consider sorting these elements. In that case, you need to convert the `linSearch` function into a `binSearch` function so you can perform a binary search on the ordered elements in the in-memory bucket array.

- The `insertItem` function inserts an item in an external hash table. The function returns `true` if the insertion is successful; otherwise, it returns `false`. The function starts by calculating the hash address of the `x` insert item. The function then reads the primary bucket with the index that is the hash address. Next, comes the insertion step, which may be one of the following cases:
  - Case 1: The primary bucket is empty. In this case, the `x` item becomes the first item inserted in the targeted bucket. The `insertItem` function performs the following tasks:
    1. Assigns 0 and 1 to the `overflowIndex` and `elemsInBucket` members, respectively.
    2. Assigns the `x` item to the first array element accessed by the `bucketArray` pointer.
    3. Writes the updated bucket by calling the `writeBucket` function.
    4. Increments the `workSize` data member.
    5. Assigns `true` to the local `ok` Boolean variable.
  - Case 2: The primary bucket is not empty. In this case, the primary task is to determine whether item `x` already exists in the targeted external hash table. This process involves searching for `x` in the bucket that was just read and possibly in all other secondary buckets that are chained to the current primary bucket. The search starts with a call to the `linSearch` function. The `insertItem` function assigns the value returned by `linSearch` to the local variable index. The `insertItem` function uses a `while` loop statement to examine the outcome of the call to `linSearch` and determine what steps to take. The `while` loop iterates when the value in index is `NO_HASH_ELEM_FOUND` and when secondary buckets are chained to the primary bucket. Each loop iteration reads the chained bucket and searches for `x` in that bucket.

    If the previous search reveals that `x` is in an external hash table, the `insertItem` function assigns `false` to the local `ok` Boolean variable and performs no data insertion. Otherwise, data insertion proceeds. There are two subcases for inserting data:

    Case 2A: The targeted bucket (which may be a primary or secondary bucket) is not full. The function performs the following tasks:

1. Assigns `x` to the proper element of the in-memory bucket array.
2. Writes the updated bucket by calling the `writeBucket` function.

Case 2B: The targeted bucket is full. This means that the inserted `x` item must be written in a new bucket. The function performs the following tasks:

1. Increments the `maxBuckets` data member.
2. Assigns the value of `maxBuckets` to the `overflowIndex` data member. This task establishes a link between the last read bucket and the new one.
3. Updates the last read bucket by calling the `writeBucket` function.
4. Assigns 0 and 1 to the `overflowIndex` data members and `elemsInBucket`, respectively.
5. Assigns the `x` item to the first element of the in-memory bucket array.
6. Writes the new bucket by calling the `writeBucket` function. Notice that the argument for the `writeAll` parameter in this call is `true` because the `insertItem` function is writing data to a new bucket.

   Once the `insertItem` function handles either of the previous two subcases, the function increments the `workSize` data member and assigns `true` to the local `ok` Boolean variable. The function returns the value of `ok`.

- The `search` function, which determines whether the `x` item resides in an external hash table. The function returns a Boolean result that reflects the outcome of the search. If the `workSize` is 0, the function promptly returns `false`; otherwise, the function performs the following tasks:

  1. Calculates the hash address of `x`.
  2. Invokes a `do/while` loop to perform the search for `x`. Each loop iteration reads a bucket, calls the `linSearch` function, and assigns the value of the `overflowIndex` member to the `hashAddress` local variable. The loop iterates as long as the value in the `overflowIndex` member is positive and the value of the local variable index is `NO_HASH_ELEM_FOUND`. These conditions indicate that `x` has not been found and that more buckets are left to search.
  3. Returns the function value based on comparing the value of the local variable index with `NO_HASH_ELEM_FOUND`.

- The `remove` function, which deletes `x` from an external hash table. The function returns `true` if `x` was found and deleted; otherwise, it returns `false`. If the `workSize` member is 0, the function promptly returns 0. Otherwise, the function performs the following tasks:

  1. Calculates the hash address of `x`.
  2. Uses a `do/while` loop to search for `x` in an external hash table. This loop is similar to the one used in the search function.
  3. If `x` is found in an external hash table, the function proceeds with the deletion. Here are the various deletion cases:
     - Case 1: The `x` item matches the last or only element of the in-memory bucket array. In this case, the `remove` function decrements the member `elemsInBucket`.
     - Case 2: The `x` item is not the last member of the in-memory bucket array. In this case, the function copies the elements of that array to overwrite the element that matches `x`. The function also decrements the member `elemsInBucket`.
  4. Writes the updated current bucket by calling the `writeBucket` function. The bucket written to the stream may be an empty bucket.
  5. Returns the function result of `true`.

- The `getFirstNode` function, which visits the first entry in an external hash table. The `x` reference parameter returns the visited item. The first entry is the first element in the first nonempty primary bucket. The function returns `true` if the hash table is not empty or `false` if it is empty. The `getFirstNode` function performs the following tasks:

  1. Assigns 0 to the `tableIndex` member. The assigned value permits the `getFirstNode` function to begin searching for the first entry in the first primary bucket.
  2. Assigns 0 to the `entryIndex` member. The assigned value specifies the index of the sought element.
  3. Reads the targeted bucket specified by the `tableIndex` member. Because there is no guarantee that the first primary bucket contains data, the function must be ready to read the subsequent primary buckets until it finds a bucket that is not empty. This task is done next.

4. Searches for a bucket that is not empty using a `while` loop statement. The loop iterates as long as the `elemsInBucket` member is 0 and the `tableIndex` member is less than `VmHashTableSize`. This condition tells the loop to read another primary bucket as long as the currently read primary bucket is empty and there are more primary buckets to read. Each loop iteration increments the `tableIndex` member and then reads the next primary bucket.
5. If the value of the `tableIndex` member is less than the value of the `VmHashTableSize` member, the function assigns the first element of the in-memory bucket array to the `x` reference parameter. The function then returns `true`.
6. If the value of `tableIndex` is equal to the value of `VmHashTableSize`, the function returns `false`.

The task of the `getFirstNode` function is easier than that of `getNextNode`. This difference is due to the fact that `getFirstNode` searches for the first element in the first primary bucket that is not empty.

- The `getNextNode` function, which visits the next data item in an external hash table. The function returns `true` if the next item is found; otherwise, it returns `false`. The `x` reference parameter returns the visited item. The `firstEntry` reference parameter indicates whether `x` is the first element in a primary bucket. The function performs the following tasks:

1. Assigns `false` to the `firstEntry` parameter. This is the default value passed by the `firstEntry` parameter.
2. Reads the last visited bucket, specified by the `visitIndex` member.
3. Increments the `entryIndex` member to search for the next element in the currently read bucket.
4. If the value of `entryIndex` is less than the value of `elemsInBucket` , the function assigns the in-memory bucket element at `entryIndex` to the `x` parameter. The function then returns `true`.

5. If the value of entryIndex is not less than the value of elemsInBucket, the function searches first in any chained buckets and then in the next primary buckets. The function uses two while loop statements to search in the chained secondary buckets and in subsequent primary buckets.

6. The first while loop iterates as long as the value of overflowIndex is positive. Each loop iteration assigns the value of overflowIndex to visitIndex, reads the bucket specified by visitIndex, and determines if the bucket just read is not empty. If elements are in the bucket, the function sets the entryIndex member to 0, copies the first element of the in-memory bucket array to the x parameter, and returns true.

7. If the previous loop does not iterate or does not locate data in secondary buckets—keep in mind that the current deletion scheme allows empty secondary buckets to exist—the function increments the tableIndex member and proceeds with the second while loop.

8. The second while loop searches for data in subsequent primary buckets. Each iteration reads a primary bucket specified by the tableIndex member, assigns 0 to the entryIndex, assigns the value of tableIndex to member visitIndex, and determines whether the currently read bucket is empty. If elements are in the bucket, the function assigns true to the parameter firstEntry, copies the first element of the in-memory bucket array to the x parameter, and returns true. If the current primary bucket is empty, the function increments the value in member tableIndex.

9. Returns false if the second while loop stops iterating.

- The setTableIndex function, which enables you to assign a new value for the tableIndex data member. The function verifies that the new value is in the range of 0 to (VmHashTableSize - 1). If this condition is true, the function assigns the new index value to tableIndex and visitIndex, assigns 0 to member entryIndex, and returns true. If the supplied index is out of range, the function returns false.

Listing 20.6. The source code for the VMHSHTBL.CPP library file.

```
//////////////////////////////////////////////////////////////////////
//                                                                  //
//              Copyright (c) 1992 Namir Clement Shammas            //
//                                                                  //
```

```
//  Version: 1.0                                    Date 7/9/1992   //
//                                                                  //
//  Purpose: implements a template class of virtual hash tables.    //
//           The following operations are implemented:              //
//                                                                  //
//           + insertion                                            //
//           + search                                               //
//           + deletion                                             //
//           + sequential visit to the hash-table entries           //
//                                                                  //
//////////////////////////////////////////////////////////////////////

#include "vmhshtbl.hpp"

/////////////////////////////////////////////////////////////////////
//
template<class T>
VmHashTable<T>::VmHashTable(unsigned maxVmHashTableSize,
                            const char* HashFilename,
                            unsigned theElemsPerBucket,
                            T& emptyElem,
                            unsigned (*aHashFunc)(T&, unsigned))
//
// Purpose: initializes a hash table.
//
// Parameters:
//
//   input: maxVmHashTableSize - the size of the hash table.
//          aHashFunc - the hash function.
//
{
    VmHashTableSize =
        (maxVmHashTableSize == 0) ? 1 : maxVmHashTableSize;
    maxBuckets = VmHashTableSize - 1;
    elemsPerBucket = (theElemsPerBucket == 0) ? 1
                                              : theElemsPerBucket;
    workSize = 0;
    bucketSize = elemsPerBucket * sizeof(T) + 2 * sizeof(unsigned);
    // assign hash function to member hfunc
    hfunc = aHashFunc;
```

continues

Listing 20.6. continued

```
    // create the hash-table buffer
    bucketArray = new T[elemsPerBucket];

    if (!bucketArray) {
      strcpy(errMsg, ALLOCATE_ERROR);
      return;
    }

    // create the buffer
    for (unsigned i = 0; i < elemsPerBucket; i++)
      *(bucketArray + i) = emptyElem;
    blankElem = emptyElem;
    overflowIndex = 0; // set default overflow overflowIndex
    elemsInBucket = 0; // initial number of elements in a bucket
    // open the stream
    f.open(HashFilename, ios::in | ios::out | ios::binary);
    if (!f.good()) {
      strcpy(errMsg, "Cannot open stream");
      return;
    }
    for (i = 0; i < VmHashTableSize; i++)
      writeBucket(i, true);
}

////////////////////////////////////////////////////////////////////
//
template<class T>
VmHashTable<T>::~VmHashTable()
//
// Purpose: removes a hash-table object.
//
{
    // remove the bucket buffer elements
    delete [] bucketArray;
    // close the stream
    f.close();
}
```

```
/////////////////////////////////////////////////////////////////////
//
template<class T>
char* VmHashTable<T>::getErrorMessage()
//
// Purpose: returns the string stored in member errMsg and
// clears the string in that member.
//
{
    string80 s;

    strcpy(s, errMsg);
    errMsg[0] = '\0';
    return s;
}

/////////////////////////////////////////////////////////////////////
//
template<class T>
void VmHashTable<T>::readBucket(unsigned bucketNumber)
//
// Purpose: reads the bucket number bucketNumber.
//
// Parameters:
//
//    input: bucketNumber - the index of the bucket read.
//
{
  T* p = bucketArray;

  f.seekg((long)bucketSize * bucketNumber);
  // read the number of elements in this bucket
  f.read((char*)&elemsInBucket, sizeof(unsigned));
  // read the bucket overflow overflowIndex
  f.read((char*)&overflowIndex, sizeof(unsigned));
  for (unsigned i = 0; i < elemsInBucket; i++, p++)
    f.read((char*)p, sizeof(T));
  for (i = elemsInBucket; i < elemsPerBucket; i++, p++)
    *p = blankElem;
}
```

continues

Listing 20.6. continued

```
////////////////////////////////////////////////////////////////////
//
template<class T>
void VmHashTable<T>::writeBucket(unsigned bucketNumber,
                                 boolean writeAll)
//
// Purpose: write data to the bucket number bucketNumber.
//
// Parameters:
//
//    input: bucketNumber - the index of the output bucket.
//           writeAll - include blank data.
//
{
  T* p = bucketArray;

  f.seekg((long)bucketSize * bucketNumber);
  // write the number of elements in this bucket
  f.write((const char*)&elemsInBucket, sizeof(unsigned));
  // write the bucket overflow overflowIndex
  f.write((const char*)&overflowIndex, sizeof(unsigned));
  for (unsigned i = 0; i < elemsInBucket; i++, p++)
    f.write((const char*)p, sizeof(T));
  if (writeAll) {
    // write balance of bucket elements using the blank element
    for (i = elemsInBucket; i < elemsPerBucket; i++)
      f.write((const char*)&blankElem, sizeof(T));
  }
}

////////////////////////////////////////////////////////////////////
//
template<class T>
unsigned VmHashTable<T>::linSearch(T& x)
//
// Purpose: performs a simple linear search to locate x in
// the array of bucket elements. The function returns the
// index of the matching element or NO_HASH_ELEM_FOUND
// if no match is found.
//
```

```
// Parameters:
//
//    input: x - the search data.
//
{
  unsigned i = 0;
  boolean notFound = true;

  while (i < elemsInBucket && notFound)
    if (x != *(bucketArray + i))
      i++;
    else
      notFound = false;

  if (notFound)
    return NO_HASH_ELEM_FOUND;
  else {
    x = *(bucketArray + i);
    return i;
  }
}

/////////////////////////////////////////////////////////////////////
//
template<class T>
boolean VmHashTable<T>::insertItem(T& x)
//
// Purpose: builds a hash table by inserting a single item.
// This routine should be called several times to build
// a complete hash table. The function returns true if the
// x item is inserted; otherwise, the function returns false.
//
// Parameters:
//
//   input: x - the data inserted in the hash table.
//
{
    unsigned hashAddress;
    unsigned index;
    boolean ok = false;
```

continues

Listing 20.6. continued

```
    // get the hash table address
    hashAddress = (*hfunc)(x, VmHashTableSize);
    readBucket(hashAddress);

    // is the table entry not empty?
    if (elemsInBucket > 0) {
      // is x not in the hash table?
      index = linSearch(x);
      while (overflowIndex > 0 &&
             index == NO_HASH_ELEM_FOUND) {
        hashAddress = overflowIndex;
        readBucket(hashAddress);
        index = linSearch(x);
      }

      // data not already in hash table?
      if (index == NO_HASH_ELEM_FOUND) {
        // insert data in the current bucket?
        if (elemsInBucket < elemsPerBucket) {
          // copy x to the next available element in bucketArray
          *(bucketArray + elemsInBucket++) = x;
          // write the bucket
          writeBucket(hashAddress, false);
        }
        else {
          // write to a new bucket
          maxBuckets++;
          // set bucket overflow index
          overflowIndex = maxBuckets;
          // update the current bucket
          writeBucket(hashAddress, false);
          // prepare a new bucket
          overflowIndex = 0;
          elemsInBucket = 1;
          *bucketArray = x;
          writeBucket(maxBuckets, true);
        }
        workSize++;
        ok = true;
      }
```

```
      else {
         ok = false;
      }
    }
    else {
      // write first element in bucket
      overflowIndex = 0;
      elemsInBucket = 1;
      *bucketArray = x;
      writeBucket(hashAddress, false);
      workSize++;
      ok = true;
    }
    return ok;
}

////////////////////////////////////////////////////////////////////
//
template<class T>
boolean VmHashTable<T>::search(T& x)
//
// Purpose: searches the hash table for a specific key. The
// x parameter returns the nonkey data for the matching
// hash-table member. The function returns true if an
// element matches or false if no match is found.
//
// Parameters:
//
//   input: x - the sought data.
//
{
    unsigned hashAddress;
    unsigned index;

    if (workSize == 0)
      return false;

    hashAddress = (*hfunc)(x, VmHashTableSize);
    do {
      // read bucket
      readBucket(hashAddress);
```

continues

Listing 20.6. continued

```
        // search for x in bucket
        index = linSearch(x);
        hashAddress = overflowIndex;
      } while (overflowIndex > 0 && index == NO_HASH_ELEM_FOUND);

      return (index != NO_HASH_ELEM_FOUND) ? true : false;
}

///////////////////////////////////////////////////////////////////////
//
template<class T>
boolean VmHashTable<T>::remove(T& x)
//
// Purpose: deletes a specific entry from the hash table. The
// function returns true if an element matches or
// false if no match is found.
//
// Parameters:
//
//   input: x - the reference to the search data.
//
{
    unsigned hashAddress;
    unsigned index;

    if (workSize == 0)
      return false;

    hashAddress = (*hfunc)(x, VmHashTableSize);
    do {
      // read bucket
      readBucket(hashAddress);
      // search for x in bucket
      index = linSearch(x);
      if (overflowIndex > 0 && index == NO_HASH_ELEM_FOUND)
        hashAddress = overflowIndex;
    } while (overflowIndex > 0 && index == NO_HASH_ELEM_FOUND);

    // found element to delete
    if (index != NO_HASH_ELEM_FOUND) {
```

```
      if (index == (elemsInBucket - 1))
        elemsInBucket--;
      else {
        // overwrite deleted element
        for (unsigned i = index; i < (elemsInBucket - 1); i++)
          *(bucketArray + i) = *(bucketArray + i + 1);
        elemsInBucket--;
      }
      // write updated bucket to the stream
      writeBucket(hashAddress, false);
      return true;
    }
    else
      return false;
}

//////////////////////////////////////////////////////////////////////
//
template<class T>
boolean VmHashTable<T>::getFirstNode(T& x)
//
// Purpose: visits the first entry in the hash table. The function
// returns true if the hash table is not empty or false if
// otherwise.
//
// Parameters:
//
//   output: x - the reference to the data in the first entry.
//
{

    if (workSize == 0)
      return false;

    tableIndex = 0;
    entryIndex = 0;
    readBucket(tableIndex);
    // search for first entry in hash table
    while (elemsInBucket == 0 &&
           tableIndex < VmHashTableSize)
        readBucket(++tableIndex);
```

continues

Listing 20.6. continued

```
    // found a hash-table entry?
    if (tableIndex < VmHashTableSize) {
       x = bucketArray[entryIndex];
       visitIndex = tableIndex;
       return true;
    }
    else
        return false;
}

////////////////////////////////////////////////////////////////////
//
template<class T>
boolean VmHashTable<T>::getNextNode(T& x,
                                    boolean& firstEntry)
//
// Purpose: visits the next entry in the hash table. The function
// returns true if the next entry was found.
//
// Parameters:
//
//   output: x - the data in the next entry.
//           firstEntry - true if visited data is the first in a
//           primary bucket. The value is significant only if
//           the function result is true.
//
{
    if (workSize == 0)
      return false;

    firstEntry = false; // default assignment
    // read last visited bucket
    readBucket(visitIndex);
    entryIndex++;
    // more elements to visit in the bucket?
    if (entryIndex < elemsInBucket) {
      x = bucketArray[entryIndex];
      return true;
    }
```

```
    else {
      // are there chained buckets?
      while (overflowIndex > 0) {
        visitIndex = overflowIndex;
        readBucket(visitIndex);
        if (elemsInBucket > 0) {
          entryIndex = 0;
          x = *bucketArray;
          return true;
        }
      }
      // read another bucket in the main hash table
      tableIndex++;
      // no more main hash-table buckets to read?
      while (tableIndex < VmHashTableSize) {
        readBucket(tableIndex);
        entryIndex = 0;
        visitIndex = tableIndex;
        if (elemsInBucket > 0) {
          firstEntry = true;
          x = *bucketArray;
          return true;
        }
        tableIndex++;
      }
      return false;
    }
}

//////////////////////////////////////////////////////////////////////
//
template<class T>
boolean VmHashTable<T>::setTableIndex(unsigned newTableIndex)
//
// Purpose: assigns a new value for the tableIndex data member
// to redirect the action of the getNextNode function. The function
// returns true if a newTableIndex is in the range
// [0..VmHashTableSize-1] or false if otherwise. An out-of-range
// value for newTableIndex leaves the data member tableIndex
// unchanged.
```

continues

Listing 20.6. continued

```
//
// Parameters:
//
//   input: newTableIndex - the new value for tableIndex.
//
{
    if (newTableIndex < VmHashTableSize) {
        tableIndex = newTableIndex;
        visitIndex = tableIndex;
        entryIndex = 0;
        return true;
    }
    else
        return false;
}
```

Testing the VmHashTable Class

Let's look at a program to test the external hash-table class. Listing 20.7 shows the source code for the TSVMHSH1.CPP test program. The program tests the `VmHashTable` class with a class of fixed strings, `String5`, defined in the program. `String5` is a minimal class that models five-character strings. The test program declares the following constants:

- `EMPTY` defines the empty data string.
- `BASE` defines the first string. All other strings are derived from `BASE` by changing the first character.
- `HASH_ONE_CHAR` is a flag used in compiling the hash function. More about the role of this constant later.
- `TEST_SIZE` defines the number of strings to insert in the tested external hash table.

The `String5` class declares a class with a single data member and a minimal set of functions. The `str` data member stores up to six characters, including the null character. The class also declares three constructors. A few functions can access the

characters in the `str` member and obtain the length of the string stored in `str`. The `String5` class also includes a variety of operators:

- The assignment operator (=), with which you can copy one instance of `String5` into another.
- The access operator (`[]`), with which you can access the characters of the `str` member. To simplify matters, I omitted any range checking for the arguments of the parameter `index`.
- The set of relational operators.
- The insertion operator (<<), which supports stream output.

I chose to code the hash function as a separate function, defined outside the `String5` class. This function contains the `#ifdef` compiler directives that examine whether the `HASH_ONE_CHAR` identifier is defined. If it's defined, the compiler directs the hash function to calculate the returned result using only the first character. In contrast, if `HASH_ONE_CHAR` is not defined, the compiler uses the `while` loop that calculates the hash address using all the characters of the `s` string.

What's the difference? When `HASH_ONE_CHAR` is defined, the `hashFunction` function gives a good result. On the other hand, when the `HASH_ONE_CHAR` is not defined, the `hashFunction` function yields the same address for all the arguments used in the program. By this mediocre performance, you can actually see chained buckets in use. For the sake of learning how external hash tables work, you may tolerate this substandard performance of the `hashFunction` function.

The `main` function creates the `h` hash table with thirteen entries and specifies that the `hashFunction` function is the hash function for the instances of the `String5` class. The program also creates the `String5` instance `s` used to insert, search, remove, and visit data in `h`.

The program tests the `VmHashTable` instance `h` by performing the following tasks:

1. Inserts `TEST_SIZE` instances of `String5` in the `h` hash table. The program uses a `for` loop statement to insert the `AAAAA` to `OAAAA` strings. Each iteration prepares

the s string and inserts it into the hash table by calling the insertItem function.

2. Searches for the AAAAA to OAAAA strings in the h hash table. The program uses a for loop to search for each string by calling the search function. If the search function returns true, the program displays the index of the matching string and the matching string itself. Otherwise, the program displays a line informing you that the searched string is absent in the hash table. The outcome of each iteration appears on a separate line. When the results of all iterations are displayed, the program waits for you to press a key.
3. Visits the hash table entries using the getFirstNode and getNextNode functions (see Figure 20.7). The output shows a map of the hash table entries. The colliding entries are displayed on the same line and separated by two dashes. The program first calls the getFirstNode function and assigns its result to the ok Boolean variable. The program then uses a while loop to iterate as long as the ok variable is true. Each iteration performs the following tasks:
    1. Displays the string of the last visited hash table entry.
    2. Calls the getNextNode function and assigns the function result to the variable ok.
    3. Emits a new line if the isfirst variable is true. Otherwise, emits two dashes when ok is true.
    4. Once the strings are displayed, the program waits for you to press a key.
4. Deletes the strings GAAAA through IAAAA. The program uses a for loop to delete the targeted strings by calling the remove function. If the remove function returns false, the program displays a warning message that the sought string was not removed because it was not found.
5. Repeats step 2 to search for strings AAAAA to OAAAA. This time, the strings deleted in the previous steps (GAAAA through IAAAA) are not found. The program informs you that these strings are not in the hash table.
6. Repeats step 3 to display the hash-table map for the trimmed hash table.

```
AAAAA--NAAAA
BAAAA--OAAAA
CAAAA
DAAAA
EAAAA
FAAAA
GAAAA
HAAAA
IAAAA
JAAAA
KAAAA
LAAAA
MAAAA

press any key to delete elements 6 through 8
```

Figure 20.7. The hash-table map.

Listing 20.7. The source code for the TSVMHSH1.CPP test program.

```
#include <iostream.h>
#include <conio.h>
#include "string.hpp"
#include "vmhshtbl.cpp"

#define EMPTY "!!!!!"
#define BASE "AAAAA"
#define HASH_ONE_CHAR

const unsigned TEST_SIZE = 15;


class String5
{
  protected:
    char str[6];

  public:
    String5()
      { memset(str, 0, 6); }
    String5(const char* s);
    String5(String5& s)
      { strcpy(str, s.str); }
```

continues

Listing 20.7. continued

```
        char* getstr()
          { return str; }
        unsigned getLen()
          { return strlen(str); }

        String5& operator =(String5& s);
        char& operator[](unsigned index)
         { return str[index]; }

        int operator <(String5& s)
          { return strcmp(str, s.str) < 0; }
        int operator <=(String5& s)
          { return strcmp(str, s.str) <= 0; }
        int operator >(String5& s)
          { return strcmp(str, s.str) > 0; }
        int operator >=(String5& s)
          { return strcmp(str, s.str) >= 0; }
        int operator ==(String5& s)
          { return strcmp(str, s.str) == 0; }
        int operator !=(String5& s)
          { return strcmp(str, s.str) != 0; }

       friend ostream& operator <<(ostream& os, String5& s);
};

String5::String5(const char* s)
{
  if (strlen(s) < 6)
    strcpy(str, s);
  else {
    memcpy(str, s, 5);
    str[6] = '\0';
  }
}

String5& String5::operator =(String5& s)
{
  strcpy(str, s.str);
  return *this;
}
```

```
ostream& operator <<(ostream& os, String5& s)
{
  os << s.str;
  return os;
}
unsigned hashFunction(String5& s, unsigned modulo)
//
// Purpose: returns the hashing address 0..modulo-1.
//
// Parameters:
//
//    input: s - string begin hashed.
//           modulo - the size of the hash table.
//
{
   unsigned i = 0, y = 0;
   char p[sizeof(String5)];

   // copy string s to p
   strcpy(p, s.getstr());

#ifdef HASH_ONE_CHAR

     y = p[0] % modulo;

#else

     while (i < 6) {
        y = (y * 17 + i + 13 * p[5 - i]) % modulo;
        i++;
     }

#endif

   return y;
}

main()
{
    char akey;
    String5 s = String5(EMPTY);
```

continues

Listing 20.7. continued

```
VmHashTable<String5> h(13, "HASH1.DAT", 2, s, hashFunction);
unsigned i;
boolean ok, isfirst;

clrscr();
s = String5(BASE);
// insert 20 elements
for(i = 0; i < TEST_SIZE; i++) {
    s[0] = char(65 + i);
    h.insertItem(s);
}
// search for the elements
for(i = 0; i < TEST_SIZE; i++) {
    s[0] = char(65 + i);
    cout.width(2);
    if (h.search(s))
        cout << i << "   " << s << '\n';
    else
        cout << "no match for " << s << '\n';
}
cout << "\npress any key to visit and map hash nodes ";
getch();
cout << '\n';
clrscr();
ok = h.getFirstNode(s); // visit first node
while (ok) {
    cout << s;
    ok = h.getNextNode(s, isfirst);
    if (isfirst)
        cout << '\n';
    else {
        if (ok)
            cout << "--";
    }
}
cout << "\n\npress any key to delete elements "
     << (TEST_SIZE / 2 - 1) << " through "
     << (TEST_SIZE / 2 + 1) << '\n';
getch(); clrscr();
clrscr();
```

```
// delete members
s = String5(BASE);
for(i = TEST_SIZE / 2 - 1;
    i <= (TEST_SIZE / 2 + 1);
    i++) {
    s[0] = char(65 + i);
    ok = h.remove(s);
    if (!ok)
        cout << "did not delete " << s << '\n';
}
if (!ok) {
    cout << "press any key ";
    getch(); cout << '\n';
}
clrscr();
// view set of strings
for(i = 0; i < TEST_SIZE; i++) {
    s = String5(BASE);
    s[0] = char(65 + i);;
    cout.width(2);
    if (h.search(s))
        cout << i << "   " <<
                s << " was found\n";
    else
        cout << i << "   " <<
                s << " was NOT found\n";
}
cout << '\n';
cout << "press any key to visit and map hash table";
getch(); clrscr();
// visit hash-table node
ok = h.getFirstNode(s);
while (ok) {
    cout << s;
    ok = h.getNextNode(s, isfirst);
    if (isfirst)
        cout << '\n';
    else {
        if (ok)
            cout << "--";
```

continues

Listing 20.7. continued

```
        }
    }
    cout << "\n\npress any key to end the program... ";
    getch();

    return 0;
}
```

Summary

Hash tables are structures that enable quick data searching. This chapter presented C++ template classes that model internal and external hash tables. The chapter discussed the basics of hashing, hash functions, and data collision.

The internal hash table supports dynamic data and offers the following operations:

- Adding data in a hash table.
- Searching for data in a hash table.
- Deleting data from a hash table.
- Visiting the data in a hash table.

The internal hash table presented in this chapter uses AVL trees, instead of the more typical linked lists, to resolve collision among data in a hash table.

This chapter also presented a class that models external hash tables. The class stores data in buckets. Each bucket contains one or more data items. In the case of multiple items in a bucket, they are basically colliding data. External hash tables use primary and secondary buckets. Primary buckets are created when the external hash table is initialized. The number of primary buckets is fixed. Secondary buckets are overflow buckets, created as needed. Secondary buckets store additional colliding data that cannot be contained in the primary buckets.

The external hash table supports fixed-sized data and offers the following operations:

- Adding data in a hash table.
- Searching for data in a hash table.
- Deleting data from a hash table.
- Visiting the data in a hash table.

The M-Way Tree and the B-Tree

Chapter 18 focused on the binary tree and its variants, the AVL-tree and the red-black tree (a clever representation of the 2-3 multiway tree using a binary tree). This chapter concentrates on the memory-based multiway (also called *m-way*) tree and the disk-based B-tree. Although these tree types share similar fundamental tree-management operations, they differ in storage schemes and the amount of handled information.

Invented by Bayer and McCreight in 1972 (Bayer also invented the red-black tree), B-tree is the result of extensive research that focused on efficient ways to manage data in secondary storage (e.g., mass storage devices).

The M-Way Tree

M-way trees are designed to store two or more data items in a node. The letter *m* represents the order of the tree—the maximum number of links in a node. The binary tree is a 2-way tree. The simplest m-way tree that has multiple data items in a node, therefore, is a 3-way tree. The maximum number of data items in an m-way tree node is m-1.

Figure 21.1 shows a sample 5-way tree. The nodes of the tree accommodate up to 4 data items (the minimum number of items is 1). The maximum and minimum number of nodes in an m-way tree is a tree design parameter. Although the maximum number of items in a node of an m-way tree is systematically set to m-1, the minimum number of items does not need to be 1 for all values of *m*. The minimum number of items in a node should increase as the value of *m* increases. The technical literature suggests an approximate value of m / 2 using the expression (m / 2 -1).

Figure 21.1 also demonstrates that each m-way tree node contains the following information:

1. A sorted array that contains data items inserted in the tree.
2. An array of pointers that links a node with its child nodes.
3. A counter that stores the number of items in a node.

The basic operations of an m-way tree are

1. Data search—this process begins in the root node (as with binary trees) and proceeds to the appropriate child nodes. A data item search in a node must compare search data with sorted data items. Using a linear search is adequate in this case because the number of data items is small. This search determines
    - Whether a matching data item was found.
    - The search index, which points to the matching node element if such an element exists. If no matching node element exists, the index points to the child node link that must be used to continue to look for the search data.
2. Data insertion—this process begins with a search for the location to insert new data. The search points to the node that receives the new data. The insertion process is executed in one of the following ways:

- If the target node has not reached its full capacity, the new data is inserted into that node. The insertion maintains the order of the array of data in the node. This is the simplest data insertion case.
- If the target node is at maximum capacity, the insertion process divides the target node into two nodes, and the median element of the original node is pushed into the parent node.

The inserted new data item ends up in a leaf node.

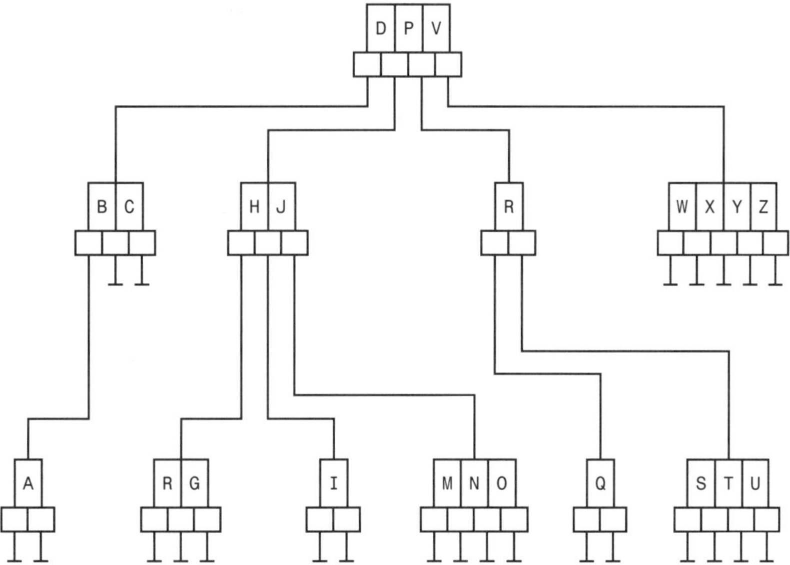

Figure 21.1. A sample m-way tree of the order 5.

3. Data deletion—this process removes a data item from a node and performs any required m-way tree rebalancing. Depending on the circumstances, delete data from an m-way tree in the following ways:
   - *Case 1: The deleted data item is in a leaf node that contains more than the minimum number of data items.* In this case, simply remove the deleted data item from its host leaf node (refer to Figure 21.2).
   - *Case 2: The deleted data item is in an internal node.* In this case, promote the successor item in the child node (refer to Figure 21.3).

- *Case 3: The deleted data item is in a leaf node that has the minimum number of data items, and at least one neighboring node has more than the minimum number of items.* In this case, pull down the successor of the deleted data item from the parent node to replace the deleted item. The successor of the pulled-down item is moved to the same parent node (refer to Figure 21.4).
- *Case 4: The deleted data item is in a leaf node that has the minimum number of data items, and all neighboring nodes contain the minimum number of items.* In this case, the m-way tree combines some of the leaf nodes with a data item in the parent node. Additional reorganization may be required to maintain a minimum number of items in higher level nodes (refer to Figure 21.5).

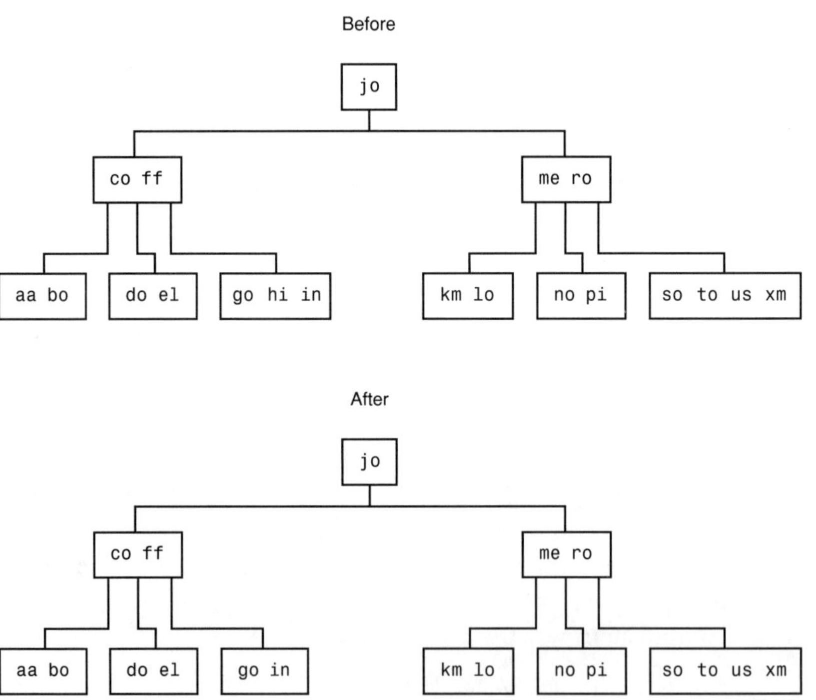

Figure 21.2. A Case 1 deletion (note the deletion of string `hi`).

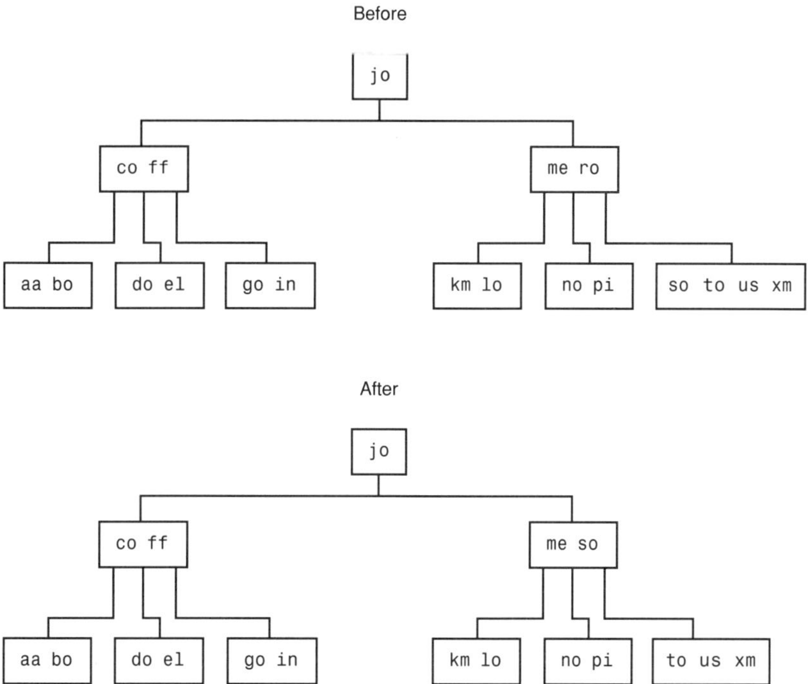

Figure 21.3. A Case 2 deletion (note the deletion of string `ro`).

The MWTree Class

It may be useful to look at a template C++ class that models the m-way tree. Listing 21.1 contains the source code for the mwtree.hpp header file. This file declares the `MWTree` class and contains the constants `MWTREE_ORDER`, `MWTREE_MAX`, and `MWTREE_MIN` to define the order, the maximum number of items in a node, and the minimum number of items in a node. The header file also declares the template structure `MWTstruct` to model an m-way tree node. The structure contains the following members:

1. The `count` member stores the number of data items in a node.
2. The array `data` stores the data items in a node. The `MWTstruct` structure declares the array size to be `MWTREE_MAX + 1`. The range of used elements is 1 to `MW_TREE_MAX`. The element at index 0 is not used.

3. The array `nodeLink` stores the pointers to the child nodes. The `MWTstruct` structure declares the array size to be `MWTREE_MAX + 1`. The range of used elements is 0 to `MW_TREE_MAX`.

4. The `marked` member stores the index of the next item to visit. This information enables the tree traversal member functions to select the next item to visit.

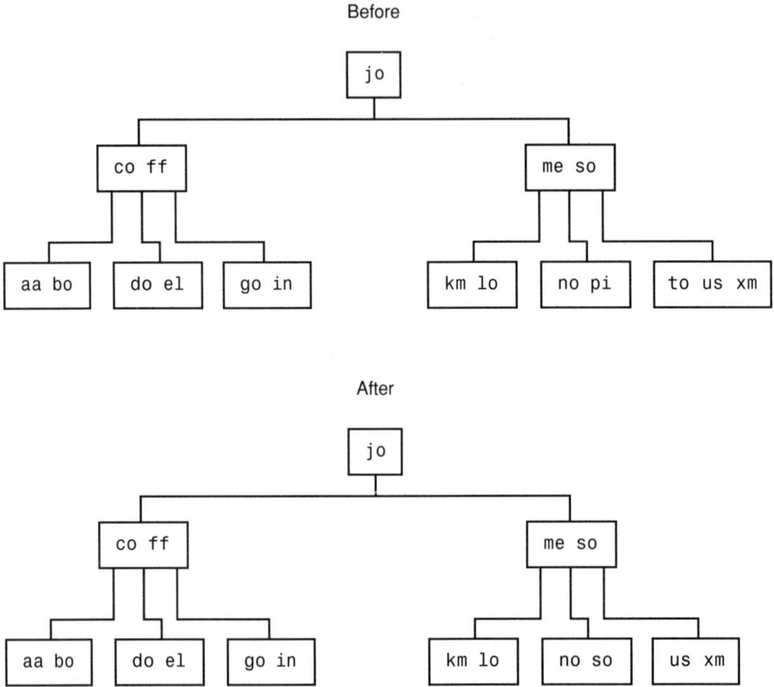

Figure 21.4. A Case 3 deletion (note the deletion of string `pi`).

The class `MWtree` declares a number of data members and member functions (note the following data members):

1. `errMsg` stores the error message text produced by various member functions.
2. `numData` stores the number of data items in an instance of class `MWtree`.
3. `numNodes` members contain the number of nodes in an instance of class `MWtree`.
4. `nodePtr` is the pointer to visited m-way tree nodes.

5. `root` is the pointer to the root node of the m-way tree.
6. `visitIndex` stores the index of the currently visited data item in the currently visited node.
7. The Boolean `seekNode` member is used as a special flag to traverse the nodes of an m-way tree.

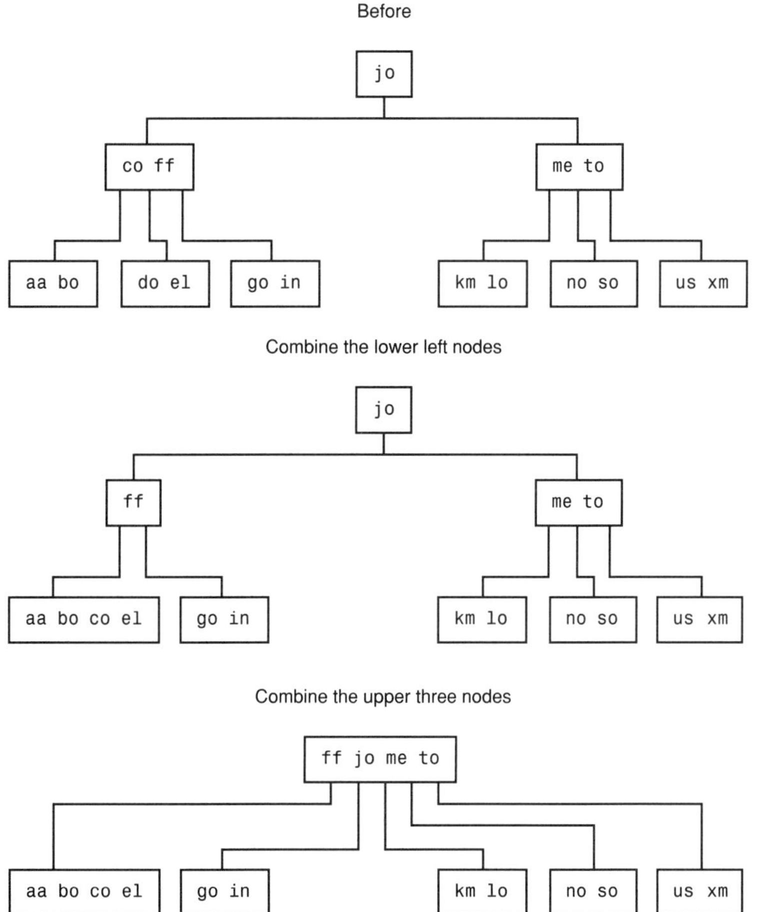

Figure 21.5. A Case 4 deletion (note the deletion of string `do`).

The class declaration contains a number of member functions. Only a few member functions, however, are defined within the class declaration:

1. A class destructor, which invokes the `clear` member function to clear an instance of the `MWtree` class.
2. `getNumData` returns the number of data items in an instance of class `MWtree`.
3. `getNumNodes` returns the number of nodes in an instance of class `MWtree`.
4. The `clear` member function, which invokes the `clearNode` member function and passes the argument of the root data member.

Listing 21.1. The source code for mwtree.hpp header file.

```
//////////////////////////////////////////////////////////////////////
//                                                                  //
//            Copyright (c) 1992 Namir Clement Shammas              //
//                                                                  //
//  Version: 1.0.0                               Date 8/11/92       //
//                                                                  //
//  Purpose: implements class of m-way trees that have the          //
//           following functionality:                               //
//                                                                  //
//             + inserts data.                                      //
//             + searches for data.                                 //
//             + deletes data.                                      //
//             + visits the nodes of the multiway tree.             //
//                                                                  //
//                                                                  //
//////////////////////////////////////////////////////////////////////

#include "comndata.h"

#ifndef _MWTREE_HPP
#define _MWTREE_HPP

const unsigned MWTREE_ORDER = 5;
const unsigned MWTREE_MAX = MWTREE_ORDER - 1;
const unsigned MWTREE_MIN = MWTREE_ORDER / 2;

template<class T>
```

```
struct MWTstruct {
    unsigned count;
    T data[MWTREE_MAX+1];
    MWTstruct<T>* nodeLink[MWTREE_MAX+1];
    unsigned marked;// visit flag
};

template<class T>
class MWtree
{

  protected:
    string80 errMsg;        // error message
    unsigned numData,
             numNodes,
             visitIndex;
    MWTstruct<T> *nodePtr;
    MWTstruct<T> *root;
    boolean seekNode;

    boolean searchMWtree(T& x,
                         MWTstruct<T> *rootPtr,
                         MWTstruct<T>* &nodePtr,
                         unsigned &pos);
    boolean searchNode(T& x,
                       MWTstruct<T> *ptr,
                       unsigned &pos);
    boolean pushDown(T& x, MWTstruct<T>* ptr,
                     T& item, MWTstruct<T>* &itemRST);
    void pushIn(T& x, MWTstruct<T>* xRST,
                MWTstruct<T>* ptr, unsigned pos);
    void cutNode(T& x, MWTstruct<T>* xRST,
                 MWTstruct<T>* ptr, unsigned pos,
                T& y, MWTstruct<T>* &yRST);
    void recDelete(T& x, MWTstruct<T> *ptr, boolean& found);
    void trim(MWTstruct<T> *ptr, unsigned pos);
    void successor(MWTstruct<T> *ptr, unsigned pos);
    void restore(MWTstruct<T> *ptr, unsigned pos);
    void shiftRight(MWTstruct<T> *ptr, unsigned pos);
    void shiftLeft(MWTstruct<T> *ptr, unsigned pos);
    void compact(MWTstruct<T> *ptr, unsigned pos);
```

continues

Listing 21.1. continued

```
    void clearNode(MWTstruct<T>* &rootPtr);
    void clearMarks(MWTstruct<T>* rootPtr);
    void visitTree(MWTstruct<T>* rootPtr,
                   MWTstruct<T>* &node);

  public:
    // ************** state manipulation methods **************
    MWtree();
    ~MWtree()
      { clear(); }

    char* getErrorMessage();
    unsigned getNumData() const
      { return numData; }
    unsigned getNumNodes() const
      { return numNodes; }

    // ************** object manipulation methods *************
    virtual boolean insert(T& x);
    virtual boolean search(T& x);
    virtual boolean remove(T& x);
    virtual boolean getFirstNode(T& x);
    virtual boolean getNextNode(T& x);
    virtual void clear()
      { clearNode(root); }
};
#endif
```

Listing 21.2 shows the source code for the MWTREE.CPP library file. This file contains the definitions for the constructor and member functions of class `MWtree`.

The `MWtree` class has a single constructor, which is the default constructor. This constructor initializes the instance of class `MWtree` by assigning `NULL` to the root member, zeros to the `numData` and `numNodes` members, and a null string to the `errMsg` member. The constructor allocates no dynamic memory.

The following subsections present the various member functions grouped by the operations they perform.

Data Search

The MWtree class has three member functions that are involved in data searches. These member functions are:

1. The search member function searches for a specific data item in the m-way tree. The current implementation of the MWtree class does not support data nodes with duplicate key information. The Boolean function returns true if the item x is found in the targeted m-way tree. If item x is not found, the function yields False. The function calls the protected member function searchMWtree to perform the search.
2. The recursive and protected searchMWtree function searches the m-way tree to locate a node that contains an item matching the search-data parameter x. The rootPtr parameter is the pointer to the currently searched node. The reference parameter nodePtr returns the pointer to the node that contains a matching data item. The reference parameter pos returns the index of the matching data item or yields the index for the appropriate insertion of a new data item. The Boolean function returns true if the item x is found in the targeted m-way tree. If item x is not found, the function yields false. If the function yields True, the reference parameters indicate the location of the matching item. If the function returns False, the same parameters yield the appropriate insertion location.
3. The Boolean protected searchNode function searches a node for an item that matches the argument for the search-data x. The parameter ptr is the pointer to the searched node. The reference parameter pos returns the index of the matching item or the index for the appropriate insertion of a new data item.

Data Insertion

The MWtree class contains a number of member functions used to insert new data items in the class instances:

1. The Boolean `insert` member function inserts the item `x` in an m-way tree. The function returns True if item `x` is successfully inserted. If item `x` is already in the m-way tree or if the possible dynamic allocation of new nodes fails, the function yields False. The function invokes the `search` member function to verify that item `x` does not already exist in the tree. The function also invokes the Boolean function `pushDown` to determine whether there is a new root (and growth in tree height).
2. The protected and recursive `pushDown` function inserts the data item `x` in an m-way tree. The parameter `ptr` is the pointer to the manipulated node. The reference parameters `item` and `itemRST`, respectively, are the median item and median-right subtrees. These parameters are used to help rebalance the tree. The Boolean function returns True if there is a need to increase the tree height. If there is no need to increase the height, the function yields False. The function calls the protected member function `pushIn` to insert a new data item or the protected member function `cutNode` if node splitting is needed.
3. The protected `pushIn` function inserts the new data item `x` and its right subtree pointer in a node. The parameter `x` and `XRST`, respectively, represent the inserted item and its right subtree pointer. The parameter `ptr` is the pointer to the manipulated node. The parameter `pos` is the insertion index. The new information is inserted at index `pos + 1`.
4. The protected `cutNode` member function splits the node accessed by parameter `ptr` with key data `x` and subtree pointer `xRST` at index `pos`. The resulting nodes are accessed by pointers `ptr` and `yRST`. The reference parameter `y` is the median key.

Data Deletion

The `MWtree` class declares the following member functions to handle both the deletion of data from the tree and the ensuing tree rebalance:

1. The Boolean `remove` function deletes the item `x` from the m-way tree. The function returns True if item `x` is successfully deleted from the tree. If item `x` does not exist in the tree, the function yields False. The function invokes the recursive member function `recDelete` to perform the requested deletion. After the `recDelete` function returns, the `remove` function decrements the `numData`

data member and handles the case of an empty root, which may result after the deletion. In this case, the function pulls a data item from the smallest child node.

2. The recursive and protected `recDelete` function removes the item `x` from an m-way tree. The parameter `ptr` is the pointer to the searched and manipulated tree. The reference parameter found is a Boolean flag returned by the function. The function calls the `searchNode` member function to search the node accessed by pointer `ptr`. If found, the function deletes the matching item from that node. If the node is a leaf, `recDelete` invokes the protected member function `trim`. If the node is not a leaf, `recDelete` calls the `successor` member function to replace the deleted item by its successor and then makes a recursive call. If the item `xis` is not found in the node accessed by pointer `ptr`, `recDelete` makes a recursive call to `search` in the appropriate child node.
3. The protected member function `trim` deletes a data item from a leaf node. The parameter `ptr` is the pointer to the targeted leaf node. The parameter `pos` is the index of deleted item.
4. The protected member function `successor` replaces a data item with its immediate successor. The parameter `ptr` is the pointer of the targeted node. The parameter `pos` is the index of the data item that is replaced by its successor.
5. The protected member function `restore` locates a data item and inserts it into a node to maintain a minimum number of items in a node. The parameter `ptr` is the pointer to the manipulated node. The parameter `pos` is the insertion index. The function deals with the case when the argument for parameter `pos` represents the leftmost, rightmost, and non-extreme keys. The function calls the member functions `shiftLeft`, `shiftRight`, and `compact` to help restore the required balance.
6. The protected member function `shiftRight` moves a data element to the right in a node. The parameter `ptr` is the pointer to the manipulated node. The parameter `pos` is the index of the shifted data item.
7. The protected member function `shiftLeft` moves a data element to the left in a node. The parameter `ptr` is the pointer to the manipulated node. The parameter `pos` is the index of the shifted data item.
8. The protected member function `compact` combines adjacent nodes. The parameter `ptr` is the pointer to the manipulated node. The parameter `pos` is the node merge index.

Clearing the M-Way Tree

The member function `clearNode` is a recursive function that is used to clear the nodes of an m-way tree. The function uses a `for` loop to recursively call itself to delete its child nodes. After the child nodes are deleted, `clearNode` deletes the current node that is accessed by the pointer `rootPtr`.

Traversing the M-Way Tree

Traversing the m-way tree is more complicated than traversing binary trees because each node contains multiple data items and links to multiple child nodes. The `MWtree` class offers the following member functions to support m-way tree traversing.

1. The recursive and protected `clearMarks` member function assigns 0 to the `mark` data member of each node. The function assigns 0 to the `mark` member of the current node and then uses a `for` loop to recursively call itself and process the child nodes.

2. The recursive and protected `visitTree` member function traverses the nodes of the m-way tree. The `rootPtr` parameter is the pointer to the currently searched tree. The reference parameter node returns the pointer to the visited node. To understand how the function `visitTree` works, refer to Figure 21.6, which contains a diagram of the general structure of an m-way tree node. Visiting each node proceeds as follows:

    - Visit the child node attached to link `L1`
    - Visit the data item `d1`
    - Visit the child node attached to link `L2`
    - Visit the data item `d2`
    - Visit the remaining child nodes and node data items by repeating the preceding pattern

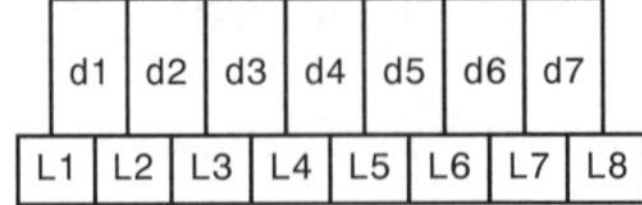

Figure 21.6. The general structure of an m-way tree node.

3. The `getFirstNode` member function initiates the m-way tree traversal. The Boolean function returns True if the visited tree is not empty. The reference parameter `x` returns the item of the first visited data item. The function calls `clearMarks` to set the marked data member in each node to 0. The function then calls `visitTree` to obtain the first data item in the tree.

4. The `getNextNode` member function retrieves the next data item in the m-way tree. The function yields True if there is a next item to retrieve. If there is no next item, the function returns False. The function calls `visitTree` to locate the next item. The `seekNode` data member is used to indicate the success or failure of the call to `visitTree`.

Listing 21.2. The source code for the MWTREE.CPP library file.

```
//////////////////////////////////////////////////////////////////////
//                                                                  //
//            Copyright (c) 1992 Namir Clement Shammas              //
//                                                                  //
//  Version: 1.0.0                                  Date 8/11/92    //
//                                                                  //
//  Purpose: implements class of m-way trees that have the          //
//           following functionality:                               //
//                                                                  //
//             + inserts data.                                      //
//             + searches for data.                                 //
//             + deletes data.                                      //
//             + visits the nodes of the multiway tree.             //
//                                                                  //
//                                                                  //
//////////////////////////////////////////////////////////////////////

#include <string.h>
#include "mwtree.hpp"

/////////////////////////////////////////////////////////////////////
//
template<class T>
MWtree<T>::MWtree()
//
// Purpose: initializes the instances of a multiway tree.  The
```

continues

Listing 21.2. continued

```
// constructor does not allocate any dynamic memory.
//
{
    root = NULL;
    numData = 0;
    numNodes = 0;
    errMsg[0] = '\0';
}

////////////////////////////////////////////////////////////////////
//
template<class T>
char* MWtree<T>::getErrorMessage()
//
// Purpose: returns the contents of the errMsg data member
// and assigns an empty string to that member.
//
//
{
    string80 s;

    strcpy(s, errMsg);
    strcpy(errMsg, "");
    return s;
};

////////////////////////////////////////////////////////////////////
//
template<class T>
boolean MWtree<T>::insert(T& x)
//
// Purpose: performs node insertion in a multiway tree.
//
//  Parameters:
//
//    input: x - the inserted data
//
{
  T r;  // data for the node that is inserted as the new root
  MWTstruct<T> *p,
```

```
               *rRST; // the right subtree of 'r'

  // if item x is in the tree exit
  if (search(x))
    return false;

  // did the tree grow in height?
  if (pushDown(x, root, r, rRST)) {
     // allocate space for a new node
     p = new MWTstruct<T>;
     if (!p) {
       strcpy(errMsg, ALLOCATE_ERROR);
       return false;
     }
     // make new root
     numNodes++;
     p->count = 1;
     p->data[1] = r;
     p->nodeLink[0] = root;
     p->nodeLink[1] = rRST;
     root = p;
  }
  numData++;
  return true;
}

//////////////////////////////////////////////////////////////////////
//
template<class T>
boolean MWtree<T>::search(T& x)
//
// Purpose: searches for a specific data in the multiway tree.
// The function returns true if item x is in the tree. Otherwise,
// the function yields false.
//
//  Parameters:
//
//   input: x - the search data data
//
{
  unsigned dummyIndex;
```

continues

Listing 21.2. continued

```
    MWTstruct<T> *dummyPtr;

    return searchMWtree(x, root, dummyPtr, dummyIndex);
  }

  ////////////////////////////////////////////////////////////////////
  //
  template<class T>
  boolean MWtree<T>::searchMWtree(T& x,
                                  MWTstruct<T> *rootPtr,
                                  MWTstruct<T>* &nodePtr,
                                  unsigned &pos)
  //
  // Purpose: recursive function that searches for specific data
  // in the multiway tree. The function returns true if item x
  // is in the tree. Otherwise, the function yields false.
  //
  //  Parameters:
  //
  //   input: x - the search
  //          rootPtr - the root of a subtree
  //          nodePtr - the pointer to the node that contains item x
  //          pos - the index of the matching element
  //
  {
    if (rootPtr) {
      if (searchNode(x, rootPtr, pos)) {
        nodePtr = rootPtr;
        return true;
      }
      else
        return searchMWtree(x, rootPtr->nodeLink[pos],
                            nodePtr, pos);
    }
    else
      return false;

  }
```

```
////////////////////////////////////////////////////////////////////
//
template<class T>
boolean MWtree<T>::searchNode(T& x,
                              MWTstruct<T> *ptr,
                              unsigned &pos)
//
// Purpose: searches a node for an element that matches item x. The
// function returns true if x is found in the searched node.
// Otherwise, the function yields false.
//
//  Parameters:
//
//   input: x - the search data data
//          ptr - the searched node
//
//   output:
//          pos - the index of the node element that matches item x
//
// Comment: the value returned by the reference parameter pos is
// significant only if the function result is true.
//
{
    // is item x in the node at all?
    if (x < ptr->data[1]) {
      pos = 0;
      return false;
    }
    else {
      // begin the serial search in the elements of the node
      pos = ptr->count;
      while (x < ptr->data[pos] && pos > 1)
        pos--;
      // return function result
      return (x == ptr->data[pos]) ? true : false;
    }
}

////////////////////////////////////////////////////////////////////
//
template<class T>
```

continues

Listing 21.2. continued

```
boolean MWtree<T>::pushDown(T& x,
                            MWTstruct<T>* ptr,
                            T& item,
                            MWTstruct<T>* &itemRST)
//
// Purpose: recursive function that inserts the item x.
// The function returns true if the height of the
// multiway tree needs to be increased. Otherwise, the function
// yields false.
//
//
// Parameters:
//
//    input: x - the inserted data
//           ptr - the pointer to the manipulated node
//
//    output:
//           item - the median element
//           itemRST - the pointer to the right subtree of the node
//             which contains item
//
{
  unsigned i;

  if (!ptr) {
    // cannot insert into an empty tree
    item = x;
    itemRST = NULL;
    return true;
  }
  else {
    // attempt to insert a duplicate key in the current node?
    if (searchNode(x, ptr, i)) {
      strcpy(errMsg, "Cannot insert duplicates");
      return false;
    }
    // reinsert the median element
    if (pushDown(x, ptr->nodeLink[i], item, itemRST)) {
      if (ptr->count < MWTREE_MAX) {
        pushIn(item, itemRST, ptr, i);
```

```
          return false;
        }
        else {
          cutNode(item, itemRST, ptr, i, item, itemRST);
          return true;
        }
      }
      else
        return false;
    }
}

////////////////////////////////////////////////////////////////////
//
template<class T>
void MWtree<T>::pushIn(T& x,
                       MWTstruct<T>* xRST,
                       MWTstruct<T>* ptr,
                       unsigned pos)
//
// Purpose: inserts the item x and the pointer xRST in the node
// accessed by pointer ptr and in the position pos.
//
// Parameters:
//
//    input: x - the inserted data
//           xRST - the inserted node pointer
//           ptr - the pointer to the manipulated node
//           pos - the index of the inserted element in the
//             manipulated node
//
{
    // move the elements and links in the manipulated node
    for (unsigned i = ptr->count; i >= (pos + 1); i--) {
      ptr->data[i+1] = ptr->data[i];
      ptr->nodeLink[i+1] = ptr->nodeLink[i];
    }
    // insert item x
    ptr->data[pos+1] = x;
    // insert pointer xRST
    ptr->nodeLink[pos+1] = xRST;
```

continues

Listing 21.2. continued

```
    // increment count of node elements
    ptr->count++;
}

////////////////////////////////////////////////////////////////////
//
template<class T>
void MWtree<T>::cutNode(T& x,
                        MWTstruct<T>* xRST,
                        MWTstruct<T>* ptr,
                        unsigned pos,
                        T& y,
                        MWTstruct<T>* &yRST)
//
// Purpose: divides the node accessed by pointer ptr that contains
// item x and pointer xRST at index pos. The new nodes are accessed
// by pointers ptr and yRST. The median element is y.
//
// Parameters:
//
//    input: x - the inserted data
//           xRST - the inserted pointer associated with item x
//           ptr - the pointer to the manipulated node
//           pos - the index of the dividing line
//
//    output:
//           y - the new median
//           yRST - the pointer to the other node.
//
{
   unsigned median;

   // calculate the median element which also determines if
   // the new inserted item x is placed in the new left or the
   // new right nodes
   median = (pos <= MWTREE_MIN) ? MWTREE_MIN : MWTREE_MIN + 1;
   // create a new tree node and put it on the right
   yRST = new MWTstruct<T>;
   numNodes++;
```

```
    // loop to move half of the keys
    for (unsigned i = median + 1; i <= MWTREE_MAX; i++) {
      yRST->data[i - median] = ptr->data[i];
      yRST->nodeLink[i - median] = ptr->nodeLink[i];
    }
    yRST->count = MWTREE_MAX - median;
    ptr->count = median;
    if (pos <= MWTREE_MIN)
      // push in the new data
      pushIn(x, xRST, ptr, pos);
    else
      pushIn(x, xRST, yRST, pos - median);
    y = ptr->data[ptr->count];
    yRST->nodeLink[0] = ptr->nodeLink[ptr->count--];
}

//////////////////////////////////////////////////////////////////////
//
template<class T>
boolean MWtree<T>::remove(T& x)
//
//
// Purpose: performs node deletion. The function returns true if
// item x was deleted from the multiway tree.
//
//  Parameters:
//
//    input: x - the data to be removed
//
{
     MWTstruct<T> *p;
     boolean found;

     recDelete(x, root, found);
     if (found) {
       numData--; // decrement data counter
       // is the node empty?
       if (root->count == 0) {
         p = root;
         root = root->nodeLink[0];
         delete p;
```

continues

Listing 21.2. continued

```
          // decrement the node counter
          numNodes--;
        }
      }
      return found;
}

////////////////////////////////////////////////////////////////////
//
template<class T>
void MWtree<T>::recDelete(T& x,
                          MWTstruct<T> *ptr,
                          boolean& found)
//
//
// Purpose: recursive function that performs node deletion.
//
//  Parameters:
//
//    input: x - the data to be removed
//
//    output:
//           found - flag that indicates whether item x was found
//
{
    unsigned i;

    // does ptr point to an NULL node?
    if (!ptr)
      found = false;
    else {
      // search for x in the current node
      found = (searchNode(x, ptr, i)) ? true : false;
      // found an element that matches item x?
      if (found) {
        // does ptr point to a leaf node?
        if (!ptr->nodeLink[i - 1])
          // remove element at index i
          trim(ptr, i);
```

```
        else {
          // replace data[i] with its successor
          successor(ptr, i);
          recDelete(ptr->data[i], ptr->nodeLink[i], found);
        }
      }
      else
        // search another node because item x is
        // not in the current node
        recDelete(x, ptr->nodeLink[i], found);

      if (ptr->nodeLink[i] &&
          ptr->nodeLink[i]->count < MWTREE_MIN)
          restore(ptr, i);
    }
}


/////////////////////////////////////////////////////////////////////
//
template<class T>
void MWtree<T>::trim(MWTstruct<T> *ptr, unsigned pos)
//
//
// Purpose: removes the element at index pos from the node accessed
// by pointer ptr.
//
//  Parameters:
//
//    input: ptr - the pointer to the trimmed node
//           pos - the index of the trimmed element
//
{
    for (unsigned i = pos + 1; i <= ptr->count; i++) {
      ptr->data[i - 1] = ptr->data[i];
      ptr->nodeLink[i - 1] = ptr->nodeLink[i];
    }
    // decrement node counter
    ptr->count--;
}
```

continues

Listing 21.2. continued

```
/////////////////////////////////////////////////////////////////////
//
template<class T>
void MWtree<T>::successor(MWTstruct<T> *ptr, unsigned pos)
//
//
// Purpose: replaces ptr->data[pos] by its immediate successor.
//
//  Parameters:
//
//    input: ptr - the pointer to the node with the replaced data
//           pos - the index of the replaced data
//
{
   MWTstruct<T> *p;

   p = ptr->nodeLink[pos];
   while (p->nodeLink[0])
     p = p->nodeLink[0];
   ptr->data[pos] = p->data[1];
}

/////////////////////////////////////////////////////////////////////
//
template<class T>
void MWtree<T>::restore(MWTstruct<T> *ptr, unsigned pos)
//
//
// Purpose: locates an item and inserts into ptr->branch[pos] in
// order to restore the minimum number of items in the targeted
// node.
//
//  Parameters:
//
//    input: ptr - the pointer to the manipulated node
//           pos - the index of the inserted element
//
{
  if (pos == 0) {
    // restore leftmost element in the current node?
```

```
    if (ptr->nodeLink[1]->count > MWTREE_MIN)
      shiftLeft(ptr, 1);
    else
      compact(ptr, 1);
  }
  // restore the rightmost element in the current node?
  else if (pos == ptr->count) {
    if (ptr->nodeLink[pos - 1]->count > MWTREE_MIN)
      shiftRight(ptr, pos);
    else
      compact(ptr, pos);
  }
  // restore other internal elements in the current node
  else {
    if (ptr->nodeLink[pos - 1]->count > MWTREE_MIN)
      shiftRight(ptr, pos);
    else if (ptr->nodeLink[pos + 1]->count > MWTREE_MIN)
      shiftLeft(ptr, pos + 1);
    else
      compact(ptr, pos);
  }
}

//////////////////////////////////////////////////////////////////////
//
template<class T>
void MWtree<T>::shiftRight(MWTstruct<T> *ptr, unsigned pos)
//
//
// Purpose: moves a data element to the right in a node.
//
//  Parameters:
//
//    input: ptr - the pointer to the manipulated node
//           pos - the index of the shifted data element
//
{
    MWTstruct<T> *p;

    p = ptr->nodeLink[pos];
    // move all the data elements to the right by one position
```

continues

Listing 21.2. continued

```
        for (unsigned i = ptr->count; i > 0; i--) {
          p->data[i + 1] = p->data[i];
          p->nodeLink[i + 1] = p->nodeLink[i];
        }
        // shift the data element from parent node and into right node
        p->nodeLink[1] = p->nodeLink[0];
        p->count++;
        p->data[1] = ptr->data[pos];

        // move the last data of the left node into the parent node
        p = ptr->nodeLink[pos - 1];
        ptr->data[pos] = p->data[p->count];
        ptr->nodeLink[pos]->nodeLink[0] = p->nodeLink[p->count];
        p->count--;
}

///////////////////////////////////////////////////////////////////
//
template<class T>
void MWtree<T>::shiftLeft(MWTstruct<T> *ptr, unsigned pos)
//
//
// Purpose: moves a data element into the left in a node.
//
//  Parameters:
//
//    input: ptr - the pointer to the manipulated node
//           pos - the index of the shifted data element
//
{
    MWTstruct<T> *p;

    // shift data element from parent node into the left node
    p = ptr->nodeLink[pos - 1];
    p->count++;
    p->data[p->count] = ptr->data[pos];
    p->nodeLink[p->count] = ptr->nodeLink[pos]->nodeLink[0];

    // shift the data element from the right node into
    // the parent node
```

```
    p = ptr->nodeLink[pos];
    ptr->data[pos] = p->data[1];
    p->nodeLink[0] = p->nodeLink[1];
    p->count--;
    // loop that shifts all of the data elements in the right node
    // by one position upward
    for (unsigned i = 1; i <= p->count; i++) {
      p->data[i] = p->data[i + 1];
      p->nodeLink[i] = p->nodeLink[i + 1];
    }
}

//////////////////////////////////////////////////////////////////////
//
template<class T>
void MWtree<T>::compact(MWTstruct<T> *ptr, unsigned pos)
//
//
// Purpose: combines adjacent nodes.
//
//  Parameters:
//
//    input: ptr - the pointer to the manipulated node
//           pos - the index of the merged right node
//
{
    MWTstruct<T> *p = ptr->nodeLink[pos - 1];
    // q is the pointer to the right node that will be made vacant
    // and then deleted
    MWTstruct<T> *q = ptr->nodeLink[pos];

    // process the left node and insert data elements from
    // the parent node
    p->count++;
    p->data[p->count] = ptr->data[pos];
    p->nodeLink[p->count] = q->nodeLink[0];
    // inserts all data elements from the right node
    for (unsigned i = 1; i <= q->count; i++) {
      p->count++;
      p->data[p->count] = q->data[i];
      p->nodeLink[p->count] = q->nodeLink[i];
```

continues

Listing 21.2. continued

```
    }

    // remove data elements from the parent node
    for (i = pos; i < ptr->count; i++) {
      ptr->data[i] = ptr->data[i + 1];
      ptr->nodeLink[i] = ptr->nodeLink[i + 1];
    }
    ptr->count--;
    // remove the empty right node
    delete q;
    numNodes--;
}

////////////////////////////////////////////////////////////////////
//
template<class T>
void MWtree<T>::clearMarks(MWTstruct<T>* rootPtr)
//
// Purpose: recursive function used to traverse the
// multiway tree and set the marked members to 0.
//
//  Parameters:
//
//    input: rootPtr - pointer to the root of the multiway tree.
//
{
    if (rootPtr) {
        rootPtr->marked = 0;
        for (unsigned i = 0; i <= rootPtr->count; i++)
          clearMarks(rootPtr->nodeLink[i]);
    }
}

////////////////////////////////////////////////////////////////////
//
template<class T>
void MWtree<T>::visitTree(MWTstruct<T>* rootPtr,
                          MWTstruct<T>* &node)
//
// Purpose: recursive function used to traverse the multiway tree.
```

```
//
//  Parameters:
//
//    input: rootPtr - pointer to the root of the multiway tree.
//
//    output: node - the pointer to the next node visited.
//
{
    unsigned n = rootPtr->marked;

    // terminate recursive traversal?
    if (n > rootPtr->count)
      // all nodes have been visited
      return;

    if (rootPtr->nodeLink[n])
      visitTree(rootPtr->nodeLink[n], node);

    if (seekNode && n < rootPtr->count) {
      rootPtr->marked++;
      node = rootPtr;
      visitIndex = rootPtr->marked;
      seekNode = false;
      //rootPtr->marked++;
      return;
    }
}

////////////////////////////////////////////////////////////////////
//
template<class T>
void MWtree<T>::clearNode(MWTstruct<T>* &rootPtr)
//
// Purpose: recursive function to delete subtrees.
//
// Parameters:
//
//    input: rootPtr - the pointer of the node to delete
//
{
    if (rootPtr) {
```

continues

Listing 21.2. continued

```
        for (unsigned i = 0; i <= rootPtr->count; i++)
          clearNode(rootPtr->nodeLink[i]);
        delete rootPtr;
    }
}

//////////////////////////////////////////////////////////////////////
//
template<class T>
boolean MWtree<T>::getFirstNode(T& x)
//
// Purpose: visits the root of the multiway tree.  The function
// returns true if the multiway tree object has a root.
//
//  Parameters:
//
//   input: x - the pointer to the data associated with the root of
//           the multiway tree.
{
    if (root) {
        seekNode = true;
        clearMarks(root);
        visitTree(root, nodePtr);
        x = nodePtr->data[visitIndex];
    }
    return (root) ? true : false;
}

//////////////////////////////////////////////////////////////////////
//
template<class T>
boolean MWtree<T>::getNextNode(T& x)
//
// Purpose: visits the next node in the multiway tree. The function
// returns true if there was a next node to visit.
//
//  Parameters:
//
//    input: x - the pointer to the data associated with the visited
//             node.
```

```
//
{
    seekNode = true;
    if (root) {
        visitTree(root, nodePtr);
        if (!seekNode)
            x = nodePtr->data[visitIndex];
    }
    return (!seekNode) ? true : false;
}
```

Testing the MWTree Class

Listing 21.3 contains the source code for the TSMWTREE.CPP test program, which manipulates instances of `MWtree` instantiated with the `cString` class. The program declares the functions `showTree`, `searchNode`, and `main`.

The `showTree` function displays the strings stored in an instance of `MWtree<cString>` in a single column. The parameter `t` specifies the m-way tree. The parameter `msg` passes the commenting text that appears at the top of the screen. The function uses the local Boolean variable `ok` to traverse the m-way tree `t` and initializes `ok` with the Boolean result of `t.getFirstNode`. The routine uses a `while` loop to examine the value of `ok`. Each iteration displays the contents of the variable `str`, a local instance of class `cString`. Each loop iteration calls the function `getNextNode` to visit the next node and assigns the Boolean function result to the variable `ok`.

The function `searchNode` searches for specific data in an m-way tree. The parameter `t` specifies the searched m-way tree. The parameter `s` passes the search string. `searchNode` assumes that the nodes of tree `t` have been displayed by the `showTree` function. The `searchNode` function calls `MWtree::search` to look for the argument of parameter `s` in the argument of `t`. The function displays text that reflects the search outcome.

The function `main` declares the object tree, an instance of `MWtree` instantiated with the class `cString`. The function also declares `country`, an array of `cString` instances, and initializes the array with the names of European countries. `country` supplies data to the tested m-way tree. To test for existing and nonexisting data in the instance of `MWtree`, `main` stores all members (except the last two, Greece and Denmark) of `country` in the m-way tree.

`main` tests the m-way tree as follows:

1. Inserts the members of the array `country` (except the last two) using a `for` loop. Each loop iteration calls the member function `MWtree::insert` to insert a `cString` instance.
2. Displays the data in the object tree by calling the function `showTree`, which displays the sorted names of the countries in a single column and waits for you to press any key.
3. Searches for the elements of `country` in the object tree. This step uses a `for` loop that calls the `searchNode` function. The loop iterates over all the elements (including Greece and Denmark) of `country`. The last two iterations, therefore, should generate a `no match` message displayed by the `searchNode` function.
4. Removes half of the nodes in the object tree. The function uses a `for` loop to call the `MWtree::remove` member function. The arguments for the `remove` function are the elements of `country`.
5. Repeats Steps 2 and 3 with the trimmed m-way tree.

Listing 21.3. The source code for the TSMWTREE.CPP test program.

```
#include <iostream.h>
#include "video.h"
#include "string.hpp"
#include "mwtree.cpp"

void showTree(MWtree<cString>& t, cString msg)
{
  cString str;
  boolean ok = t.getFirstNode(str);

  clrscr();
  cout << msg
       << " (tree has " << t.getNumNodes() << " nodes)"
       << "\n\n";
  while (ok) {
    cout << str << '\n';
    ok = t.getNextNode(str);
  }
  gotoxy(1, 23);
```

```
  cout << "Press any key ... ";
  getch();
}

void searchNode(MWtree<cString>& t, cString& s)
{
  gotoxy(1, 23);
  clreol();
  gotoxy(1, 22);
  cout << "Press any key to search for " << s;
  getch();
  gotoxy(1, 22);
  clreol();
  if (t.search(s))
    cout << "Found " << s << " in tree\n";
  else
    cout << "No match for " << s << '\n';
  cout << "Press any key to continue ... ";
  getch();
}

main()
{
  MWtree<cString> tree;
  cString country[] = { "France",
                        "Germany",
                        "Sweden",
                        "Ireland",
                        "Italy",
                        "Spain",
                        "Portugal",
                        "Switzerland",
                        "Belgium",
                        "England",
                        "Monaco",
                        "Andora",
                        "Luxembourg",
                        "Greece",   // not inserted in tree
                        "Denmark"   // not inserted in tree
                      };
  unsigned count = sizeof(country) / sizeof(cString);
```

continues

Listing 21.3. continued

```
    unsigned testSize = count - 2;

    // insert the names of the countries
    for (unsigned i = 0; i < testSize; i++)
      tree.insert(country[i]);

    // display AVL-tree
    showTree(tree, "Complete m-way tree is:");

    for (i = 0; i < count; i++)
      searchNode(tree, country[i]);

    for (i = 0; i < count / 2; i++)
      tree.remove(country[i]);

     // display AVL-tree
    showTree(tree, "Trimmed m-way tree is:");

    for (i = 0; i < count; i++)
      searchNode(tree, country[i]);

    gotoxy(1, 22); clreol();
    gotoxy(1, 23); clreol();

    return 0;
}
```

The B-Tree

The B-tree data structure is a disk-based version of the multiway tree. The B-tree shares the same basic algorithms with the m-way tree. These trees, however, differ in implementation. The pointer access in the m-way tree is replaced by a disk read or write operation. The m-way tree node pointers, consequentially, are replaced with B-tree indices used in file I/O.

The Btree Class

This section concentrates on the class `Btree` that models a B-tree. Listing 21.4 contains the source code for the btree.hpp header file, which file contains the following constants:

1. `BTREE_NIL`, which defines an index value that is equivalent to the pointer `NULL`. A node link with a `BTREE_NIL` value does not refer at any node stored on disk.
2. `BTREE_ORDER`, which defines the order of the B-tree.
3. `BTREE_MAX` and `BTREE_MIN`, which define the maximum and minimum number of data items in a node.
4. `BTREE_MIN_DEL_ARRAY`, which defines the initial size of an array that tracks the deleted nodes.
5. `BTREE_DEL_ARRAY_INCR`, which specifies the increment in the size of the array that tracks the deleted nodes.

The header file also declares `Bstruct`, the template structure that models a B-tree node. Similar to the `MWTstruct` structure, it declares the following members:

1. `count`, which stores the number of actual data items in a node.
2. `data`, which stores data items in a node. `Bstruct` declares the array size as `BTREE_MAX + 1`. The used elements range is 1 to `BTREE_MAX`. The element at index 0 is not used.
3. `nodeLink`, which stores the indices that refer to the child nodes. `Bstruct` declares the array size as `BTREE_MAX + 1`. The used elements range is 0 to `BTREE_MAX`.
4. `marked`, which stores the index of the next item to visit. This information enables the tree traversal member functions to select the next item to visit.

Remember that the template class `T` must not contain relevant data members that are pointers. This requirement must be observed to accommodate data storage in streams.

The class `Btree` declares a number of data members (and member functions):

1. `errMsg` stores the error message text generated by the various member functions.
2. `numData` stores the number of data items in an instance of the class `MWtree`.
3. `numNodes` contains the number of nodes in an instance of the class `MWtree`.
4. `nodeSize` stores the size of the structure `Bstruct`.
5. `visitIndex` stores the index of the currently visited data item in the currently visited node.
6. `nodePtr` is the index of the visited m-way tree nodes.
7. `root` is the index of the root node of the m-way tree.
8. `numDelNodes` stores the number of deleted nodes.
9. `countDelNodeArray` stores the current maximum size of the array `delNodeArray`.
10. `highNodeIndex` stores the index of the last node stored in the supporting stream.
11. `delNodeArray` is the pointer to the dynamic array of the deleted nodes' indices. The dynamic array, accessed by `delNodeArray`, enables the instances of `Btree` to reuse the disk space of deleted nodes.
12. The Boolean `seekNode` is used as a special flag to traverse the nodes of a B-tree.
13. `f` is the supporting stream.

The class declaration contains a rich set of member functions. Only a few member functions are defined within the class declaration:

1. The class destructor, which invokes the `clear` member function to clear an instance of the `MWtree` class.
2. The `getNumData` function returns the number of data items in an instance of class `MWtree`.
3. The `getNumNodes` function returns the number of nodes in an instance of class `MWtree`.
4. The `clear` member function deletes the dynamic array `delNodeArray` and closes the supporting stream `f`.

Listing 21.4. The source code for the btree.hpp header file.

```
////////////////////////////////////////////////////////////////////
//                                                                //
//           Copyright (c) 1992 Namir Clement Shammas             //
//                                                                //
//  Version: 1.0.0                               Date 8/12/92     //
//                                                                //
//  Purpose: implements class of B-trees that have the            //
//           following functionality:                             //
//                                                                //
//             + inserts data.                                    //
//             + searches for data.                               //
//             + deletes data.                                    //
//             + visits the nodes of the multiway tree.           //
//                                                                //
//                                                                //
////////////////////////////////////////////////////////////////////

#include "comndata.h"
#include <fstream.h>

#ifndef _BTREE_HPP
#define _BTREE_HPP

const unsigned BTREE_NIL = 0xffff;
const unsigned BTREE_ORDER = 5;
const unsigned BTREE_MAX = BTREE_ORDER - 1;
const unsigned BTREE_MIN = BTREE_ORDER / 2;
const unsigned BTREE_MIN_DEL_ARRAY = 50;
const unsigned BTREE_DEL_ARRAY_INCR = 20;

template<class T>
struct Bstruct {
    unsigned count;
    T data[BTREE_MAX+1];
    unsigned nodeLink[BTREE_MAX+1];
    unsigned marked; // visit flag
};

template<class T>
```

continues

Listing 21.4. continued

```
class Btree
{

  protected:
    string80 errMsg;             // error message
    unsigned numData,            // number of data items in B-tree
             numNodes,           // number of nodes in B-tree
             nodeSize,           // size of each node
             visitIndex,         // visit index
             nodePtr,            // visit node index
             root,               // index to root page
             numDelNodes,        // number of deleted nodes
             countDelNodeArray,  // number of elements in delNodeArray
             highNodeIndex;      // highest node index
    unsigned* delNodeArray;      // array of deleted node indices
    boolean seekNode;            // search flag
    fstream f;                   // supporting stream

    boolean searchBtree(T& x,
                        unsigned rootPtr,
                        unsigned &nodePtr,
                        unsigned &pos);
    boolean searchNode(T& x,
                       Bstruct<T> *ptr,
                       unsigned &pos);
    boolean pushDown(T& x, unsigned ptr,
                     T& item, unsigned &itemRST);
    void pushIn(T& x, unsigned xRST,
                Bstruct<T> *ptr, unsigned pos);
    void cutNode(T& x, unsigned xRST,
                 unsigned ptr, unsigned pos,
                 T& y, unsigned &yRST);
    void recDelete(T& x, unsigned ptr, boolean& found);
    void trim(Bstruct<T> *ptr, unsigned pos);
    void successor(Bstruct<T> *ptr, unsigned pos);
    void restore(Bstruct<T> *ptr, unsigned pos);
    void shiftRight(Bstruct<T> *ptr, unsigned pos);
    void shiftLeft(Bstruct<T> *ptr, unsigned pos);
    void compact(Bstruct<T> *ptr, unsigned pos);
```

```
    void clearMarks(unsigned rootPtr);
    void visitTree(unsigned rootPtr, unsigned &node);

    void writeNode(Bstruct<T> *node, unsigned nodeNum);
    void readNode(Bstruct<T> *node, unsigned nodeNum);
    void expandDelNodeArray();
    unsigned getNodeIndex();

  public:
    // ************** state manipulation methods **************
    Btree(const char* filename);
    ~Btree()
      { clear(); }

    char* getErrorMessage();
    unsigned getNumData() const
      { return numData; }
    unsigned getNumNodes() const
      { return numNodes; }
    void getPage(Bstruct<T> *node, unsigned pageNum)
      { readNode(node, pageNum); }

    // ************** object manipulation methods *************
    virtual boolean insert(T& x);
    virtual boolean search(T& x);
    virtual boolean remove(T& x);
    virtual boolean getFirstNode(T& x);
    virtual boolean getNextNode(T& x);
    virtual void clear()
      {
        delete [] delNodeArray;
        f.close();
      }
};

#endif
```

Listing 21.5 shows the source code for the BTREE.CPP library file, which contains the definition of the class constructor and most of the member functions.

I derived the `Btree` class from the `MWtree` class. The `Btree` class, therefore, contains a number of member functions that are similar to those in `MWtree`. `Btree`, however, is different in the following ways:

- The use of disk I/O that replaces pointer access to store and access data. The functions that perform node I/O use dynamic instances of the structure `Bstruct` to minimize the stack space requirement.
- Some B-tree member functions use unsigned-typed parameters instead of pointers to structures.
- The nodes indices are compared with the constant `BTREE_NIL` to indicate whether or not they refer to a valid node.
- The `searchBtree` function (similar to the recursive `searchMWtree` function) is non-recursive. This coding scheme reduces the stack space requirements.
- The `clearMarks` function is implemented as a non-recursive member function. The `Btree::clearMarks` function performs serial node I/O to assign 0 to the marked member of each node. This initialization method is straightforward.

The member functions `trim`, `successor`, `restore`, `shiftRight`, `shiftLeft`, and `compact` use code that is similar to their counterparts in class `MWtree`.

The `Btree` class declares a single constructor. The constructor requires the name of the file that is opened as a stream for binary I/O. The constructor initializes the data members `root`, `numData`, `numNodes`, `numDelNodes`, `errMsg`, and `countDelNodeArray`. The constructor opens the supporting stream and creates the dynamic array to keep track of deleted nodes. If there is any error in opening the stream or allocating the dynamic array, the constructor assigns an error message to the `errMsg` data member.

Node I/O

The `Btree` class contains two protected member functions, `writeNode` and `readNode`, that perform node I/O. The parameter node is the pointer to the node that is being written or read. The `nodeNum` parameter is the index of the node being written or read. Both node I/O functions use the `seekg` stream function to move the stream pointer to the beginning of the targeted node. This node is located at `nodeNum * nodeSize` bytes from the beginning of the stream. The node I/O functions perform their task using a single call to the stream `write` or `read` function.

Managing Node Indices

The `Btree` class contains two member functions that manage the node indices:

1. The `getNodeIndex` function returns a node index for a new node and returns the index 0 when you call it to create the very first node in an instance of class `Btree`. Subsequent calls return a node index using the following criteria:
   - There are no deleted nodes. The function returns the incremented value of the `highNodeIndex` data member. This scheme yields indices in an increasing sequence of numbers.
   - There is at least one deleted node. The function returns the index stored in the element `delNodeArray[numDelNode]`.
2. The `expandDelNodeArray` function expands the size of the dynamic array accessed by pointer `delNodeArray`. The array is increased by `BTREE_DEL_ARRAY_INCR` elements. If the dynamic allocation of the new array fails, the function assigns an error message to the `errMsg` data member. The function creates the new array using the local pointer `newArray`. The function then copies the values from the old array, accessed by `delNodeArray`, to the new array. The function then deletes the old array and assigns the address of the new array to the `delNodeArray` member.

Listing 21.5. The source code for the BTREE.CPP library file.

```
////////////////////////////////////////////////////////////////////////
//                                                                  //
//              Copyright (c) 1992 Namir Clement Shammas            //
//                                                                  //
//  Version: 1.0.0                                  Date 8/12/92    //
//                                                                  //
//  Purpose: implements class of B-trees that have the              //
//           following functionality:                               //
//                                                                  //
//             + inserts data.                                      //
//             + searches for data.                                 //
//             + deletes data.                                      //
//             + visits the nodes of the B-tree.                    //
//                                                                  //
//                                                                  //
```

continues

Listing 21.5. continued

```
//////////////////////////////////////////////////////////////////////

#include <string.h>
#include "btree.hpp"

/////////////////////////////////////////////////////////////////////
//
template<class T>
Btree<T>::Btree(const char* filename)
//
// Purpose: initializes the instances of a B-tree. The
// constructor allocates dynamic memory for the array that tracks
// the deleted nodes.
//
// Parameters:
//
//     input: filename - the name of the supporting file.
//
{
    root = BTREE_NIL;
    numData = 0;
    numNodes = 0;
    numDelNodes = 0;
    // create the array that tracks the deleted nodes
    countDelNodeArray = BTREE_MIN_DEL_ARRAY;
    delNodeArray = new unsigned[countDelNodeArray];
    if (!delNodeArray) {
      strcpy(errMsg, ALLOCATE_ERROR);
      return;
    }
    // assign BTREE_NIL to the elements of the array delNodeArray
    for (unsigned i = 0; i < countDelNodeArray; i++)
      *(delNodeArray + i) = BTREE_NIL;
    errMsg[0] = '\0';
    nodeSize = sizeof(Bstruct<T>);
    // open the stream for binary I/O
    f.open(filename, ios::binary | ios::in | ios::out);
    if (!f.good()) {
      strcpy(errMsg, "Cannot open file ");
      strcat(errMsg, filename);
```

```
    }
}

//////////////////////////////////////////////////////////////////////
//
template<class T>
char* Btree<T>::getErrorMessage()
//
// Purpose: returns the contents of the errMsg data member
// and assigns an empty string to that member.
//
//
{
    string80 s;

    strcpy(s, errMsg);
    strcpy(errMsg, "");
    return s;
}

//////////////////////////////////////////////////////////////////////
//
template<class T>
void Btree<T>::writeNode(Bstruct<T> *node, unsigned nodeNum)
//
// Purpose: writes a node to the stream.
//
// Parameters:
//
//    input: node - the node written to the stream.
//           nodeNum - the node index
//
{
  f.seekg(nodeNum * nodeSize);
  // write node in one swoop
  f.write((unsigned char*) node, nodeSize);
}

//////////////////////////////////////////////////////////////////////
//
template<class T>
```

continues

Listing 21.5. continued

```
void Btree<T>::readNode(Bstruct<T> *node, unsigned nodeNum)
//
// Purpose: reads a node from the stream.
//
// Parameters:
//
//    input: node - the node read from the stream.
//           nodeNum - the node index
//
{
  f.seekg(nodeNum * nodeSize);
  // read the node in one swoop
  f.read((unsigned char*) node, nodeSize);
}

////////////////////////////////////////////////////////////////////////
//
template<class T>
void Btree<T>::expandDelNodeArray()
//
// Purpose: expands the size of the delNodeArray.
//
{
    unsigned *newArray;
    unsigned newSize = countDelNodeArray + BTREE_DEL_ARRAY_INCR;

    // create new array
    newArray = new unsigned[newSize];
    // copy values from the old array
    for (unsigned i = 0; i < countDelNodeArray; i++)
      *(newArray + i) = *(delNodeArray + i);
    // delete the old array
    delete [] delNodeArray;
    // assign delNodeArray pointer to access the new array
    delNodeArray = newArray;
    // update the current size of the delNodeArray
    countDelNodeArray = newSize;
}

////////////////////////////////////////////////////////////////////////
```

```
//
template<class T>
unsigned Btree<T>::getNodeIndex()
//
// Purpose: returns the index for the next node.
//
{
  // are there no deleted nodes?
  if (numDelNodes == 0) {
    highNodeIndex = (numNodes > 0) ? highNodeIndex + 1 : 0;
    return highNodeIndex;
  }
  else
    // get node index from the delNodeArray
    return *(delNodeArray + numDelNodes-- - 1);
}

//////////////////////////////////////////////////////////////////////
//
template<class T>
boolean Btree<T>::insert(T& x)
//
// Purpose: performs node insertion in a B-tree.
//
//  Parameters:
//
//    input: x - the inserted data
//
{
  T r;  // data for the node that is inserted as the new root
  unsigned p, rRST; // the right subtree of 'r'
  Bstruct<T> *buf;

  // if item x is in the tree exit
  if (search(x))
    return false;

  // did the tree grow in height?
  if (pushDown(x, root, r, rRST)) {
     // get the index of a new node
     p = getNodeIndex();
```

continues

Listing 21.5. continued

```
      // make new root
      buf = new Bstruct<T>;
      numNodes++;
      buf->count = 1;
      buf->data[1] = r;
      buf->nodeLink[0] = root;
      buf->nodeLink[1] = rRST;
      for (unsigned i = 2; i <= BTREE_MAX; i++)
        buf->nodeLink[i] = BTREE_NIL;
      root = p;
      // save the new node
      writeNode(buf, p);
      delete buf;
    }
    numData++;
    return true;
}

////////////////////////////////////////////////////////////////////
//
template<class T>
boolean Btree<T>::search(T& x)
//
// Purpose: searches for specific data in the B-tree.
// The function returns true if item x is in the tree. Otherwise,
// the function yields false.
//
//  Parameters:
//
//   input: x - the search data data
//
{
  unsigned dummyIndex;
  unsigned dummyPtr;

  return searchBtree(x, root, dummyPtr, dummyIndex);
}

////////////////////////////////////////////////////////////////////
```

```
//
template<class T>
boolean Btree<T>::searchBtree(T& x,
                              unsigned rootPtr,
                              unsigned &nodePtr,
                              unsigned &pos)
//
// Purpose: recursive function that searches for specific data
// in the B-tree. The function returns true if item x
// is in the tree. Otherwise, the function yields false.
//
//  Parameters:
//
//   input: x - the search
//          rootPtr - the index to the root of a subtree
//          nodePtr - the index to the node that contains item x
//          pos - the index of the matching element
//
{
  boolean iterate = true;
  boolean found = false;
  Bstruct<T> *buf = new Bstruct<T>;

  while (iterate) {
    if (rootPtr == BTREE_NIL)
      iterate = false;
    else {
      readNode(buf, rootPtr);
      found = searchNode(x, buf, pos);
      if (found) {
        nodePtr = rootPtr;
        iterate = false;
      }
      else
        rootPtr = buf->nodeLink[pos];
    }
  }
  delete buf;
  return found;
}
```

continues

Listing 21.5. continued

```
////////////////////////////////////////////////////////////////////
//
template<class T>
boolean Btree<T>::searchNode(T& x,
                             Bstruct<T> *ptr,
                             unsigned &pos)
//
// Purpose: searches a node for an element that matches item x. The
// function returns true if x is found in the searched node.
// Otherwise, the function yields false.
//
//  Parameters:
//
//   input: x - the search data
//          ptr - the pointer to the searched node
//
//   output:
//          pos - the index of the node element that matches item x
//
// Comment:  the value returned by the reference parameter pos is
// significant only if the function result is true.
//
{
    // is item x in the node at all?
    if (x < ptr->data[1]) {
      pos = 0;
      return false;
    }
    else {
      // begin the serial search in the elements of the node
      pos = ptr->count;
      while (x < ptr->data[pos] && pos > 1)
        pos--;
      // return the function's result
      return (x == ptr->data[pos]) ? true : false;
    }
}

////////////////////////////////////////////////////////////////////
//
```

```
template<class T>
boolean Btree<T>::pushDown(T& x,
                           unsigned ptr,
                           T& item,
                           unsigned &itemRST)
//
// Purpose:  recursive function that inserts item x in the B-tree.
// The function returns true if the height of the B-tree needs
// to be increased. Otherwise, the function yields false.
//
// Parameters:
//
//    input: x - the inserted data
//           ptr - the index to the manipulated node
//
//    output:
//           item - the median element
//           itemRST - the index to the right subtree of the node
//             which contains item
//
{
  unsigned i;
  Bstruct<T> *buf;

  if (ptr == BTREE_NIL) {
    // cannot insert into an empty tree
    item = x;
    itemRST = BTREE_NIL;
    return true;
  }
  else {
    buf = new Bstruct<T>;
    readNode(buf, ptr);
    // attempt to insert a duplicate key in the current node?
    if (searchNode(x, buf, i)) {
      strcpy(errMsg, "Cannot insert duplicates");
      return false;
    }
    // reinsert the median element
    if (pushDown(x, buf->nodeLink[i], item, itemRST)) {
      if (buf->count < BTREE_MAX) {
```

continues

Listing 21.5. continued

```
          pushIn(item, itemRST, buf, i);
          writeNode(buf, ptr);
          delete buf;
          return false;
        }
        else {
          cutNode(item, itemRST, ptr, i, item, itemRST);
          delete buf;
          return true;
        }
      }
      else {
        delete buf;
        return false;
      }
    }
  }
}

//////////////////////////////////////////////////////////////////////
//
template<class T>
void Btree<T>::pushIn(T& x,
                      unsigned xRST,
                      Bstruct<T> *ptr,
                      unsigned pos)
//
// Purpose: inserts the item x and the index xRST in the node
// accessed by index ptr and in the position pos.
//
// Parameters:
//
//    input: x - the inserted data
//           xRST - the inserted node index
//           ptr - the index to the manipulated node
//           pos - the index of the inserted element in the
//             manipulated node
//
{
    // move the elements and links in the manipulated node
```

```
    for (unsigned i = ptr->count; i >= (pos + 1); i--) {
      ptr->data[i+1] = ptr->data[i];
      ptr->nodeLink[i+1] = ptr->nodeLink[i];
    }
    // insert item x
    ptr->data[pos+1] = x;
    // insert index xRST
    ptr->nodeLink[pos+1] = xRST;
    // increment count of node elements
    ptr->count++;
}

////////////////////////////////////////////////////////////////////
//
template<class T>
void Btree<T>::cutNode(T& x,
                      unsigned xRST,
                      unsigned ptr,
                      unsigned pos,
                      T& y,
                      unsigned &yRST)
//
// Purpose: divides the node accessed by index ptr that contains
// item x and index xRST at index pos. The new nodes are accessed
// by pointers ptr and yRST. The median element is y.
//
// Parameters:
//
//    input: x - the inserted data
//           xRST - the inserted index associated with item x
//           ptr - the index to the manipulated node
//           pos - the index of the dividing line
//
//    output:
//           y - the new median
//           yRST - the index to the other node.
//
{
   unsigned median, idx;
   Bstruct<T> *buf1, *buf2;
```

continues

Listing 21.5. continued

```
    buf1 = new Bstruct<T>;
    buf2 = new Bstruct<T>;
    readNode(buf1, ptr);
    // calculate the median element which also determines if
    // the new inserted item x is placed in the new left or the
    // new right nodes
    median = (pos <= BTREE_MIN) ? BTREE_MIN : BTREE_MIN + 1;
    // create a new tree node and put it on the right
    yRST = getNodeIndex();
    for (unsigned i = 0; i <= BTREE_MAX; i++)
      buf2->nodeLink[i] = BTREE_NIL;
    numNodes++;

    // loop to move half of the keys
    for (i = median + 1; i <= BTREE_MAX; i++) {
      buf2->data[i - median] = buf1->data[i];
      buf2->nodeLink[i - median] = buf1->nodeLink[i];
    }
    buf2->count = BTREE_MAX - median;
    buf1->count = median;
    // push in the new data
    if (pos <= BTREE_MIN)
      pushIn(x, xRST, buf1, pos);
    else
      pushIn(x, xRST, buf2, pos - median);
    y = buf1->data[buf1->count];
    buf2->nodeLink[0] = buf1->nodeLink[buf1->count--];
    writeNode(buf1, ptr);
    writeNode(buf2, yRST);
    delete buf1;
    delete buf2;
}

//////////////////////////////////////////////////////////////////////
//
template<class T>
boolean Btree<T>::remove(T& x)
//
//
// Purpose: performs node deletion. The function returns true if
```

```
// item x was deleted from the B-tree.
//
//  Parameters:
//
//    input: x - the data to be removed
//
{
    Bstruct<T> *buf = new Bstruct<T>;
    unsigned p;
    boolean found;

     recDelete(x, root, found);
    if (found) {
      numData--; // decrement data counter
      readNode(buf, root);
      // is the node empty?
      if (buf->count == 0) {
        p = root;
        root = buf->nodeLink[0];
        // delete node at index p
        numDelNodes++; // increment the counter for the number
                       // of deleted nodes
        // does the array delNodeArray need to expand?
        if (numDelNodes == countDelNodeArray)
          expandDelNodeArray();
        // assign index q to an element of array delNodeArray
        *(delNodeArray + numDelNodes - 1) = p;
        // decrement the node counter
        numNodes--;
      }
    }
    delete buf;
    return found;
}

//////////////////////////////////////////////////////////////////////
//
template<class T>
void Btree<T>::recDelete(T& x,
                         unsigned ptr,
                         boolean& found)
```

continues

Listing 21.5. continued

```
//
//
// Purpose: function that performs node deletion.
//
//  Parameters:
//
//    input: x - the data to be removed
//
//    output:
//           found - flag that indicates whether item x was found
//
{
    Bstruct<T> *buf, *buf2;
    unsigned i, ss;

    if (ptr == BTREE_NIL)
       found = false;
    else {
      buf = new Bstruct<T>;
      readNode(buf, ptr);
      // search for x in the current node
      found = (searchNode(x, buf, i)) ? true : false;
      // found an element that matches item x?
      if (found) {
        // does ptr point to a leaf node?
        if (buf->nodeLink[i - 1] == BTREE_NIL) {
          // remove element at index i
          trim(buf, i);
          writeNode(buf, ptr);
        }
        else {
          // replace data[i] with its successor in node ptr
          successor(buf, i);
          writeNode(buf, ptr);
          recDelete(buf->data[i], buf->nodeLink[i], found);
        }
      }
      else
        recDelete(x, buf->nodeLink[i], found);
```

```
        if (buf->nodeLink[i] != BTREE_NIL) {
          buf2 = new Bstruct<T>;
          readNode(buf2, buf->nodeLink[i]);
          if (buf2->count < BTREE_MIN) {
            restore(buf, i);
            writeNode(buf, ptr);
          }
          delete buf2;
        }
        delete buf;
      }
}


//////////////////////////////////////////////////////////////////////
//
template<class T>
void Btree<T>::trim(Bstruct<T> *ptr, unsigned pos)
//
//
// Purpose: removes the element at index pos from the node accessed
// by index ptr.
//
//  Parameters:
//
//    input: ptr - the pointer of the trimmed node
//           pos - the index of the trimmed element
//
{
    for (unsigned i = pos + 1; i <= ptr->count; i++) {
      ptr->data[i - 1] = ptr->data[i];
      ptr->nodeLink[i - 1] = ptr->nodeLink[i];
    }
    // decrement node counter
    ptr->count--;
}

//////////////////////////////////////////////////////////////////////
//
template<class T>
void Btree<T>::successor(Bstruct<T> *ptr, unsigned pos)
```

continues

Listing 21.5. continued

```
//
//
// Purpose: replaces ptr->data[pos] with its immediate successor.
//
//  Parameters:
//
//    input: ptr - the pointer to the node with the replaced data
//           pos - the index of the replaced data
//
{
   Bstruct<T> *bufP;
   unsigned p, n;
   bufP = new Bstruct<T>;
   p = ptr->nodeLink[pos];
   readNode(bufP, p);
   while (bufP->nodeLink[0] != BTREE_NIL) {
     n = bufP->nodeLink[0];
     readNode(bufP, n);
   }
   ptr->data[pos] = bufP->data[1];
   delete bufP;
}

////////////////////////////////////////////////////////////////////
//
template<class T>
void Btree<T>::restore(Bstruct<T> *ptr, unsigned pos)
//
//
// Purpose: locates an item and inserts into nodeLink[pos] of
// node ptr in order to restore the minimum number of items in
// the targeted node.
//
//  Parameters:
//
//    input: ptr - the pointer to the manipulated node
//           pos - the index of the inserted element
//
{
  Bstruct<T> *childBuf, *childBuf2;
```

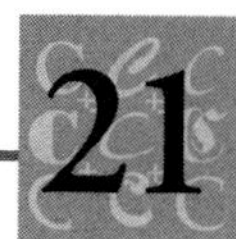

```
  childBuf = new Bstruct<T>;
  if (pos == 0) {
    readNode(childBuf, ptr->nodeLink[1]);
    // restore leftmost element in the current node?
    if (childBuf->count > BTREE_MIN)
      shiftLeft(ptr, 1);
    else
      compact(ptr, 1);
  }
  // restore the rightmost element in the current node?
  else if (pos == ptr->count) {
    readNode(childBuf, ptr->nodeLink[pos - 1]);
    if (childBuf->count > BTREE_MIN)
      shiftRight(ptr, pos);
    else
      compact(ptr, pos);
  }
  // restore other internal elements in the current node?
  else {
    childBuf2 = new Bstruct<T>;
    readNode(childBuf, ptr->nodeLink[pos - 1]);
    readNode(childBuf2, ptr->nodeLink[pos + 1]);
    if (childBuf->count > BTREE_MIN)
      shiftRight(ptr, pos);
    else if (childBuf2->count > BTREE_MIN)
      shiftLeft(ptr, pos + 1);
    else
      compact(ptr, pos);
    delete childBuf2;
  }
  delete childBuf;
}

//////////////////////////////////////////////////////////////////////
//
template<class T>
void Btree<T>::shiftRight(Bstruct<T> *ptr, unsigned pos)
//
//
// Purpose: moves a data element to the right in a node.
//
```

continues

Listing 21.5. continued

```
//  Parameters:
//
//    input: ptr - the pointer to the manipulated node
//           pos - the index of the shifted data element
//
{
    Bstruct<T> *bufP = new Bstruct<T>;
    Bstruct<T> *bufQ = new Bstruct<T>;
    unsigned p, q;

    p = ptr->nodeLink[pos];
    readNode(bufP, p);
    // move all the data elements to the right by one position
    for (unsigned i = bufP->count; i > 0; i--) {
      bufP->data[i + 1] = bufP->data[i];
      bufP->nodeLink[i + 1] = bufP->nodeLink[i];
    }
    // shift the data element from parent node and into right node
    bufP->nodeLink[1] = bufP->nodeLink[0];
    bufP->count++;
    bufP->data[1] = ptr->data[pos];
    writeNode(bufP, p);

    // move the last data of the left node into the parent node
    p = ptr->nodeLink[pos - 1];
    readNode(bufP, p);
    ptr->data[pos] = bufP->data[bufP->count];
    q = ptr->nodeLink[pos];
    readNode(bufQ, q);
    bufQ->nodeLink[0] = bufP->nodeLink[bufP->count];
    bufP->count--;
    // update nodes p and ptr in the stream
    writeNode(bufP, p);
    writeNode(bufQ, q);
    delete bufP;
    delete bufQ;
}

//////////////////////////////////////////////////////////////////////
//
```

```
template<class T>
void Btree<T>::shiftLeft(Bstruct<T> *ptr, unsigned pos)
//
//
// Purpose: moves a data element into the left node.
//
//  Parameters:
//
//    input: ptr - the index to the manipulated node
//           pos - the index of the shifted data element
//
{
    Bstruct<T> *bufP = new Bstruct<T>;
    Bstruct<T> *bufQ = new Bstruct<T>;
    unsigned p, q;

    // shift data element from parent node into the left node
    p = ptr->nodeLink[pos - 1];
    readNode(bufP, p);
    bufP->count++;
    bufP->data[bufP->count] = ptr->data[pos];
    q = ptr->nodeLink[pos];
    readNode(bufQ, q);
    bufP->nodeLink[bufP->count] = bufQ->nodeLink[0];
    writeNode(bufP, p);

    // shift the data element from the right node into
    // the parent node
    p = ptr->nodeLink[pos];
    readNode(bufP, p);
    ptr->data[pos] = bufP->data[1];
    bufP->nodeLink[0] = bufP->nodeLink[1];
    bufP->count--;
    // loop that shifts all of the data elements in the right node
    // by one position upward
    for (unsigned i = 1; i <= bufP->count; i++) {
      bufP->data[i] = bufP->data[i + 1];
      bufP->nodeLink[i] = bufP->nodeLink[i + 1];
    }
    // update nodes p and ptr in the stream
    writeNode(bufP, p);
```

continues

Listing 21.5. continued

```
        delete bufP;
        delete bufQ;
    }

    ///////////////////////////////////////////////////////////////////////
    //
    template<class T>
    void Btree<T>::compact(Bstruct<T> *ptr, unsigned pos)
    //
    // Purpose: combines adjacent nodes.
    //
    //  Parameters:
    //
    //    input: ptr - the pointer to the manipulated node
    //           pos - the index of the merged right node
    //
    {
        Bstruct<T> *bufP = new Bstruct<T>;
        Bstruct<T> *bufQ = new Bstruct<T>;
        unsigned p, q;

        p = ptr->nodeLink[pos - 1];
        readNode(bufP, p);
        // q is the index to the right node that will be made vacant
        // and then deleted
        q = ptr->nodeLink[pos];
        readNode(bufQ, q);

        // process the left node and insert data elements from
        // the parent node
        bufP->count++;
        bufP->data[bufP->count] = ptr->data[pos];
        bufP->nodeLink[bufP->count] = bufQ->nodeLink[0];
        // inserts all data elements from the right node
        for (unsigned i = 1; i <= bufQ->count; i++) {
          bufP->count++;
          bufP->data[bufP->count] = bufQ->data[i];
          bufP->nodeLink[bufP->count] = bufQ->nodeLink[i];
        }
```

```
    // remove data elements from the parent node
    for (i = pos; i < ptr->count; i++) {
      ptr->data[i] = ptr->data[i + 1];
      ptr->nodeLink[i] = ptr->nodeLink[i + 1];
    }
    ptr->count--;
    // remove the empty right node
    numDelNodes++; // increment the counter for the number
                   // of deleted nodes
    // does the array delNodeArray need to expand?
    if (numDelNodes == countDelNodeArray)
      expandDelNodeArray();
    // assign index q to an element of array delNodeArray
    *(delNodeArray + numDelNodes - 1) = q;
    numNodes--;
    writeNode(bufP, p);
    delete bufQ;
    delete bufP;
}

////////////////////////////////////////////////////////////////////
//
template<class T>
void Btree<T>::clearMarks(unsigned rootPtr)
//
// Purpose: function used to traverse the B-tree and set the
// marked member of each node to 0.
//
//  Parameters:
//
//    input: rootPtr - index to the root of the B-tree.
//
{
    Bstruct<T> *buf;

    if (rootPtr != BTREE_NIL) {
        buf = new Bstruct<T>;
        // write to all the pages systematically
        for (unsigned i = 0; i <= highNodeIndex; i++) {
          readNode(buf, i);
          buf->marked = 0;
```

continues

Listing 21.5. continued

```
            // update data in the stream
            writeNode(buf, i);
          }
          delete buf;
      }
  }

  ////////////////////////////////////////////////////////////////////////
  //
  template<class T>
  void Btree<T>::visitTree(unsigned rootPtr,
                           unsigned &node)
  //
  // Purpose: recursive function used to traverse the B-tree.
  //
  //  Parameters:
  //
  //    input: rootPtr - index to the root of the B-tree.
  //
  //    output: node - the index to the next node visited.
  //
  {
      Bstruct<T> *buf = new Bstruct<T>;
      unsigned n;

      readNode(buf, rootPtr);
      n = buf->marked;

      // terminate recursive traversal?
      if (n > buf->count) {
        delete buf;
        // all nodes have been visited
        return;
      }

      if (buf->nodeLink[n] != BTREE_NIL)
        visitTree(buf->nodeLink[n], node);

      if (seekNode && n < buf->count) {
        buf->marked++;
```

```
        node = rootPtr;
        visitIndex = buf->marked;
        seekNode = false;
        writeNode(buf, rootPtr);
    }
    delete buf;
}

////////////////////////////////////////////////////////////////////
//
template<class T>
boolean Btree<T>::getFirstNode(T& x)
//
// Purpose: visits the root of the B-tree. The function
// returns true if the B-tree object has a root.
//
//  Parameters:
//
//   input: x - the index to the data associated with the root of
//           the B-tree.
{
    Bstruct<T> *buf;

    if (root != BTREE_NIL) {
        seekNode = true;
        clearMarks(root);
        visitTree(root, nodePtr);
        buf = new Bstruct<T>;
        readNode(buf, nodePtr);
        x = buf->data[visitIndex];
        delete buf;
    }
    return (root != BTREE_NIL) ? true : false;
}

////////////////////////////////////////////////////////////////////
//
template<class T>
boolean Btree<T>::getNextNode(T& x)
//
// Purpose: visits the next node in the B-tree. The function
```

continues

Listing 21.5. continued

```
// returns true if there was a next node to visit.
//
//  Parameters:
//
//    input: x - the index to the data associated with the visited
//             node.
//
{
    Bstruct<T> *buf;

    seekNode = true;
    if (root != BTREE_NIL) {
        visitTree(root, nodePtr);
        buf = new Bstruct<T>;
        readNode(buf, nodePtr);
        if (!seekNode)
            x = buf->data[visitIndex];
        delete buf;
    }
    return (!seekNode) ? true : false;
}
```

Testing the Btree Class

Let me present a program that tests the `Btree` class. Listing 21.6 contains the source code for the TSBTREE.CPP test program. The program uses a custom string class, `LString`, that models fixed-size strings. Such a class is needed to accommodate the storage scheme of the `Btree` class. The class `LString` declares a class with a single data member and a minimal set of member functions. The `str` data member stores up to 12 characters (including the null character). The class also declares three constructors. There are a few member functions to access the characters in member `str` and obtain the length of the string stored in member `str`. The `LString` class also includes a variety of operators:

1. The = operator enables you to copy one instance of `LString` onto another.

2. The [] operator enables you to access the characters of the str member. (To simplify matters, I omitted any range checking for the arguments of the parameter index.)
3. The set of relational operators.
4. The friend << operator supports stream output.

The test program manipulates instances of Btree instantiated using the LString class. The program declares the functions showTree, searchNode, displayLink, showPages, and main.

The showTree function displays the strings stored in an instance of Btree<LString> in a single column. The parameter t specifies the B-tree. The parameter msg passes the commenting text that appears at the top of the screen. The function uses the local Boolean variable ok to traverse the B-tree t and initializes the variable ok with the Boolean result of t.getFirstNode. The routine uses a while loop to examine the value of variable ok. Each iteration displays the contents of variable str, a local instance of class LString. Each loop iteration also calls the function getNextNode to visit the next node and assigns the Boolean function result to the variable ok.

The function searchNode searches for specific data in a B-tree. The parameter t specifies the searched B-tree. The parameter s passes the search string. The searchNode function assumes that the nodes of tree t have been displayed by the showTree function. searchNode calls the Btree::search function to look for the argument of parameter s in the argument of t. The function displays text that reflects the search outcome.

The function showPages displays the nodes of a Btree instance. The parameter t specifies the Btree instance displayed by the function. The parameter msg passes a commenting message that appears at the top line of the screen. The parameter s passes an instance of class LString. The function showPages displays the data items of each node on a separate line. The general format for each line is:

```
Page <number> : (link[0]) data[1] (link[1]) data[2] ...
```

The function displayLink displays the index of the child node or NIL if there is no child node.

The function main declares the object tree, an instance of Btree instantiated with the class LString. The function also declares country, an array of LString instances, and initializes the array with the names of European countries. The array country supplies data to the tested B-tree. To test for existing and nonexisting data in the instance of `Btree`, `main` stores all members (except the last two, Greece and Denmark) of `country` in the B-tree. `main` tests the B-tree as follows:

1. Inserts the members of `country` (except the last two) using a `for` loop. Each loop iteration calls the following functions:

   - `Btree::insert` to insert an `LString` instance.
   - `showPages` to display the current nodes of the `Btree` instance tree.

   The following output is generated by the first loop iteration and shows one page with one item:

   ```
   After inserting France
   Page 0 : (NIL) France (NIL)


   Press any key to continue
   ```

   The following output is generated by the last loop iteration (after the program inserts the country England):

   ```
   After inserting England
   Page 0 : (NIL) Andora (NIL) Belgium (NIL)
   Page 1 : (NIL) Sweden (NIL) Switzerland (NIL)
   Page 2 : (0) England (4) Ireland (3) Spain (1)
   Page 3 : (NIL) Italy (NIL) Luxembourg (NIL) Monaco (NIL) Portugal
             (NIL)
   Page 4 : (NIL) France (NIL) Germany (NIL)


   Press any key to continue
   ```

2. Displays the data in the object tree by calling the function `showTree`. The function displays the sorted names of the countries in a single column and waits for you to press any key.

3. Searches for the elements of `country` in the object tree. This step uses a `for` loop that calls the `searchNode` function. The loop iterates over all the elements of `country` (including Greece and Denmark). The last two iterations, therefore, should generate a `no match` message displayed by the `searchNode` function.

4. Removes half of the nodes in the object tree. The function uses a `for` loop to call the following functions:

- Btree::remove (the arguments for the remove function are the elements of thc array country)
- showPages to display the current nodes of the Btree instance tree

5. Repeats steps 2 and 3 with the trimmed B-tree.

Listing 21.6. The source code for the TSBTREE.CPP test program.

```
#include <iostream.h>
#include "video.h"
#include "btree.cpp"

const MAX_STRING = 12;

class LString
{
   protected:
     char str[MAX_STRING];

   public:
     LString()
       { memset(str, 0, MAX_STRING); }
     LString(const char* s);
     LString(LString& s)
       { strcpy(str, s.str); }
     char* getstr()
       { return str; }
     unsigned getLen()
       { return strlen(str); }

     LString& operator =(LString& s);
     char& operator[](unsigned index)
      { return str[index]; }

     int operator <(LString& s)
       { return strcmp(str, s.str) < 0; }
     int operator <=(LString& s)
       { return strcmp(str, s.str) <= 0; }
     int operator >(LString& s)
```

continues

Listing 21.6. continued

```
        { return strcmp(str, s.str) > 0; }
      int operator >=(LString& s)
        { return strcmp(str, s.str) >= 0; }
      int operator ==(LString& s)
        { return strcmp(str, s.str) == 0; }
      int operator !=(LString& s)
        { return strcmp(str, s.str) != 0; }

    friend ostream& operator <<(ostream& os, LString& s);
};

LString::LString(const char* s)
{
  if (strlen(s) < MAX_STRING)
    strcpy(str, s);
  else {
    memcpy(str, s, MAX_STRING - 1);
    str[MAX_STRING] = '\0';
  }
}

LString& LString::operator =(LString& s)
{
  strcpy(str, s.str);
  return *this;
}

ostream& operator <<(ostream& os, LString& s)
{
  os << s.str;
  return os;
}


void showTree(Btree<LString>& t, const char* msg)
{
  LString str;
  boolean ok = t.getFirstNode(str);
```

```
  clrscr();
  cout << msg
       << " (tree has " << t.getNumNodes() << " nodes)"
       << "\n\n";
  while (ok) {
    cout << str << '\n';
    ok = t.getNextNode(str);
  }
  gotoxy(1, 23);
  cout << "Press any key ... ";
  getch();
}

void searchNode(Btree<LString>& t, LString& s)
{
  gotoxy(1, 23);
  clreol();
  gotoxy(1, 22);
  cout << "Press any key to search for " << s;
  getch();
  gotoxy(1, 22);
  clreol();
  if (t.search(s))
    cout << "Found " << s << " in tree\n";
  else
    cout << "No match for " << s << '\n';
  cout << "Press any key to continue ... ";
  getch();
}

void displayLink(unsigned n)
{
  if (n != BTREE_NIL)
    cout << '(' << n << ") ";
  else
    cout << "(NIL) ";
}

void showPages(Btree<LString>& t, const char* msg, LString& s)
// displays the tree nodes for a B-tree with no deleted nodes
{
```

continues

Listing 21.6. continued

```
    Bstruct<LString> page;
    clrscr();
    cout << msg << s << '\n';
    for (unsigned i = 0; i < t.getNumNodes(); i++) {
      t.getPage(&page, i);
      cout << "Page " << i << " : ";
      for (unsigned j = 0; j <= page.count; j++) {
        if (j > 0)
          cout << page.data[j] << " ";
        displayLink(page.nodeLink[j]);
      }
      cout << '\n';
    }
    cout << "\n\nPress any key to continue";
    getch();
}

main()
{
  Btree<LString> tree("tsbtree.dat");
  LString country[] = { "France",
                        "Sweden",
                        "Spain",
                        "Portugal",
                        "Switzerland",
                        "Belgium",
                        "Ireland",
                        "Italy",
                        "Monaco",
                        "Andora",
                        "Luxembourg",
                        "Germany",
                        "England",
                        "Greece",    // not inserted in tree
                        "Denmark"    // not inserted in tree
                       };
  unsigned count = sizeof(country) / sizeof(LString);
  unsigned testSize = count - 2;
  unsigned numDelete = count / 2;
```

```
  // insert the names of the countries
  for (unsigned i = 0; i < testSize; i++) {
    tree.insert(country[i]);
    showPages(tree, "After inserting ", country[i]);
  }

  // display B-tree
  showTree(tree, "Complete B-tree is:");

  for (i = 0; i < count; i++)
    searchNode(tree, country[i]);

  for (i = 0; i < numDelete; i++) {
    tree.remove(country[i]);
    showPages(tree, "After deleting ", country[i]);
  }

   // display AVL-tree
  showTree(tree, "Trimmed B-tree is:");

  for (i = 0; i < count; i++)
    searchNode(tree, country[i]);

  gotoxy(1, 22); clreol();
  gotoxy(1, 23); clreol();

  return 0;
}
```

Summary

This chapter presents the memory-based multiway tree (also called the m-way tree) and the stream-based B-tree and covers the following topics:

- The basic specifications and operations of an m-way tree. The operations include searching for data, inserting data, and deleting data.

- The `MWtree` class that models an m-way tree. The class operations consist of searching for data in nodes and among nodes, inserting data, deleting data, rebalancing tree nodes, and traversing the nodes.
- The `Btree` class that models the B-tree. The class operations consist of searching for data in nodes and among nodes, inserting data, deleting data, managing the space of deleted nodes, rebalancing tree nodes, and traversing the nodes.

Index

Symbols

A

B

C

D

E

F

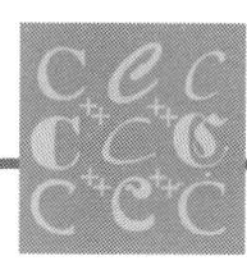

G

H

I

J-K

L

M

N

O

P

Q-R

S

T

U-V

W

X-Z

What's on the Disk?

This book's companion disk contains valuable general and template classes:

- An extensive string class library.
- Classes for manipulating words, items, tokens, and character sets.
- A template class for double-linked lists.
- Template binary tree classes, including one that uses a dynamic array.
- A template class for AVL trees.
- Template classes for a memory-based multi-way tree and its disk-based counterpart, the B-tree.
- A template class for the memory-based (internal) hash tables.
- A template class for the disk-based (external) hash tables.
- A template for dynamic arrays that contains extensive sorting and searching member functions.

Installing the Disk

The companion disk contains the self-extracting file CODE.EXE. To install the files in that archive, perform the following steps:

1. Insert the companion disk in drive A: or B:.
2. Create a subdirectory, ADVCPP for example, that is attached to the directory of your C++ compiler.
3. Move to the subdirectory you just created.
4. At the DOS prompt, enter either

   ```
   a:code
   ```

   if the companion disk is in drive A:, or

   ```
   b:code
   ```

   if the companion disk is in drive B:.

The CODE.EXE file will unpack the files in the current directory.